LIBRARY OF NEW TESTAMENT STUDIES

663

Formerly Journal for the Study of the New Testament Supplement Series

Editor
Chris Keith

Editorial Board
Dale C. Allison, Lynn H. Cohick, R. Alan Culpepper, Craig A. Evans, Jennifer Eyl, Robert Fowler, Simon J. Gathercole, Juan Hernández Jr., John S. Kloppenborg, Michael Labahn, Matthew V. Novenson, Love L. Sechrest, Robert Wall, Catrin H. Williams, Brittany E. Wilson

EXODUS IN THE NEW TESTAMENT

Edited by

Seth M. Ehorn

LONDON • NEW YORK • OXFORD • NEW DELHI • SYDNEY

T&T CLARK

Bloomsbury Publishing Plc

50 Bedford Square, London, WC1B 3DP, UK
1385 Broadway, New York, NY 10018, USA
29 Earlsfort Terrace, Dublin 2, Ireland

BLOOMSBURY, T&T CLARK and the T&T Clark logo
are trademarks of Bloomsbury Publishing Plc

First published in Great Britain 2022

Copyright © Seth M. Ehorn and contributors, 2022
Paperback edition published 2023

Seth M. Ehorn has asserted his right under the Copyright, Designs and Patents Act, 1988, to be
identified as Editor of this work.

All rights reserved. No part of this publication may be reproduced or transmitted in any form or by
any means, electronic or mechanical, including photocopying, recording, or any information storage
or retrieval system, without prior permission in writing from the publishers.

Bloomsbury Publishing Plc does not have any control over, or responsibility for, any third-party
websites referred to or in this book. All internet addresses given in this book were correct at the
time of going to press. The author and publisher regret any inconvenience caused if addresses have
changed or sites have ceased to exist, but can accept no responsibility for any such changes.

A catalogue record for this book is available from the British Library.

Library of Congress Cataloging-in-Publication Data

Names: Ehorn, Seth, editor.
Title: Exodus in the New Testament / edited by Seth M. Ehorn.
Description: London ; New York : T&T Clark, 2021. | Series: The library of New Testament studies,
2513-8790 ; 663 | Includes bibliographical references and index. | Summary: "This book examines
citations and allusions to Exodus (and Exodus traditions) within the New Testament"--
Provided by publisher.
Identifiers: LCCN 2021052327 (print) | LCCN 2021052328 (ebook) | ISBN
9780567702777 (hb) | ISBN 9780567702784 (epdf) | ISBN 9780567702807 (epub)
Subjects: LCSH: Bible. Exodus--Quotations in the New Testament. | Bible.
Exodus--Criticism, interpretation, etc. | Bible. Exodus--Relation to the New Testament. |
Bible. New Testament--Relation to Exodus.
Classification: LCC BS1245.55 .E965 2021 (print) | LCC BS1245.55 (ebook) |
DDC 222/.12--dc23/eng/20211202
LC record available at https://lccn.loc.gov/2021052327
LC ebook record available at https://lccn.loc.gov/2021052328

ISBN:	HB:	978-0-5677-0277-7
	PB:	978-0-5677-0281-4
	ePDF:	978-0-5677-0278-4
	ePUB:	978-0-5677-0280-7

Series: Library of New Testament Studies, volume 663
ISSN 2513-8790

Typeset by: Trans.form.ed SAS

To find out more about our authors and books visit www.bloomsbury.com
and sign up for our newsletters.

Contents

Preface   vii
Abbreviations   ix

INTRODUCTION
   Seth M. Ehorn   1

Chapter 1
EXODUS IN THE SECOND TEMPLE PERIOD
   Drew Longacre   6

Chapter 2
EXODUS IN MATTHEW'S GOSPEL
   Jeannine K. Brown   31

Chapter 3
'OLD EXODUS' AND 'NEW EXODUS' IN THE GOSPEL OF MARK
   Daniel M. Gurtner   48

Chapter 4
EXODUS IN LUKE-ACTS
   Brian J. Tabb and Steve Walton   61

Chapter 5
EXODUS IN JOHN
   Andreas J. Köstenberger   88

Chapter 6
EXODUS IN THE PAULINE LETTERS
   David M. Westfall   109

Chapter 7
EXODUS IN THE DISPUTED PAULINE LETTERS
   Seth M. Ehorn   127

Chapter 8
EXODUS IN HEBREWS
   David M. Moffitt   146

Chapter 9
EXODUS IN THE GENERAL LETTERS
   Katie Marcar   164

Chapter 10
READING EXODUS IN REVELATION
   Michelle Fletcher   182

Chapter 11
REVIEW ESSAY:
EXODUS IN THE NEW TESTAMENT
   Carmen Joy Imes   202

Bibliography   211
Contributors   233
Index of References   235
Index of Authors   255

Preface

Several years ago Steve Moyise, the external examiner for my doctoral thesis, suggested that I take up a project that he and Maarten Menken began. The present volume, *Exodus in the New Testament*, is that project. The volume follows the pattern established by Moyise and Menken's volumes also published by Bloomsbury T&T Clark on *Genesis in the New Testament*, *Psalms in the New Testament*, etc. The notable exception is that this volume is not linked to the Seminar on the Use of the Old Testament in New Testament, hosted annually in Hawarden, Wales. I wish to thank Susan Docherty, convener of the seminar, for consulting with me about the project.

For several reasons, including a global pandemic, the publication of this volume took longer than expected. I am grateful to all the contributors for their patience and endurance throughout the long journey. I trust we are all happy to be out of the wilderness!

Seth M. Ehorn

Abbreviations

AB	Anchor Bible
AC	*L'Antiquité classique*
ACCSNT	Ancient Christian Commentary on Scripture New Testament
AGJU	Arbeiten zur Geschichte des antiken Judentums und des Urchristentums
AnaPap	*Analecta papyrologica*
AnBib	Analecta Biblica
ANTC	Abingdon New Testament Commentaries
ANTS	Apostolos New Testament Studies
ArBib	Aramaic Bible
AS	*Aramaic Studies*
ATANT	Abhandlungen zur Theologie des Alten und Neuen Testaments
AUSS	*Andrews University Seminary Studies*
BASOR	*Bulletin of American Schools of Oriental Research*
BBB	Bonner biblische Beiträge
BBC	Blackwell Bible Commentaries
BBR	*Bulletin for Biblical Research*
BDAG	F. W. Danker, W. Bauer, W. F. Arndt, and F. W. Gingrich (eds.), *Greek-English Lexicon of the New Testament and Other Early Christian Literature* (Chicago: University of Chicago, 3rd edn, 2000).
BDBAT	Beihefte zu den Dielheimer Blättern zum Alten Testament
BEB	Biblioteca Estudios Bíblicos
BECNT	Baker Exegetical Commentary on the New Testament
BegC	*The Beginnings of Christianity. Part 1: The Acts of the Apostles.* Edited by Frederick J. Foakes-Jackson and Kirsopp Lake. 5 vols. London: Macmillan, 1922. Repr. under the subtitle, Grand Rapids: Baker, 1977
BETL	Bibliotheca Ephemeridum Theologicarum Lovaniensium
BHD	*Bible History Daily*
BHGNT	Baylor Handbook on the Greek New Testament
BHQ	*Biblia Hebraica Quinta*
BHS	*Biblia Hebraica Stuttgartensia*
Bib	*Biblica*
BIOSCS	*Bulletin of the International Organization for Septuagint and Cognate Studies*
BIS	Biblical Interpretation Series
BNTC	Black's New Testament Commentaries
BSac	*Bibliotheca Sacra*
BSCS	Brill Septuagint Commentary Series
BSL	Biblical Studies Library

BTNT	Biblical Theology of the New Testament Series
BZAW	Beihefte zur Zeitschrift für die alttestamentliche Wissenschaft
BZNW	Beihefte zur Zeitschrift für die neutestamentliche Wissenschaft
CBET	Contributions to Biblical Exegesis and Theology
CBQ	*Catholic Biblical Quarterly*
CBR	*Currents in Biblical Research*
CGTC	Cambridge Greek Testament Commentary
ConBNT	Coiectanea Neotestamentica
ConcC	Concordia Commentary
ConJ	*Concordia Journal*
COQG	Christian Origins and the Question of God
DCH	D. J. A. Clines, *Dictionary of Classical Hebrew* (9 vols.; Sheffield: Sheffield Phoenix, 1993–2014)
DJD	Discoveries in the Judaean Desert
DSD	*Dead Sea Discoveries*
ÉBib	Études bibliques
EBS	Encountering Biblical Studies
EC	*Early Christianity*
EKKNT	Evangelisch-katholischer Kommentar zum Neuen Testament
ExpTim	*Expository Times*
FRLANT	Forschungen zur Religion und Literatur des Alten und Neuen Testaments
GE	F. Montanari, *The Greek Dictionary of Ancient Greek* (Leiden: Brill, 2015)
GKC	*Gesenius' Hebrew Grammar* (ed. Emil Kautzsch; trans. Arthur E. Cowley; Oxford: Clarendon, 2nd edn, 1910)
HB	Hebrew Bible
HBAI	*Hebrew Bible and Ancient Israel*
HBCE	*The Hebrew Bible: A Critical Edition*
HNT	Hanbuch zum Neuen Testament
HSS	Harvard Semitic Studies
HThKAT	Herders Theologischer Kommentar zum Alten Testament
HThKNT	Herders Theologischer Kommentar zum Neuen Testament
HUBP	Hebrew University Bible Project
ICC	International Critical Commentary
IJASP	Internationales Jahrbuch für die Altertumskunde Syrien-Palästinas
Int	Interpretation Commentary Series
Int	*Interpretation*
IOSOT	International Organization for the Study of the Old Testament
JAJSup	Supplements to Journal of Ancient Judaism
JAOS	*Journal of the American Oriental Society*
JBL	*Journal of Biblical Literature*
JCS	*Journal of Cuneiform Studies*
JDT	*Jahrbuch für deutsche Theologie*
JETS	*Journal of the Evangelical Theological Society*
JNSL	*Journal of Northwest Semitic Languages*
JSJSup	Supplements to Journal for the Study of Judaism in the Persian, Hellenistic, and Roman Periods
JSNT	*Journal for the Study of the New Testament*
JSNTSup	Journal for the Study of the New Testament Supplement Series
JSOT	*Journal for the Study of the Old Testament*

JSOTSup	Journal for the Study of the Old *Testament* Supplement Series
JSP	*Journal for the Study of the Pseudepigrapha*
JSPL	*Journal for the Study of Paul and His Letters*
JTS	*Journal of Theological Studies*
KEK	Kritisch-exegetischer Kommentar über das Neue Testament (Meyer-Kommentar)
KEL	Kregel Exegetical Library
LCL	Loeb Classical Library
LNTS	Library of New Testament Studies
LXX	Septuagint
MS(S)	Manuscript(s)
MSU	Mitteilungen des Septuaginta-Unternehmens
MT	Masoretic Text
NA^{28}	Nestle-Aland, *Novum Testamentum Graece* (28th edn)
NAC	New American Commentary
NAS	New American Standard
Neot	*Neotestimentica*
NETS	New English Translation of the Septuagint
NIB	New Interpreter's Bible
NICNT	New International Commentary on the New Testament
NICOT	New International Commentary on the Old Testament
NIGTC	New International Greek Testament Commentary
NIVAC	New International Version Application Commentary
NovT	*Novum Testamentum*
NovTSup	Supplements to Novum Testamentum
NRSV	New Revised Standard Version
NSBT	New Studies in Biblical Theology
NT	New Testament
NTL	New Testament Library
NTS	*New Testament Studies*
OTL	Old Testament Library
OTS	Old Testament Studies
PBM	Paternoster Biblical Monographs
PNTC	Pillar New Testament Commentary
PRSt	*Perspectives in Religious Studies*
RevExp	*Review and Expositor*
RevQ	*Revue de Qumran*
RNT	Regensburger Neues Testament
SBG	Studies in Biblical Greek
SBLDS	Society of Biblical Studies Dissertation Series
SBLSymS	Society of Biblical Literature Symposium Series
SBT	Studies in Biblical Theology
SCS	Septuagint and Cognate Studies
SKKNT	Stuttgarter Kleiner Kommentar, Neues Testament
SNTSMS	Society for New Testament Studies Monograph Series
SP	Samaritan Pentateuch
SPhiloM	Studies in Philo of Alexandria and Mediterranean Antiquity
SR	*Studies in Religion*
SSU	Studia Semitica Upsaliensia

STDJ	Studies on the Texts of the Desert of Judah
TDNT	G. Kittel and G. Friedrich (eds.), *Theological Dictionary of the New Testament* (trans. G. W. Bromiley; 10 vols.; Grand Rapids: Eerdmans, 1964–76)
Tg	Targum
Theod.	Theodotian
THKNT	Theologischer Handkommentar zum Neuen Testament
THNTC	Two Horizons New Testament Commentary
TLOT	E. Jenni, with assistance from C. Westermann (eds.), *Theological Lexicon of the Old Testament* (trans. M. E. Biddle; 3 vols.; Peabody, MA: Hendrickson, 1997)
TS	Texts and Studies
TSK	*Theologische Studien und Kritiken*
TTCS	Teach the Text Commentary Series
TynBul	*Tyndale Bulletin*
TZ	*Theologische Zeitschrift*
UBS[5]	United Bible Society, *Greek New Testament* (5th edn)
VT	*Vetus Testamentum*
VTSup	Supplements to Vetus Testamentum
Vulg	Vulgate
WBC	Word Biblical Commentary
WTJ	*Westminster Theological Journal*
WUNT	Wissenschaftliche Untersuchungen zum Neuen Testament
ZAW	*Zeitschrift für die alttestamentliche Wissenschaft*
ZECNT	Zondervan Exegetical Commentary on the New Testament
ZRGG	*Zeitschrift für Religions- und Geistesgeschichte*

Introduction

Seth M. Ehorn

The book of Exodus and its traditions played a significant role in the identity formation of the Jewish people. Even now the story of Israel's deliverance from its oppressors in Egypt continues to serve as a pattern for human struggle, suffering, and redemption. Its utility is well-suited to many contexts. For example, Lin-Manuel Miranda's musical, *Hamilton*, recasts the early American struggle for independence by evoking the exodus story as a paradigm of people freeing themselves from their oppressors and gaining a new promised land. Likewise, Martin Luther King, Jr. evoked the exodus story during the American civil rights movement by simply stating 'I've been to the mountaintop', positioning himself as a Moses-like figure as part of his emerging prophetic persona.[1] And, the exodus story is trivialized in works like Thomas Hardy's *Jude the Obscure*, where the lead character, Jude, compares the study of Greek and Latin to 'a labour like that of Israel in Egypt'.[2] As the chapters in this volume will show, the range of responses and reuses of Exodus and exodus tradition in modern works is mirrored also in antiquity.

References to Exodus and exodus tradition appear throughout the Jewish Scriptures, especially in Deuteronomy, various historical books, the Prophets, and Psalms.[3] This is not surprising because the paradigmatic significance of the exodus event is established already in the book of Exodus itself:[4]

---

[1] From a sermon delivered 27 January 1957. See esp. G. S. Selby, *Martin Luther King and the Rhetoric of Freedom: The Exodus Narrative in America's Struggle for Civil Rights* (Waco, TX: Baylor University Press, 2008), pp. 115–36.

[2] T. Hardy, *Jude the Obscure: A Critical Edition* (ed. Norman Page; London: Norton & Co., 2nd edn, 1999), p. 27.

[3] For detailed studies, see, e.g., C. Kupfer, *Mit Israel auf dem Weg durch die Wüste: Eine leserorientierte Exegese der Rebellionstexte in Exodus 15:22–17:7 und Numeri 11:1–20:13* (OTS, 61; Leiden: Brill, 2012); T. Römer, 'Exode et Anti-Exode: La nostalgie de l'Egypte dans les traditions du désert', in T. Römer (ed.), *Lectio difficilior probabilior? L'exégèse comme expérience de décloisonnement* (BDBAT, 12; Heidelberg: Wiss.-theol. Seminar, 1991), pp. 155–72; R. G. S. Idestrom, 'Echoes of the Book of Exodus in Ezekiel', *JSOT* 33 (2009), pp. 489–510; P. Milne, 'Psalm 23: Echoes of the Exodus', *SR* 4/3 (1974), pp. 237–47; A. R. Ceresko, 'The Rhetorical Strategy of the Fourth Servant Song (Isaiah 52:13–53:12): Poetry and Exodus–New Exodus', *CBQ* 56 (1994), pp. 42–55; R. E. Watts, *Isaiah's New Exodus in Mark* (WUNT, 2/88; Tübingen: Mohr Siebeck, 1997).

[4] On this point, see P. Barmash, 'Out of the Mists of History: The Exaltation of the Exodus in the Bible', in P. Barmash and W. D. Nelson (eds.), *Exodus in the Jewish Experience: Echoes and Reverberations* (New York: Lexington Books, 2015), pp. 1–22.

When the LORD has brought you into the land of the Canaanites, as he swore to you and your ancestors, and has given it to you, ¹² you shall set apart to the LORD all that first opens the womb. All the firstborn of your livestock that are males shall be the LORD's. ¹³ But every firstborn donkey you shall redeem with a sheep; if you do not redeem it, you must break its neck. Every firstborn male among your children you shall redeem. ¹⁴ When in the future your child asks you, 'What does this mean?' you shall answer, 'By strength of hand the LORD brought us out of Egypt, from the house of slavery. ¹⁵ When Pharaoh stubbornly refused to let us go, the LORD killed all the firstborn in the land of Egypt, from human firstborn to the firstborn of animals. Therefore I sacrifice to the LORD every male that first opens the womb, but every firstborn of my sons I redeem.' ¹⁶ It shall serve as a sign on your hand and as an emblem on your forehead that by strength of hand the LORD brought us out of Egypt. (Exod. 13.11-16, NRSV)

In the wider context of this passage, the call to '*remember* this day on which you came out of Egypt' (Exod. 13.3) is mirrored by the refrain that Israel must not '*forget* the Lord, who brought you out of the land of Egypt, out of the house of slavery' (Deut. 6.12; 8.14; 9.7; Ps. 106.21).[5] Integral to the God of Israel's very identity is this act of redemption from slavery in Egypt. It comes as no surprise, then, that Israel's exodus featured prominently in Jewish reflection during the Second Temple period. Indeed, Michael Fishbane suggests that 'the exodus tradition was used, from the first, as a paradigmatic teaching for present and future generations'.[6] The chapters in this volume survey only a limited range of these 'future generations'—namely those that comprise the New Testament.[7]

Although engagement with a scriptural source text is sometimes gauged by counting quotations and putative allusions, it is clear that the influence of the book of Exodus in the New Testament cannot be evaluated solely on the basis of a counting exercise. As several chapters in this volume demonstrate, the general storyline of Exodus, including reference to key figures and events, provides a narrative framework for several of the New Testament texts. Indeed, some New Testament scholarship has even emphasized the hope for a new exodus as an ongoing reality in the first century CE.[8] Therefore, evaluating the use of Exodus in the New Testament requires careful attention to the text of Exodus as

---

[5] See, especially, B. G. Wold, 'Memory in the Dead Sea Scrolls: Exodus, Creation and Cosmos', in S. C. Barton, L. T. Stuckenbruck, and B. G. Wold (eds.), *Memory in the Bible and Antiquity: The Fifth Durham-Tübingen Research Symposium (Durham, September 2004)* (WUNT, 1/212; Tübingen: Mohr Siebeck, 2007), pp. 47–74.

[6] M. Fishbane, 'The "Exodus" Motif/The Paradigm of Historical Renewal', in M. Fishbane (ed.), *Text and Texture: A Literary Reading of Selected Texts* (Oxford: One World, 1998), pp. 121–40 (121).

[7] See E. S. Gruen, *Heritage and Hellenism: The Reinvention of Jewish Tradition* (Berkeley: University of California Press, 1998), pp. 41–72, for a fascinating survey of references to Exodus in Greco-Roman sources.

[8] E.g., N. T. Wright, *The New Testament and the People of God* (COQG, 1; Minneapolis: Fortress, 1992); D. L. Smith, 'The Uses of "New Exodus" in New Testament Scholarship: Preparing a Way through the Wilderness', *CBR* 14 (2016), pp. 207–43.

well as the reception of the tradition in its various forms. Following the pattern of prior books in the series *The New Testament and the Scriptures of Israel*,[9] contributors have been allowed to work within their own preferred intertextual framework(s) and any unique aspects of their approach(es) are explained in their chapters. To borrow language from Steve Moyise and Maarten Menken, 'just as there is variety in the reception of [Exodus] in the New Testament, so there is variety among scholars writing on this subject. Some focus on the textual form of the Old Testament passages that have been quoted; others on the role or function that they have in the new work.'[10] The contributions in this volume showcase not only the rich ways that Exodus and its traditions inform the writings of the New Testament, but also the multiple methodological approaches that generate fresh insights into ancient texts. An overview of the contributors and chapters follows.

In Chapter 1, Drew Longacre summarizes the uses of Exodus in Judaism of the Second Temple period. After briefly overviewing Exodus' contents and key themes, he discusses the various issues surrounding the composition of Exodus, including discussion of the so-called Documentary Hypothesis and the grouping of Exodus with parts of the Hebrew Bible (e.g., the Pentateuch). This is followed by detailed discussion of the Hebrew and Greek text(s) of Exodus, including discussion of the structure and translation technique of the book. Longacre argues that a single common ancestor, dated no later than the fourth century BCE, best explains the homogeneity of the Hebrew textual tradition. After acknowledging that the Greek versions of Exodus are the important starting point for analyzing the use of the Exodus in the New Testament, Longacre draws a significant conclusion: 'Textual pluriformity thus appears to have been the norm in the late Second Temple period ... This reality is foundational to accurate analysis of New Testament uses of the Old Testament' (p. 26).

In Chapter 2 Jeannine Brown explores the use of Exodus in Matthew's Gospel by tracking thematic movements and motifs. This approach—rather than a simple survey of quotations and allusions—allows Brown to highlight the significant ways that Exodus informs and undergirds the storyline of Matthew. Brown considers a layered typology of Moses and Israel; the new exodus theme in Matthew's genealogy, passion narrative, and healing narratives; the theme of safety and provision in Jesus' ministry and the significance of Torah (including Exodus) in Jesus' teaching; and the related narrative themes of tabernacle/temple and divine presence. Through this narrative or storied approach, Brown demonstrates that the Gospel of Matthew closely corresponds to the framework of Exodus.

---

[9] S. Moyise and M. J. J. Menken (eds.), *The Psalms in the New Testament* (London: T&T Clark, 2004); S. Moyise and M. J. J. Menken (eds.), *Isaiah in the New Testament* (London: T&T Clark, 2005); S. Moyise and M. J. J. Menken (eds.), *Deuteronomy in the New Testament* (LNTS, 358; London: T&T Clark, 2007); M. J. J. Menken and S. Moyise (eds.), *The Minor Prophets in the New Testament* (LNTS, 377; London: T&T Clark, 2009); M. J. J. Menken and S. Moyise (eds.), *Genesis in the New Testament* (LNTS, 466; London: T&T Clark, 2012).

[10] Moyise and Menken, *Psalms in the New Testament*, p. 3.

Daniel Gurtner's (Chapter 3) study on Mark's Gospel considers four quotations and five allusions to Exodus in Mark's Gospel. Throughout the study, Gurtner is attuned to the issue of discerning whether Mark's use of Exodus texts and traditions come mediated through an interpretive filter (e.g., Isaiah) or whether Mark's engagement is more directly connected to Exodus itself. Gurtner shows that reducing all uses to a singular framework cannot explain the 'complexities and variances' of Mark's usage (p. 60).

In Chapter 4, Brian Tabb and Steve Walton discuss texts, imagery, and major events and themes from Exodus that appear in Luke-Acts. Tabb discusses six such examples in Luke, including quotations (Lk. 2.22-23; 7.27; 18.20) and allusions (9.28-33; 13.14; 20.37). Two of the quotations concern matters of Jewish law, including purification offerings (Exod. 13.2, 12) and a commandment from the Decalogue (Exod. 20.12-16). Walton considers a plethora of examples in Acts—many from Stephen's speech in Acts 7—where the author quotes (Acts 23.5), alludes (Acts 3.13; 14.15; 15.10; 17.24), or re-narrates from Exodus (Acts 7). The primary uses of Exodus involve an appeal to the enduring significance of the exodus (e.g., Lk. 20.38; Acts 7), including the development of a new exodus theme in several specific texts (e.g., Lk. 2.25; 7.27; 9.31; 13.12-16). They show how the author of Luke-Acts adopts and adapts Exodus traditions in order to narrate his two-part work, frame the responses of characters (e.g., Lk. 20.37; Acts 23.5), and establish Jesus' role in a new exodus deliverance.

Andreas Köstenberger's chapter on the Gospel of John (Chapter 5) concludes that the exodus theme is used 'to demonstrate that Jesus is the climax of God's self-disclosure to his people' (p. 107). While this contribution follows the traditional division into the Book of Signs (1.19–12.50) and the Book of Exaltation/ Glory (13.1–21.25), the majority of discussion appears in the former, including analysis of John the Baptist (Jn 1.23, 29, 36), typological fulfillments (Jn 3.14; 6.1-15), and broad narrative patterns that may correspond to Exodus or, at least, to Moses (e.g., Jn 6.20; 7.19, 22, 31; 8.12; 12.13). The farewell discourse (Jn 13–17) is briefly discussed in comparison with Moses' parting words. Finally, Köstenberger considers the role that Exodus plays in John's Passion narrative, including reference to piercing Jesus' side rather than breaking his legs (Jn 19.24), to present Jesus as a paschal offering.

In Chapter 6, David Westfall explores the undisputed Pauline letters for traces of Exodus. After discussing Galatians, 1–2 Corinthians, and Romans, he concludes that although quotations are relatively sparse, the book of Exodus played a significant role in Paul's theological imagination. Significant events like the covenant at Sinai and the golden calf incident help Paul to articulate his theological convictions and convey both hostility and hope about patterns of disobedience found in his fledgling churches.

In Chapter 7, Seth Ehorn explores several possible allusions to Exodus and exodus tradition as well as a quotation from the Decalogue in the disputed Pauline letters. Unlike the undisputed Pauline letters, Exodus does not play a major role in the scriptural matrix that informs these letters. Nevertheless, the author(s) of the disputed letters still find ongoing significance in the text of

Exodus and/or in its narrative that helps make sense of present circumstances. A quotation of Exod. 20.12 supports the household code teaching in Eph. 6.2-3 by showing why it is 'right' (δίκαιος) that children obey their parents. Moreover, a fleeting reference to Jannes and Jambres in 2 Tim. 3.8-9 shows that the exodus story (and its later reception) provided resources for the author to understand a current struggle against opponents and the threat(s) of false teaching.

David Moffitt's chapter on Exodus in Hebrews (Chapter 8) considers how the book of Exodus provides a structural framework to the early chapters of Hebrews. This includes the author's extended wilderness typology as well as the author's emphasis on the tabernacle. According to Moffitt, the author not only draws upon but adapts Exodus and its traditions for its moral and theological instructions.

In Chapter 9, Katie Marcar explores the quotations and allusions to the book of Exodus (and its traditions) in the General Letters. She concludes that the letters 'do not demonstrate a systematic or sustained interest in Exodus or exodus traditions. Rather, the Exodus material reflected in the General Letters seems to reflect the contemporary Jewish and Christian interpretive environment' (p. 181).

In her chapter of Revelation (Chapter 10), Michelle Fletcher proposes to read Revelation 'with Exodus' rather than 'for Exodus'. This distinction follows from the nature of Revelation's textual evocation(s) itself and also reflects her methodological assumptions about how intertextuality functions. Fletcher notes the seminal significance of Exodus resulted in its reuse in earlier Jewish writings (e.g., HB) and this must be taken into consideration when discussing any exodus traditions that surface in Revelation. Among the traditions she discusses are the divine name (Rev. 1.4), manna (Rev. 2.17), the Lamb (Rev. 5), the Song of Moses (Rev. 15), and the plagues (Rev. 16). Through these studies, Fletcher helpfully draws attention to the complexity of Revelation's relationship with Exodus because 'Revelation's evocations are alive with a plurality of reference' (p. 201).

Following these studies, Carmen Imes provides a reflection on the volume from her perspective as a scholar of the Hebrew Bible. In addition to drawing attention to several themes that emerged across the chapters, she offers two case studies that illustrate the pitfalls and prospects of studying the use of Exodus in the New Testament.[11]

---

[11] I wish to thank Carmen Imes for offering not only this reflection but also for providing helpful editorial feedback on several essays prior to publication.

Chapter 1

Exodus in the Second Temple Period

Drew Longacre

1. Introduction

The book of Exodus is known in Hebrew as שמות ('the names'), based on the first words of the book. In Greek the book is known as ἔξοδος ('exit, way out') or ἐξαγωγή ('leading out'), from the former of which comes the Latinized English title Exodus. The book of Exodus was a foundational book for the people of Israel, rehearsing their deliverance from Egypt and confirmation as the Lord's chosen, covenant people, as well as the giving of the divine law regulating that covenant relationship. Because of its importance for both Jews and Christians, Exodus has an extremely rich and complex history that must be taken into consideration when studying the reception of the book by New Testament authors.

2. Contents of Exodus

It is difficult to define the limits of a literary tradition like the book of Exodus that was constantly developing, but the preserved documentary evidence suggests that—despite sometimes significant differences—there was already in the late Second Temple period a generally recognized common core of textual material that defined the structure and sequence of the book of Exodus. This literary work consisted of three parts, with only relatively minor internal variation in the tradition.

a. Israel in Egypt (1.1–12.42)

Exodus begins with the people of Israel in Egypt, having immigrated during Joseph's lifetime to survive famine in Canaan. Many years later, a new king arises who subjugates the Israelites and conscripts them for his building projects. Yahweh, the God of the Israelites, raises up a leader from among his people named

Moses, who becomes his prophet and messenger to bring the Israelites out of Egypt and back to the land of Canaan promised to the patriarchs. After a series of conflicts between God and the stubborn Egyptian Pharaoh where God strikes Egypt with devastating plagues, the Pharaoh finally agrees to let Israel go free from their bondage.

b. Israel on the Road to Sinai (12.43–18.27)

The Israelites begin their long trek towards Canaan, but Pharaoh changes his mind and pursues them, catching them at the shore of the sea. The Lord causes the sea to open before the Israelites, who cross on dry land to safety on the other side. The Egyptians pursue, but are destroyed when the Lord makes the waters return. The Israelites continue to Mt. Sinai, complaining despite supernatural provision from the Lord.

c. Israel Encamped at Sinai (19.1–40.38)

When the Israelites reach Mt. Sinai, God appears to them and makes a covenant with them. Israel must remain faithful to Yahweh and him alone and obey his commandments, and in return Israel will be blessed as his special people. Disobedience, however, will bring severe punishment upon Israel's heads, as is seen when Israel falls into idolatry by constructing and worshipping a golden calf. The Lord then commands the construction of a portable tabernacle, where he will abide in the midst of Israel during their wandering. The book ends with the completion of this tabernacle and the Lord's presence with Israel.

3. Key Themes in Exodus

Several recurring themes permeate the book of Exodus. Though it would be impossible to do full justice to the complex thematic contents of the book in such a short survey, I here highlight four repeated and significant themes that find reflexes in later reception of Exodus.

a. God's Righteous Judgment

One important theme in Exodus is God's righteous judgment as an indication of his superiority over his enemies. The plagues sent by God against Egypt were in fact targeted attacks against the gods of Egypt (12.12; 15.11; cf. Num. 33.4).[1] In his conflict with Pharaoh, the Lord demonstrates his superiority in raising Pharaoh up (9.16) and hardening his heart (9.12; 10.1, 20, 27; 11.10; 14.8) in order to devastate him. The Lord fights on behalf of his people Israel against their enemies (12.14, 25) and delivers Israel with great acts of judgment (6.6; 7.4). The severity

---

[1] Many scholars have pointed out parallels between certain plagues and prominent characteristics of significant Egyptian deities. For an overview, see Z. Zevit, 'Exodus in the Bible and the Egyptian Plagues', *BHD* (2011), n.p., https://www.biblicalarchaeology.org/daily/biblical-topics/exodus/exodus-in-the-bible-and-the-egyptian-plagues/.

of his punishment is repeatedly indicated by references to his strong hand and outstretched arm (3.19-20; 6.1, 6; 7.4-5; 9.3, 15; 13.3, 9, 14, 16; 15.6, 9, 12, 16; 32.11). The Lord's victories demonstrate his absolute superiority and incomparability (8.10; 9.14; 15.11; 18.11).

Even God's own people are not immune from his holy wrath. In an enigmatic paragraph, God tries to kill Moses, apparently due to Moses' failure to circumcise his own son, but his judgment is averted by Zipporah's quick response (4.24-26). The Lord intends to destroy Israel entirely and restart with Moses after the people worship the golden calf. However, because of Moses' mediation he relents, leading to the less extensive judgment by the swords of the Levites (32.10, 26-29). God will blot out of his book whoever sins against him (32.33). To Moses, the Lord reveals himself as slow to anger, but also one who does not withhold punishment from the guilty (34.6-7).

b. Deliverance/Redemption

God's supernatural deliverance and redemption is another major theme of the book of Exodus. God heard the cry of Israel and decided to act on their behalf (2.23-25; 3.7-10, 16; 4.31; 6.5). He fights for his people Israel, inflicting mighty acts of judgment on their enemies (6.6-7; 7.4-5; 14.25, 30; 15.3). The people of Israel, however, were spared from God's judgments (8.22; 9.4, 6-7, 26; 10.23; 11.7; 12.27). Exodus 15.1-18 is a victory song commemorating divine victory against the Egyptians. As a result, Israel is 'brought out' from their bondage in Egypt to newfound freedom (3.10-12; 6.6-7, 13, 26-27; 7.4-5; 12.17, 39, 41-42, 51; 13.3-4, 8-9, 14, 16; 14.8, 11; 16.1, 6, 32; 18.1; 19.1; 20.2; 23.15; 29.46; 32.11-12; 34.18). The redemption of Israel was foundational for Israel coming to know Yahweh as their covenant Lord and the establishment of his covenant with them (6.7; 20.2; 29.46). The law provided that, just as the Lord killed the firstborn of the Egyptians, the firstborn of every animal should be sacrificed, but the firstborn of every Israelite woman should be redeemed (13.13-15; 34.20). Israel was also commanded to treat the foreigners within its midst fairly, because they too had experienced the difficulties of being resident aliens in Egypt (22.20 [Heb.]; 23.9). In the end, God intended to bring his redeemed people to the promised land (3.8, 17; 6.8; 15.13; 33.1).

c. The Covenant at Sinai

In chs. 19–40, we have a long narrative about the inauguration of a covenant between Yahweh and Israel that is mediated by Moses. This covenant is in response to Yahweh's recollection of and faithfulness to his previous covenant with the patriarchs Abraham, Isaac, and Jacob (2.24; 6.4; 32.13), as well as his awareness of Israel's suffering in Egypt (6.5). Though the whole earth is the Lord's, he offers Israel an exclusive covenant relationship as his special possession, a kingdom of priests, and a holy nation (19.5-6). Israel is God's firstborn son (4.22-23). The core stipulations of this covenant are the Ten Commandments written on stone tablets to be deposited in the ark of the covenant (20.1-17), but covenant obedience also entailed submission to other regulations (20.22–23.33; 34.11-28), including the requirement to keep the Sabbath day holy (16.23-26; 20.8-11; 31.14-16; 35.2-3). A distinctive stipulation of this covenant is that Israel may not join in covenants with other gods or peoples (20.2-6, 23; 23.13, 24, 32-33; 32.8, 31; 34.12, 15-16). Yahweh is jealous for the affections of his people (20.5; 34.14). In response, Yahweh will do great wonders on behalf of Israel (34.10). Israel agrees to the terms of the covenant and ratifies it (19.8; 24.3, 7-8), but already in Exodus they break the terms of the covenant (32.1-35). Only by Moses' intercession and God's grace are some of the Israelites spared. At the conclusion of the book, God takes up residence with his covenant people in the tabernacle designed to mediate his presence (40.34).

d. The Revelation and Glory of the Lord

Throughout the book of Exodus, Yahweh is progressively revealed to Pharaoh, Egypt, Jethro, Moses, and Israel. Pharaoh refuses to release the Israelites because he does not yet know Yahweh (5.2). The Egyptians do not yet fear Yahweh as they should (9.30). But God's intervention to devastate the Egyptians and liberate the Israelites means that the Egyptians will come to know that he is Yahweh (7.5, 17; 8.18 [Heb.]; 14.4, 18). Egypt comes to realize that Yahweh is unique (9.14), rules over all the world (9.29), and favors his people, Israel (11.7).

God had appeared to the patriarchs as El-Shaddai, but they did not yet know him as Yahweh as the Israelites in the time of the Exodus would (6.3).[2] Through the wonders God does in Egypt and the wilderness, the Israelites will come to know that he is Yahweh (10.2; 16.12)[3] and that he is the one who brought them out of Egypt (16.6). When God dwells in the midst of his special people Israel,

---

[2] As mentioned below in the section on the composition of the book of Exodus, this verse is often used by source and redaction critics to suggest that P believed that the patriarchs did not yet know or use the name Yahweh. A similar case has been made for 3.13-15 and E. The fact that these verses are part of such a prominent theme of coming to know Yahweh throughout the book of Exodus cautions against simplistic referential appropriations of these verses in support of various models for the formation of the book. In Exodus, knowledge of the name Yahweh may not be primarily linguistic, but experiential. At question is not cognitive awareness of the name Yahweh, but rather the full experience of his power, presence, and covenant faithfulness. Thus, even those who have heard the name of Yahweh can still not know him as Yahweh (e.g., 5.2; 6.7; 7.5, 17; 8.18 [Heb.]; 10.2; 14.4, 18; 16.12; 29.46; 33.13). This theme is also picked up in later books with the same sense, even long after everyone is presumed to have heard the name Yahweh (e.g., Isa. 52.6; Jer. 16.21).

Alternatively, the latter half of 6.3 has been interpreted as a rhetorical question 'And was I not known to them by my name, Yahweh?' Interrogative sentences (especially negative ones) connected to a preceding sentence by ו are typically not marked with an interrogative ה, which normally marks questions in Hebrew (GKC §150a). This would render this sentence not as denigrating the knowledge of the patriarchs, but actually reinforcing the common knowledge of Yahweh by both the patriarchs and the Israelites in Egypt, which fits the context and rhetorical aim of this section well. For a recent discussion of unmarked questions in Biblical Hebrew, see E. Robar, 'Unmarked Modality and Rhetorical Questions in Biblical Hebrew', in N. Vidro, R. Vollandt, E.-M. Wagner, and J. Olszowy-Schlanger (eds.), *Studies in Semitic Linguistics and Manuscripts: A Liber Discipulorum in Honour of Professor Geoffrey Khan* (SSU, 30; Uppsala: Uppsala University Press, 2018), pp. 75–97.

[3] The Septuagint also reads this (proleptically?) in 2.25.

they will know that he is Yahweh their God (6.7; 29.46). Moses' father-in-law, the Midianite priest Jethro, also comes to know that Yahweh is greater than all the gods (18.11). God reveals himself especially to Moses to make himself known as Yahweh in the fullness of his character (3.13-15; 33.13; 34.5-8).

This process of self-revelation serves to increase the glory of Yahweh. God raised up Pharaoh and brought him low again to bring glory to himself through devastating Pharaoh and the Egyptians (14.4, 17-18). God's glory puts fear into the hearts of Israel and Moses (3.6; 34.29-35). Yet Yahweh reveals his glory to Israel through his wonders (16.7) and his presence among his people (16.10; 24.16-17; 29.43; 33.18–34.7; 40.34-35).

4. Composition

The book of Exodus is, strictly speaking, anonymous, as was common in the literature of the ancient Near East. God himself is said to have written the first tablets of the Ten Commandments (24.12; 31.18; 32.16; 34.1). Within Exodus, Moses is said to have written a number of documents (17.14; 24.4, 7; 34.27-28), but he is never said to have written the entire book as we now have it. Later Jewish and Christian authors attributed the book of Exodus (and the rest of the Pentateuch) to Moses, who probably would have died around either the fifteenth or thirteenth centuries BCE. Some early Jewish and Christian authors did, however, suggest that parts of the Pentateuch may have been written after the time of Moses, such as by Joshua or Ezra.

Modern critical scholars have largely rejected this attribution of the book to Moses, because of elements within the Pentateuch which seem incompatible with Mosaic authorship and because of textual clues that suggest composition of the text in stages. A few illustrative examples from Exodus will be helpful. Exodus 13.17 and 23.31 mention the Philistines, but the Philistines are commonly thought to have come to the land only after the time of Moses. Exodus 1.11 and 12.37 mention a city named Rameses, which most scholars suggest was named after Rameses II from the thirteenth century BCE, which is problematic for those who argue for an early date for the exodus in the fifteenth century. Exodus 16.35 may imply awareness of the cessation of manna from heaven, which does not occur until after the death of Moses in Josh. 5.12. Exodus 16.36 provides a ratio for conversion between measurements for later readers unfamiliar with the earlier measurement.

Potential discrepancies within the text of Exodus have further led most scholars to suppose that the book of Exodus was composed in stages. For example, the text of Exod. 15.1b-18 appears to reflect a stage in the development of the Hebrew language significantly earlier than the rest of the book. Moses' Midianite father-in-law is once called Reuel (2.18; so also Num. 10.29; Judg. 1.16 and 4.11 say the Kenite Hobab was Moses' father-in-law), but otherwise called Jethro. The mountain where God made the covenant with Israel is sometimes called Horeb (3.1; 33.6; so also repeatedly in Deuteronomy), but otherwise called Sinai.

Many scholars have interpreted Exod. 6.3 as saying that the name Yahweh was unknown to the patriarchs, which would conflict with the use of this divine name in Genesis.[4]

Based on such observations, many scholars have suggested that Exodus (and the Pentateuch as a whole) was compiled from multiple independent sources. The most famous form of the Documentary Hypothesis (popularized by Wellhausen)[5] suggested that the book of Exodus was composed of three main independent source documents telling the history of Israel (D does not substantially affect the text of Exodus) labeled J, E, and P. According to this theory, a redactor combined the narratives of J and E (creating JE), and then a subsequent redactor combined P with JE, yielding the book of Exodus as we know it.

Many recent studies have called into question the nature of each of these sources as complete, coherent, independent documents. There is widespread (though not universal) agreement on which material should be ascribed to P in Exodus, but scholars continue to debate whether it existed as an independent document or merely reflects the work of a redactor (or a series of like-minded redactors) rewriting the prior non-P material. The material reconstructed for E is very fragmentary, which has led many scholars to say that E never was an independent document, but rather was the work of a redactor rewriting earlier material. If E ever was an independent document, it must have been used only selectively in the creation of JE. There is also debate about whether J—which is also somewhat fragmentary—was a single document that determined the shape of the Pentateuch or a series of fragments arranged according to the structure determined by P.[6] Thus, though there is much disagreement in the details of the various models proposed for the composition of the book of Exodus, there is general agreement among critical scholars that the book was composed in stages, with at least an identifiable Priestly author/redactor being added to prior non-Priestly material. Scholars differ widely on both the detail and confidence with which they suppose that the compositional history of the book can be reconstructed.

Though Exodus is often treated as a book in its own right, in its current form it is integrally related literarily with other books of the Hebrew Bible/Old Testament (HB/OT). Exodus is the second book of a series of interrelated books, which continues the narrative of the book of Genesis and flows directly into the

---

[4] But see n. 2, above.
[5] J. Wellhausen, *Die Composition des Hexateuchs und der historischen Bücher des Alten Testaments* (Berlin: G. Reimer, 3rd edn, 1899). For a recent reformulation of the Documentary Hypothesis, see J. S. Baden, *The Composition of the Pentateuch: Renewing the Documentary Hypothesis* (New Haven: Yale University Press, 2012).
[6] This summary of current debates in Pentateuchal Criticism is largely based on R. G. Kratz, 'The Analysis of the Pentateuch: An Attempt to Overcome Barriers of Thinking', *ZAW* 128 (2016), pp. 529–61, as well as an unpublished paper by Hans Debel (presented orally at the IOSOT 2013 meeting in Munich), which he kindly sent me for personal use. For a shorter, published paper from the same perspective, see H. Debel, 'Envisioning the "Editions" of Exodus: Reconstructing the Growth of a Literary Chain of Tradition', in H. Ausloos and B. Lemmelijn (eds.), *A Pillar of Cloud to Guide: Text-critical, Redactional, and Linguistic Perspectives on the Old Testament in Honour of Marc Vervenne* (BETL, 269; Leuven: Peeters, 2014), pp. 363–78.

narrative of the book of Leviticus, such that Exodus should be read in light of its larger literary context. Scholars debate how far the narrative history of Israel for which Exodus was composed extends, suggesting either a Tritoteuch (three books = Genesis–Leviticus), Tetrateuch (four books = Genesis–Numbers), Pentateuch (five books = Genesis–Deuteronomy), Hexateuch (six books = Genesis–Joshua), Heptateuch (seven books = Genesis–Judges), or Enneateuch (nine books = Genesis–Judges plus Samuel and Kings).[7]

In later tradition, Exodus was most closely identified with the Pentateuch (the five books of Moses), known in Hebrew as the Torah (תורה = 'instruction', from which is derived the concept of 'law') or in Greek as the Law (ὁ νόμος). Presumably the five books of the Pentateuch were first written separately on five medium-sized scrolls in a multi-volume series. But the Dead Sea Scrolls (in particular 4QExod-Lev^f) suggest that by the third century BCE at the latest, these books may frequently have been written together on a single large scroll, as is the case with medieval and modern Torah scrolls. From the fourth century CE, Christians began occasionally making complete Bibles in Greek, containing both the Old and New Testaments (and sometimes also other books). In Greek Christian circles, Exodus came to be frequently written in large codices containing the Octateuch (8 books = Genesis–Judges plus Ruth). Jewish scribes began occasionally copying Exodus as part of large codices containing the entire Hebrew Bible (equivalent to the Christian OT) in Hebrew at the latest in the tenth century CE.

Exodus is considered sacred scripture by Jews and Christians alike. It has been and continues to be an undisputed part of the canon of the HB for all Jewish and Samaritan (the latter accept only the Pentateuch) groups and part of the OT canon for almost all Christian groups (some Christian heresies like that of Marcion rejected the OT).

5. The Text of Exodus in Hebrew

a. Ancient Evidence

After its composition into a form that would be recognizable as the book of Exodus to modern readers, the book continued to undergo certain changes that can be documented in the manuscript tradition. I have argued that the high degree of homogeneity in the tradition and the patterns of readings in our extant manuscripts suggest that all of our extant textual witnesses ultimately descend primarily (if not exclusively) from a single common ancestor—an archetype—which can be dated no later than the fourth century BCE.[8] Already by the third century BCE, however, Exodus was preserved in diverse text forms that show evidence of continuing minor literary development beyond the core text common

---

[7] For a recent discussion, see T. B. Dozeman, T. Römer, and K. Schmid (eds.), *Pentateuch, Hexateuch, or Enneateuch? Identifying Literary Works in Genesis through Kings* (Atlanta: Society of Biblical Literature, 2011).

[8] D. Longacre, 'A Contextualized Approach to the Hebrew Dead Sea Scrolls Containing Exodus' (Ph.D. diss., University of Birmingham, 2015), pp. 229–36.

to all witnesses, most frequently with harmonistic or interpretive expansions. Preserved Greek texts (to be discussed below) suggest that in the early third century there probably was a now-lost Hebrew version of the construction of the tabernacle in chs. 25–40 that was shorter than the presently known Hebrew texts and differently arranged. All surviving Hebrew manuscripts, however, follow one of two alternative arrangements of these chapters—both of which must have been circulating already in the third century—which expand the text to create greater correspondence between the commands and the reports of their execution.[9] Most ancient and medieval Jewish Hebrew manuscripts (the former often called proto-Masoretic or M[asoretic]-like) have the arrangement of the tabernacle account essentially as known in modern English translations. A significant minority of the Dead Sea Scrolls (especially 4QpaleoExod^m) and all Samaritan manuscripts, however, move the instructions for making the altar of incense (Exod. 30.1-10) from their position as an appendix to the instructions to incorporate them in a more appropriate location after the other implements of the tabernacle (after 26.35).

The latter branch of the tradition—often called 'pre-Samaritan'—further distinguishes itself from the relatively conservative general tradition with numerous harmonistic expansions (e.g., 6.9b; 7.18b, 29b; 8.1b, 19b; 9.5b, 19b; 10.2b; 11.3b; 18.25+; 20.19a; 20.21b; 32.10+; 39.21+),[10] which create greater correspondence between: (1) commands and their executions and (2) narrated speeches/events and other references to them. The typologically later Samaritan Pentateuch further adds an additional partisan commandment (20.17b) requiring worship on Mt. Gerizim based on texts from Deuteronomy (Deut. 5.18b or 11.29; 27.2-7; 11.30), and in Exod. 20.24 it limits sacrificial worship to that one location and changes God's decree about the worship center to a past-tense statement.[11]

---

[9] A theory of textual relations popularized by William F. Albright and Frank Moore Cross and defended in more recent times by Nathan Jastram suggests that the Samaritan Pentateuch (SP) and Septuagint (LXX) descended from a common Palestinian branch of the textual tradition apart from the Masoretic text (MT). See W. F. Albright, 'New Light on Early Recensions of the Hebrew Bible', in F. M. Cross and S. Talmon (eds.), *Qumran and the History of the Biblical Text* (Cambridge, MA: Harvard University Press, 1975), pp. 140–46; F. M. Cross, 'The Evolution of a Theory of Local Texts', and 'The History of the Biblical Text in the Light of Discoveries in the Judaean Desert', in *Qumran and the History*, pp. pp. 306–20 and 177–95, respectively; N. Jastram, 'A Comparison of Two "Proto-Samaritan" Texts from Qumran: 4QpaleoExod^m and 4QNum^b', *DSD* 5, no. 3 (1998), pp. 264–89. On the other hand, J. E. Sanderson, *An Exodus Scroll from Qumran: 4QpaleoExod^m and the Samaritan Tradition* (HSS, 30; Atlanta: Scholars Press, 1986); J. R. Davila, 'Text-Type and Terminology: Genesis and Exodus as Test Cases', *RevQ* 16, no. 61 (1993), pp. 3–37; and K. Kim, 'Studies in the Relationship between the Samaritan Pentateuch and the Septuagint' (Ph.D. diss., Hebrew University of Jerusalem, 1994), argue that MT and SP are more closely related to each other than to LXX, and the secondary agreements between SP and LXX, though numerous, are mostly superficial harmonizations. The close agreement between MT and SP against LXX in the tabernacle accounts strongly supports this latter opinion.

[10] Here the plus sign (+) marks the expansions.

[11] While scholars continue to debate the parallel situation in Deuteronomy (where the Samaritan Pentateuch and some other witnesses state that God had already chosen the worship center, while other witnesses state that that decision would be made in the future), the non-classical hybrid form אזכרתי of the Samaritan Pentateuch in Exod. 20.24 is obviously secondary.

Several related manuscripts from Qumran preserve running texts of Exodus with frequent harmonistic and midrashic expansions and rearrangements (4Q158, 4Q364, 4Q365, and 4Q366). Scholars continue to debate whether these so-called (Reworked) Pentateuch manuscripts (4QRP[a-d]) were intended as revisions of the book of Exodus or one or more new, derivative works based on Exodus, as well as whether or not they may have been accepted as sacred scripture within the Qumran community.[12] But there is a growing consensus that these texts at least continued a process of literary development evident already within the clearly documented history of the book of Exodus.

As with the rest of the Pentateuch, the copies of Exodus from the Judean Desert reflect an interesting pattern. Manuscripts discovered at sites other than Qumran (in the case of Exodus, only Mur1) agree extremely closely with later, Jewish manuscripts (MT), whereas the manuscripts discovered in the Qumran caves display somewhat more variety and difference, even in those that follow the same general text type as the MT. This has led some scholars to argue that there must have been a particular text preserved in, preferred by, and promulgated by Jerusalem temple circles.[13] Others, however, have argued that textual pluriformity was ubiquitous across the spectrum of Jewish groups.[14]

Below is a list of all the continuous-text Hebrew copies of the book of Exodus recovered from the Judean Desert.[15] Most of these scrolls were written in the square Jewish script (2Q3 and 4Q20 have only the tetragrammaton in paleo-Hebrew), but two were written entirely in paleo-Hebrew (4Q11 and 4Q22).

---

[12] In addition to the DJD editions, see the extensive discussions in D. K. Falk, *The Parabiblical Texts: Strategies for Extending the Scriptures in the Dead Sea Scrolls* (London: T&T Clark, 2007); S. W. Crawford, *Rewriting Scripture in Second Temple Times* (Grand Rapids: Eerdmans, 2008); E. Tov, 'From 4QReworked Pentateuch to 4QPentateuch (?)', in M. Popović (ed.), *Authoritative Scriptures in Ancient Judaism* (JSJSup, 141; Leiden: Brill, 2010), pp. 73–91; M. Zahn, *Rethinking Rewritten Scripture: Composition and Exegesis in the 4QReworked Pentateuch Manuscripts* (STDJ, 95; Leiden: Brill, 2011); E. Ulrich, *The Dead Sea Scrolls and the Developmental Composition of the Bible* (VTSup, 169; Leiden: Brill, 2015), pp. 187–94.

[13] E.g., E. Tov, 'The Dead Sea Scrolls and the Textual History of the Masoretic Bible', in N. Dávid, A. Lange, K. de Troyer, and S. Tzoref (eds.), *The Hebrew Bible in Light of the Dead Sea Scrolls* (FRLANT, 239; Göttingen: Vandenhoeck & Ruprecht, 2012), pp. 41–53 (47–48); A. van der Kooij, 'Preservation and Promulgation: The Dead Sea Scrolls and the Textual History of the Hebrew Bible', in Dávid, Lange, de Troyer, and Tzoref (eds.), *The Hebrew Bible in Light of the Dead Sea Scrolls*, pp. 29–40.

[14] Ulrich, *Dead Sea Scrolls*, pp. 21–25.

[15] It should also be noted that several additional Dead Sea Scrolls-like fragments of Exodus have recently come into the hands of three private collections: the Museum of the Bible (MOTB) collection; the Martin Schøyen collection; and the Southwestern Baptist Theological Seminary collection. These fragments, however, are of questionable provenance and authenticity, having appeared on the market along with many fragments now considered to be modern fakes by some specialists. See my review of the volume publishing the fragments from the MOTB collection: D. Longacre, review of *Dea Sea Scrolls Fragments in the Museum Collection*, edited by E. Tov, K. Davis, and R. Duke, *JTS* 69, no. 1 (2018), pp. 265–67. For more detailed arguments against the authenticity of at least some of the newly purchased fragments, see K. Davis, 'Caves of Dispute: Patterns of Correspondence and Suspicion in the Post-2002 "Dead Sea Scrolls" Fragments', *DSD* 24, no. 2 (2017), pp. 229–70; K. Davis et al., 'Nine Dubious "Dead Sea Scrolls" Fragments from the Twenty-First Century', *DSD* 24, no. 2 (2017), pp. 189–228.

They are all published in the official Discoveries in the Judaean Desert series, published by Oxford University Press (volume numbers indicated below).

ID	Name	Assigned Date	Textual Affiliation	DJD
1Q2	1QExod	1–50 CE	Insufficient data; close to MT	I
2Q2	2QExod[a]	50–68 CE	Close to LXX or independent	III
2Q3	2QExod[b]	1–68 CE	Probably a heavily reworked manuscript; possibly a series of excerpts	III
2Q4	2QExod[c]	75–1 BCE	Insufficient data	III
4Q1	4QGen-Exod[a]	125–100 BCE	Conservative; close to MT	XII
4Q11	4QpaleoGen-Exod[l]	100–25 BCE	Conservative; closely aligned with 4Q14	IX
4Q13	4QExod[b]	30 BCE–20 CE	Close to LXX or independent	XII
4Q14	4QExod[c]	50–25 BCE	Conservative; closely aligned with 4Q11	XII
4Q17	4QExod-Lev[f]	250–175 BCE	Harmonistic; pre-SP	XII
4Q18	4QExod[g]	c. 50 BCE	Insufficient data; close to MT	XII
4Q19	4QExod[h]	50–1 BCE	Insufficient data	XII
4Q20	4QExod[j]	1–25 CE	Probably to be reconstructed pre-SP	XII
4Q21	4QExod[k]	50–68 CE	Insufficient data	XII
4Q22	4QpaleoExod[m]	100–25 BCE	Harmonistic; pre-SP	IX
4Q158	4Q(Reworked) Pentateuch[a]	50–1 BCE	Heavily reworked	V
4Q364	4Q(Reworked) Pentateuch[b]	75–50 BCE	Heavily reworked	XIII
4Q365	4Q(Reworked) Pentateuch[c]	75–50 BCE	Heavily reworked	XIII
4Q366	4Q(Reworked) Pentateuch[d]	75–50 BCE	Heavily reworked	XIII
Mur1	MurGen-Exod.Num[a]	100–125 CE	Conservative; identical to MT	II

Portions of Exodus (mostly from chs. 12–13 and 15) can also be found in excerpt manuscripts, such as 4Q15 (4QExod^d), 4Q16 (4QExod^e), 4Q37 (4QDeut^j), 4Q175 (4QTestimonia), and numerous *tefillin* and *mezuzot*. The discovery of an Aramaic translation of Leviticus at Qumran suggests that we should probably presume that Exodus also circulated in Aramaic translation, though no ancient manuscript evidence survives.

b. Modern Editions of Hebrew Exodus

Exodus has not yet appeared in any of the major ongoing text-critical series: *The Hebrew Bible: A Critical Edition* (*HBCE*), *Biblia Hebraica Quinta* (*BHQ*), or the Hebrew University Bible Project (HUBP). Thus, the current standard scholarly Hebrew text edition of Exodus remains *Biblia Hebraica Stuttgartensia* (*BHS*), which reproduces diplomatically the text of the famous Leningrad Codex along with critically edited Masoretic notes and an apparatus of variant readings. This resource is important for quick reference, but must be used with caution for detailed textual scholarship. Most importantly, *BHS* does not include the many readings from the Dead Sea Scrolls, and its treatment of the Greek tradition is often insufficient or misleading. Thus, scholars studying New Testament citations of Exodus must carefully examine these corpora for themselves. Wevers' edition mentioned in the section on the Greek text of Exodus remains the standard point of reference for the Old Greek and variant readings within the Greek tradition (and daughter versions). For quick and convenient checks of whether or not the fragmentary Qumran scrolls preserve a particular passage under consideration, see now the reference work of Ulrich,[16] though of course more detailed investigation requires reference to their principal editions in the Discoveries in the Judaean Desert series.

For the Samaritan Pentateuch, the edition of von Gall remains indispensable.[17] Von Gall's critically edited base text does not adequately reflect Samaritan orthography and grammar and occasionally makes emendations against all Samaritan manuscripts. Nevertheless, used judiciously, it remains the most important source for understanding the Samaritan tradition, given the breadth of its coverage. Another helpful resource is the edition of Tal and Florentin,[18] whose base text more accurately reflects the Samaritan manuscript tradition, but without the extensive documentation found in von Gall. The forthcoming large critical edition of Schorch will soon replace both von Gall and Tal and Florentin as the standard reference text for the Samaritan Pentateuch.[19]

---

[16] E. Ulrich, *The Biblical Qumran Scrolls: Transcriptions and Textual Variants* (VTSup, 134; Leiden: Brill, 2010). Note, however, that this reference work does not include the scrolls found at sites other than the eleven scroll caves around Qumran, which for Exodus means MurGen-Exod.Num^a.

[17] A. F. von Gall, *Der Hebräische Pentateuch der Samaritaner* (Giessen: Töpelmann, 1918).

[18] A. Tal and M. Florentin, *The Pentateuch: The Samaritan Version and the Masoretic Version* (Tel Aviv: Haim Rubin, 2010 [Hebrew]).

[19] S. Schorch, 'A Critical *editio maior* of the Samaritan Pentateuch: State of Research, Principles, and Problems', *HBAI* 2/1 (2013), pp. 100–20.

6. The Text of Exodus in Greek

Since the New Testament was written in Greek and the authors cited their scriptures in Greek, it is only natural that the starting point for analyzing their uses of the Old Testament should likewise be with the Greek scriptures. For this reason, we will linger somewhat longer than in other sections on the nature of the Greek scriptures in the time of the New Testament authors.[20]

a. Origins

In the beginning of the third century BCE, there was a significant diasporan Jewish community located in Greek-speaking Alexandria. With the ever-decreasing knowledge of Hebrew among its members, this community made the momentous decision to translate the Hebrew Pentateuch into Greek. The *Letter of Aristeas* claims that the king Ptolemy II commissioned the translation for the famous library of Alexandria and that it was realized by 72 Judean translators (later forms of the story mention 70 translators). Most scholars today, however, are convinced that it was a product largely by and for the benefit of the expat Jewish community in the early third century BCE.

In the middle of the twentieth century, Paul Kahle suggested that there were originally many different popular Greek translations, which were gradually lost as the diversity of early texts was homogenized into a single, standardized version.[21] Recent manuscript discoveries (both in Israel and Egypt) and evidence for processes of revision towards contemporary Hebrew texts, however, have led most scholars today to the conclusion that there was indeed a single, influential translation that served as the foundation for later developments in the Greek tradition.[22]

b. Translation Technique

Based on systematic differences between books in the ways the texts were translated from Hebrew to Greek, it appears that each book of the Pentateuch was translated separately by a different person. The translator of Exodus is widely recognized from his work as one of the best translators of the scriptures into Greek, based on his ability to understand his Hebrew base text and bring across the meaning in a contextually sensitive way into relatively good Greek by the standards of his time. While he often translated the Hebrew text by giving word-for-word equivalents in Greek when it was not problematic, he nevertheless

---

[20] For further introductory discussion on the Septuagint of Exodus, see A. Salvesen, 'Exodus', in J. K. Aitken (ed.), *T&T Clark Companion to the Septuagint* (London: Bloomsbury T&T Clark, 2015), pp. 29–42.
[21] P. E. Kahle, 'Untersuchungen zur Geschichte des Pentateuchtextes', *TSK* 88 (1915), pp. 399–439; P. E. Kahle, *The Cairo Geniza* (Oxford: Blackwell, 2nd edn, 1959).
[22] See especially the influential work of D. Barthélemy on the Minor Prophets scroll, *Les devanciers d'Aquila* (VTSup, 10; Leiden: Brill, 1963). Cf. A. Aejmelaeus and Tuukka Kauhanen (eds.), *The Legacy of Barthélemy: 50 Years after Les Devanciers d'Aquila* (Göttingen: Vandenhoeck & Ruprecht, 2017).

tried to ensure that his translation was readable, clear, and stylistically pleasing. For example, he might add words to clarify ambiguous texts, leave out Hebrew words that were unnecessary in the Greek, or vary his choice of lexical equivalents for semantic or stylistic reasons. Furthermore, the translator of Exodus used Greek conjunctions very freely in order to explicate his perception of the logical structure of the text, such as when the Hebrew has the simple conjunction ו ('and') without explicitly stating how the clauses on either side of the conjunction are connected. An illuminating example of this translator's technique can be seen in Exod. 1.16:

Masoretic Text and Septuagint of Exodus 1.16	
ויאמר בילדכן את העבריות וראיתן על האבנים אם בן הוא והמתן אתו ואם בת היא וחיה	καὶ εἶπεν Ὅταν μαιοῦσθε τὰς Ἑβραίας καὶ ὦσιν πρὸς τῷ τίκτειν, ἐὰν μὲν ἄρσεν ᾖ, ἀποκτείνατε αὐτό, ἐὰν δὲ θῆλυ, περιποιεῖσθε αὐτό.
And he said, 'When you act as midwives to the Hebrew women and you see *them* on the stones[?], if it is a son, then you shall kill him, and if it is a daughter, then she shall live'.	And he said, 'Whenever you act as midwives to the Hebrew women and they are about to give birth, if it is a male, kill him, but if a female, spare her'.

Several characteristic translation decisions can be seen in this instructive example. First he translates ויאמר with the simple Greek equivalent καὶ εἶπεν. But the first Hebrew word of the quotation of Pharaoh's words (בילדכן, lit. 'in your acting as midwives to') presents a challenge for the translator, since the syntactical construction ב plus an infinitive construct plus a subjective personal pronoun for a temporal clause (i.e., 'when you are acting as midwives to') would be somewhat awkward if translated literally into Greek. Instead, he translates the more idiomatic Ὅταν μαιοῦσθε to bring across correctly and in a more natural Greek way the idea that the midwives were supposed to do their gruesome duty each time (i.e., 'whenever') they were acting as midwives. The translator then chooses not to represent the Hebrew direct object marker את in את העבריות, since it is unnecessary in Greek, where the accusative case has the same function. In the obscure Hebrew idiom וראיתן על האבנים (lit. 'and you see [on] the stones[?]'), the 'stones' are commonly interpreted as referring to some sort of birthing stool on which the laboring women sat, but may alternatively be understood as the 'genitals' of the babies by which the midwives would check the sex.[23] This difficult idiom would make no sense to Greek readers literally translated—and, uncharacteristically, may not have even been understood correctly by the translator—so he translated it according to his interpretation

---

[23] A. Aejmelaeus, 'What Can We Know about the Hebrew *Vorlage* of the Septuagint?', in *On the Trail of the Septuagint Translators: Collected Essays* (Leuven: Peeters, rev. edn, 2007 [originally published 1987]), pp. 71–106 (94).

with a normal Greek equivalent καὶ ὦσιν πρὸς τῷ τίκτειν, 'they are about to give birth'. He completely changes the words and the syntactic structure, but he still brings across the perceived (or guessed) meaning for his Greek readers.

The translator shows a similar degree of freedom in the next part of the verse. First, he translates אם בן הוא ('if it is a son') with ἐὰν μὲν ἄρσεν ᾖ ('if it is a male'). This translation uses the obvious equivalent אם = ἐάν ('if') for the conditional clause, but the translator adds the conjunction μέν that has no equivalent in the Hebrew, since the μέν ... δέ construction is the normal way of introducing two possible options as in 'on the one hand...on the other hand...' He further chooses not to translate בן as υἱός ('son'), but rather uses the more appropriate Greek word ἄρσεν ('male'), since in the context it is the sex of the child that is emphasized, rather than a familial relationship. The pronoun הוא is ignored in the Greek, which instead adds the subjunctive verb ᾖ ('it is'), which is expected in such a Greek conditional construction. והמתן אתו ('then you shall kill him') is rendered in a fairly straightforward way as ἀποκτείνατε αὐτό ('kill him'), though the translator uses an aorist imperative rather than a future to represent the Hebrew *weqatal*-form verb and does not render the Hebrew conjunction ו, since Greek does not use a conjunction in apodoses to conditional clauses. The protasis of the second conditional clause ואם בת היא ('and if it is a daughter') is translated as ἐὰν δὲ θῆλυ ('but if a female'), which uses the postpositive δέ as equivalent to the Hebrew conjunction ו to complete the idiomatic μέν...δέ construction, even though it requires changing the word order and translating ו—which has been translated with καί earlier in the sentence—with a different word. Here the translator shows that he is concerned more with bringing across the logical structure of the text than reproducing every Hebrew conjunction with the same Greek equivalent. The use of θῆλυ ('female') for בת ('daughter') again stresses the sex of the baby over against familial relationships. And again, the pronoun היא is ignored in the translation as unnecessary in good Greek. Finally, the *weqatal*-form verb וחיה ('and she will live') is translated with another imperative περιποιεῖσθε αὐτό ('spare her'), which brings across the correct meaning, but with a different root ('spare' vs. 'live') and syntax. The example of 1.16 gives an impression of the translator's skillful reworking of the text to bring across the meaning in good Greek in small-scale translation units.

Complicating this general picture of a skillful translator reworking the text into relatively good Greek is the possibility that there may have been more than one hand at work behind the Greek text as we now know it. Particularly in the account of the construction of the tabernacle in chs. 35–40 as opposed to the rest of the book, scholars have noticed differences in lexical equivalents, different understandings of Hebrew technical vocabulary, and large-scale quantitative differences in chs. 35–40 when compared to the Hebrew, which some have explained as resulting from two different translators[24] or a single translator

---

[24] J. Popper, *Der biblische Bericht über die Stiftshütte: ein Beitrag zur Geschichte der Composition und Diaskeue des Pentateuch* (Leipzig: Heinrich Hunger, 1862); J. W. Wevers, *Text History of the Greek Exodus* (MSU, 21; Göttingen: Vandenhoeck & Ruprecht, 1992); J. W. Wevers, 'The

with subsequent revision.²⁵ Perhaps most noteworthy among these differences is the dilemma that the tabernacle seems to be oriented differently in the different sections, according to Bogaert.²⁶ Other scholars continue to argue that the entire book appears to have been translated by a single translator.²⁷

c. Hebrew Source Text

Closely connected with the debate over the number of translators evident in the Old Greek of Exodus is the question of the Hebrew source text from which it was translated. While the Greek text of most of the book is quite close to known Hebrew texts, in the tabernacle accounts—particularly chs. 35–40—there are significant differences from all known Hebrew manuscripts in both contents and order. See the 'Synoptic Overview of the Tabernacle Accounts' below, which arranges the instructions for (chs. 25–31) and narrated construction of (chs. 35–40) the tabernacle and its accoutrements in parallel and highlights substantial discrepancies in order or contents between witnesses.²⁸ Perhaps the most noteworthy differences between the Old Greek and extant Hebrew witnesses are:²⁹

1. The Greek text lacks a substantial amount of text concerning the breastplate that is found in the Hebrew witnesses (MT 28.23-28).
2. The Greek text places the fashioning of the priestly garments (MT 39.2-31 || LXX 36.8b-40) before the construction of the tabernacle, rather than after it.
3. The Greek text has a substantially shorter version of the construction of the tabernacle structure itself (MT 36.8-34 || LXX 37.1-6; 38.18-21), which is divided into two sections.
4. The Greek text places the fashioning of the courtyard (MT 38.9-23 || LXX 37.7-21) immediately after the construction of the tabernacle, rather than after the items within the courtyard.

Building of the Tabernacle', *JNSL* 19 (1993), pp. 123–31; D. Fraenkel, 'Übersetzungsnorm und literarische Gestaltung—Spuren individueller Übersetzungstechnik in Exodus 25ff. + 35ff.', in L. Greenspoon and O. Munnich (eds.), *VIII Congress of the International Organization for Septuagint and Cognate Studies, Paris, 1992* (SCS, 41; Atlanta: Scholars Press, 1995), pp. 73–87; M. L. Wade, *Consistency of Translation Techniques in the Tabernacle Accounts of Exodus in the Old Greek* (SCS, 49; Atlanta: SBL, 2003).

25. D. W. Gooding, *The Account of the Tabernacle: Translation and Textual Problems of the Greek Exodus* (TS, 6; Cambridge: Cambridge University Press, 1959).
26. P.-M. Bogaert, 'L'orientation du parvis du sanctuaire dans la version grecque de l'Exode (*Ex.*, 27,9-13 LXX)', *AC* 50 (1981), pp. 79–85.
27. A. H. Finn, 'The Tabernacle Chapters', *JTS* 16 (1915), pp. 449–82; A. Aejmelaeus, 'Septuagintal Translation Techniques – A Solution to the Problem of the Tabernacle Account', in *On the Trail of Septuagint Translators: Collected Essays* (Leuven: Peeters, rev. edn, 2007 [originally published in 1990]), pp. 107–21.
28. Major content and structural differences are **underlined and in bold**.
29. || means that the passages are parallel, where the verse numbering differs in the Hebrew and Greek editions.

5. The Greek text lacks a substantial amount of material concerning the construction of the items for the tabernacle (MT 37.1–38.7 ∥ LXX 38.1-17, 22-24), completely lacking a focused account of the construction of the incense altar (MT 37.25-28), though it does mention the incense altar elsewhere (LXX 39.16; 40.5, 24).
6. The Greek text of the concluding summary also differs considerably in many ways (MT 39.32–40.38 ∥ LXX 39.14–40.32).

Synoptic Overview of the Tabernacle Accounts					
Contents	*MT 25–31*	*SP 25–31*	*LXX 25–31*	*MT/SP 35–40*	*LXX 35–40*
A. Offering	25.1-9	as MT	25.1-8	35.1-29	35.1-29
B. Bezalel and Oholiab				35.30–36.7	35.30–36.7
				36.8a	**36.8a**
C. Priestly Vestments					**36.8b-40**
D. Tabernacle				**36.8b-38**	**37.1-6**
E. Courtyard					**37.7-21**
F. Ark	25.10-22	as MT	25.9-21	**37.1-9**	**38.1-9**
G. Table	25.23-30	as MT	25.22-29	**37.10-16**	**38.9-12**
H. Candlestick	25.31-40	as MT	25.30-40	**37.17-24**	**38.13-17**
I. Incense Altar				**37.25-28**	
J. Anointing Oil				**37.29**	
K. Tabernacle	**26.1-35**	**as MT**	**26.1-35**		**38.18-20**
L. Courtyard					**38.21**
M. Incense Altar		**30.1-10**			
N. Tabernacle	26.36-37	as MT	26.36-37		
O. Altar of Burnt Offerings	27.1-8	as MT	27.1-8	**38.1-7**	**38.22-24**
P. Anointing Oil and Incense					**38.25**
Q. Bronze Basin				38.8	38.26
R. Courtyard	27.9-19	as MT	27.9-19	**38.9-20**	
S. Bezalel and Oholiab				**38.21-23**	
T. Materials Used for Tabernacle				38.24-31	39.1-12
U. Oil for Lamp	27.20-21	as MT	27.20-21		
V. Garments for High Priest	28.1-4	as MT	28.1-4	39.1	39.13
W. Priestly Vestments	**28.5-43**	**as MT**	**28.5-39**	**39.2-31**	

X. Consecration of Priests	29.1-37	as MT	29.1-37		
Y. Regular Sacrifices	29.38-46	as MT	29.38-46		
Z. Incense Altar	**30.1-10**		**30.1-10**		
AA. Atonement Money	30.11-16	as MT	30.11-16		
BB. Bronze Basin	30.17-21	as MT	30.17-21		
CC. Anointing Oil	30.22-33	as MT	30.22-33		
DD. Anointing Oil	30.34-38	as MT	30.34-38		
EE. Bezalel and Oholiab	31.1-11	as MT	31.1-11		
FF. Construction				39.32-43	39.14-23
GG. Concluding Summary				**40.1-38**	**40.1-32**

In addition to these large-scale differences, there are many smaller differences where the Old Greek is typically shorter than the MT and/or differs in the formulation of details. The net effect of all these differences between the Old Greek tabernacle account and known Hebrew texts is threefold:

1. The Greek text is significantly shorter than known Hebrew texts.
2. The Greek text is generally structured according to the principle of grouping items made of similar materials according to the assigned division of labor (i.e., fabrics by Oholiab/Eliab first, followed by metal work by Bezalel), rather than moving outward from the tabernacle and its implements to the courtyard and its furnishings and finally to the priestly vestments as in known Hebrew texts.
3. Passages in the Greek text about the construction of the tabernacle and its accoutrements (chs. 35–40) typically correspond less closely to the wording of parallel passages where God instructs Moses how to construct them (chs. 25–31) than is the case in known Hebrew texts.

Based on such observations, scholars have attributed these differences either to the translation technique of the translator(s),[30] the work of a subsequent reviser,[31] or a divergent Hebrew source text for the Old Greek, commonly referred to by the German noun *Vorlage*, namely the Hebrew text that lay before the translator.[32]

---

[30] Finn, 'The Tabernacle Chapters'; Wevers, *Text History*; Wevers, 'The Building'; J. Cook, 'Exodus 38 and Proverbs 31: A Case of Different Order of Verses and Chapters in the Septuagint', in M. Vervenne (ed.), *Studies in the Book of Exodus: Redaction–Reception–Interpretation* (Leuven: Leuven University Press, 1996), pp. 537–49.

[31] Gooding, *The Account*.

[32] Popper, *Der biblische Bericht*; R. D. Nelson, 'Studies in the Development of the Text of the Tabernacle Account' (Ph.D. diss., Harvard University, 1986); Aejmelaeus, 'Septuagintal Translation Techniques'; P.-M. Bogaert, 'L'importance de la Septante et du "Monacensis" de la Vetus Latina

Aejmelaeus argues that—even though the translator practices a high degree of freedom in his translation technique—it would not have been the role of the translator to make editorial changes,[33] but others suggest that the translator could be expected to make the same kinds of editorial changes as scribes working in the Hebrew tradition.[34]

Of course, it is important to recognize that there are exceptions to these general tendencies and that these kinds of differences affect chs. 25–31 as well as chs. 35–40 (though to a lesser extent). These facts perhaps caution against explaining the differences based on a theory of two different translators. Furthermore, there is a common scribal tendency within the documented Hebrew tradition to harmonize parallel commands and the executions of those commands by assimilating the wording of one to that of its parallel. Many of the longer, more detailed texts in known Hebrew witnesses can be easily explained as the work of scribes making the wording of commands and their corresponding executions match more closely than in the Greek text. The fact that so many of the large-scale differences between the traditions can be explained by such a well-documented process also increases the chances that the major differences should be attributed to a Hebrew source text for the Old Greek translation that was generally typologically earlier than currently known Hebrew texts. The contrary theory of a translator or reviser significantly abbreviating and restructuring is based on a model that is not as well-documented, and scholars have struggled to come up with compelling reasons behind many of the changes in this scenario. Nevertheless, real problems and inconsistencies in our extant Greek texts continue to give pause, and it is not even entirely certain that the true Old Greek version of the tabernacle account has survived *in toto*. Bogaert, for instance, argues that an Old Latin codex (translated from an early Greek text) witnesses to an earlier form of the Greek text than is preserved in any surviving Greek manuscripts.[35] Furthermore, the Old Greek itself (and possibly also its *Vorlage*) is characterized by frequent harmonizations, and occasionally even significant editorial changes (e.g., claiming that the Hebrews built Heliopolis in Egypt [1.11] and stating that the bronze altar was built from the bronze of the censors from Korah's rebellion [LXX 38.22, based on MT/LXX Num 17.1-5]), so it clearly cannot be considered the direct predecessor of the Masoretic text, even if one concludes that it is generally typologically earlier. The relationship between textual witnesses and the editorial development of the tabernacle account of Exodus remains one of the most complex and contentious questions in biblical textual scholarship.

---

pour l'exégèse du livre de l'Exode (chap. 35–40)', in Verveene (ed.), *Studies in the Book of Exodus*, pp. 399–428; E. Tov, *Textual Criticism of the Hebrew Bible* (Minneapolis; Fortress, 3rd edn, 2012), pp. 316–17; B. Bruning, 'The Making of the Mishkan' (Ph.D. diss., University of Notre Dame, 2014); Ulrich, *Dead Sea Scrolls*, p. 234.

[33] Aejmelaeus, 'Septuagintal Translation Techniques'.
[34] Wade, *Consistency of Translation Techniques*; J. Screnock, *Traductor Scriptor: The Old Greek Translation of Exodus 1–14 as Scribal Activity* (VTSup, 174; Leiden: Brill, 2017), though Screnock focuses on the earlier chapters of the book.
[35] Bogaert, 'L'importance de la Septant'.

d. Transmission

After the Old Greek translation of the Pentateuch in the first half of the third century BCE, the Greek text underwent a long and complex history of transmission. Copyists, as always, made mistakes when copying the text, creating differences within Greek copies of the book. The significant differences between the Greek and Hebrew texts also caused problems for early scholars who compared them. For instance, the church father Origen lamented the great differences already in the third century CE in his famous *Letter to Africanus*.

Some ancient scholars compared their Greek texts with contemporary Hebrew texts and made revisions to the Greek to conform it more closely to the Hebrew. Still others compared their own Greek texts with these revised Greek texts and made occasional revisions. That such processes were already underway by the second century BCE is evident from two small fragments of a papyrus manuscript from cave 7 at Qumran in the Judean Desert. Given the number 805 in the standard Rahlfs numbering system (= 7Q1 or 7QpapLXXExod in the standard terminology for the study of the Dead Sea Scrolls), it is dated paleographically to approximately 100 BCE, making it the earliest preserved Greek copy of Exodus and the only pre-Christian one yet discovered. MS 805 gives early evidence of revision of the Old Greek tabernacle account towards a contemporary Hebrew text.[36]

Exodus 28.4b-7		
Masoretic Text	*Rahlfs 805 = 7Q1*	*Wevers' Old Greek*
	και	και
ועשו בגדי קדש	ποιησουσιν στολας αγιας Αα	ποιήσουσιν στολὰς ἁγίας Ἀα
לאהרן <u>אחיך</u>	ρων τω α]δ̲[ελ]φ̲[ω σου και	ρων _____ καὶ
	τοις	τοῖς
ולבניו לכהנו	υιοις α]υ̲του __ ιερα[τευειν <u>αυ</u>	υἱοῖς αὐτοῦ <u>εἰς τὸ</u> ἱερατεύειν _
לי : והם יקחו	<u>τον μ</u>]οι ⁵ και αυ[τοι λημψον	____ μοι. ⁵ καὶ αὐτοὶ λήμψον
את הזהב ואת	ται] το χρυσιον[και την υα	ται τὸ χρυσίον καὶ τὴν ὑά
התכלת ואת הארגמן	κιν]θον και τη[ν πορφυραν	κινθον καὶ τὴν πορφύραν
ואת תולעת השני ואת	και] το κοκκι[νον και την	καὶ τὸ κόκκινον καὶ τὴν
השש : ⁶ ועשו	βυσσο]ν ⁶ Κα[ι ποιησου	βύσσον. ⁶ καὶ ποιήσου
את האפד <u>זהב</u>	σιν την ε]πω̲[μιδα εκ <u>χρυ</u>	σιν τὴν ἐπωμίδα ἐκ _____
<u>תכלת וארגמן</u>	<u>σιου και υα</u>]<u>κιν</u>[<u>θου και πορ</u>	
<u>תולעת שני</u>	<u>φυρας και κοκκινου νενη</u>	
ושש משזר	σμενου και βυσσου κεκλω	_____ βύσσου κεκλω
מעשה חשב :	σμενης, εργον υφαντον ποι	σμένης, ἔργον ὑφαντὸν ποι
⁷ שתי כתפת	κιλτου· ⁷ δυο επωμιδες συν	κιλτοῦ, ⁷ δύο ἐπωμίδες συν
חברת יהיה לו	εχουσαι ε]σ̲ον̲[ται αυτω	έχουσαι ἔσονται αὐτῷ
	ετερα την ε]<u>τερα</u>[ν, επι τοις	<u>ἑτέρα τὴν ἑτέραν</u>, ἐπὶ τοῖς
אל שני קצותיו וחבר :	δυσιν μερεσιν εξηρτημεναι·	δυσὶ μέρεσιν ἐξηρτημέναι,

---

[36] So also J. W. Wevers, 'PreOrigen Recensional Activity in the Greek Exodus', in D. Fraenkel, U. Quast, and J. W. Wevers (eds.), *Studien zur Septuaginta—Robert Hanhart zu Ehren. Aus Anlaß seines 65. Geburtstages* (MSU, 20; Göttingen: Vandenhoeck & Ruprecht, 1990), pp. 121-39.

> Composite translation:
> ⁴ When they make these sacred vestments for <u>your brother</u> Aaron and his sons to serve me as priests, ⁵ they shall use gold, blue, purple, and crimson yarns, and fine linen. ⁶ They shall make the ephod <u>of gold, of blue, purple, and crimson yarns, and</u> of fine twisted linen, skillfully worked. ⁷ It shall have two shoulder-pieces attached to its two edges, <u>one to the other,</u> so that it may be joined together.

Several important textual differences illustrate this phenomenon. First, the letter traces on the first line of MS 805 (marked in black ink, as opposed to reconstructed text in gray) do not fit with letters we would expect at that location based on the Old Greek, but they do fit perfectly with the additional expression 'your brother' (underlined in each column, including a blank when not present). This expression is not found in the Old Greek, but it appears to have been added to bring the text closer to the contemporary Hebrew text that had it. The same revision towards the Hebrew appears in two closely related medieval Greek MSS 72 and 376, and the Arabic,[37] Armenian, and Syrohexaplaric translations, and notes in the margins of several medieval Greek manuscripts (85, 321, 130, and 344) claim that the early revisers Aquila, Symmachus, and Theodotion also included the phrase in their Greek texts.[38]

Second, MS 805 lacks the εἰς τό ('in order to') of the Old Greek, and reconstruction based on average line lengths strongly suggests that it added αυτον ('him') after ιερα[τευειν ('to minister') in agreement with the Hebrew, which has a third person pronominal suffix after its infinitive in לכהנו ('in order that he might minister as priest'). The second change in particular is stylistically unnecessary in the Greek and gives evidence of a scribe adding words to the Old Greek base text to make it closer to the Hebrew. This change is once again found in MSS 72, 376, and the Syrohexapla, as well as MS 318, and this correction towards the Hebrew is again marked in marginal notes in copies of the Syrohexapla as readings from the early revisers.

Third, at the bottom of the first fragment of MS 805, the ink traces fit υα]χιν[θου better than any letters that would be expected based on reconstruction according to the Old Greek. If this is correct, then it seems that a significant amount of text not in the Old Greek was added at this point to make it agree with the Hebrew. Many other manuscripts agree with this change—including a medieval correction to MS F; the *O* group of manuscripts; MS 318; the closely related MSS 128, 630, and 628; marginal notes in the Latin codices 91, 94–96; an Ethiopic manuscript; and the Arabic, Armenian, and Syrohexaplaric translations—several of which claim that this revision goes back to the early revisers.

---

[37] It is possible that the Arabic was translated directly from the Hebrew, rather than the Septuagint, in which case this would not technically qualify as a revision of the Septuagint. Thanks to an anonymous reviewer for this clarification.

[38] According to Wevers' apparatus, MS 344 also states that the expression was found in o′, which normally means the Septuagint, but this is unlikely to be the true Old Greek reading.

Thus, at three significant points, MS 805 seems to evidence early revision of the Old Greek text towards a contemporary Hebrew text. The close verbal agreement with the Old Greek in many details, however—see especially the highly distinctive idiomatic, clarifying addition ἑτέρα τὴν ἑτέραν ('one to the other') of 28.7, which has no equivalent in the Hebrew—proves that MS 805 is not a completely new Greek translation, but rather a revision of the Old Greek.

In this way, MS 805 serves as an early predecessor for the famous later revisers Aquila, Symmachus, and Theodotion, who were themselves the inspiration behind the important text-critical work of the church father Origen in the third century CE. Based on the work of the early revisers, Origen's six-columned synopsis of the Hebrew and Greek texts available to him—called the 'Hexapla'—led to the diffusion of many corrections towards the Hebrew into the mainstream Greek tradition and daughter versions, most notably by supplementing the Greek text where large passages in the Hebrew were lacking (see especially MT 28.23-28 after LXX 28.22; MT 36.8-34 after LXX 37.2; MT 37.10b-15 after LXX 38.11; MT 37.17-28 after LXX 38.17). In the process of comparing readings in different manuscripts and adopting corrections according to the Hebrew into Greek texts, the Greek manuscripts became very eclectic and mixed in their textual character, greatly complicating any attempts to reconstruct the history of transmission of the Greek text and the relationships between manuscripts in the Greek tradition.

Textual pluriformity thus appears to have been the norm in the late Second Temple period, and the New Testament authors may have had access to a bewildering array of Old Testament texts. This likely included Hebrew texts that sometimes differed from each other significantly and various Greek texts based on the Old Greek translation, but which may have been affected by revisions towards contemporary Hebrew texts. This reality is foundational to accurate analysis of New Testament uses of the Old Testament.

e. Secondary Reception of the Greek Exodus

The reception of the Old Greek translation of Exodus in other works is evident from very early in its history. Three fragments of Demetrius the Chronographer, apparently from the end of the third century BCE, are based on the Septuagint translation of Exodus and attempt to resolve exegetical problems arising in the Greek text. The fragmentarily preserved *Exagoge* of Ezekiel the Tragedian, probably from the second century BCE, similarly uses the Old Greek translation and rewrites the story of the Exodus in Greek poetic meter with embellishments.

The Greek text of Exodus is one of the books most frequently quoted and referred to in the books of the New Testament, and also frequently features prominently in the works of Philo of Alexandria and Flavius Josephus. The Septuagint has been the dominant form of the book of Exodus (although sometimes in revised form) used by the Greek-speaking church from the patristic writers up until today, as well as the basis for the translations used in many other eastern national churches (Ethiopic, Arabic[?], Armenian, Coptic—in the Achmimic, Boharic, Fayumic, and Sahidic dialects—Palestinian-Syriac, and the Syrohexapla). Old Latin texts translated from the Septuagint dominated the western church until they were superseded by Jerome's Vulgate (based on the Hebrew) in the late antique and early medieval periods. With the adoption of the Septuagint by the Greek-speaking church, it quickly fell out of favor in Rabbinic Jewish circles.

f. Modern Editions

Several modern editions of the Septuagint of Exodus are available. Two editorial projects followed the principle of presenting the main text of the edition as found in Codex Vaticanus, with variants collated from other witnesses given in apparatuses. The edition of Swete is now a relatively dated hand edition of the entire Greek Old Testament with minimal apparatus.[39] The Cambridge edition of Brooke and McLean offers much more information, but it too is mostly outdated.[40]

The short hand edition of Rahlfs (corrected by Hanhart), in contrast, presents an eclectically reconstructed main text, with variants from the major majuscule manuscripts in an apparatus.[41] Following in this eclectic editorial tradition, the current standard critical edition of the Septuagint of Exodus is the so-called Göttingen edition of Wevers.[42] Wevers incorporates nearly all known textual evidence for the Septuagint text of Exodus and its subsequent revisions into an edition with a main text and two apparatuses. The main text consists of a single critically constructed text, which represents Wevers' best attempt to reconstruct the text of the purported original Old Greek translation. The first apparatus lists all of the textual evidence of variants within the Greek manuscript tradition, as well as translations and authors dependent on the Septuagint. The second apparatus lists the readings attributed to the early revisers in the manuscripts. Wevers has also published two companion volumes, one on the textual history of the Greek Exodus,[43] and another of collected notes on selected passages in the Greek tradition.[44] While additional important textual materials have come to light since Wevers published his edition (most notably the large Exodus papyrus codex 866)[45] and some of the readings selected for his critical text may be legitimately

---

[39] H. B. Swete, *The Old Testament in Greek according to the Septuagint, Vol. 1* (Cambridge: Cambridge University Press, 1901).

[40] A. E. Brooke and N. McLean, *The Old Testament in Greek According to the Septuagint, Vol. 1, Part II* (Cambridge: Cambridge University Press, 1909).

[41] A. Rahlfs and R. Hanhart, *Septuaginta* (Stuttgart: Deutsche Bibelgesellschaft, rev. edn, 2006).

[42] J. W. Wevers, with the help of U. Quast, *Septuaginta: Vetus Testamentum Graecum Auctoritate Academiae Scientiarum Gottingensis editum, vol. II, 1 – Exodus* (Göttingen: Vandenhoeck & Ruprecht, 1991).

[43] Wevers, *Text History*.

[44] J. W. Wevers, *Notes on the Greek Text of Exodus* (SCS, 30; Atlanta: Scholars Press, 1990).

[45] For the most substantial portions published to date, see D. Minutoli and R. Pintaudi, '*Esodo* (IV 16-VII 21) in un codice di papiro della collezione Martin Schøyen (*MS* 187)', *AnaPap* 23-24 (2011–2012), pp. 17–55; K. De Troyer, 'The Textual Character of the *Exodus Codex* of the Schøyen Collection (*MS* 187; RA 866)', *AnaPap* 23–24 (2011–2012), pp. 57–79. Additional fragments were published by D. A. deSilva with M. P. Adams, 'Seven Papyrus Fragments of a Greek Manuscript of Exodus', *VT* 56 (2006), pp. 143–70; D. A. deSilva, 'Five More Papyrus Fragments from a Greek

questioned, this edition undoubtedly remains the starting point for scholarly interaction with the Greek tradition of Exodus.

Several important projects have also recently produced translations of the Septuagint of Exodus into modern languages. The *New English Translation of the Septuagint* (NETS) of Exodus (with introduction) by Larry Perkins is now the standard English translation,[46] replacing the outdated translation by Brenton. The *Lexham English Septugatint* was published more recently and adopts a different theoretical translation perspective than NETS.[47] Daniel Gurtner has also published an English translation and commentary, based on the Greek text of Codex Vaticanus.[48] The French *La Bible d'Alexandrie* translation of Exodus by Le Boulluec and Sandevoir provides a wealth of discussion on the language of the Septuagint and its reception in patristic authors.[49] Other modern-language translations include German and Spanish.[50] The recent upsurge in interest in the Septuagint both as an important early witness to the text of the Hebrew book of Exodus and as a significant literary development in its own right has rightly increased the profile of the Septuagint in every aspect of Biblical Studies and makes Septuagint studies a lively and vital field of inquiry.

7. Reception

Because Exodus was so foundational in Jewish identity, many ancient authors interacted closely with the book, both in terms of its general traditions and its specific text. At the most general level, the traditional storyline could be called into service without reference to any specific text. For instance, in 1QM 11.9-10, the author artfully elaborates on the coming punishment of the community's enemies with a reference to the destruction of the Egyptians in Exodus: 'You [God] shall treat them like Pharaoh, like the officers of his chariots in the Red Sea'.[51] In 4Q504 1-2 ii 8-12, the deliverance from Egypt is called upon as evidence of God's covenant faithfulness towards his exiled people:

Codex of Exodus', *BIOSCS* 40 (2007), pp. 1–29. At least two more fragments are in the process of publication (from the Yale and Museum of the Bible collections), but the current locations of other parts of the codex are unknown.

[46] L. J. Perkins, 'Exodus', in A. Pietersma and B. G. Wright (eds.), *A New English Translation of the Septuagint* (Oxford: Oxford University Press, 2007), pp. 43–81; for an online version of NETS including the latest corrections, see http://ccat.sas.upenn.edu/nets/edition/ (accessed 8 November 2016).

[47] K. Penner (ed.), *The Lexham English Septuagint* (Bellingham: Lexham, 2019).

[48] D. M. Gurtner, *Exodus: A Commentary on the Greek Text of Codex Vaticanus* (BSCS; Leiden: Brill, 2013).

[49] A. Le Boulluec and P. Sandevoir, *La Bible d'Alexandrie 2: L'Exode* (Paris: Cerf, 1989).

[50] W. Kraus and M. Karrer, *Septuaginta Deutsch* (Stuttgart: German Bible Society, 2009), for an online version, see https://www.academic-bible.com/en/home/scholarly-editions/septuagint/septuaginta-deutsch/ (accessed 8 November 2016); N. F. Marcos and M. V. S. Díaz-Caro (eds.), *La Biblia griega Septuaginta I: Pentateuco* (BEB, 125; Salamanca: Ediciones Sígueme, 2008).

[51] Translation by F. G. Martínez and E. J. C. Tigchelaar, *The Dead Sea Scrolls Study Edition* (Leiden: Brill, 1999), p. 131.

Surely You alone are the living God; beside You is none other. You have remembered Your covenant whereby You brought us forth from Egypt while the nations looked on. You have not abandoned us among the nations; rather, You have shown covenant mercies to Your people Israel in all [the] lands to which You have exiled them...[52]

At other times, ancient authors made implicit or explicit use of specific passages of Exodus in their writings. 4Q175 includes an excerpt from Exod. 20.21 in a collection of related passages with parallels to the *testimonia* that have been proposed to explain a series of Old Testament quotations by New Testament writers. Other works explicitly cite passages in Exodus as proof texts, such as the citation of Exod. 23.7 in 1QS 5.15. Philo of Alexandria (*Leg. All.* 1.40) uses Exod. 7.1 ('I have made you God to Pharaoh') allegorically in his discussion of the inspiration of the human mind and soul.

Another common way of more extensively using the book of Exodus in the Second Temple period was to selectively retell (or 'rewrite') substantial portions of the narrative (or possibly also legal sections) for literary (e.g., Ezekiel the Tragedian) or (more frequently) exegetical purposes, resolving difficult interpretive problems and expanding the tradition along the way. Key examples of this phenomenon include Jubilees, the Temple Scroll, Pseudo-Philo's *Liber antiquitatum biblicarum*, Josephus' *Antiquities*, and possibly the 4Q(Reworked) Pentateuch manuscripts and/or later Aramaic Targums.

A substantial number of secondary references to Exodus in Second Temple Jewish literature were collected by Armin Lange and Matthias Weigold, which is a helpful starting point, though these references should be scrutinized and supplemented.[53] Katell Berthelot and Thierry Legrand have also prepared a helpful anthology of Qumran texts that relate thematically or textually to Exodus.[54] Recent years have seen a proliferation of specialized studies on the use of Exodus in other works, highlighting the richness of this field of study.[55]

8. Conclusion

The history of the reception and transmission of the book of Exodus is extremely rich and complex, and there remains much detailed work to be done. Scholars studying NT uses of the OT must be aware of a bewildering array of textual

---

[52] Translation according to the Accordance Non-Biblical Scrolls module.
[53] A. Lange and M. Weigold, *Biblical Quotations and Allusions in Second Temple Jewish Literature* (Göttingen: Vandenhoek & Ruprecht, 2011).
[54] K. Berthelot and T. Legrand, *La bibliothèque de Qumrân, vol. 2, Torah: Exode - Lévitique - Nombres: Édition et traduction des manuscrits hébreux, araméens et grecs* (Paris: Cerf, 2010).
[55] E.g., P. Enns, *Exodus Retold: Ancient Exegesis of the Departure from Egypt in Wis 10:15-21 and 19:1-9* (HSS, 57; Atlanta: Scholars Press, 1997); R. M. Fox (ed.), *The Reverberations of the Exodus in Scripture* (Eugene, OR: Pickwick, 2014); B. Halpern-Amaru, *The Perspective from Mt. Sinai: The Book of Jubilees and Exodus* (JAJSup, 21; Göttingen: Vandenhoeck & Ruprecht, 2015); N. LaCoste, 'Waters of the Exodus: Jewish Experiences with Water in Ptolemaic and Roman Egypt' (Ph.D. diss., University of Toronto, 2016).

diversity and intricate webs of intertextual relationships. Nevertheless, the evidence and resources currently available put modern scholars in a good position to undertake this work and make significant contributions to our understanding of the book of Exodus and its ancient (and modern) interpretations.

Chapter 2

EXODUS IN MATTHEW'S GOSPEL

Jeannine K. Brown

The book of Exodus finds its way into Matthew's Gospel at a number of levels. Possibly most obvious are the citations that appear across this Gospel, with quite a number pointing to the importance of the Decalogue (Exod. 20) for the evangelist. The text of Exodus appears in the Gospel in other ways as well. References to important proper nouns from Exodus populate the First Gospel: (1) seven references to its protagonist, Moses; (2) a cluster of references to Egypt in Matthew 2—that place of original exile; and (3) references to the primary festival of both Exodus and Matthew, Passover, which provides the temporal setting for Jesus' death. Exodus appears even more subtlety in type scenes, such as the wilderness testing (of Jesus, like Israel), two great feedings of the people, and the crossing (taming) of dangerous waters. Indeed, the event from which the book is named[1]—the exodus from Egypt—appears as a significant typological event in the life of Jesus—he goes to Egypt as Israel did and returns to the land as a sign of God's protection (2.15).

Because the storyline of Exodus seems to hold some relevance for its use in Matthew, I have arranged this chapter by attending in a general fashion to the major thematic movements of that Old Testament book and beginning with an analysis of key personages common to Exodus and Matthew: (1) Moses, Israel, and Jesus; (2) Exodus Redemption; (3) Wilderness and Torah; and (4) Tabernacle and Presence.[2] While it is quite possible to organize in another manner (e.g., via

---

[1] The book's title in the Septuagint is ἔξοδος. The Matthean citations and allusions from Exodus that are discussed in this chapter are quite clearly drawn from the LXX of that book.
[2] A three-part outline of Exodus that corresponds to #2–4 here is typical; Enns, for example, outlines the book in the following three movements: (1) Departure from Egypt (chs. 1–15); (2) Mount Sinai: Law (chs. 16–24); and (3) Mount Sinai: Tabernacle (chs. 25–40). P. Enns, *Exodus* (NIVAC; Grand Rapids: Zondervan, 2000), p. 33.

Matthew's sequence; or via the categories of citations, allusions/echoes, persons/places),[3] I have found attending to the storied shape of Exodus to contribute to greater clarity for the ways Matthew draws on themes and motifs of the Exodus narrative for his own story of Jesus. In this move, I do not claim that Matthew is using Exodus as a literary whole, only that he may be interacting with these particular Exodus traditions or stories in fairly discrete ways.

A narrative outline for this topic also coheres with a methodology for intertextuality that highlights the storied nature of metaleptic analysis.[4] An underlying assumption of this method is that New Testament authors might cite or allude to (a brief part of) another text for the purpose of evoking its backstory.[5] I will argue that this is the case for the exile motif of Matthew 1–2, with its 'new exodus' connotations (see §2 below). Another prong of a storied metaleptic analysis is recognition that New Testament authors frequently access the events represented in antecedent texts to inform their own narration of Jesus' life and ministry.[6] Such 'narrative patterns', as Mallen calls them, may have fewer linguistic connections than have typically been 'required' for authentication of citations and allusions. As Mallen defines it, a narrative pattern is 'a series of events or interactions between characters whose similarity to those in an earlier text is apparent although the specific details and the language of expression may vary'.[7] I explore (§3 below) possible narrative patterns between Exodus and Matthew in Jesus' feeding miracles and his authority over the waters.

1. Moses, Israel, and Jesus

A first area for exploration is the pattern of typological relationships between Jesus and Moses and Jesus and Israel. There are numerous potential connections between the Matthean Jesus and Moses as portrayed in Exodus; and these have been comprehensively identified and addressed by Allison.[8] What I want to highlight in my brief analysis is the way that the typological uses of Moses and of

---

[3] I have followed the latter pattern in J. K. Brown, 'Genesis in Matthew's Gospel', in M. J. J. Menken and S. Moyise (eds.), *Genesis in the New Testament* (LNTS, 466; London: Bloomsbury T&T Clark, 2012), pp. 42–59.

[4] J. K. Brown, 'Metalepsis: The Intersection of Two Stories', in B. J. Oropeza and S. Moyise (eds.), *Exploring Intertextuality: Diverse Strategies for New Testament Interpretation of Texts* (Eugene, OR: Cascade, 2016), pp. 29–41.

[5] J. K. Brown, *Scripture as Communication: Introducing Biblical Hermeneutics* (Grand Rapids: Baker Academic, 2nd edn, 2021), p. 100. It is important also to recognize that an author may reference another text for multiple purposes. Beaton helpfully identifies this multipurpose intention with the terminology of a citation's 'bi-referentiality'. R. Beaton, *Isaiah's Christ in Matthew's Gospel* (SNTSMS, 123; Cambridge: Cambridge University Press, 2002), pp. 5, 120.

[6] Patterns of setting and characters are also possible and are an object of study within a storied metaleptic approach; see Brown, 'Metalepsis: The Intersection of Two Stories', pp. 31–32.

[7] P. Mallen, *The Reading and Transformation of Isaiah in Luke-Acts* (LNTS, 367; London: T&T Clark, 2008), p. 24.

[8] D. C. Allison Jr., *The New Moses: A Matthean Typology* (Minneapolis: Fortress, 1993). The scope of this chapter is focused on Exodus in Matthew, while a full exploration of a Moses typology would extend beyond Exodus to include other Old Testament books as well, most notably Numbers and Deuteronomy.

Israel for understanding Matthean Christology are inescapably intertwined in the early chapters of the Gospel, suggesting that the two might function in a fairly unified fashion.

a. Matthew 2

In Matthew 2, the storied association between Jesus and Moses revolves around the threat to their young lives by a ruthless king (Exod. 1.22; Mt. 2.13, 16). This is followed in Matthew by a fairly clear allusion to Exod. 4.19 (LXX) in Mt. 2.20. When (the adult) Moses expresses his desire to return to Egypt following his asylum in Midian, the Lord says, 'Leave and return to Egypt, *for all those who sought your life are dead*' (LXX). Matthew mirrors closely the final clause in his narration of the angel's words to Joseph after Herod's death: 'Get up and take the child and his mother and go to the land of Israel, *for those who sought the child's life are dead*' (Mt. 2.20).[9]

Exod. 4.19   τεθνήκασιν γὰρ πάντες οἱ ζητοῦντές σου τὴν ψυχήν.

Mt. 2.20   τεθνήκασιν γὰρ οἱ ζητοῦντες τὴν ψυχὴν τοῦ παιδίου.

While this allusion could be marshalled as clear evidence for a Moses–Jesus typology, the differences between the two texts are important to consider. It is the *adult Moses* who returns *to Egypt* after the death of those seeking to kill him for killing one of their own countrymen (Exod. 2.11-15). In Matthew, the *child Jesus* is brought back to *the land of Israel* after asylum in Egypt. Therefore, while Exodus' Moses and Matthew's Jesus share some storied similarities (e.g., precarious infancies under despotic kings, asylum in another country), they also differ in important ways (e.g., reasons for and countries of asylum), suggesting that Jesus is not being portrayed in Matthew 2 (or elsewhere in Matthew) *primarily* as 'the new and better Moses'.[10] Instead, Matthew has layered this connection with his Israel–Jesus typology, which is the more central association in this part of Matthew.[11]

A signal that Matthew's primary typological lens from Exodus for Jesus is Israel (more than Moses) comes in Mt. 2.15, in the citation from Hos. 11.1: 'Out of Egypt I have called my son'. This reference itself is a storied allusion to the exodus event from Exodus 14–15 (cf. Exod. 4.22-23: 'Israel is my firstborn son').[12] That Hosea refers to the past event of Yahweh's deliverance of Israel

---

[9] All translations of biblical texts are my own, unless otherwise indicated.
[10] The language comes from D. Platt, *Exalting Jesus in Matthew* (Nashville, TN: B&H Academic, 2013), pp. 92–93. Allison is judicious in his assessment of the purposes of Matthew's Moses typology, concluding that the evangelist does nothing to denigrate Moses in comparison to Jesus; in fact, he suggests that '[i]t was Moses' very greatness that allowed honor to pass from him to his superior look-alike' (*New Moses*, p. 276).
[11] Allison notes that 'in Matthew 2 the evangelist glossed the traditional Moses typology with an Israel typology' (*New Moses*, p. 166) and indicates that it is likely that Matthew 'construe[d] Jesus' status as the new Israel and his identity as another Moses as correlative conceptions' (p. 142).
[12] R. B. Hays, *Echoes of Scripture in the Gospels* (Waco, TX: Baylor University Press, 2016), p. 113.

(the referent of 'my son') is clear from his previous line: 'When Israel was a child, I loved him' (Hos. 11.1a, NRSV).[13] Matthew draws on the exodus event (via Hosea) to accent the important similarities between Israel's story and Jesus' life. They are both in Egypt, away from the 'promised' land. From that place, God brings them back to 'the land of Israel' (Mt. 2.20 and 21), with Matthew signaling a parallel between God's restoration in the exodus event and in the present arrival of Jesus the Messiah. The primacy here of Israel-Christology (over Moses-Christology) emerges from the evangelist's use of the exodus event to focus attention on Israel's (and Jesus') identity as God's son, rather than on parallels between Jesus and Moses. In this way, Matthew's allusions to Moses via story and text appear to reference Exodus in a general way, with more particular attention being given to Israel-Christology.

b. Matthew 4.2

Outside of the infancy narrative, Matthew draws on Exodus typologically at Mt. 4.2, with scholars arguing for either a Moses or Israel typology (or both) in that allusion as well. The relevant language from Matthew involves the phrase describing Jesus' activity of fasting 'forty days and forty nights" (ἡμέρας τεσσεράκοντα καὶ νύκτας τεσσεράκοντα). The same language (though in different word order, with the adjectives preceding the nouns) occurs in the Septuagint of Exod. 34.28, where Moses is on Mount Sinai before the Lord for 'forty days and forty nights' without eating or drinking (see also 24.18). This motif, with identical language, also occurs at Deut. 9.9, and given the thematic use of Deuteronomy 6–8 in Matthew's temptation scene (4.4, 7, 10), it could be argued that the Deuteronomy text provides the source for the allusion at Mt. 4.2. Nevertheless, the Exodus narrative is the basis for the Deuteronomy reference, with the latter being 'but a recollection of the original events described twice in Exodus' (24.18; 34.28).[14] In other words, Exodus provides the prototype event for the narration of Jesus' fasting in the wilderness.[15]

Yet there is another layer to this allusion, one that picks up on the temporal reference to 'forty [days]' along with the locative setting of 'the wilderness' (Mt. 4.1). Given that Matthew will consistently highlight a comparison (and specifically a contrast) between Jesus *and Israel* in the temptation narrative,[16] it is likely that an allusion is intended to the forty years of Israel's wilderness wandering within the lead-in to this pericope at 4.1-2 (see Num. 14.32-34; cf.

---

[13] Beale argues that, in his use of Hosea, 'Matthew was assuming a presupposition of corporate solidarity between Christ and Israel'. G. K. Beale, 'The Cognitive Peripheral Vision of Biblical Authors', *WTJ* 76 (2014), pp. 263–93 (277).

[14] D. M. Gurtner, '"Fasting" and "Forty nights": The Matthean Temptation Narrative (4:1-11) and Moses Typology', in C. A. Evans and H. D. Zacharias (eds.), *'What Does the Scripture Say': Studies in the Function of Scripture in Early Judaism and Christianity, vol. 1: The Synoptic Gospels* (LNTS, 470; London: Bloomsbury T&T Clark, 2012), pp. 1–11 (5).

[15] Numerous scholars see an allusion to both Exodus and Deuteronomy here in Matthew; e.g., U. Luz, J. E. Crouch, and H. Koester, *Matthew 1–7: A Commentary* (Minneapolis: Fortress, 2007), p. 151; D. A. Hagner, *Matthew* (WBC, 33A-B; 2 vols.; Dallas, TX: Word Books, 1993, 1995), p. 1:64; J. Nolland, *The Gospel of Matthew* (NIGTC; Grand Rapids, MI: Eerdmans, 2005), p. 163.

[16] See J. K. Brown, *Matthew* (TTCS; Grand Rapids, MI: Baker, 2015), pp. 34–39.

Exod. 16.35; Deut. 8.2).[17] This possibility gains traction via the testimony of select Second Temple Jewish writings that seem to generalize Moses' experience of fasting forty days/nights to make it an *Israel experience*.[18] In the *Life of Adam and Eve*, Adam is portrayed as committing to a forty-day fast for repentance after expulsion from paradise (6.1). Abraham takes similar action—fasting for 'forty days and nights' on Mount Horeb accompanied by an angel, according to the *Apocalypse of Abraham* (12.1-2). Isaac is characterized as fasting for forty-day periods as evidence of his piety in the *Testament of Isaac* (4.4).[19] It is telling that these foundational figures of Judaism are each portrayed in line with the biblical portrait of Moses fasting for forty days (and forty nights).[20]

While it would be fair to argue that these biblical figures are portrayed as taking on the appearance of Moses,[21] it is just as possible to argue that Moses' experience is being generalized to Israel's representative figures. This makes sense especially if Moses himself is understood representatively for Israel, as he seems to be in the biblical material (e.g., Exod. 32.9-14, 30-32; 33.12-17).[22] If this representative (typological) function—Moses like Israel and Israel like Moses—is a Jewish phenomenon, Matthew's comparison of Jesus in his forty days of wilderness fasting to Israel's forty-year wilderness experience is only heightened by these Moses allusions. As Allison frames Matthew's perspective, 'Jesus' experience of another exodus made him both like Israel and like Moses'.[23] And Matthew's focus in his early chapters seems to land more squarely on *Jesus as Israel* than on *Jesus as Moses*. As Donaldson suggests, '[l]ike Israel of old, Jesus has been called by God out of Egypt to a life of humble obedience; like Israel, this calling was put to the test in the wilderness. The hope of the story is that, unlike Israel, Jesus will remain faithful where Israel was disobedient'.[24] As we have seen in Matthew 2, a Moses typology might be nested within the evangelist's more prominent Israel-Christology.

---

[17] Carter understands Matthew to be echoing both Exod. 34.28 (Moses) and Israel's forty-year wilderness experience. W. Carter, *Matthew and the Margins: A Socio-political and Religious Reading* (Sheffield: Sheffield Academic, 2000), p. 108.

[18] See references in Allison, *New Moses*, pp. 168–69.

[19] '[Isaac] would also fast the three forty-day periods, every time the forty-day period came around' (4.4) (Stinespring's translation, in 'Testament of Isaac', p. 907). This text suggests a pattern of fasting, although it is not clear the context in which this pattern emerges (i.e., Egyptian Judaism or Coptic Christianity, which has exerted some influence on this 1–2 century CE text); W. F. Stinespring, 'Testament of Isaac: A New Translation and Introduction', in J. H. Charlesworth (ed.), *The Old Testament Pseudepigrapha* (2 vols.; New York: Doubleday, 1983, 1985), pp. 1:903–11 (904).

[20] In *3 Bar.* 4.14, the first-person narrator recounts how Noah prays and laments for forty days (though no mention of fasting is included).

[21] E.g., Gurtner, 'Moses Typology', pp. 8–9.

[22] Hays (*Echoes of Scripture in the Gospels*, p. 117) highlights the intercessory (i.e., representative) role that Moses has in the Old Testament (e.g., Deut. 9.25-26).

[23] Allison, *New Moses*, p. 142. The difference between my view and Allison's has to do with relative emphasis. I understand Matthew nesting moments of Moses typology within his more prominent Israel-Christology. Alternatively, Allison suggests that in Mt. 4 'the evangelist overlaid the existing Israel typology with specifically Mosaic motifs' (p. 166).

[24] T. L. Donaldson, 'The Vindicated Son: A Narrative Approach to Matthean Christology', in R. N. Longenecker (ed.), *Contours of Christology in the New Testament* (Grand Rapids, MI: Eerdmans, 2005), pp. 110–21 (116).

2. Exodus Redemption

Matthew introduces early in his Gospel (2.15) the exodus event to show Jesus to be a type of Israel. Yet the motif of the exodus may already begin in the first chapter of Matthew, if we understand the evangelist making a connection between his prominent exile theme and the motif of a (new) exodus.

Matthew signals a clear exilic theme in the opening genealogy; one of its two key junctures is the Babylonian exile, with the reference to 'exile' or 'deportation' occurring twice in this terse genealogical genre (μετοικεσία; 1.11-12). In fact, the shape of the genealogy as interpreted by the evangelist (1.17) moves from establishment of the covenant people (beginning with Abraham, 1.2) and of its kingship (with David, 1.6) to loss of land and kingship during the time of exile (1.11-12), to the restoration of the people and of kingship in Jesus the Messiah (1.16). Restoration from exile becomes tied to exodus motifs with the repetition of the phrase 'of his brothers' (1.2, 11).[25] This phrase connects two moments in Israel's history when the people were displaced from the land—during their time in Egypt (1.2) and during Babylonian exile (1.11). This connection offers the implication that the final turn of the genealogy—the arrival of the Messiah and of restoration—is a kind of new exodus, a return from exile to the promised land (cf. 2.19-21).

This is confirmed by the evangelist's use of intertexts in Matthew 2 as well as the narrative flow of that chapter. Matthew's use of Micah and Jeremiah, as well as Hosea with its allusions to the exodus event (above), each revolve around the motif of return from exile.[26] Additionally, the plot of Matthew 2 highlights the parallel between Israel's sojourn from Egypt back to their land and Jesus' similar path from Egypt back to 'the land of Israel' (repeated at 2.20, 21). According to Matthew, Jesus as Messiah inaugurates a return from exile—a new exodus—that promises restoration for the people of Israel and the nations beyond.[27]

Matthew's passion narrative provides the climax of the motif of new exodus. He locates Jesus' missional death during the feast of Passover (26.2, 17) and fosters a theological connection between the two to accent Matthew's 'new exodus typology'.[28] At Jesus' final meal with his disciples, his words allude to the ratification ceremony of the covenant between Yahweh and Israel in Exodus 24 (LXX):

> Mt. 26.28 'For this is my blood of the covenant [τοῦτο γάρ ἐστιν τὸ αἷμά μου τῆς διαθήκης] which is poured out for many for the forgiveness of sins'.

---

[25] The two names in Matthew's genealogy that surface in Exodus are Amminadab and Nahshon (father and brother of Elisheba, who was married to Aaron; see Exod. 6.23).
[26] Brown, *Matthew*, pp. 22–27.
[27] Brown, *Matthew*, p. 25.
[28] W. D. Davies and D. C. Allison Jr., *Matthew* (ICC; 3 vols.; London: T&T Clark, 1988, 1991, 1997), p. 3:437.

Exod. 24.8 'Look, the blood of the covenant [Ἰδοὺ τὸ αἷμα τῆς διαθήκης], which the Lord made with you concerning all these words'.

The scene in Exodus has Israel professing their covenantal loyalty to Yahweh and their obedience to God's commands ('all these words'). Thus, Matthew's allusion to Exod. 24.8 (cf. also 24.6) 'recalls the original basis of Israel's life as the special people of God'.[29] For the evangelist, Jesus' missional death brings about a renewal of that same covenant, with covenantal disobedience being addressed by Jesus' own blood—his representative death—and resulting in forgiveness and life. And while Matthew avoids using language of 'new' covenant (cf. Lk. 22.20; 1 Cor. 11.25), by drawing on Exod. 24.8 in this way he confirms the renewal of the covenant as Israel's new exodus.[30] As Carter expresses it, 'a new exodus, this time involving a world dominated by Roman not Egyptian power, is under way'.[31]

Some commentators have also seen an echo of the exodus event in the ten miracles of Matthew 8–9, as a parallel with the ten plagues of Exodus 7–12. For example, Grundmann draws upon *m. 'Abot* 5.4-5, which highlights the importance of the number ten in relation to the Exodus miracles, to suggest that Matthew connects these ten plagues ('ten wonders') with the 'ten wonders of the messianic era', thereby accenting the connection between Moses and Jesus.[32] Gundry also raises this possible connection and notes that the potential significance of the number ten is heightened by the likelihood that 'Matthew has combined two exorcisms into one and two healings of blind men into one'.[33] If so, then Matthew 8–9, like Matthew 5–7, would contribute to Jesus 'as the greater Moses'.[34] Yet, in the end, Gundry suggests that this possibility is not particularly likely.[35]

One of the determining factors for this question of the significance of ten miracles is whether Matthew, in the intercalation of the accounts of the healing of a young girl (9.18-19, 23-26) and of a woman with chronic bleeding (9.20-22), intends one or two healings to be counted. If these two healings are viewed as a single account, then there are nine miracles across Matthew 8–9, rather nicely arranged in groups of threes (8.1-17; 8.23–9:8; 9.18-34), with discipleship-themed sections interspersed (8.18-22; 9.9-17).[36] If the healings of the young

---

[29] R. T. France, *Matthew* (NICNT; Grand Rapids: Eerdmans, 2007), p. 994.
[30] Hays adds to this allusion an echo of Exod. 24.9-11, where Moses and Israel's leaders eat together: 'The fact that these words of institution occur in the context of a *meal* is also directly reminiscent of Exodus 24:9-11' (*Echoes of Scripture in the Gospels*, p. 134).
[31] Carter, *Matthew and the Margins*, p. 506.
[32] W. Grundmann, *Das Evangelium nach Matthäus* (HThKNT, 1; Berlin: Evangelische Verlagsanstalt, 1968), pp. 245–46 (author's translation). See also discussion in C. S. Keener, *A Commentary on the Gospel of Matthew* (Grand Rapids: Eerdmans, 1999), p. 258.
[33] R. H. Gundry, *Matthew: A Commentary on His Literary and Theological Art* (Grand Rapids: Eerdmans, 1982), p. 136.
[34] Gundry, *Matthew*, p. 136.
[35] He suggests that the many healings of Mt. 8.16 make any definitive counting of the miracles of chs. 8–9 tenuous.
[36] Davies and Allison, *Matthew*, pp. 2:1–2; see also pp. 1:86–87. But note Allison's reconsideration (though not change of mind) in *New Moses*, given the Exodus arrangement of the ten plagues in three groups of three, with a final, single plague (pp. 209–13).

girl and the woman are understood (and communicated) as two accounts by Matthew, then there are ten miracles in Matthew 8–9 and the possibility that the evangelist is evoking the ten plagues increases. If Matthew is pointing to the ten plagues with these ten miracles of Jesus, then a significant reversal could be in view. While Exodus portrays ten moments of destruction as a part of Israel's redemption from Egypt, Matthew represents Jesus as the Messiah of Israel's restoration from sickness (8.17) and even from death (9.18-26). This, then, would fit with Matthew's accent on Jesus as enacting Israel's new exodus.

3. Wilderness and Torah

a. Wilderness Safety and Provision

We have already seen that the wilderness motif, drawn from Israel's experience, is used by Matthew to signal his Israel-Christology (4.1-11). The evangelist also draws on specific references to Israel's exodus and wilderness experiences to signal the theme of God's provision for Israel through Jesus' Galilean ministry. Specifically, Jesus' act of rescue from the dangers of the waters and his provision of food for the people evoke similar Exodus motifs. As Keener comments on Jesus' miraculous actions in 14.13-33, '[t]he God of the Exodus, who divided waters (Ex 14:21) and provided manna from heaven (Ex 16:14-18), was at work in history again'.[37]

Jesus is portrayed as the one who rescues his followers from the chaotic waters in Mt. 8.23-27 and 14.22-33. As Senior notes, '[w]ithin the biblical world, the fearsome power of the sea was associated with demonic forces. To exert power over the sea was, therefore, a symptom of the divine presence.'[38] In Mt. 8.23-27, a storm threatens Jesus' disciples and they fear they will drown. In Mt. 14.22-33, the wind and waves pound their boat (14.24; cf. 8.24). Jesus by his presence and power tames the waters (Mt. 8.26; 14.32). This picture may evoke God's rescue of Israel from Egypt through power over the waters: 'the Lord drove the sea back' (Exod. 14.21; cf. 15.8). Jesus rescues his disciples as Yahweh had saved Israel (Exod. 14.30; cf. Mt. 8.25; 14.30).[39] This connection finds support in Jesus' words to his disciples at Mt. 14.27: 'Take courage! It is I [ἐγώ εἰμι]. Do not fear.' The affirmation, ἐγώ εἰμι, appears to evoke the words of the God who addresses Moses at the burning bush and provides the self-identification, Ἐγώ εἰμι ὁ ὤν ('I am who I am', Exod. 3.14).[40]

Matthew also characterizes Jesus' ministry as one of miraculous, material provision for his people, similar to Yahweh's provision of food (quail and manna) for Israel through Moses during their wilderness journeys (e.g., Exod. 16.1-18).

---

[37] Keener, *Gospel of Matthew*, p. 404.
[38] D. Senior, *Matthew* (ANTC; Nashville: Abingdon, 1998), p. 102.
[39] Senior too suggests Exod. 14.13-31 as a possible allusion: 'Walking upon the sea is also depicted as a manifestation of divine power over the chaos of the waters... The dramatic Exodus event where the Israelites march dry-shod through the sea may be an influence [in Matthew 14]' (*Matthew*, pp. 171–72).
[40] Davies and Allison, *Matthew*, p. 2:506; Senior, *Matthew*, p. 171.

Both Matthean feedings (5,000 in 14.15-21; and 4,000 in 15.32-39) 'echo the story of Moses providing food for Israel in their wilderness wanderings'.[41]

5,000 Fed (Mt. 14.15-21)	4,000 Fed (Mt. 15.32-39)	Echoing of Exodus
In a 'deserted' (ἔρημος) place (14.15)	In a 'deserted' (ἐρημία) place (15.33)	In the 'desert' of Sin (ἔρημος) Exod. 16.1, 3; LXX)
People have no food (14.15)	People have no food (15.32)	People have no food (Exod. 16.3)
Five loaves and two fish (14.17)	Seven loaves and a few fish (15.34)	Manna and quail (Exod. 16.13-14)
All ate and were full (14.20)	All ate and were full (15.37)	All had what they needed (Exod. 16.18)

Other potential allusive connections to Exodus in this regard are worth noting. Matthew's added phrase in the two feedings to the number being fed 'besides women and children' (14.21; 15.38; cf. Mark 6.44; 8.9) may evoke Exod. 12.37, which indicates the number of Israelites leaving Egypt: about 600,000 men 'besides women and children' (12.37, RSV).[42] Hagner offers that Matthew may have found it desirable to preserve these two feedings (from Mark) in order to parallel the two feedings of Moses in Exodus 16 and Numbers 11.[43] It is also intriguing in the healing summary introducing the second feeding (Mt. 15.29-31) that Matthew narrates the response of the crowd as praising 'the God of Israel' (τὸν θεὸν Ἰσραήλ, 15.31). This way of referring to Yahweh, common enough in the Old Testament (e.g., Judg. 5.3; 1 Kgs 1.48; Ps. 41.13 [LXX: 40.14]), occurs at Exod. 5.1: 'So says the Lord, the God of Israel [ὁ θεὸς Ισραηλ]'.

Given that some of the shared details between the feedings recur during the Passover meal Jesus will eat with his disciples (Mt. 26.20-30),[44] the Exodus narrative echoes gain even greater prominence.[45]

> Through these multidirectional interconnections, Matthew signals that the feeding miracles should be interpreted through the lens of Israel's experience in the wilderness. As Israel was led from slavery to freedom by their God, so now Israel's God is acting in their history to bring about a new exodus or return from exile, already prophesied by Isaiah (e.g., 40:1-11). For Matthew, Jesus is the one who inaugurates this new exodus from

---

[41] J. K. Brown and K. A. Roberts, *Matthew* (THNTC; Grand Rapids: Eerdmans, 2019), p. 139, from which the chart is derived. Turner concurs, noting the likelihood 'that Matthew intends this story to remind his readers of the past miraculous feeding of the Israelites with manna in the wilderness'. D. L. Turner, *Matthew* (BECNT; Grand Rapids: Baker Academic, 2008), p. 369. See also Carter, *Matthew and the Margins*, pp. 306, 328.
[42] Davies and Allison, *Matthew*, pp. 2:493.
[43] Hagner, *Matthew*, p. 450.
[44] For a detailed analysis, see Brown and Roberts, *Matthew*, p. 139.
[45] See prior discussion of the Exodus Passover allusions in Mt. 26.20-30 and 26.28 particularly.

beginning (see Matt 3:2) to end—from his ministry of provision for his people [in the feedings] to his provision of forgiveness through his death at the time of Passover (26:28).[46]

b. Torah

Quite a number of citations or obvious allusions to Exodus appear in Matthew in connection to the Torah. The first location where these Torah texts emerge is in the 'antitheses' of the Sermon on the Mount (Mt. 5.21-46).

Exod. 20.13 (LXX) οὐ φονεύσεις
'You shall not commit murder'

Mt. 5.21 'You have heard that it was said to the people of ancient times, "You shall not commit murder"' (οὐ φονεύσεις)

Exod. 20.14 (LXX) οὐ μοιχεύσεις
'You shall not commit adultery'

Mt. 5.27 'You have heard that it was said, "You shall commit adultery"' (οὐ μοιχεύσεις)

Exod. 21.24 (LXX) ὀφθαλμὸν ἀντὶ ὀφθαλμοῦ, ὀδόντα ἀντὶ ὀδόντος
'...an eye for eye, a tooth for tooth...'

Mt. 5.38 You have heard that it was said, "An eye for an eye and a tooth for a tooth..."' (ὀφθαλμὸν ἀντὶ ὀφθαλμοῦ καὶ ὀδόντα ἀντὶ ὀδόντος)

In these citations, Matthew uses the Septuagint consistently with little variation; only the addition of καί in Mt. 5.38 distinguishes these three references from their Exodus counterparts (LXX). Matthew's use of these three Torah stipulations in the flow of the Sermon on the Mount is significant. The evangelist draws on a number of foundational teachings from the Torah to demonstrate that Jesus applies the Torah by intensifying its original messages. In these citations, Matthew's Jesus draws a comparison between a Torah prohibition or command and his own corresponding teaching as an intensification of it.[47] Allen describes this intensification as a 'next step' hermeneutic, demonstrating that the relationship between Old Testament instruction and Jesus' teaching is not one of antithesis or direct contrast

---

[46] Brown and Roberts, *Matthew*, pp. 139–40. Carter (*Matthew and the Margins*, p. 326) highlights how the feeding of the 4,000 in Matthew 'exhibits the new creation in which in God's empire there is abundant food for all'.

[47] Because of this movement toward intensification (versus contradiction), Boxall suggests that these six comparisons could be referred to as 'hypertheses'. I. Boxall, *Discovering Matthew: Content, Interpretation, Reception* (Grand Rapids: Eerdmans, 2015), p. 129.

but of extension.⁴⁸ In other terms, Jesus is 'making a fence around the Torah', a Jewish practice of broadening the scope of a command or limiting further a prohibition to protect it from transgression (e.g., *m. 'Abot* 1.1).

In extending the prohibition against murder to disavowing even anger, Matthew's Jesus does not contradict the Old Testament command. Instead, he raises the bar for his followers: they are not only to obey the prohibition against murder but are also to eschew the anger and disdain that could lead to murder.⁴⁹ With this connection, Jesus emphasizes the importance of authentic 'alignment of disposition and action, of motive and behavior'.⁵⁰ This calibration of disposition and behavior runs across the six comparisons ('antitheses') of 5.21-48. It can be seen in the second comparison between the Old Testament command against adultery (Exod. 20.14) and Jesus' prohibition against even lusting after or desiring a woman (Mt. 5.27-28). In the fifth comparison (the final one which draws upon Exodus), Jesus cites the *lex talionis*—'the law of retribution' (Exod. 21.24), whose purpose was to limit a punishment to fit a crime and not exceed it. This role of the *lex talionis* in limiting retribution and so curbing revenge is likely in view in Jesus' citation of it (see Philo, *Spec. Leg.* 3.182, for a reference to the equality of the Torah seen in this command). Jesus provides an intensification of that teaching for his disciples—they are not even to 'oppose' (or 'violently oppose') those doing evil toward them (5.39).⁵¹

The emphasis on alignment of disposition and behavior across these six comparisons culminates in the final one commending love of even one's enemy (5.43-44),⁵² which finds its source in God's disposition and action (5.45-48): 'Be complete and whole as your Father in heaven is complete and whole' (τέλειος, 5.48).⁵³ Divine integrity—alignment of motive and behavior—is to shape a life of integrity for any who would be a disciple of Jesus. Jesus, in the Sermon on the Mount, has already introduced this motif in the sixth beatitude: 'Blessed are those whose hearts are undivided, for they will see God' (5.8).

Just as the Decalogue is essential for Jesus' early teachings on the Torah and its right interpretation (5.21-48), so Matthew continues to portray Jesus returning to these foundational teachings across his ministry. When confronted with

---

⁴⁸ O. W. Allen, *Fortress Biblical Preaching Commentaries: Matthew* (Lanham: Fortress, 2013), p. 60.

⁴⁹ This tie between anger and murder is more apparent if there is an allusion at Mt. 5.21-26 to Gen. 4.1-12—the story of Cain's anger toward and subsequent murder of Abel. See Brown, 'Genesis in Matthew', p. 50, drawing on D. C. Allison, Jr., *Studies in Matthew: Interpretation Past and Present* (Grand Rapids: Baker, 2005), pp. 65–78.

⁵⁰ Brown and Roberts, *Matthew*, p. 62.

⁵¹ Wink suggests that the verb ἀνθίστημι is best understood as denoting violent resistance. W. Wink, 'Beyond Just War and Pacifism: Jesus' Nonviolent Way', *RevExp* 89 (1992), pp. 197–214 (199). Louw and Nida offer 'fight back against' as an appropriate translation equivalent for ἀνθίστημι. J. P. Louw and E. A. Nida, *Greek-English Lexicon of the New Testament Based on Semantic Domains* (New York: United Bible Societies, 2nd edn, 1989), p. 49.

⁵² Jesus' teaching here is anticipated by Exod. 23.4-5: 'When you come upon your enemy's ox or donkey going astray, you shall bring it back. When you see the donkey of one who hates you lying under its burden and you would hold back from setting it free, you must help to set it free' (NRSV). Yet Matthew's exhortation moves beyond the OT ethic and is 'revolutionary in its newness' (Hagner, *Matthew*, p. 134).

⁵³ For discussion of this translation of τέλειος, see Brown and Roberts, *Matthew*, pp. 66, 346.

Pharisees from Jerusalem who accuse his disciples of ignoring purity regulations established by the elders (15.1-2), Jesus counters by identifying their disobedience to the very commands of God in their efforts to obey such human traditions (15.3-9). In the process, he cites parts of both Exod. 20.12 and 21.17 (numbered in the LXX as 21.16) to indicate the fundamental importance of caring for father and mother:

> Exod. 20.12   τίμα τὸν πατέρα σου καὶ τὴν μητέρα …
> 'Honor your father and mother'

> Exod. 21.16 (LXX)   ὁ κακολογῶν πατέρα αὐτοῦ ἢ μητέρα αὐτοῦ τελευτήσει θανάτῳ (cf. 21.17 in MT/English)
> 'The one who speaks evil of their father or their mother shall be put to death'

> Mt. 15.4   ὁ γὰρ θεὸς εἶπεν· τίμα τὸν πατέρα καὶ τὴν μητέρα, καί· ὁ κακολογῶν πατέρα ἢ μητέρα θανάτῳ τελευτάτω.
> '"Honor your father and mother", and "The one who speaks evil of their father or mother must be put to death"'[54]

In his use of these key Exodus commands across his story of Jesus,[55] the evangelist highlights narratively *Jesus as consummate interpreter of the Torah*. Across Matthew, this narrative-Christological emphasis routinely emerges in contrast to Israel's teachers—the scribes and the Pharisees. The evangelist portrays these teachers—those who 'sit in Moses' seat' (23.2) and so *should* be interpreting the Torah rightly—as misguided and so as 'guides who are blind' (15.14; 23.16, 24).[56] As he introduces the antitheses, Jesus has already indicated that scribes and Pharisees are not paragons of Torah adherence (or interpretation): 'For I tell to you that unless your covenant loyalty (δικαιοσύνη) exceeds that of the

---

[54] The omission of the pronouns in Matthew's rendering of the Septuagintal texts does not seem significant, as the Greek article can stand in for pronouns in any case. See D. B. Wallace, *Grammar beyond the Basics: An Exegetical Syntax of the New Testament* (Grand Rapids: Zondervan, 1996), p. 211. Nolland suggests that their omission is due to Matthean economizing of space (*Gospel of Matthew*, p. 616).

[55] Jesus also refers to the Decalogue at 19.18-19; see below.

[56] It is worth noting the references to Moses in Matthew are primarily focused on the contest between the Jewish leadership and Jesus as to who rightly represents and interprets the Torah understood as coming from Moses. The Pharisees and scribes reference Moses' teaching (Deut. 24.1-4) for their interpretation of divorce (Mt. 19.7), while Jesus counters with his own interpretation of that teaching of Moses (Mt. 19.8). The Sadducees cite Moses' teaching from Deut. 25.5-6 to create a scenario to test Jesus' as Torah interpreter (Mt. 22.24). And while Jesus technically affirms the role of the Pharisees and scribes as sitting in 'Moses' seat', it is Jesus himself in his teaching role ('listen to him') who at his transfiguration is affirmed by the divine voice in the presence of Moses and Elijah (17.3-5). Jesus also encourages obedience to the Torah by exhorting the man he has healed from a skin disease to 'offer the gift commanded by Moses' (8.4). Nilsen notes that, in the controversy stories of the Gospels, the personage of Moses 'becomes almost synonymous with the "law", which clearly is the Torah' (p. 306). She concludes, 'Moses, then, is remembered as a prophet foreshadowing Jesus, a lawgiver and the law itself' (p. 307); T. D. Nilsen, 'Memories of Moses: A Survey through Genres', *JSOT* 41 (2017), pp. 287–312.

scribes and the Pharisees you will certainly never enter the kingdom of heaven' (Mt. 5.20).[57] Jesus, on the other hand, interprets the Torah rightly by doing so through the lens of the prophets (see 'the Law and/or the Prophets' at 5.17; 7.12; 22.40; cf. 11.13). His prophetic interpretation of Torah is discernable at Mt. 9.13; 12.17 (Hos. 6.6) and 23.23 (Mic. 6.8). In the process, Jesus prioritizes the Torah's central or 'weightier matters' (Mt. 23.23). This kind of debate around the relative centrality of various laws was commonplace in Judaism (e.g., *m. 'Abot* 2.1).[58]

We can see attention to a prioritization of Torah commands in the story of the rich man and Jesus at Mt. 19.16-22. In response to the man's question about gaining eternal life, Jesus calls him to keep the commandments (19.17). The man's question, 'Which ones?', is more than likely 'focused on prioritization (which are most important?) than exclusion (which am I free to ignore?)'[59] Jesus answers by again returning to the Decalogue; he cites particularly commands that address how one should act toward neighbor (Exod. 20.12-16)[60] and concludes with the more general call to love neighbor from Leviticus (19.18; cf. Mt. 22.34-40).[61] In this listing, Jesus has omitted the commands focused on allegiance to God, namely, the prohibitions against worshiping other gods, against images, and against misuse of the name of Yahweh, along with the command regarding Sabbath observance (Exod. 20.3-11). This omission may be significant since the rich man will walk away from discipleship when complete allegiance is required of him—divesting of possessions for the poor to follow Jesus (19.21-22; cf. 6.24). As Brown and Roberts note, '[t]he man does not *attach* himself to Jesus because he is unable to *detach* himself from his many possessions for the sake of the kingdom'.[62]

4. Tabernacle and Presence

a. Tabernacle/Temple

The final major narrative movement of Exodus involves the instructions for building the tabernacle, where Israel's God then comes to live among the people (Exod. 25–40).[63] While references to the temple in Matthew do not necessarily find their origins in Exodus, some of the particulars of the temple structures and accessories can be traced back to that book. Additionally, Exodus references for financial support of the tabernacle make their way into Matthew's narrative in ch. 17.

---

[57] For δικαιοσύνη as a covenantal term, in Judaism and in Matthew, see J. K. Brown, 'Justice, Righteousness', in J. B. Green, J. K. Brown, and N. Perrin (eds.), *Dictionary of Jesus and the Gospels* (Downers Grove: InterVarsity, 2nd edn, 2013), pp. 463–67.

[58] G. Burge, 'Commandment', in Green, Brown, and Perrin (eds.), *Dictionary of Jesus and the Gospels*, pp. 149–52 (151).

[59] Brown and Roberts, *Matthew*, pp. 179–80.

[60] Matthew's listing differs in order but not in wording from the Septuagint (other than the omission of the pronoun in relation to parents, similar to Mt. 15.4 discussed above).

[61] This concluding note is missing from the evangelist's Markan source (10.19).

[62] Brown and Roberts, *Matthew*, p. 180.

[63] Enns, *Exodus*, p. 33.

The account of the temple tax, unique to Matthew (17.24-27), alludes to Exod. 30.13-16 (cf. 38.26), with its reference to the half-shekel requirement for support for the tabernacle (and subsequently for the temple). In Matthew, those who collect the temple tax ('the two-drachma', τὰ δίδραχμα; 17.24) inquire as to whether Jesus pays it.[64] It seems that Jews of Jesus' era were not obligated to pay the tax.[65] After the temple's destruction in 70 CE, Rome absorbed this tax, claiming it for their own purposes (the *fiscus judaicus*).[66] Jesus claims exemption for himself and his disciples, in a move similar to other Jewish groups. In Jesus' case, he provides a kingdom rationale in which the children or sons of the kingdom are free from such taxation: 'the word "sons" [υἱοί, *huioi*, "children, sons"] invites us to reflect on Jesus' special relationship with the God whose temple the tax was meant to service'.[67] Nevertheless, this brief pericope concludes with Jesus choosing to pay the tax to avoid causing others to stumble (in this case, those collecting the tax), an important motif in the subsequent Community Discourse (18.6-9).[68]

Echoes of the Exodus tabernacle also emerge in Matthew 23, within Jesus' prophetic critique of scribes and Pharisees. At 23.16-22, Jesus criticizes the hypocritical practice of taking oaths in capricious or arbitrary ways (potentially to extract oneself from an oath when it became inconvenient to keep). Philo provides a window into this kind of behavior when he indicates that he knows of people who 'swear at length and make whole speeches consisting of a string of oaths and thus, by their misuse of the many forms of the divine name in places where they ought not to do so, show their impiety' (*Dec.* 94). Jesus censures those who would invalidate swearing by the temple while claiming that to swear by the gold of the temple is binding (Mt. 23.16). The reference to '[the temple's] gold' (χρυσός) points back to the instructions for and description of the building the tabernacle in Exodus 25–39, where gold (χρυσίον) is used extensively in the tabernacle and its furnishings (e.g., 25.11-13, 17-18, 24-26, 28-31, 36-39).[69] Jesus argues that the gold of the temple cannot be the basis of a stronger oath, since the temple (or in the case of Exodus, the tabernacle) is greater than the gold used in its service.[70]

Jesus provides a similar argument in 23.18-19 against any who would invalidate swearing by the (temple's) altar (θυσιαστήριον) while considering an oath

---

[64] The τὰ δίδραχμα being the Matthean contemporary equivalent of the half-shekel.

[65] D. E. Garland, 'The Temple Tax in Matthew and the Principle of Not Giving Offense', in D. Bauer and M. Alan Powell (eds.), *Treasures New and Old: Recent Contributions to Matthean Studies* (Atlanta: Scholars Press, 1996), pp. 68–98 (74–75).

[66] This raises the question of whether Matthew is drawing on this account for his own audience after the temple's destruction to provide instruction about payment of this Roman tax; W. Carter, 'Paying the Tax to Rome as Subversive Praxis: Matthew 17.24-27', *JSNT* 76 (1999), pp. 3–31.

[67] France, *Matthew*, p. 666.

[68] The collectors of the temple tax should not be subsumed within the category of tax-collectors (for Rome) or within Matthew's characterization of Jewish leadership. Instead, it is likely that Jewish 'communities had certain persons assigned to make the collections and forward them to Jerusalem' (*m. Šeqal.* 2.1; Garland, 'Temple Tax', p. 69 n. 1).

[69] Unsurprisingly, the Greek, ναός ('temple') does not occur in the Septuagint of Exodus; instead, σκηνή ('tabernacle') occurs across chs. 25–40.

[70] Jesus' central teaching on oaths comes earlier in Matthew, in the Sermon on the Mount, where Jesus disavows frivolous oaths altogether and calls his followers to let their 'word stand as either "Yes" or "No"' (5.37).

binding if it is sworn by a gift (δῶρον) offered on that same altar. Jesus contends that, because the altar 'consecrates the gift' (23.19), the altar is greater than the gift. Exodus 29 is relevant to Jesus' argument, as it highlights the 'most holy' status of the altar in the tabernacle (and later, the temple):

> ...you shall offer a sin offering for the altar (θυσιαστήριον), when you make atonement for it, and shall anoint it, to consecrate it. Seven days you shall make atonement for the altar, and consecrate it, and the altar shall be most holy; whatever touches the altar shall become holy. (29.26b-37, NRSV)

A final and most significant Matthean reference to an element of the temple comes at the climax of the Gospel—at Jesus' death by crucifixion. Immediately upon breathing his last (Mt. 27.50), 'the curtain in the temple ripped in two from top to bottom' (27.51).[71] The curtain (καταπέτασμα) referenced here likely refers to the inner curtain of the temple (and formerly in the tabernacle). As Gurtner notes, the inner curtain is the only one of the three tabernacle curtains whose Hebrew term is uniformly translated by καταπέτασμα in the Septuagint so that it functions as the 'default' term for that inner curtain.[72]

This inner curtain separated the most holy place from the rest of the tabernacle (and later, the temple). As the Exodus instructions read, 'You shall hang the curtain under the clasps, and bring the ark of the covenant in there, within the curtain; and the curtain shall separate for you the holy place from the most holy' (Exod. 26.33, NRSV). Given this expressed function, it is most likely that Matthew's reference to the rending of the καταπέτασμα has to do with overcoming such separation. As Gurtner suggests, '[t]he accomplishment of atonement by the death of Jesus necessarily leads to the accessibility of humanity to God, depicted in Matthew not just as a person entering God's presence...but also as God's being "with us" (Emmanuel, 1:23)'.[73]

---

[71] The other phenomena the evangelist narrates include an earthquake (Mt. 27.51) and resurrection (resuscitation) of 'many holy people' (27.52-53). The former, according to Luz, accords with the Old Testament's witness to earthquakes as one locus of divine revelation (e.g., Exod. 19.18 and the quaking of Sinai at the presence of Yahweh; U. Luz and H. Koester, *Matthew 21–28: A Commentary* [Minneapolis: Fortress, 2005], p. 566). On the latter (holy ones raised), see Brown, *Matthew*, p. 312.

[72] D. M. Gurtner, *The Torn Veil: Matthew's Exposition of the Death of Jesus* (SNTSMS, 139; Cambridge: Cambridge University Press, 2007), p. 46; see also pp. 199–201. Gurtner elsewhere argues that 'καταπέτασμα is the "default" term for the inner veil in the LXX, and where καταπέτασμα is used for a curtain other than the inner veil, the LXX translator indicates so by the use of a locative genitive' (noting that the NT authors omit using a locative genitive and so reference the inner veil); D. M. Gurtner, 'LXX Syntax and the Identity of the NT Veil', *NovT* 47 (2005), pp. 344–53 (345).
The three curtains identified in the Septuagint of Exodus with the term καταπέτασμα are: (1) the curtain at the entrance of the tabernacle (e.g., 26.36-37 LXX); (2) the curtain at the entrance to the courtyard (e.g., 39.19 LXX); and (3) the curtain within the tabernacle dividing the holy place from the holiest place (e.g., 26.31-33; 30.6; 40.3, 21 LXX). This overlap of terminology is understandable given that '[t]he tabernacle is basically a series of curtains and frames' (Enns, *Exodus*, p. 519).

[73] Gurtner, *The Torn Veil*, p. 189.

b. Presence

This particular tabernacle (temple) allusion leads fairly seamlessly into a final Exodus category for consideration, that of presence, and specifically the divine presence among the people of God. Matthew offers a clear and potent *inclusio* for this motif in his affirmation of Jesus as 'Emmanuel... God with us' (1.23) and in Jesus' concluding promise, 'I am with you always' (ἐγὼ μεθ' ὑμῶν εἰμι, 28.20). These final words of Jesus resonate with Exod. 3.12, where Yahweh promises Moses, 'I will be with you' (Ἔσομαι μετὰ σοῦ).[74] This theme of God dwelling with Israel runs across Exodus and is the *raison d'être* of the tabernacle: 'And have them make me a sanctuary, so that I may dwell among them' (Exod. 25.8). As Kupp suggests, this theme actually begins with the Sinai narrative (Exodus 16–24): 'Within the narrative purposes of Exodus, then, the tabernacle is continuous with Sinai; its role is, in a sense, to be a portable Sinai... [T]he Sinai presence now accompanies Israel in the midst of the people.'[75] In Exodus, Sinai and tabernacle are both about presence.

Matthew brings together these two Exodus traditions—Sinai and tabernacle—at the conclusion of his Gospel,[76] where he commends discipleship by 'teaching [the nations] to obey everything that I have commanded you. And remember I am with you always, even to the end of the age' (28.20). The motif of 'everything that I have commanded you' echoes a similar refrain from Exodus (7.2; 25.22; 29.35; cf. also Deut. 1.3), highlighting loyalty to the Torah (Exodus) and to Jesus' teachings on it (Matthew).

Mt. 28.20	πάντα ὅσα ἐνετειλάμην ὑμῖν
Exod. 7.2	πάντα, ὅσα σοι ἐντέλλομαι
Exod. 25.22	πάντα, ὅσα ἂν ἐντείλωμαί σοι
Exod. 29.35	πάντα, ὅσα ἐνετειλάμην σοι

The motif of presence ('I am with you always'—in line with the tabernacle) and of teaching ('obey everything I have commanded you'—in line with Sinai) come together in a single, climactic moment in Matthew. As Kupp observes, 'Matthew appears to have revisited quite deliberately the Sinai paradigm here [in Mt. 28.20], where the giving of the law, the formation of community and the presence of YHWH came together'.[77]

---

[74] Given that this is a common Old Testament refrain, it is difficult to argue for an intentional allusion to Exodus specifically.

[75] D. D. Kupp, *Matthew's Emmanuel: Divine Presence and God's People in the First Gospel* (New York: Cambridge University Press, 1996), pp. 128–29.

[76] Kupp, *Matthew's Emmanuel*, p. 216.

[77] Kupp, *Matthew's Emmanuel*, p. 216. Matthew also interweaves community and presence (and possibly Torah) in 18.20, a central affirmation of the Community Discourse: 'For wherever two or three are gathered in my name, I am there in their midst'. Kupp and others (Turner, *Matthew*, p. 446) have cautiously noted the (later) rabbinic parallel (*m. 'Abot* 3.2, 6): 'If two sit together and the words between them are of Torah, then the *Shekhinah* (presence/glory) is in their midst' (Kupp, *Matthew's Emmanuel*, p. 192). For a critique of this application, see Garland, *Matthew*, p. 196.

5. Conclusion

From a storied perspective, Matthew's reflections on Exodus traditions and texts can be understood within the broad framework of exodus redemption, Torah at Sinai, and tabernacle (following the structure of Exodus). Through this lens, Matthew's own narrative interests emerge. He portrays Jesus as Israel's representative who comes out of Egypt into (the land of) restoration, highlighting the new exodus that brings restoration from exile and covenant renewal through Jesus' missional death. Matthew characterizes Jesus as the authentic interpreter of Torah, who presses toward a higher ethic implicit in it (clarifying it via the prophets) and teaches his followers to live out covenant loyalty fully. Jesus also mirrors Yahweh's role of rescue and provision and, ultimately, fulfills the divine promise of presence: 'I am with you always, even to the end of the age' (28.20b).

Chapter 3

'OLD EXODUS' AND 'NEW EXODUS' IN THE GOSPEL OF MARK

Daniel M. Gurtner

1. Introduction

Since Rikki Watts' important monograph on the Isaianic 'New Exodus' in Mark, scholars have frequently interpreted Markan appropriation of Exodus themes through an Isaianic lens.[1] Without detracting from the importance of this reading, I want to revisit the underlying textual foundations from Exodus itself and the bearing they have on the Markan narrative; perhaps not all Mark's appropriations of Exodus material are Isaianic in nature. To address this we must examine citations and verbal allusions to Exodus found in Mark, to elucidate the function of Exodus texts upon the overall *bios* of Mark. Yet clear citations of Exodus are sparse in the Gospel of Mark. As Hays observes, unlike Matthew, 'Mark rarely points explicitly to correspondences between Israel's Scripture' in his narrative of Jesus.[2] Hays himself categorizes what he calls 'scriptural intertextual references in the Gospels' into quotations, allusions, and echoes.[3] One could add a sub-category to the first of so-called composite citations.[4] Despite the utility of these classifications, the

---

* An earlier draft of this paper was presented at the Midwest Region SBL Meeting (11 February 2017; South Bend, Indiana).
[1] R. E. Watts, *Isaiah's New Exodus in Mark* (WUNT, 2/88; Tübingen: Mohr Siebeck, 1997).
[2] R. B. Hays, *Echoes of Scripture in the Gospels* (Waco, TX: Baylor University Press, 2016), p. 15.
[3] Hays, *Echoes of Scripture in the Gospels*, p. 10.
[4] See S. A. Adams and S. M. Ehorn (eds.), *Composite Citations in Antiquity*. Vol. 1, *Jewish, Graeco-Roman, and Early Christian Uses* (LNTS, 525; London: Bloomsbury T&T Clark, 2016), pp. 1–16. Moyise observes that the Mark contains nine examples where words from more than a single OT text are conflated (e.g., Mk 1.2-3, 11; 7.10; 10.19; 11.17; 12.19, 32; 13.24-26; 14.62). S. Moyise, 'Composite Citations in the Gospel of Mark', in S. A. Adams and S. M. Ehorn (eds.), *Composite Citations in Antiquity*. Vol. 2, *New Testament Uses* (LNTS, 593; London: Bloomsbury T&T Clark, 2018), pp. 16–33.

distinctions between them are not always so clear and they are perhaps unnecessary. If the evangelists are as steeped in the textual traditions of Israel's Scripture as most scholars seem to recognize, it would seem natural that more than one textual reference may conflate in their minds as they pen their narratives.

Little work has been devoted exclusively to what Perkins calls 'embedded Exodus materials' in Mark.[5] For Perkins—to date the only treatment of the subject—Mark's appropriation of this material is particularly pertinent in helping readers understand more fully the evangelist's development of the themes of the kingdom of God, messianic authority, and the re-constitution of God's people.[6] Perkins rightly points to the importance of the breadth of Mark's use of Exodus material for his gospel, rather than a singular context of Mark's narrative.[7] But this must be augmented by the breadth of the Exodus contexts from which Mark draws as well. For just as Mark's use of Exodus cannot be reduced to a simple Markan citation, it likewise cannot be reduced to a single Exodus context. In this manner one can acquire a more complete appreciation for the intertextual complexities of Mark's composition.

Perkins frames his analysis of Exodus in Mark in terms of three points of inquiry. First, he investigates the degree to which Mark purposely incorporates Exodus into his story because he wanted the reader to reflect upon key elements of Israel's experience. Second, he explores the relationships between Exodus motifs and the Markan narrative. Third, he examines whether or not Mark expects his readers to read the Exodus references through the grid of Isaiah 40–55 as a 'new exodus'.[8] While a careful treatment of Exodus in Mark must address all these points, I want to begin with a more neutral posture, one in which the scope of Mark's appropriation of Exodus is canvased to see where the evidence leads. In this more rudimentary exercise, I will examine Mark's use of Exodus in broad brush strokes, utilizing the cross-references found in the NA[28] and UBS[5] critical editions. This is far from comprehensive and admittedly lacking in sophistication, but it does give us some raw data from which to work in the first instance. Next, we consider the context from the Exodus text, and finally, we reflect upon the context in which it is appropriated by Mark. This allows us to cover the breadth of texts and contexts from Exodus and their respective contributions to the Markan narrative from which further assessments can be made and questions posed. It also allows us to step back and draw from a set of such identifications, purely for heuristic purposes, to facilitate future work on the necessarily more refined, subsequent tasks of contending for what constitutes a citation (composite or otherwise), allusion, or echo to Exodus in Mark.

---

[5] L. Perkins, 'Kingdom, Messianic Authority and the Re-constituting of God's People – Tracing the Function of Exodus Material in Mark's Narrative', in T. R. Hatina (ed.), *Biblical Interpretation in Early Christian Gospels.* Vol. 1, *The Gospel of Mark* (LNTS, 304; London: T&T Clark, 2006), pp. 100–115 (100).

[6] Perkins, 'Re-Constituting of God's People', p. 100. Here Perkins draws from W. R. Stegner, 'Jesus' Walking on the Water: Mark 6.45-52', in C. A. Evans and W. R. Stegner (eds.), *The Gospels and the Scriptures of Israel* (JSNTSup, 104; Sheffield: Sheffield Academic, 1994), pp. 212–34.

[7] Perkins, 'Re-Constituting of God's People', pp. 100–101.

[8] Perkins, 'Re-Constituting of God's People', p. 101.

2. Quotations of Exodus in Mark

The critical editions indicate four citations of Exodus in Mark and 21 allusions or verbal parallels that draw from 30 locations in Exodus. We will begin with a careful treatment of the few citations (Mk 1.2 [Exod. 23.20]; Mk 7.10 [Exod. 20.12; 21.16]; Mk 10.19 [Exod. 20.12-16]; Mk 12.26 [Exod. 3.6, 15]) before a survey of the allusions.

a. Mark 1.2 (Exodus 23.20)

At the outset of his narrative, Mark articulates the beginning of the good news about Jesus Christ in terms of what is written in Israel's Scriptures. Among other complicated aspects of this passage,[9] Mark utilizes a text from Exodus (23.20) that is reappropriated, almost verbatim, in Malachi (3.1):[10]

> Mk 1.2   ἰδοὺ[11] ἀποστέλλω τὸν ἄγγελόν μου πρὸ προσώπου σου, ὃς κατασκευάσει τὴν ὁδόν σου·
>
> Exod. 23.20   καὶ ἰδοὺ ἐγὼ ἀποστέλλω τὸν ἄγγελόν μου πρὸ προσώπου σου ἵνα φυλάξῃ σε ἐν τῇ ὁδῷ ...
>
> Mal. 3.1   ἰδοὺ ἐγὼ ἐξαποστέλλω τὸν ἄγγελόν μου καὶ ἐπιβλέψεται ὁδὸν πρὸ προσώπου μου ...[12]

Mark's wording is in some ways distinct from known Exodus texts. LXX Exodus begins with an announcement by the Lord in the first person with the emphatic ἐγώ plus the first singular ἀποστέλλω ('I am sending'; MT אנכי שלח). This reading is also attested in all extant Hebrew witnesses to this verse (אנכי; SP; not attested at Qumran), as well as the Targumim (Tg. Neof., Ps.-J., Tg. Onq.: אנא) and Peshitta (ܐܢܐ). Mark is one of only a few traditions that omit ἐγώ[13] (so

---

[9] The first citation is complicated by the fact that it is unclear whether it constitutes a citation or allusion. To make matters still more challenging, Mark introduces the citation in v. 2 as Isaianic (ἐν τῷ Ἠσαΐᾳ τῷ προφήτῃ), though he does not actually cite Isaiah until v. 3. Some manuscript traditions, perhaps in recognition of this difficulty, remove the reference to Isaiah and render the ascription in the plural: τοῖς προφήταις (K P* P A M G^sup M U W P^c 118 f^13 2 28 579 1424). Some omit the article before the name Isaiah (D Q f^1 700 1071), while one (L) spells the name Ἰησαΐα and reads τό before προφήτῃ.

[10] NA^28 marginal notation; J. Marcus, *Mark 1–8: A New Translation with Introduction and Commentary* (AB, 27A; New Haven, CT: Yale University Press, 2010), p. 143.

[11] Some manuscripts insert ἐγώ, conforming to the Exodus/Malachi context: 69* A M G^sup K L M P U W P f f^13 2 33 579 700 1971 1424 t).

[12] This reading is close to the MT's הנני שלח מלאכי ופנה־דרך לפני.

[13] Whether or not Exodus' *Vorlage* contained אנכ, LXX Exodus tends to supply ἐγώ in such instances. J. W. Wevers (*Text History of the Greek Exodus* [MSU, 21; Göttingen: Vandenhoeck & Ruprecht, 1992], p. 185) notes this as a translational commonplace for LXX Exodus whereby the present tense is accompanied by ἐγώ or σύ for the personal pronoun plus participle in Hebrew (cf. also J. W. Wevers, *Notes on the Greek Text of Exodus* [SCS, 30; Atlanta: Scholars Press, 1990], p. 369).

also Philo, *Migr. Abr.* 1.174; Ethiopic; Boharic).[14] Mark's account of sending '*my* angel' (τὸν ἄγγελόν μου) follows extant texts of LXX Exodus (as well as SP [מלאכי] and Tg. Onq.), whereas MT simply reads 'an angel' (מלאך; also Tg. Neof., Tg. Ps.-J.; Syr.).[15]

Mark's πρὸ προσώπου σου[16] is found in Exodus (MT לפניך; Symmachus: προαγοντα σε), though Mark omits Exodus' purpose statement for the angel as such, 'to guard you on the way' (LXX: ἵνα φυλάξῃ σε ἐν τῇ ὁδῷ; MT: לשמרך בדרך). Instead, Mark creates a unique, simplified reading otherwise unattested in Exodus witnesses: He reads the relative pronoun ὅς with τὸν ἄγγελον as the antecedent, retaining the function of the messenger but drawing attention slightly from the purpose of him being sent to his identity as one who will prepare (κατασκευάσει).[17]

Exodus 23.20 is repeated almost verbatim in Mal. 3.1. Like Mark, however, Malachi does not indicate the purpose of the sending (ἵνα φυλάξῃ σε ἐν τῇ ὁδῷ, Exod. 23.20). Instead, Malachi emphasizes the role of the angel to 'oversee the way' (NETS; καὶ ἐπιβλέψεται ὁδόν). But Mark does not include this reading, nor does he include the ἐγώ from LXX Mal. 3.1 (not attested in MT here). Finally, Mark prefers the simplex ἀποστέλλω to Malachi's compound ἐξαποστέλλω.[18]

In the context of the Exodus citation (Exod. 23.20) the messenger is the 'angel of the Lord' (LXX ὁ ἄγγελος τοῦ θεοῦ; MT מלאך האלהים) who is to go before the Israelites in their departure from Egypt (Exod. 14.19; see also 23.20, 23; 32.34; 33.2).[19] In Mark, the place of Israel is taken by Jesus,[20] and the 'angel of the Lord' becomes the messenger, John. The context of Malachi is the Lord's (יהוה) announcement that he will send a messenger, Elijah (Mal. 4.5; MT 3.23) ahead of his own coming at the day of the Lord (cf. Ezek. 43.2-4; Hag. 1.8).[21]

---

[14] J. W. Wevers, with the help of U. Quast, *Septuaginta: Vetus Testamentum Graecum Auctoritate Academiae Scientiarum Gottingensis editum*, vol. II, 1 – *Exodus* (Göttingen: Vandenhoeck & Ruprecht, 1991), p. 271.

[15] Exodus' reading clarifies the connection between the angel and its sender (so also SP, Vulg.; cf. 23.23; 32.34).

[16] Decker observes that Mark's πρὸ προσώπου is temporal, indicating John's ministry as the appropriate preparation before Jesus' ministry began. R. J. Decker, *Temporal Deixis of the Greek Verb in the Gospel of Mark with Reference to Verbal Aspect* (SBG, 10; New York: Lang, 2001), p. 89. Though, he notes, it may be special elsewhere, such as Lk. 10.1.

[17] See D. M. Gurtner, *Exodus: A Commentary on the Greek Text of Codex Vaticanus* (BSCS; Leiden: Brill, 2013).

[18] However, the manuscript evidence for the inclusion or omission of ἐγώ is mixed. Some include it (א A K L P W Γ Δ f[1.13] 28ᶜ 33 579 700 892 1241 1424 2542. etc.) others omit it (B D Θ 28* 565).

[19] It is also the angel of the Lord (ἄγγελος κυρίου) who appears to Moses in the burning bush (cf. also 3.24) and protects Israel from the pursuing Egyptians (cf. also Exod. 23.23; 32.34; 33.2) and is part of what Durham calls God's 'presence' motif 'that dominates the narrative of Exod. 1–20'. J. I. Durham, *Exodus* (WBC, 3; Waco, TX: Word, 1987), p. 335.

[20] R. H. Gundry, *Mark: A Commentary on His Apology for the Cross* (Grand Rapids: Eerdmans, 2000), p. 35.

[21] R. A. Guelich, *Mark 1–8:26* (WBC, 34A; Grand Rapids: Zondervan, 2015), p. 11; *pace* M. D. Hooker, *The Gospel According to St. Mark* (BNTC; Peabody, MA; Hendrickson, 1992), p. 35, who attributes the interpretation of the messenger of Mal. 3 who prepares the way identified with the Elijah of Mal. 4.5 to 'later rabbinic interpretation'. This observation is likewise made by C. E. B. Cranfield (*The Gospel According to Saint Mark* [CGTC, 2; Cambridge: Cambridge University Press, 1963], p. 39), who further observes the connection made in Mark (6.15; 8.28; 9.11-13).

The messenger will come as a 'refiner's fire' to purify the Levites (3.3a) so that the Lord will establish a renewed priesthood to bring 'offerings in righteousness' that 'will be acceptable to the Lord' (3.3b-4a, NAS). In Mark, Elijah is John the Baptist,[22] which suggests that the coming of Jesus indicates the arrival of the Lord. The conflation of these texts in Mark does not so much seem to indicate the inauguration of an exodus-like deliverance[23] as it affirms the identification of John as Elijah, God's eschatological messenger, in anticipation of the coming of the Lord.

The attribution to Isaiah is sometimes taken to indicate the composite citation is to be read as a culmination of God's returning to Zion and restoration of exiled Israel.[24] But what of the Exodus citation? Hays frames it more modestly when he reminds readers about the Exodus context, in which God promises to send an angel to lead Israel into the promised land.[25] In this respect the Exodus text, in its Markan appropriation, is perhaps invoking a 'new Exodus' motif.[26] But whether Mark here provides a 'conceptual framework' for that motif requires closer scrutiny of the other Exodus contexts from which Mark draws.[27]

b. Mark 7.10 (Exodus 20.12; 21.16)

In Mark 7 Jesus criticizes the Pharisees and scribes for neglecting the commands of God in favor of human traditions (Mark 7.8-9). In doing so, Jesus cites two examples: honoring one's parents and speaking evil of one's parents. This entails the citation of two texts, both utilizing Exodus.

(1) Mark 7.10a (Exodus 20.12). First, Mark's τίμα τὸν πατέρα σου καὶ τὴν μητέρα σου (Mark 7.10a) comes from two texts: Exod. 20.12 and Deut. 5.16. These two are nearly identical,[28] with the only difference in the LXX being the inclusion (Deut.) or exclusion (Exod.) of σου.

Mk 7.10a   τίμα τὸν πατέρα σου καὶ τὴν μητέρα σου

Exod. 20.12   τίμα τὸν πατέρα σου καὶ τὴν μητέρα ἵνα ...

Deut. 5.16   τίμα τὸν πατέρα σου καὶ τὴν μητέρα σου ὃν ...

This omission by LXX Exodus may simply be because σου is obviously implied by the context.[29] But the translator of Exodus does not seem to have problems, in

---

[22] A. Y. Collins, *Mark* (Hermeneia; Minneapolis: Fortress, 2007), pp. 135–36.
[23] *Pace* Hays, *Echoes of Scripture in the Gospels*, p. 21.
[24] Hays, *Echoes of Scripture in the Gospels*, p. 21; cf. p. 63.
[25] Hays, *Echoes of Scripture in the Gospels*, p. 22.
[26] Perkins ('Re-Constituting of God's People', p. 104) calls this conflation a 'revised exodus paradigm'.
[27] Watts, *Isaiah's New Exodus in Mark*, p. 370.
[28] Except that Deuteronomy inserts 'as the Lord your God commanded you' (ὃν τρόπον ἐνετείλατό σοι κύριος ὁ θεός σου, Deut. 5.16).
[29] Wevers, *Notes*, p. 313.

general, with repeating the obvious from his *Vorlage*. Furthermore, the inclusion of the second singular pronominal suffix after both father and mother is attested in all other witnesses, including the MT and SP (את־אביך ואת־אמך; not attested in DSS) as well as the Targumim (דאבוהי...דאימיה; Tg. Ps.-J., Tg. Onq., Tg. Neof.). Notably, it is also present in all extant Syriac witnesses (ܐܒܘܟ ܘܐܡܟ), which are typically translated from the Greek. Perhaps Mark's inclusion of σου may point to a Greek witness not otherwise attested, or simply align him more closely with Deut. 5.16 (cf. Mk 10.19; Lk. 18.20). Whether Mark draws from Exodus or Deuteronomy here, he clearly departs from his source in that he omits the purpose statements that follow in the respective contexts.[30] Instead, Mark continues with the second citation: 'the one speaking evil of father or mother must surely die' (ὁ κακολογῶν πατέρα ἢ μητέρα θανάτῳ τελευτάτω, Mk 7.10b).

(2) Mark 7.10b (Exodus 21.16). The second half of Mk 7.10 resembles a reading found in Leviticus (20.9),[31] but most clearly draws from Exod. 21.16[32] (MT 21.17[33]).

Mk 7.10b   <u>ὁ κακολογῶν πατέρα ἢ μητέρα</u> θανάτῳ τελευτάτω

Exod. 21.16   <u>ὁ κακολογῶν πατέρα</u> αὐτοῦ <u>ἢ μητέρα</u> αὐτοῦ
τελευτήσει θανάτῳ.

Mark removes Exodus' αὐτοῦ (twice), a reading attested in some LXX witnesses (MSS 707 16-25-126-414' *b* 125 628 76), as well as Matthew (15.4) and Philo (*Fug.* 1.83; *Spec. Leg.* 2.243; *Hyp.* 7.2), though its inclusion is present in the MT and other Semitic texts.[34] Mark follows Exodus' κακολογῶν ('abusing' or 'bad-mouthing'; Vulg.: *maledixeit*), which is softer than the MT's מקלל ('cursing').[35] Furthermore, Mark reverses Exodus' verb and noun (τελευτάω and θάνατος), and instead of Exodus' future tense verb (τελευτήσει), a common LXX rendering of a Hebrew imperfect verb, Mark uses the imperative τελευτάτω.

---

[30] '[S]o that it may be well with you and so that you may be long-lived on the good land that the Lord your God is giving you' (Exod. 20.12b, NETS) or 'as the Lord your God commanded you, so that it may be well with you and that you may be long-lived in the land that the Lord your God is giving you' (Deut. 5.16, NETS).
[31] ἄνθρωπος ἄνθρωπος ὃς ἂν κακῶς εἴπῃ <u>τὸν πατέρα αὐτοῦ ἢ τὴν μητέρα αὐτοῦ θανάτῳ θανατούσθω</u> πατέρα αὐτοῦ ἢ μητέρα αὐτοῦ κακῶς εἶπεν ἔνοχος ἔσται.
[32] Also Collins, *Mark*, p. 351.
[33] ὁ κακολογῶν πατέρα αὐτοῦ ἢ μητέρα αὐτοῦ τελευτήσει θανάτῳ. Wevers (*Notes*, p. 330) observes that LXX Exodus alone among ancient witnesses transposes vv. 16 and 17, presumably bringing the two capital crimes against parents together.
[34] MT, SP: אביו ואמו; Tg. Ps.-J.: לאבוי ולאימיה; Peshitta: ܐܒܘܗܝ ܘܐܡܗ.
[35] This is the only time in the LXX that verb is used for the Hebrew *piel* קלל. Most commonly קלל in the *piel* is translated in the LXX with καταράσθαι (30 out of 36 occurrences in the MT). Gen. 8.21; 12.3; Lev. 24.11, 14, 15, 23; Deut. 23.4(5); Judg. 9.27; 1 Kgdms 17.43; 2 Kgdms 16.5, 7, 9, 10, 11, 13; 19.21(22); 3 Kgdms 2.8; 3.1 (2.8); 4 Kgdms 2.24; Neh. 13.2, 25; Job 3.1; Pss. 62(61).4; 109(108).28; Prov. 24.33 (30.10); 24.34 (30.11); Eccl. 7.22(21); 7.23(22); 10.20; Jer. 15.10. Other renderings include ἀδοξία (Sir. 3.11), ἀρᾶσθαι (Josh. 24.9), κακολογέω (Exod. 22.28 [MT 22.27]; 1 Kgdms 3.13; Prov. 20.20) and κακῶς λέγω (Lev. 20.9).

These citations seem to indicate Markan familiarity with some variations in traditions. The respective contexts are decidedly legal in nature from the setting of the Sinai covenant. Here is where the stipulations of covenant obligations for Israel are, in part, spelled out. Jesus is here confronting Jews for their neglect of these particular covenant obligations, presumably with a view toward the abiding validity of these regulations.

c. Mark 10.19 (Exodus 20.12-16)

In Mark 10, a rich young man approaches Jesus with questions about attaining eternal life. Jesus responds by listing a series of commandments (Mk. 10.19), which are drawn from Exod. 20.12-16 (cf. Deut. 5.16-20). As is the case above, there is an assumption about the abiding validity of these regulations, which the young man says he has observed since his youth (Mk 10.20). Mark's citation, however, exhibits distinct variation both with respect to specific wording and the order in which items are presented. Both Mark and the LXX use second person singular verbs. Yet whereas in the LXX each verb is preceded by οὐ and the verb itself is in the future active indicative, second person singular (μοιχεύσεις, κλέψεις, φονεύσεις, ψευδομαρτυρήσεις), Mark uses μή and renders each verb as an aorist active subjunctive (φονεύσῃς, μοιχεύσῃς, κλέψῃς, ψευδομαρτυρήσῃς, ἀποστερήσῃς). Furthermore, while Mark retains Exodus' prohibition against bearing false witness, he removes the prepositional phrase 'against your neighbor with false witness' (NETS; κατὰ τοῦ πλησίον σου μαρτυρίαν ψευδῆ).[36]

Mark's addition about defrauding (μὴ ἀποστερήσῃς) is not attested in Exodus, nor anywhere in the LXX. The verb itself (ἀποστερέω) is found only nine times in the LXX,[37] with the closest verbal parallel found in Sir. 4.1: 'My son, deprive not (μὴ ἀποστερήσῃς) the poor of his living, and do not keep needy eyes waiting' (RSV). Collins suggests it is a summary of Lev. 6.1-7 (5.20-26 LXX) or of a judgment text from Mal. 3.9 (LXX) against injustice.[38]

The list of offenses in Mark's account is part of a broad tradition of variation in order. First, however, Mark's placement of honoring one's father and mother (τίμα τὸν πατέρα σου καὶ τὴν μητέρα) at the end of the list is otherwise unattested; in all extant traditions it is placed first. Mark's order ('murder', 'adultery', 'steal', 'bear false witness', then the unattested 'defraud') follows that order of the MT ('murder', 'adultery', 'steal'; תענה, 'bear false witness'; also at Deut. 5.16-20). This order is also followed by Semitic traditions (SP, Tg. Neof., Tg. Ps.-J., Tg. Onq.; not attested in DSS), as one would expect. It is also found in the Greek recensions of Aquila, Symmachus, and Theodotian, as well as the Syriac.[39] The

---

[36] This is a cumbersome rendering of the Hebrew (לא־תענה ברעך עד שקר).
[37] The verb occurs in the LXX at Exod. 21.10; Deut. 15.7; *4 Macc.* 8.23; Sir. 4.1; 29.6, 7; 34.21, 22; Mal. 3.5.
[38] Collins, *Mark*, p. 478.
[39] The order of the Syriac following that of the MT, as well as Aquila, Symmachus, and Theodotion, may infer a Greek *Vorlage* that corresponds to those recensions (ܩܛܠ, 'murder'; ܓܘܪ, 'adultery'; ܓܢܒ, 'steal').

LXX, as well as Origen, differs (μοιχεύσεις, 'adultery'; κλέψεις, 'steal'; φονεύσεις, 'murder'; ψευδομαρτυρήσεις, 'bear false witness').[40]

Adela Collins suggests the placement of the command to honor one's parents evokes for Mark's readers Jesus' saying about circumventing this command by the Corban vow (Mk 7.11). This kind of defrauding of one's parents, she suggests, may have been viewed as a temptation especially for the wealthy,[41] such as the young man in Mark 10. These obligations likewise come from covenantal stipulations from Sinai. Jesus demands more of him though, not less. What lacks in the man is not his ability to fulfill these Mosaic covenant obligations, but his willingness to give up all his wealth and follow Jesus. Again the commands are presumed to have some kind of binding authority in the Markan context, though simply following them without requisite allegiance to Jesus, falls short.

d. Mark 12.26 (Exodus 3.6; 3.15)

In Mark 12 Jesus counters the Sadducees about the nature of the resurrection by citing Exodus as the 'book of Moses' (τῇ βίβλῳ Μωϋσέως) when referencing the event of the burning bush (Mk 12.26; Exod. 3.2; cf. Exod. 3.6). The citation in Mk 12.26 could have come from Exod. 3.6 or 3.15. In Mark's rendering (ἐγὼ ὁ θεὸς Ἀβραὰμ καὶ [ὁ] θεὸς Ἰσαὰκ καὶ [ὁ] θεὸς Ἰακώβ) there is textual uncertainty about the second and third articles before θεός. Use of the article only in the first use of θεός is attested at Exod. 3.6, whereas no article is used in 3.15. Mark uses the first person personal pronoun, like Exod. 3.6 but omitted at Exod 3.15. Mark also omits the expansive εἰμι ὁ θεὸς τοῦ πατρός σου ('I am the God of your father'; MT אנכי אלהי אביך)[42] of Exod. 3.6, also absent in Exod. 3.15. The κύριος (MT, SP, Tg. Ps.-J., Tg. Neof.; Tg. Onq.: יהוה; Syr.: ܡܪܝܐ ܐܠܗܐ) at the beginning of 3.15[43] is also omitted by Mark (and Tg. Neof.). Mark's inclusion of the first person personal pronoun (ἐγώ) suggests Exod. 3.6 is preferred. Here Mark draws explicitly from a context in Exodus where God issues a call to Moses and identifies himself. Its placement at the early stages of the impending deliverance is ripe for expansion toward a New Exodus in Jesus. And yet Mark does not do so. Instead, he utilizes Exodus' statement about Israel's God as a means to affirm Jesus' teaching on resurrection. Israel's God was then—and is now—the God of the living (cf. *4 Macc.* 7.19; 16.25; *Pr. Man.* 1.1; *1 En.* 70.4).[44]

---

[40] LXX Deut. 5.17-20 reads: μοιχεύσεις, 'adultery'; φονεύσεις, 'murder'; κλέψεις, 'steal'; ψευδομαρτυρήσεις, 'bear false witness'. See Wevers, *Notes*, p. 314.

[41] Collins, *Mark*, p. 479.

[42] The Hebrew here uses a singular 'your father' (אביך), though three names are listed. LXX Exod follows suit (τοῦ πατρός σου; Tg. Ps.-J. singular דאבהתכון), though SP uses the plural 'your fathers' (אבתיך; cf. Acts 7.32). See Wevers, *Notes*, p. 28.

[43] Qumran evidence for Exod. 3.15 follows the MT, with variation only in orthography. 4QGen-Exodᵃ, frg. 19 ii lines 10-11: [יהוה]אלהי[אבתיכם]אלהי אברהם אלהי[יצחק וא[ל]הי]. 4QExodᵇ, frgs. 3 ii, 5-6 i lines 4-5: יהוה אל[והי אבותיכם אלוהי] אברהם אלוהי יצחוק ואלהי יעקב.

[44] 4QpaleoGen-Exodˡ (4Q11; DJD 9.27; cf. 4QExodᵇ [4Q13] DJD 12.90).

3. Allusions to Exodus in Mark

As noted above, there are numerous allusions to Exodus suggested for Mark's Gospel.[45] My purpose here is not to define 'allusions' or even to provide a comprehensive account of putative allusions in Mark. Instead, I will canvas what are generally considered to be allusions to Exodus in Mark and, corresponding to my treatment of quotations above, bring attention to the respective contexts from which Mark draws.[46]

The first proposed allusion is found in Mark's brief temptation narrative, where Jesus is 'in the wilderness forty days being tempted by Satan' (ἐν τῇ ἐρήμῳ τεσσεράκοντα ἡμέρας πειραζόμενος ὑπὸ τοῦ σατανᾶ, Mk 1.13), likely recalling the Israelites eating manna in the wilderness for forty years (ἔφαγον τὸ μαν ἔτη τεσσαράκοντα, Exod. 16.35).[47] Mark (uniquely) mentions the presence of wild animals (καὶ ἦν μετὰ τῶν θηρίων) but makes no mention of lacking food or drink (Lk. 4.2; Mt. 4.2). The omission suggests Mark may be less interested in the Moses typology evident in Matthew, where the inclusion is augmented by other Exodus allusions (cf. Exod. 24.18; 34.28).[48] Nowhere in Exodus do we find Mark's (unique) use of ἐκβάλλω in proximity to εἰς τὴν ἔρημον. Rather, ἐκβάλλω is used by the Lord (κύριος) who will use plagues to cause the hard-hearted Pharaoh (and Egyptians, 12.33) not simply to permit the Israelites to leave Egypt, but he will throw them out of Egypt (6.1; 11.1)! Ἐκβάλλω is also used in Exodus for the Lord's work in driving out of nations before Israel (23.18, 28, 29, 30, 31; 33.2; 34.11, 24). Regardless, the Exodus context to which Mark seems to allude is that of Israel's wandering in the wilderness, corresponding to Jesus' presence in the wilderness.

Other potential allusions draw from a variety of contexts. In Mk 2.7, Jesus is charged with blasphemy for claiming to forgive sins (Isa. 43.25; cf. Exod. 34.7). Here Mark may recall the Lord's declaration to Moses in a private theophany

---

[45] Mk 1.2 = Exod. 23.20; Mk 1.13 = Exod. 16.35; 24.18; Mk 2.7 = Exod. 34.7; Mk 2.24 = Exod. 31.13-17; 34.21; Mk 2.26 = Exod. 40.23; Mk 2.27 = Exod. 20.8-10; 23.12; Mk 3.6 = Exod. 31.14; Mk 3.14 = Exod. 18.25; Mk 6.48 = Exod. 34.6; Mk 6.50 = Exod. 14.13; Mk 9.2 = Exod. 24.1, 9, 15-16; Mk 9.7 = Exod. 40.34; Mk 9.49 = Exod. 30.35; Mk 12.26 = Exod. 3.1-2, 6, 15-16; Mk 12.40 = Exod. 22.10; Mk 13.11 = Exod. 4.15; Mk 13.19 = Exod. 9.18; 10.14; 11.6; Mk 14.12 = Exod. 12.6, 14-20; Mk 14.24 = Exod. 24.8; Mk 15.38 = Exod. 26.31-33.

[46] Perkins ('Re-constituting of God's People', p. 106) cautiously suggests potential allusions in three specific instances (Mk 2.27 [Exod. 20.8-10]; Mk 14.12-13 [Exod. 12.6, 14-20]; Mk 14.24 [Exod. 24.8]). He omits two additional instances mentioned by H. C. Kee ('The Function of Scriptural Quotations and Allusions in Mark 11–16', in E. E. Ellis and E. Gräßer [eds.], *Jesus and Paulus* [Festschrift W. G. Kümmel; Göttingen: Vandenhoeck & Ruprecht, 1975], pp. 165–88 [169–71]): the splitting of the temple curtain (Exod. 26.31; Mk 15.38) because there does not seem to be any allusion to the Exodus context; and Exod. 4.1 in Mk 13.11b because of the dissimilar contexts (Perkins, 'Re-constituting of God's People', p. 105 n. 27).

[47] Perhaps a connotation of instruction by God may be inferred (cf. *Jub.* 1.4). At Qumran Exod. 16.35 is extant only in fragmentary Hebrew texts that generally follow the MT (4Q11 [4QpaleoGen-Exod¹]; 4Q22 [4QpaleoExodᵐ]; DJD 9.38, 92–93)

[48] *Pace* Collins, *Mark*, p. 151. See D. M. Gurtner, '"Fasting" and "Forty Nights": The Matthean Temptation Narrative (4.1-11) and Moses Typology', in C. A. Evans (ed.), *'What Does the Scripture Say?' Studies in the Function of Scripture in Early Judaism and Christianity*. Vol. 1, *The Synoptic Gospels* (LNTS, 470; London: Bloomsbury T&T Clark, 2012), pp. 1–11.

(Exod. 34.5-7). In this setting Moses ascends Sinai a second time with stone tablets on which God will write to replace those broken by Moses earlier (Exod. 34.1-4). As he does so, the Lord descends in a cloud and passes before Moses, proclaiming: 'The LORD, the LORD, a God merciful and gracious, slow to anger, and abounding in steadfast love and faithfulness, keeping steadfast love for thousands, forgiving iniquity and transgression and sin, but who will by no means clear the guilty, visiting the iniquity of the fathers upon the children and the children's children, to the third and the fourth generation' (Exod. 34.6b-7, RSV). The uniqueness of God's identity in these proclamations is underscored in Moses' response: 'And Moses made haste to bow his head toward the earth, and worshiped' (Exod. 34.8, RSV). Presumably Jesus' opponents are taking his claim to forgive sins as a prerogative exclusively belonging to God. Yet the context here is a theophany to Moses at Sinai, where the identity of Israel's God is center stage. For Mark, it seems that identity here is likewise important in that the opponents question 'who' is able to forgive sins but God alone (τίς δύναται ἀφιέναι ἁμαρτίας εἰ μὴ εἷς ὁ θεός, Mk 2.7). Who indeed! As the ensuing narrative dramatically illustrates, Jesus' declaration of forgiving sins is both expressed and effective (Mk 2.8-12). When the Pharisees question the legality of the disciples' activities on the sabbath (Mk 2.24), allusion is made to prohibitions in Exodus (20.10; 31.13, 15; 34.21). These legal texts are alluded to as covenantal obligations in Israel's relationship with God (e.g., *Jub.* 2.17-19, 21, 23-27; 50.7; cf. *LAB* 11.8).[49] Jesus then explains (Mk 2.26-27) by describing the events of David and his companions eating the bread of the presence (1 Sam. 21.1; Exod. 40.23[50]). The pericope concludes with two points of emphasis. First, the sabbath is for people. Second, Jesus exercises lordship over the sabbath (Mk 3.27-28). Thus the covenantal stipulations seem to remain in place, but in the case of an urgent need—such as that of God—or the lordship of Christ, the regulations can be suspended. Yet the Pharisees presumably fail to grasp this. Instead, they intend to destroy Jesus (ἀπολέσωσιν, Mk 3.6), which may allude to a legal context with instructions to put to death one who violates the sabbath (θανάτῳ θανατωθήσεται; MT מות יומת; Exod. 31.14; cf. *Jub.* 2.25).[51]

Like the statement about God's exclusive prerogative to forgive sins above (Mk 2.7; Exod. 34.7), the scene where Jesus walks on water and, curiously, intends to pass by the disciples (ἤθελεν παρελθεῖν αὐτούς, Mk 6.48) strongly

---

[49] Exod. 20.10 has only fragmentary representation at Qumran (4Qmez[a] [149]; DJD 6.80–81). Exod. 31.13, 15 is attested in 4Q22 (4QpaleoExod[m]; DJD 9.122), and generally follows the MT. Exod. 34.21 is attested in a fragmentary segment of 4Q22 (4QpaleoExod[m]; DJD 9.128), which follows the MT generally.

[50] At Qumran Exod. 40.23 is found in 4Q17 (4QExod-Lev[f]; DJD 12.140–41), which follows the MT.

[51] Collins (*Mark*, p. 210) is doubtful this is the case. At Qumran Exod. 31.14 is found in 4Q22 (4QpaleoExod[m]; DJD 1.122), which follows the MT. It may be that Mark's account of the appointing of the Twelve (ἐποίησεν δώδεκα, Mk 3.14) draws from Moses' appointment of selecting leaders over Israel (ἐπέλεξεν Μωυσῆς ἄνδρας δυνατούς, Exod. 18.25; cf. 1Q28a 1.28–2.1; 2.21-22; 1 Macc. 3.55; 11Q19 57.4). At Qumran Exod. 18.25 is found in 4Q22 (4QpaleoExod[m]; DJD 9.97), where it includes an addition like that of SP. Collins (*Mark*, pp. 215–18) sees this appointment, alongside that of the Temple Scroll, as an anticipation of the restoration of the twelve tribes in the last days (cf. Isa. 49.5-6 LXX; Sir. 48.10; Josephus, *Ant.* 11.5.2 §133).

recalls the Lord passing by Moses (παρῆλθεν κύριος πρὸ προσώπου αὐτοῦ, Exod. 34.6; cf. Exod. 14.24).[52] To this Collins adds divine theophanies of 'passing by' Elijah (3 Kgdms 19.11 LXX) to suggest that Jesus may be appearing to the disciples in a way analogous to God's appearance to Moses and Elijah.[53] For her, then, this fits well with the Markan depiction of Jesus walking on the sea, which itself depicts him as the agent of God, a king exercising divine power.[54]

The response to the theophany in fear, followed by a word of encouragement (θαρσεῖτε, ἐγώ εἰμι· μὴ φοβεῖσθε, Mk 6.50) in part resembles Isa. 43.2. In that passage the faithful are encouraged by a promise for some future event, whereas here there is an exhortation in response to a theophany unlike that of Isaiah. In Exodus one finds Moses' response to the theophany in fear (ἀπέστρεψεν δὲ Μωυσῆς τὸ πρόσωπον αὐτοῦ εὐλαβεῖτο γὰρ κατεμβλέψαι ἐνώπιον τοῦ θεοῦ, Exod. 3.6), but no exhortation like that of Mark. Instead, Exodus words the exhortation not in response to God (e.g., Dan. 10.12 LXX) but the impending confrontation with Pharaoh (cf. *3 Macc.* 6.4). Furthermore, Mark's 'be of good courage' (θαρσεῖτε) recalls the same exhortation to Moses (θαρσεῖτε) in anticipation of the confrontation with Pharaoh (Exod. 14.13) and Moses' exhortation to Israel at Sinai (Exod. 20.20). Finally, the ground for the exhortation both to courage and not fear is in the identity of the one seen on the water (ἐγώ εἰμι; cf. Exod. 3.14 LXX; Deut. 32.39 LXX; Isa. 41.4 LXX).[55] Like above, the allusion to Exodus pertains to the identity of Israel's God, and Mark likewise seems to present Jesus not in a setting of deliverance but as a display of divine identity.

Allusion to Exodus may be found in Mark's transfiguration account (Mk 9.2-7),[56] where Jesus and select disciples ascend a high mountain (ἀναφέρει αὐτοὺς εἰς ὄρος ὑψηλὸν, Mk 9.2), like Moses does with his companions at Sinai (ἀνέβη Μωυσῆς..., Exod. 24.9;[57] ἀνέβη Μωυσῆς καὶ Ἰησοῦς εἰς τὸ ὄρος, Exod. 23.14). In Mark a cloud overshadows them (ἐγένετο νεφέλη ἐπισκιάζουσα αὐτοῖς, Mk 9.7), as it does over the whole mountain for Moses (ἐκάλυψεν αὐτὸ ἡ νεφέλη, Exod. 24.15; cf. 4Q377 frg. 2 col. 2.10-11). From there the Lord spoke to Jesus' disciples (καὶ ἐγένετο φωνὴ ἐκ τῆς νεφέλης· οὗτός ἐστιν ὁ υἱός μου ὁ ἀγαπητός, ἀκούετε αὐτοῦ, Mk 9.7), as God spoke to Moses out of the cloud at Sinai (ἐκάλεσεν κύριος τὸν Μωυσῆν τῇ ἡμέρᾳ τῇ ἑβδόμῃ ἐκ μέσου τῆς νεφέλης, Exod. 24.16; cf. Exod. 40.34; 2 Macc. 2.8; 2 Bar. 59.3).[58] Like above, the setting of Sinai connotes a context of the establishment of a covenant between the Lord and Israel.

---

[52] Some have argued the primary texts in view are from Exod. 14.21-22 and 15.19. Hays (*Echoes of Scripture in the Gospels*, pp. 71–72) observes that the former texts depict God parting the waters and leading people '*on dry ground*' (emphasis original), whereas Job 9.8 (LXX) is more suitable in its depiction of God 'walking *atop* the waters of the sea' (emphasis original). Why Hays does not consider Exod. 34.6 is unclear.

[53] Collins, *Mark*, p. 334.

[54] Collins, *Mark*, p. 334.

[55] See Collins, *Mark*, pp. 334–35.

[56] So also Collins, *Mark*, p. 420.

[57] A fragmentary text of this passage is attested in 4Q22 (4QpaleoExod^m; DJD 9.108), which at times follows SP (for 24.1-4, 6-11)

[58] So also Collins, *Mark*, p. 425. Mark's cryptic statement about being 'salted with fire' (πυρὶ ἁλισθήσεται, Mk 9.49) may allude to the seasoning of incense (Exod. 30.35).

In Mark's account of the Last Supper (Mk 14.12-25) a number of items from Exodus come to the surface. The disciples inquire about celebrating the Unleavened Bread with Jesus (Mk 14.12), which commemorates the Passover as it is instituted in Exodus (12.6, 14-20). This event was instituted by God to Moses as a commandment for all Israel to memorialize God's deliverance of Israel from the land of Egypt (Exod. 12.17). Mark presents Jesus and his disciples continuing the biblically mandated institution. While at the meal Jesus distributes the bread and the cup (Mk 14.22-23). The latter he identifies as 'my blood of the covenant which is poured out for many' (τοῦτό ἐστιν τὸ αἷμά μου τῆς διαθήκης τὸ ἐκχυννόμενον ὑπὲρ πολλῶν, Mk 14.24).[59] Mark's language of 'blood of the covenant' (τὸ αἷμά...τῆς διαθήκης, Mk 14.24) draws clearly from Exod. 24.8, where Moses sprinkles blood upon the people and declares it to be 'blood of the covenant' (τὸ αἷμα τῆς διαθήκης, דם הברית, Exod. 24.8; cf. *Jub.* 6.11). Mark's addition of μου (τὸ αἷμά μου τῆς διαθήκης) to the Exodus text identifies the covenant blood explicitly with Jesus. The context of Exodus indicates the covenantal relationship between God and Israel, particularly the ratification of that covenant. In the Markan context, as Perkins indicates, as Jesus' 'followers partake of the bread and wine... they proleptically participate in the covenant that God establishes through Jesus' death'.[60] This notion of sacrifice, Perkins continues, is already found in Mk 10.45, where the Son of Man is pouring out his blood for many. As Perkins notes, '[t]he conclusion is hard to avoid that Jesus in the Markan narrative wants his followers to interpret his coming death typologically with reference to the annual Passover sacrifice'.[61]

4. Conclusions to Mark's Use of Exodus

No doubt further allusions, echoes, and quotations could be added to this cursory list.[62] Yet even in the few citations Mark exhibits familiarity not only with the book of Exodus, but also some variations in textual traditions pertaining to that book. Furthermore, he is capable of utilizing his own innovations with Exodus traditions for his purposes. And of course there is certainly no shortage of Exodus

---

[59] Perkins ('Re-Constituting of God's People', pp. 107–8) observes that Mark's verbal form connotes a violent death not found in Exodus but elsewhere in the LXX to describe the fate of the prophets. For him, this infers how the new covenant, while similar, is also distinct from the old.

[60] Perkins, 'Re-Constituting of God's People', p. 106.

[61] Perkins, 'Re-Constituting of God's People', p. 106.

[62] E.g., Mk 13.11, where Jesus informs his disciples that the Holy Spirit will speak through them in their witness (οὐ γάρ ἐστε ὑμεῖς οἱ λαλοῦντες ἀλλὰ τὸ πνεῦμα τὸ ἅγιον), which resembles the charge that Moses will put words in Aaron's mouth for the confrontation with Pharaoh, and that God will be open both their mouths (δώσεις τὰ ῥήματά μου εἰς τὸ στόμα αὐτοῦ ... καὶ ἐγὼ ἀνοίξω τὸ στόμα σου καὶ τὸ στόμα αὐτοῦ, Exod. 4.15). Here the LXX reading (ἐγὼ ἀνοίξω τὸ στόμα σου, 'I will open your mouth') differs from MT (ואנכי אהיה עם פיך, 'I will be with your mouth'). The anticipation of a great, unprecedented tribulation (θλῖψις, Mk 13.19) may allude to the plagues of Exodus (9.18; 10.14; 11.6; cf. Wis. 16.9). The veil of the temple (τὸ καταπέτασμα τοῦ ναοῦ) torn at Jesus' death (Mk 15.38), likely the inner veil to the holy of holies, is identified first and most fully in the Exodus tabernacle texts (καταπέτασμα, פרכת, Exod. 26.31-33; cf. *Jos. Asen.* 2.8; *2 Bar.* 6.7; 1 Macc. 4.51; Josephus, *War* 5.5.4-5 §§212–219; 6.5.3 §§288–300; *Ant.* 3.6.4 §§122-29). The text is found in 4Q364 (DJD 13.223) with some variances in orthography.

texts that Mark could quote toward a New Exodus motif. Mark does draw from a deliverance text early in his gospel which, when conflated with a citation from Malachi, brings the reader's attention to John the Baptist's role to prepare the way for Jesus. But not all Exodus texts embedded in Mark bear out the notion of deliverance. Where Mark cites a deliverance context from Exodus 3, he seems to use it in a manner that underscores the nature of God in a conflict about resurrection. The notion of a narrative strategy of retelling Israel's story is not immediately apparent. Mark's familiarity with legal texts from Exodus likewise gives little indication of deliverance but instead underscore stipulations of Israel's covenantal relationship with God. All this suggests that while Mark may indeed advance a motif of an Isaianic New Exodus (Watts), or other shared motifs,[63] his use of the 'old' Exodus does not seem to accommodate such singularity of purpose. The complexities and variances of context problematize an effort to 'superimpose' one narrative upon another.[64] Not all of Mark's citations, allusions, or echoes to Exodus are through an Isaianic lens.

---

[63] Perkins, 'Re-Constituting of God's People', pp. 109–12.
[64] Hays, *Echoes of Scripture in the Gospels*, p. 103.

Chapter 4

EXODUS IN LUKE-ACTS

Brian J. Tabb and Steve Walton

1. Introduction

The Third Gospel's opening verse refers to 'the things fulfilled among us', and the risen Jesus declares in Lk. 24.44 that 'everything written about me in the Law of Moses and the Prophets and the Psalms must be fulfilled'. Following the outpouring of the Holy Spirit at Pentecost, the apostles and others proclaim how Jesus 'fulfils' Israel's Scriptures in various ways. Luke and Acts consistently present the teaching and actions of Jesus and his followers as the continuation and fulfillment of the Creator God's dealings with Israel and the nations in the Scriptures.

This chapter considers how Luke and Acts appropriate Exodus tradition. In multiple places, Luke's Gospel cites specific *Exodus texts*: the passage about the bush (Lk. 20.37), what is '*written* in the Law' (2.23; 7.27), and 'the commandments' (18.20). The programmatic speeches by Mary and Zechariah invoke *Exodus imagery* by declaring that Israel's God 'has shown strength with his arm' (ἐποίησεν κράτος ἐν βραχίονι αὐτοῦ, Lk. 1.51; cf. Exod. 6.1) and 'has visited and redeemed his people' (ἐπεσκέψατο καὶ ἐποίησεν λύτρωσιν τῷ λαῷ αὐτοῦ, Lk. 1.68; cf. Exod. 3.16; 4.31; 6.6 LXX). However, Luke and Acts also commonly draw attention to *major events* and *themes* of the Exodus narrative, including YHWH's promises to the patriarchs, his power to save his people from slavery, his glorious presence and enduring revelation to Moses at Sinai, as well as Israel's stubborn rebellion against God and his chosen leaders. Stephen's sermon references every major event in Exodus: (1) Israel multiplied in Egypt and then experienced oppression from Pharaoh (Acts 7.17-19); (2) God preserved Moses as an infant and planned to save Israel by his hand (7.20-21, 25); (3) years after Moses fled from Egypt, God's angel appeared to Moses in the burning bush (7.30); (4) Moses led Israel out of Egypt 'performing wonders and signs in Egypt and at the Red Sea and in the wilderness for forty years' (7.36); (5) he received divine oracles at Sinai (7.38); (6) he endured Israel's rebellion with the golden calf; and (7) he set up the tent of witness in the wilderness (7.44). According to Luke and Acts, God has sent Jesus, the prophet like Moses, to fulfill his ancient promises and secure a greater deliverance for his people. Yet Jesus is not simply Moses *redivivus*; he is ὁ κύριος, 'the Lord', who shares in the name, identity, character, and activity of Israel's God.[1]

Given the expansive scope of Luke's diptych and numerous subtle resonances with the Exodus narrative and also the 'new exodus' motif in Isaiah and elsewhere,[2] the present study focuses on direct citations and clear allusions to the Exodus text itself.[3] Section 2 considers six texts in Luke's Gospel that exhibit substantial verbal and conceptual parallels to the book of Exodus: (1) Lk. 2.22-23, cf. Exod. 13.2, 12; (2) Lk. 7.27, cf. Exod. 23.20; (3) Lk. 9.28-33, cf. Exodus tradition; (4) Lk. 13.14, cf. Exod. 20.8-9; (5) Lk. 18.18-20, cf. Exod. 20.12-16; and (6) Lk. 20.37-38, cf. Exod. 3.6, 15. Section 3 considers the following clear quotations or allusions to Exodus in Acts: (1) Acts 3.13, cf. Exod. 3.6, 15-16; (2) Acts 7, cf. Exodus tradition; (3) Acts 14.15 and 17.24, cf. Exod. 20.11; (4) Acts 15.10, cf. Exod. 17.2; and (5) Acts 23.5, cf. Exod. 22.27. Section 4 concludes the study with brief summary reflections on our findings.

2. Exodus Tradition in the Gospel of Luke

There is little consensus on how many times Luke alludes to the book of Exodus. UBS[5] lists twenty allusions and verbal parallels to Exodus in the Third Gospel, but this taxonomy is questionable in what it includes and omits. Six of the UBS[5] parallels are general references to Passover or the Feast of Unleavened Bread in Exodus 12 (Lk. 2.41; 22.1, 7 [×3]). Several other proposed parallels include general references to Mosaic laws concerning rest on the seventh day (Lk. 23.56; cf. Exod. 12.16; 20.10), fourfold repayment for stolen property (Lk. 19.8; cf. Exod. 22.1), and priests burning incense (Lk. 1.9; cf. Exod. 30.7). Two of the UBS[5] parallels echo Exodus language—'the finger of God' (Lk. 11.20; cf. Exod. 8.19) and 'gird your loins' (Lk. 12.35; cf. Exod. 12.11).

Other proposed allusions in UBS[5] do not stand up to close scrutiny. Jesus' question in Lk. 12.14 ('Man, who made me a judge or arbitrator over you?') shares two rather common words with Exod. 2.14 (Τίς...κατέστησεν), but Luke is hardly signaling a parallel between Jesus and Moses' opponent. Jesus' call to 'rejoice that your names are written in heaven' (Lk. 10.20) lacks a verbal correspondence with Moses' intercessory petition in Exod. 32.32. An allusion to 'the blood of the covenant' in Exod. 24.8 is much less clear in Lk. 22.20 than in the

---

[1] See C. K. Rowe, *Early Narrative Christology: The Lord in the Gospel of Luke* (Grand Rapids: Baker, 2009), pp. 243–64; R. B. Hays, *Echoes of Scripture in the Gospels* (Waco, TX: Baylor University Press, 2016), pp. 253–54.

[2] See D. W. Pao, *Acts and the Isaianic New Exodus* (BSL; Grand Rapids: Baker, 2002).

[3] For discussions on wider echoes of the exodus events in Luke–Acts, see B. D. Estelle, *Echoes of Exodus: Tracing a Biblical Motif* (Downers Grove, IL: InterVarsity, 2018), pp. 236–62; A. J. Roberts and A. Wilson, *Echoes of Exodus: Tracing Themes of Redemption through Scripture* (Wheaton, IL: Crossway, 2018), Chapters 18–20.

first Evangelist's account of the Last Supper (Mt. 26.28). Likewise, it is suspect to call the rending of the temple veil in Lk. 23.45 an allusion to the instructions for making the tabernacle veil in Exod. 26.31-33.

Surprisingly, UBS[5] omits three of the most significant Lukan allusions to Exodus: (1) Jesus' consecration according to 'the Law of the Lord' in Lk. 2.22-23, which reflects the prescriptions in Exod. 13.2, 12;[4] (2) Luke's provocative reference to Jesus' 'departure' (ἔξοδος) in 9.31; and (3) Jesus' appeal in Lk. 20.37 to God's self-designation as 'God of Abraham and God of Isaac and God of Jacob' (Exod. 3.6, 15).[5]

This section focuses on six texts in the Gospel of Luke where there is a clear quotation, whether or not signaled by an introductory formula, or a clear allusion to the book of Exodus.

a. Jesus' Consecration (Exodus 13.2, 12 in Luke 2.22-23)[6]

Exod. 13.2, 12, LXX	Lk. 2.22b-23
2 Ἁγίασόν μοι **πᾶν** πρωτότοκον πρωτογενὲς **διανοῖγον** πᾶσαν **μήτραν** ἐν τοῖς υἱοῖς Ισραηλ ἀπὸ ἀνθρώπου ἕως κτήνους· ἐμοί ἐστιν. 12 καὶ ἀφελεῖς **πᾶν διανοῖγον μήτραν**, τὰ <u>ἀρσενικά</u>, **τῷ κυρίῳ**· **πᾶν διανοῖγον μήτραν** ἐκ τῶν βουκολίων ἢ ἐν τοῖς κτήνεσίν σου, ὅσα ἂν γένηταί σοι, τὰ <u>ἀρσενικὰ</u> <u>ἁγιάσεις</u> **τῷ κυρίῳ**. Consecrate to me **every** firstborn, first produced, **opening** every **womb** among the sons of Israel, from person to animal; it belongs to me. And you shall also separate **every one opening the womb**—the <u>males</u>—**to the Lord**; **every one opening the womb** from the herds or among your livestock, whatever there may be to you, <u>consecrate</u> the <u>males</u> **to the Lord**.	ἀνήγαγον αὐτὸν εἰς Ἱεροσόλυμα παραστῆσαι τῷ κυρίῳ, καθὼς γέγραπται ἐν νόμῳ κυρίου ὅτι **πᾶν** <u>ἄρσεν</u> **διανοῖγον μήτραν** <u>ἅγιον</u> **τῷ κυρίῳ** κληθήσεται. They brought him up to Jerusalem to present him to the Lord, as it is written in the Law of the Lord, '**Every** <u>male</u> **who opens the womb** shall be called <u>holy</u> **to the Lord**'.

---

[4] This allusion is noted in NA[28] margin and by C. A. Evans, *Ancient Texts for New Testament Studies: A Guide to the Background Literature* (Peabody, MA: Hendrickson, 2005), p. 362.
[5] This allusion is noted in NA[28] margin.
[6] Exact parallels are **emboldened**; close but not-exact parallels (e.g., the same word[s] but in different cases or tenses) are <u>underlined</u>. Translations throughout are our own. We cite LXX Exodus from the edition by J. W. Wevers, with the help of U. Quast, *Septuaginta: Vetus Testamentum Graecum Auctoritate Academiae Scientiarum Gottingensis editum*, vol. II, 1 – *Exodus* (Göttingen: Vandenhoeck & Ruprecht, 1991).

After Jesus' birth in Bethlehem, his parents circumcise him on the eighth day and present him to the Lord in Jerusalem (Lk. 2.21-22). The Evangelist stresses that the holy family scrupulously follows the Law of the Lord or Moses (vv. 22, 23, 24, 27). Luke commonly highlights the fulfillment of OT prophecies and patterns, but here he simply reports 'that Jesus' parents did what the law required'.[7]

'Their purification' (τοῦ καθαρισμοῦ αὐτῶν) in v. 22 and the sacrifice of turtledoves or pigeons in v. 24 refer to the Law's requirements in Lev. 12.6, 8 for women to undergo ceremonial purification after childbirth. In between these references to Leviticus 12, Lk. 2.22b-23 states that Jesus' parents 'brought him up to Jerusalem to present him to the Lord, as it is written in the Law of the Lord, "Every male who opens the womb shall be called holy to the Lord"'. The plural αὐτῶν in v. 22 is difficult, since Lev. 12.6 requires only the mother's purification. It may suggest that Luke ties together the mother's cleansing and the offering of the child 'into one act'.[8]

Luke 2.23 loosely cites Exod. 13.2, 12 LXX, where Moses commands Israel to consecrate every firstborn male to YHWH as a reminder that YHWH delivered Israel from slavery in Egypt and killed all the firstborn in Egypt but spared those in Israel (Exod. 13.14-15; cf. 12.27). However, there are three important differences between Lk. 2.23 and the consecration of the firstborn in Exodus 13 that taken together have christological significance. First, in place of the imperative Ἁγίασον ('consecrate', Exod. 13.2 LXX), v. 23 uses the future indicative ἅγιον τῷ κυρίῳ κληθήσεται ('he will be called holy to the Lord'). This formula unmistakably recalls the angel's words to Mary in 1.35: 'therefore the child to be born will be called holy—the Son of God' (ἅγιον κληθήσεται υἱὸς θεοῦ). Second, in 2.24, Jesus' parents offer the sacrifice required for the mother's purification after childbirth (Lev. 12.8), not the five shekels to redeem the firstborn (Exod. 13.13-14; Num. 18.15-16). However, the offering of 'a pair of turtledoves, or two young pigeons' is similar to the sacrifice for the cleansing of a Nazirite who was dedicated to the Lord (Num. 6.10).[9] Third, Mary and Joseph bring Jesus to the temple (cf. 2.27), which Exodus 13 does not specify for consecrating and redeeming the firstborn.

Thus, Lk. 2.22-24 emphasizes the piety of Jesus and his family, who follow the Law's requirements.[10] Further, Luke modifies the citation of Exod. 13.2, 12 to reflect the angelic pronouncement in 1.35. Jesus is 'holy to the Lord' in a unique

---

[7] J. B. Green, 'The Problem of a Beginning: Israel's Scriptures in Luke 1–2', *BBR* 4 (1994), pp. 61–85 (76).

[8] I. H. Marshall, *Gospel of Luke: A Commentary on the Greek Text* (NIGTC; Exeter: Paternoster, 1978), p. 116. Alternatively, J. Fitzmyer argues that αὐτῶν must refer to Joseph and Mary, in *Luke* (AB, 28A-B; 2 vols.; Garden City, NY: Doubleday, 1981, 1985), vol. 1, p. 424. For additional discussion, see D. L. Bock, *Proclamation from Prophecy and Pattern: Lucan Old Testament Christology* (JSNTSup, 12; Sheffield: JSOT, 1987), pp. 83–84.

[9] F. Bovon, *Luke* (trans. C. M. Thomas; Hermeneia; 3 vols.; Minneapolis: Fortress, 2002, 2012, 2013), vol. 1, p. 99.

[10] Cf. Hays, *Echoes of Scripture in the Gospels*, p. 248.

sense as the Son of God, and his presentation to the Lord in the temple may stress 'Jesus' lifelong dedication to God'.[11]

b. The Lord's Messenger (Exodus 23.20 and Malachi 3.1 in Luke 7.27)

Exod. 23.20, LXX	Mal. 3.1, LXX	Lk. 7.27
Καὶ ἰδοὺ ἐγὼ ἀποστέλλω τὸν ἄγγελόν μου πρὸ προσώπου σου, ἵνα φυλάξῃ σε ἐν τῇ ὁδῷ, ὅπως εἰσαγάγῃ σε εἰς τὴν γῆν, ἣν ἡτοίμασά σοι.	ἰδοὺ ἐγὼ ἐξαποστέλλω τὸν ἄγγελόν μου, καὶ ἐπιβλέψεται ὁδὸν πρὸ προσώπου μου ...	οὗτός ἐστιν περὶ οὗ γέγραπται· ἰδοὺ ἀποστέλλω τὸν ἄγγελόν μου πρὸ προσώπου σου, ὃς κατασκευάσει τὴν ὁδόν σου ἔμπροσθέν σου.
And **behold, I send my messenger before you** to guard you in the <u>way</u>, in order to lead you into the land that I prepared for you.	**Behold, I send my messenger**, and he will oversee the <u>way</u> before me.	This is he concerning whom it is written, '**Behold, I send my messenger before you**, who will prepare your <u>way</u> before you'.

After 'the Lord' has compassion on the widow and raises her dead son (Lk. 9.12-15), the amazed crowd concludes, 'A great prophet has arisen among us!' and 'God has visited his people!' (v. 16). This recalls Zechariah's prophecy in Lk. 1.68, 78 and prepares for Jesus' exchange with John's disciples (7.18-23) and his teaching on John's role and reception in 'this generation' (7.24-35). Jesus' signs confirm that he indeed is 'the one who is to come' (7.19-20), and Jesus' combined citation of Exod. 23.20 and Mal. 3.1 supports his claim that John the Baptist is 'more than a prophet' (7.26).

The first half of the quotation in Lk. 7.27 agrees verbatim with Exod. 23.20a LXX (omitting ἐγώ) and is also close to Mal. 3.1 LXX. Exodus 23.20-33 concludes the Book of the Covenant (20.22–23.33) with two emphases that relate to the larger Exodus narrative. First, YHWH's messenger (LXX: ἄγγελος μου) will guard and go before Israel 'on the way', bringing them into the land he has prepared and driving out their enemies (23.20, 23).[12] Second, Israel must obey YHWH's voice and not make a covenant with the nations and their gods (23.22, 32).

---

[11] D. W. Pao and E. Schnabel, 'Luke', in G. K. Beale and D. A. Carson (eds.), *Commentary on the New Testament Use of the Old Testament* (Grand Rapids: Baker, 2007), pp. 251–414 (269).

[12] On the differences between Exod. 23.20 MT and LXX, see D. M. Gurtner, *Exodus: A Commentary on the Greek Text of Codex Vaticanus* (BSCS; Leiden: Brill, 2013), p. 404.

The precise relationship between YHWH and his messenger (ἄγγελος, מלאך) is ambiguous in 23.20-23 and elsewhere in Exodus (3.2; 14.19; 32.24; 33.2). Durham calls this messenger 'an extension of Yahweh's own person and Presence',[13] though Garrett argues that the messenger is a heavenly being subordinate to YHWH that serves as his agent.[14]

In Mal. 3.1, YHWH responds to the people's wearisome question, 'Where is the God of justice?' (2.17), announcing that he will send his messenger to prepare for the awesome 'day of his coming' (3.2). Malachi 3.1 alludes to Exod. 23.20 but significantly changes לפניך ('before *you*') to לפני ('before *me*'). Malachi 3.22 (4.5 EVV) identifies this 'messenger' as Elijah, whose coming precedes 'the great and awesome day of YHWH'.

By form, Lk. 7.27 is closer to Exod. 23.20, but the re-use of Exod. 23.20 in Mal. 3.1 contributes to Jesus' application of this text to John. Luke 1.17 presents John's calling in terms of Mal. 3.22-23 LXX (4.5-6 EVV): he will go 'in the spirit and power of Elijah' to turn the people's hearts and ready them for the Lord.

The combined Scripture citation in Lk. 7.27 explicates John the Baptist's unique salvation-historical role. John is the promised prophet like Elijah, who prepares the way for *the Lord Jesus*, in the fulfilment of God's new exodus program of judgment and salvation (3.3-17).[15] Jesus identifies John as the greatest 'among those born of women' (7.28), yet John belongs to the old era of promise and not the new era of eschatological fulfilment, the age of the kingdom.[16]

c. Jesus' 'Exodus' and Glory (Exodus in Luke 9.28-33)

In Lk. 9.18-20, Jesus asks the disciples who the crowds say that he is, and Peter confesses that Jesus is God's Messiah, not John, Elijah, or a prophet of old. Jesus then charges them not to tell this to anyone and predicts his impending suffering (vv. 21-22). He then teaches about the cost of discipleship and promises that the Son of Man will come in glory (vv. 23-27). In the very next scene, Peter, James, and John behold Jesus' transfigured glory, and a heavenly voice confirms Jesus' identity and commands that the disciples 'listen to him' (v. 35; cf. Deut. 18.15). The transfiguration serves as initial fulfillment of Jesus' promise that some present 'will not taste death until they see the kingdom of God' (v. 27) and prepares for Jesus' journey to Jerusalem in v. 51. The Lukan transfiguration account includes a number of allusions to the book of Exodus that clarify Jesus' identity and mission.

First, the phrase ἀνέβη εἰς τὸ ὄρος in Lk. 9.28 alludes to Moses going up to the mountain of God (Exod. 19.3; 24.13, 18; 34.4; cf. Deut. 5.5; 10.3 LXX). In Lk. 9.28 and throughout Exodus (beginning at 3.1), the mountain is a place of divine presence and revelation.

---

[13] J. I. Durham, *Exodus* (WBC, 3; Waco, TX: Word, 1987), p. 335. Similarly B. Childs speaks of 'the virtual identification of the angel with God himself', in *The Book of Exodus: A Critical, Theological Commentary* (OTL; Philadelphia: Westminster, 1974), p. 487.
[14] D. A. Garrett, *A Commentary on Exodus* (KEL; Grand Rapids: Kregel Academic, 2014), p. 537.
[15] Cf. Hays, *Echoes of Scripture in the Gospels*, p. 248.
[16] D. L. Bock, *Luke* (BECNT; 2 vols.; Grand Rapids: Baker, 1994, 1996), vol. 1, p. 675.

Second, the glorious change in Jesus' face (Lk. 9.29) may recall Exod. 34.29-30, where the appearance of Moses' face 'was charged with glory' (NETS), or the manifestation of YHWH's glory in 24.17 (τὸ...εἶδος τῆς δόξης κυρίου).[17] The disciples then behold Jesus' glory (εἶδον τὴν δόξαν αὐτοῦ, Lk. 9.32), which conceptually parallels the frequent displays of YHWH's glory in Exodus (16.7, 10; 24.16-17; 40.28-29) and especially Moses' request that YHWH show his glory (33.18).

Third, a cloud overshadowed Peter and the others on the mountain (νεφέλη ... ἐπεσκίαζεν αὐτούς, Lk. 9.34; cf. Mk 9.7).[18] The cloud in the book of Exodus frequently represents YHWH's glorious presence with his people at the exodus from Egypt (13.21-22; 14.19, 24) and during their wilderness journeys (16.10; 40.31-32 LXX [40.37-38 MT]). The precise phrase ἐπεσκίαζεν...ἡ νεφέλη occurs uniquely in the LXX at Exod. 40.29 (40.35 MT), where the cloud 'overshadowed' the tent of witness that was filled with divine glory. Further, the disciples 'entered the cloud' (εἰσελθεῖν...εἰς τὴν νεφέλην) as Moses did at Sinai in Exod. 24.18 LXX (εἰσῆλθεν Μωυσῆς εἰς τὸ μέσον τῆς νεφέλης). Moreover, the voice from the cloud in Lk. 9.35 recalls YHWH's words to Moses ἐκ μέσου τῆς νεφέλης in Exod. 24.16 LXX.

Fourth, Moses and Elijah appeared in glory on the mountain and spoke with Jesus about '*his departure* (τὴν ἔξοδον αὐτοῦ) that he was about to fulfill in Jerusalem' (Lk. 9.31). While all of the Synoptics record the appearance of Moses and Elijah with Jesus, only Luke refers to Jesus' ἔξοδος.[19] The term ἔξοδος denotes the 'departure' of Israel from the land of Egypt in Exod. 19.1 and elsewhere in the LXX (Num. 33.38; 3 Kgdms 6.1; Pss. 104.38; 113.1). Other Jewish and Christian writers also refer to this well-known event as ἡ ἔξοδος.[20] Jesus' ἔξοδος in Lk. 9.31 is not his journey to Jerusalem but more likely denotes his 'departure' from this world at death and subsequent ascension (cf. v. 51).[21] Additionally, Lk. 9.31 presents Jesus' departure 'as a fulfillment event' using the verb πληρόω ('accomplish'),[22] which refers to the scriptural fulfillment in Lk. 24.44. The ἔξοδος of Jesus recalls Israel's departure from Egypt, and the fulfillment language

---

[17] Pao and Schnabel, 'Luke', p. 311. An allusion to Exod. 34.29-25 is questioned by Fitzmyer, *Luke*, vol. 1, p. 799. If Lk. 9.29 does allude to Moses' face in Exod. 34.29, it indicates 'contrast as well as comparison', as noted by M. L. Strauss, *The Davidic Messiah in Luke–Acts: The Promise and its Fulfillment in Lukan Christology* (JSNTSup, 110; Sheffield: Sheffield Academic, 1995), p. 270. On the extended allusion to Exod. 34 in 2 Cor. 3.7-16, see D. A. Garrett, 'Veiled Hearts: The Translation and Interpretation of 2 Corinthians 3', *JETS* 53 (2010), pp. 729–72.

[18] Outside of the transfiguration accounts, the only NT occurrences of ἐπισκιάζω are in Lk. 1.35, with reference to the Most High's power, and Acts 5.15, with reference to Peter's shadow.

[19] 'This verse is almost completely a Lukan formulation', according to J. Nolland, *Luke 9:21–18:34* (WBC, 35B; Dallas, TX: Word, 1993), p. 499.

[20] Philo, *Vit. Mos.* 1.105; 2.248; Josephus, *Ant.* 2.309, 312, 320, 325; 5.72; *T. Sim.* 9:1; *T. Benj.* 12:4; Aristob. 1.17; Heb. 11.22.

[21] Contra S. H. Ringe, 'Luke 9:28-36: The Beginning of an Exodus', *Semeia* 28 (1983), pp. 83–99 (94); rightly Nolland, *Luke 9:21–18:34*, p. 500; Bovon, *Luke*, vol. 1, p. 376. For ἔξοδος as a euphemism for death, cf. Wis. 3.2.

[22] M. Wolter, *The Gospel According to Luke* (Baylor-Mohr Siebeck Studies in Early Christianity; 2 vols.; Waco, TX: Baylor University Press, 2016–2017), vol. 1, p. 393.

suggests that Jesus is accomplishing a greater work of salvation according to the divine plan.[23]

Cumulatively, these parallels suggest that Luke intends readers to draw connections between Jesus' glorious transfiguration and YHWH's glorious revelation to Moses. Luke does not primarily cast Jesus as a new Moses but as God's 'Son' and 'Chosen One' (9.35) who shares in the divine glory and accomplishes the divine will through his ἔξοδος. Jesus will soon set his face to go to Jerusalem (v. 51) where he 'will suffer many things' and 'be delivered into human hands' (vv. 22, 44). However, the revelation of Jesus' transfigured glory on the mountain confirms that Jesus speaks with divine authority as God's Son and previews the glory that Jesus will attain 'through his death, resurrection, ascension and exaltation' (cf. 24.26).[24]

d. The True Sabbath (Exodus 20.8-9 in Luke 13.14)

Exod. 20.8-9, LXX	Lk. 13.14
μνήσθητι <u>τὴν ἡμέραν τῶν σαββάτων</u> ἁγιάζειν αὐτήν. <u>ἓξ ἡμέρας ἐργᾷ</u> καὶ ποιήσεις πάντα τὰ ἔργα σου· Remember <u>the Sabbath day</u> to consecrate it. For <u>six days you shall work</u> and do all your work.	Ἀποκριθεὶς δὲ ὁ ἀρχισυνάγωγος, ἀγανακτῶν ὅτι τῷ σαββάτῳ ἐθεράπευσεν ὁ Ἰησοῦς, ἔλεγεν τῷ ὄχλῳ ὅτι <u>ἓξ ἡμέραι</u> εἰσὶν ἐν αἷς δεῖ <u>ἐργάζεσθαι</u>· ἐν αὐταῖς οὖν ἐρχόμενοι θεραπεύεσθε καὶ μὴ <u>τῇ ἡμέρᾳ τοῦ σαββάτου</u>. And the synagogue ruler, being indignant that Jesus had healed on the Sabbath, answered and said to the crowd, 'There are <u>six days</u> in which it is necessary <u>to work</u>. Therefore, on these come and be healed and not on <u>the Sabbath day</u>'.

The Sabbath in Jesus' ministry is not only a day for consecrated rest but also for controversy. Luke regularly presents Jesus teaching in the synagogue on the Sabbath (4.16, 31; 6.6; 13.10) and records at least four Sabbath healings (4.31-37; 6.6-11; 13.10-17; 14.1-6).[25] Jesus asserts his authority as 'Lord of the Sabbath' in 6.5, and his teaching and healing activity on the Sabbath reveal the true purpose of the seventh day.

Luke sets the stage for a dramatic Sabbath controversy in the midst of the Travel Narrative: Jesus resumes his customary teaching 'in one of the synagogues

---

[23] Similarly, S. R. Garrett, 'Exodus from Bondage: Luke 9:31 and Acts 12:1-24', *CBQ* 52 (1990), pp. 656–80 (656); Bock, *Luke*, vol. 1, p. 869.
[24] Strauss, *Davidic*, p. 263.
[25] The healing of Peter's mother-in-law in Lk. 4.38-39 also likely occurred on the Sabbath, though Luke does not make this explicit.

on the Sabbath', then Luke introduces a woman with 'a spirit of weakness', who was bent over and unable to straighten herself (13.10-11). Jesus sees her, declares that she is released (ἀπολύω) from her weakness, lays hands on her, and she is made straight and glorifies God (vv. 12-13). Then the synagogue ruler[26] responds with indignation and instructs the people present to heed the fourth commandment: 'There are six days in which it is necessary to work. Therefore, on these come and be healed and not on the Sabbath day' (v. 14; cf. Exod. 20.8-9; Deut. 5.12-13 LXX). The ruler does not argue for his understanding of the Sabbath commandment but presents it as the self-evident will of God.[27]

Jesus 'the Lord' (ὁ κύριος) challenges the ruler's interpretation and exposes his opponents' hypocrisy by noting how each of them would 'loose' (λύω) their animals from the manger and give them water to drink (v. 15). Jesus' pairing of 'ox or donkey' is infrequent in the LXX and may allude to Isa. 32.20: 'Blessed are those who sow by every water, where ox and donkey (βοῦς καὶ ὄνος) tread'.[28] In context, such freedom of the household animals comes in a time of restoration, when 'the Spirit from on high comes upon you' and God's people 'live in a city of peace and dwell in trust' (Isa. 32.15, 18).

Jesus takes issue with the ruler's interpretation and application of the fourth commandment, which in the context extends the restriction of Sabbath work to 'your ox and your donkey and every one of your animals' (Exod. 20.10 LXX). The Lord reasons from the lesser to the greater:[29] if the people untie and water their animals on the day of rest, how much more necessary is it then for 'a daughter of Abraham whom Satan bound for eighteen years' to be 'loosed' (λύω) on the Sabbath (Lk. 13.16). According to the Lord of the Sabbath, it is not merely permitted to free this woman on the seventh day, it is *necessary* (δεῖ).[30] This is in keeping with Jesus' mission to proclaim good news to the poor and liberty to the captives and oppressed (Lk. 4.18; cf. Isa. 61.1-2).[31]

In v. 17, Luke records that Jesus' opponents 'were put to shame' while the crowd rejoiced 'because of all the marvels (τοῖς ἐνδόξοις) he was doing'. The adjective ἔνδοξος, used as a noun only here in the NT, denotes YHWH's mighty deeds at the exodus and conquest of the land in Exod. 34.10 and Deut. 10.21 LXX. This suggests that 'Luke has the Exodus theme on his mind'[32] and signals that Jesus 'the Lord' brings a new exodus salvation that brings freedom and joy to his people.

---

[26] Nina Collins argues that the historical opposition to Jesus following the healing of the bent woman came not from the leader of the synagogue but from Jewish peasant farmers (*Jesus, the Sabbath and the Jewish Debate: Healing on the Sabbath in the 1st and 2nd Centuries CE* [LNTS, 474; London: Bloomsbury T&T Clark, 2014], pp. 203, 205, 208). For a thorough response and critique of Collins' reading on historical and literary grounds, see J. J. Ryan, 'Jesus and Synagogue Disputes: Recovering the Institutional Context of Luke 13:10-17', *CBQ* 79 (2017), pp. 41–59.

[27] J. B. Green, *The Gospel of Luke* (NICNT; Grand Rapids: Eerdmans, 1997), p. 523.

[28] Pao and Schnabel, 'Luke', pp. 333–34.

[29] Noted also by Ryan, 'Jesus and Synagogue Disputes', p. 58.

[30] Green, *Luke*, p. 524.

[31] D. Hamm, 'The Freeing of the Bent Woman and the Restoration of Israel: Luke 13:10-17 as Narrative Theology', *JSNT* 31 (1987), pp. 23–44 (34).

[32] Hamm, 'Freeing', p. 27.

e. The Commandments and Life (Exodus 20.12-16 in Luke 18.20)

Exod. 20.12-16 LXX	Lk. 18.20
τίμα τὸν πατέρα σου καὶ τὴν μητέρα, ἵνα εὖ σοι γένηται, καὶ ἵνα μακροχρόνιος γένῃ ἐπὶ τῆς γῆς τῆς ἀγαθῆς, ἧς κύριος ὁ θεός σου δίδωσίν σοι. <u>οὐ μοιχεύσεις. οὐ κλέψεις. οὐ φονεύσεις. οὐ ψευδομαρτυρήσεις</u> κατὰ τοῦ πλησίον σου μαρτυρίαν ψευδῆ.	τὰς ἐντολὰς οἶδας· <u>μὴ μοιχεύσῃς, μὴ φονεύσῃς, μὴ κλέψῃς, μὴ ψευδομαρτυρήσῃς</u>, **τίμα τὸν πατέρα σου καὶ τὴν μητέρα.**
Honor your father and mother, in order that it may be well with you, and in order that you may be long-lived in the good land that the Lord your God is giving you. <u>You shall not commit adultery. You shall not steal. You shall not murder. You shall not testify falsely</u> against your neighbour with false testimony.	You know the commandments: '<u>Do not commit adultery, do not murder, do not steal, do not testify falsely</u>, **honor your father and mother**'.

Luke's account of the rich ruler includes Jesus' only direct OT citation in the Gospel's central section.[33] The exchange between the ruler (ἄρχων) and Jesus in 18.18-23 follows the parable of the Pharisee and tax collector (vv. 9-14) and Jesus' teaching concerning children and the kingdom (vv. 15-17). The ruler departs in sorrow because he is unwilling to sell his possessions and follow Jesus (vv. 22-23), in contrast to Peter and others who have left homes and family for the sake of God's kingdom (vv. 28-29). Jesus promises that those who willingly embrace the cost of discipleship will receive blessing 'in this time, and in the age to come eternal life' (v. 30).

The ruler's question in v. 18, 'Good Teacher, what must I do to inherit eternal life?', parallels the lawyer's query in 10.25.[34] Jesus responds, 'You know the commandments: "Do not commit adultery, do not murder, do not steal, do not bear false witness, honor your father and mother"' (v. 20). In Luke's account, Jesus cites commandments five through nine from the Decalogue (Exod. 20.12-16; cf. Deut. 5.16-20).[35] The Ten Words are 'the words of the covenant' YHWH established with Israel at Sinai after rescuing Israel from bondage in

---

[33] Pao and Schnabel, 'Luke', p. 351.

[34] On 'eternal life' in early Judaism, see S. J. Gathercole, 'Torah, Life, and Salvation: Leviticus 18:5 in Early Judaism and the New Testament', in C. A. Evans (ed.), *From Prophecy to Testament: The Function of the Old Testament in the New* (Peabody, MA: Hendrickson, 2004), pp. 126–45.

[35] On the textual differences between the Decalogue and Mt. 19.18-19, Mk 10.19, and Lk. 18.20, see D. L. Hakala, 'Jesus Said, "Keep the Commandments", and the Rich Man Asked, "Which Ones?": The Decalogue as a Law Summary in the Story of the Rich Man', in C. A. Evans and J. J. Johnston (eds.), *Searching the Scriptures: Studies in Context and Intertextuality* (LNTS, 543; London: Bloomsbury T&T Clark, 2015), pp. 171–90 (175–76).

Egypt (Exod. 20.2; 34.28), and 'they stand in a foundational position at the head of all other instructions in Exodus and Deuteronomy'.[36]

While Jesus affirms the abiding authority of these widely known commands, he also shows that keeping the Law alone does not qualify one to inherit eternal life. Rather, one must *receive* the kingdom of God like a child (18.16-17) and *follow* Jesus (v. 20) to enter the kingdom and experience eternal life (vv. 25, 30).

f. The God of the Living (Exodus 3.6, 15 in Luke 20.37)

Exod. 3.6a, 15a, LXX	Lk. 20.37
⁶ᵃ καὶ εἶπεν αὐτῷ Ἐγώ εἰμι ὁ θεὸς τοῦ πατρός σου, θεὸς **Ἀβρααμ** καὶ θεὸς **Ισαακ** καὶ θεὸς **Ιακωβ**.	ὅτι δὲ ἐγείρονται οἱ νεκροί, καὶ Μωϋσῆς ἐμήνυσεν ἐπὶ τῆς βάτου, ὡς λέγει κύριον τὸν θεὸν Ἀβραὰμ καὶ θεὸν Ἰσαὰκ καὶ θεὸν Ἰακώβ.
And he said, 'I am the God of your ancestors, God of Abraham and God of Isaac and God of Jacob'.	But that the dead are raised, even Moses made known in the passage about the bush, where he says the Lord is the God of Abraham and the God of Isaac and the God of Jacob.
¹⁵ᵃ καὶ εἶπεν ὁ θεὸς πάλιν πρὸς Μωυσῆν Οὕτως ἐρεῖς τοῖς υἱοῖς Ισραηλ Κύριος ὁ θεὸς τῶν πατέρων ὑμῶν, θεὸς **Ἀβρααμ** καὶ θεὸς **Ισαακ** καὶ θεὸς **Ιακωβ**, ἀπέσταλκέν με πρὸς ὑμᾶς.	
And God said again to Moses, 'Thus you shall say to the sons of Israel: The Lord, the God of your ancestors, God of Abraham and God of Isaac and God of Jacob, has sent me to you'.	

After confrontations between Jesus and the chief priests, scribes, and elders in Lk. 20.1-26, the Sadducees come to Jesus in v. 27. The Sadducees appear only here in the Third Gospel (cf. Acts 4.1; 5.17; 23.6-8). The evangelist introduces them as 'those who deny that there is a resurrection' (v. 27; cf. Mt. 22.23; Mk 12.18), which signals that their hypothetical question about the resurrection is wholly disingenuous (v. 33). Jesus' interlocutors begin by piously appealing to what 'Moses wrote' concerning levirate marriage (v. 28; cf. Deut. 25.5 LXX). Then they pose a scenario where one woman has seven husbands (six by levirate marriage) but no children, and they ask whose wife she will be in 'the resurrection' (vv. 29-33). Jesus explains that there is no marriage and no death in the age

---

[36] J. S. DeRouchie, 'Making the Ten Count: Reflections on the Lasting Message of the Decalogue', in J. S. DeRouchie, J. Gile and K. J. Turner (eds.), *For Our Good Always: Studies on the Message and Influence of Deuteronomy in Honor of Daniel I. Block* (Winona Lake, IN: Eisenbrauns, 2013), pp. 415–40 (415).

to come (vv. 34-36). He appeals to 'the passage about the bush' (Exod. 3.1–4.17) to refute the Sadducees and demonstrate from the Law of Moses that God raises the dead and 'is not the God of the dead, but of the living' (vv. 37-38).

Exodus 3 is a foundational passage that 'combines three traditions that define Israel: the patriarchs, the exodus, and Sinai'.[37] At this theophany on 'the mountain of God', YHWH reveals to Moses his name and his purposes to deliver his people out of Egypt and into the promised land. The parallel in Mk. 12.26 clearly cites Exod. 3.6, but the opening κύριον in Lk. 20.37 may suggest a reference to the restatement of YHWH's name in Exod. 3.15. Luke 20.37 modifies the wording of Exod. 3.15 (or 3.6) LXX by presenting YHWH's self-identification in the accusative, rather than the nominative (as in the LXX and Mk 12.26). This subtle grammatical change, along with the present tense λέγει ('says'), allows Jesus to appeal more directly to Moses' authority in response to the Sadducees' challenge.

While Exodus 3 does not explicitly refer to the resurrection, YHWH's identification as the God of the patriarchs long after their deaths suggests that they must still exist.[38] Jesus draws out this implication in 20.38: 'Now he is not God of the dead, but of the living, for all live to him'. Fourth Maccabees 7.19 similarly affirms that the patriarchs and other faithful Jews 'do not die to God but live to God' (cf. 16.25).[39] Thus, Jesus 'fully and completely grasps its meaning as "transfer" from the past and present into the future'.[40] YHWH's covenant love for Abraham that led to the exodus from Egypt 'can only mean that Abraham will be forever with God', thus ensuring the resurrection.[41] Jesus thus affirms the abiding authority of Exod. 3.6 and bases the hope of future resurrection squarely on God's identity, reputation, and secure promise to his covenant people.

3. Exodus Tradition in Acts

The number of clear quotations and allusions in Acts to the book of Exodus is impressive. UBS[5] identifies twelve quotations plus 32 allusions and verbal parallels, which is more both numerically and proportionately than any other NT book. Undoubtedly this is due in large measure to the cluster of Moses echoes in Stephen's speech (Acts 7), but there are also quotations in 3.13 and 23.5. If we add allusions identified by other sources,[42] the number of possible allusions grows

---

[37] Pao and Schnabel, 'Luke', p. 368. Stephen refers to the burning bush incident in Acts 7.30-34, discussed below.

[38] Cf. Fitzmyer, *Luke*, vol. 2, p. 1306.

[39] For discussion of immortality and resurrection in *4 Maccabees*, see B. J. Tabb, *Suffering in Ancient Worldview: Luke, Seneca and 4 Maccabees in Dialogue* (LNTS, 569; London: Bloomsbury T&T Clark, 2017), pp. 114–19.

[40] Pao and Schnabel, 'Luke', p. 369. Cf. O. Schwankl, *Die Sadduzäerfrage (Mk 12, 18-27 parr): Eine exegetisch-theologische Studie zur Auferstehungserwartung* (BBB, 66; Frankfurt: Athenäum, 1987), pp. 392–95.

[41] J. J. Kilgallen, 'The Sadducees and Resurrection from the Dead: Luke 20,27-40', *Bib* 67 (1986), pp. 478–95 (488–89).

[42] NA[28] margins; G. Archer and G. Chirichigno, *Old Testament Quotations in the New Testament* (Chicago: Moody, 1983); Evans, *Ancient Texts*, pp. 373–78; H. Gough, *The New Testament*

to over forty. This discussion focuses on cases where there is a clear quotation, whether or not signaled by an introductory formula, or a clear allusion to the book of Exodus.

a. The God of the Patriarchs Raised Jesus (Exodus 3.6a, 15-16 in Acts 3.13)

Exod. 3.6a, 15-16 LXX	Acts 3.13
⁶ᵃ καὶ εἶπεν αὐτῷ Ἐγώ εἰμι ὁ θεὸς τοῦ πατρός σου, θεὸς Ἀβραὰμ καὶ θεὸς Ἰσαὰκ καὶ θεὸς Ἰακώβ.	¹³ ὁ θεὸς Ἀβραὰμ καὶ (ὁ θεὸς) Ἰσαὰκ καὶ (ὁ θεὸς) Ἰακώβ, ὁ θεὸς τῶν πατέρων ἡμῶν
And he said to him, 'I am the God of your ancestor, God of Abraham and God of Isaac and God of Jacob'.	The God of Abraham and [the God] of Isaac and [the God] of Jacob, the God of our ancestors
¹⁵⁻¹⁶ καὶ εἶπεν ὁ θεὸς πάλιν πρὸς Μωυσῆν Οὕτως ἐρεῖς τοῖς υἱοῖς Ισραηλ Κύριος ὁ θεὸς τῶν πατέρων ὑμῶν, θεὸς Ἀβραὰμ καὶ θεὸς Ἰσαὰκ καὶ θεὸς Ἰακώβ, ἀπέσταλκέν με πρὸς ὑμᾶς·...συνάγαγε τὴν γερουσίαν τῶν υἱῶν Ἰσραὴλ καὶ ἐρεῖς πρὸς αὐτούς Κύριος ὁ θεὸς τῶν πατέρων ὑμῶν ὦπταί μοι, θεὸς Ἀβραὰμ καὶ θεὸς Ἰσαὰκ καὶ θεὸς Ἰακώβ	
And God spoke again to Moses, 'This is the way you shall speak to the sons of Israel: "The Lord, **God of** your **ancestors, God of Abraham and God of Isaac and God of Jacob**, has sent me to you"; ...assemble the elders of the sons of Israel and you shall say to them, "The Lord, **the God of** your **ancestors** has appeared to me, **God of Abraham and God of Isaac and God of Jacob**"'.	

Peter's speech, provoked by the healing of the man with a congenital disability (3.1-10), explains why Jesus, through whose name the man was healed, is now the focus of God's actions. Peter begins by denying that he and John had healed the man (3.12). He then moves to describe how their ancestral God has now acted in raising Jesus from the dead (3.15) and stresses that it is through 'faith in his

---

Quotations Collated with the Scriptures of the Old Testament (London: Walton & Maberly, 1855), pp. 26–56, 304–7; I. H. Marshall, 'Acts', in G. K. Beale and D. A. Carson (eds.), *Commentary on the New Testament Use of the Old Testament* (Grand Rapids: Baker, 2007), pp. 513–606.

name' (3.16) that the man is now healed. This leads to an exposition of Scripture (3.17-26)[43] in which Peter calls the people to repentance (3.19).

In this context, Peter uses the sonorous title 'the God of Abraham and Isaac and Jacob, the God of our ancestors', echoing Exod. 3.6, 15, 16. Verse 6 has 'of your ancestor' (τοῦ πατρός σου, singular in both cases), whereas vv. 15, 16 have 'of your ancestors' (τῶν πατέρων ὑμῶν, plural in both cases), the latter being the form in Acts 3.13. The variant reading in Acts 3.13, which includes 'the God' (ὁ θεός) before each patriarch's name, may reflect the formula in Exodus 3, which in all three uses have θεός used similarly (although without an article, which is present in the variant in Acts 3.13).[44]

This appellation of YHWH is revealed in Scripture in Moses' encounter with God at the burning bush, from which the echo comes; it is familiar from the OT[45] and Second Temple Judaism[46] as a description of the God of Israel, including in other NT writings (e.g., Mt. 22.32; Lk. 13.28; 20.37). It will be repeated in Acts 7.32, again in the context of the call of Moses. The description signals God's covenant commitment to his people, rooted in his promises to Abraham (e.g., Gen. 12.1-3). Its use here highlights the continuity of God's action, from the patriarchs to Jesus. God is not now doing something entirely new; the redeeming act that is happening in and through Jesus and his people is the fulfillment of God's promises to the patriarchs and is an act of God's faithfulness to the ancient covenant. As YHWH delivered Israel from Egypt through the agency of Moses, so he is now delivering his people through Jesus. In the setting of the temple, itself a stone embodiment of YHWH's covenant and faithfulness, it is vital that the apostles explain how Jesus stands in continuity with YHWH's ancient works and words. Indeed, other parts of this speech use christological descriptions which fell into disuse (e.g., 'servant/child', v. 13; 'the holy and righteous one', v. 14; 'the author of life', v. 15; the prophet-like-Moses, vv. 22-23), presumably because they were less accessible as the believing communities became more gentile in character.[47]

This God has 'glorified his servant Jesus', which could denote the resurrection of Jesus or the healing of the man at the Beautiful Gate (or both, with the latter as an example of the power of the former).[48] Unusually for Luke-Acts, the one being

---

[43] Peter quotes from Deut. 18.5, 18-19 (vv. 22-23) and Gen. 22.18; 26.4 (v. 25). For discussion see (respectively) D. Rusam, 'Deuteronomy in Luke–Acts', in S. Moyise and M. J. J. Menken (eds.), *Deuteronomy in the New Testament* (LNTS, 358; London: Bloomsbury T&T Clark, 2007), pp. 63–81 (75–80); P. Mallen, 'Genesis in Luke–Acts', in M. J. J. Menken and S. Moyise (eds.), *Genesis in the New Testament* (LNTS, 466; London: Bloomsbury T&T Clark, 2012), pp. 60–82 (70–74).

[44] The manuscript evidence is divided, with weighty manuscripts for each reading: e.g., $\mathfrak{P}^{74}$ ℵ C include ὁ θεός for all three patriarchs; B E Ψ include ὁ θεός only with Ἀβραάμ; A D include ὁ θεός with Ἀβραάμ and only θεός with Ἰσαάκ and Ἰακώβ. The fuller form also introduces the first of the Eighteen Benedictions. Similar variants occur in Lk. 20.37 and Acts 7.32.

[45] E.g., Gen. 31.53; Exod. 4.5; *Odes* 12.1; cf. Deut. 6.10; 29.13; 2 Macc. 1.2.

[46] E.g., *T. Mos.* 3.9; *Jub.* 27.22; *Pr. Man.* 1.

[47] See the classic article J. A. T. Robinson, 'The Most Primitive Christology of All?', *JTS* n.s. 7 (1956), pp. 177–89, and the cogent critique of C. F. D. Moule, 'The Christology of Acts', in L. E. Keck and J. L. Martyn (eds.), *Studies in Luke–Acts* (London: SPCK, 1968), pp. 159–85 (167–70).

[48] For discussion, see K. L. Anderson, *"But God Raised Him from the Dead": The Theology of Jesus' Resurrection in Luke–Acts* (PBM; Milton Keynes: Paternoster, 2006), p. 223 (resurrection only);

glorified is not God,[49] but Jesus, and—more strikingly—Jesus is being glorified by God.[50] Thus '[t]o understand the meaning of the miracle...is to come to grips with who Jesus is'.[51] The reference to Exodus here is ultimately christologically focused, as it points to the identity and status of Jesus, the one whom the God of the ancestors, the God of Abraham, Isaac and Jacob, glorifies.

b. The Faithful God of Israel and His Faithless People (Exodus in Acts 7)

Stephen's speech (Acts 7.2-53)—the longest in Acts—recites the history of God's engagement with Israel in response to the accusation that Stephen speaks against the temple, the Torah, and customs handed on from Moses (6.13-14). Stephen begins with God's call of Abraham (7.2-8) and goes on to the patriarchs (7.9-16) before spending the largest part of the speech on the time of Moses and the exodus (7.17-44). The latter part moves speedily through the monarchy to the present and critiques the implied idolatry of the temple practised by present-day Israel (7.45-53).[52] The section of the speech concerning Moses and the exodus is our focus, where there are echoes of Exodus 1–3 and 32–34 in addition to other places in Exodus. This section engages with the charge that Stephen speaks against the Mosaic law and Mosaic customs by showing that what God is now doing through Jesus is in continuity with God's actions through Moses. The table below provides an extended comparison of Acts 7 with the Exodus texts.

Exodus	*Acts 7*
2.22 When the woman became pregnant she bore a son, and Moses gave him the name Gershom, saying, 'I am <u>a resident alien in a land belonging to others</u> (Πάροικός εἰμι ἐν γῇ ἀλλοτρίᾳ)' (cf. Gen. 15.13-14).	6 God spoke in this way, 'Your seed will be **resident aliens in a land belonging to others** (πάροικον ἐν γῇ ἀλλοτρίᾳ), and they will enslave them and treat them badly for four hundred years'.
3.12 <u>God said</u> (εἶπεν...ὁ θεός) to Moses, 'I will be with you, and this will be the sign for you, that I call you out; when you <u>have led</u> (ἐν τῷ ἐξαγαγεῖν σε) my people out from Egypt, <u>you will worship God</u> **on this** mountain (λατρεύσετε τῷ θεῷ **ἐν τῷ** ὄρει **τούτῳ**)'.	7 Yet I myself will judge the nation which enslaves them, <u>God said</u> (ὁ θεὸς εἶπεν), 'And after these things <u>they will come out</u> (ἐξελεύσονται) and <u>they will worship me</u> **in this** place (λατρεύσουσίν μοι **ἐν τῷ** τόπῳ **τούτῳ**)'.

D. Hamm, 'Acts 3:12-26: Peter's Speech and the Healing of the Man Born Lame', *PRSt* 11 (1984), pp. 199–217 (202) (the healing, at least in part); Bock, *Proclamation*, p. 189 (both).

[49] Lk. 2.20; 5.25; 7.16; 13.13; 17.15; 18.43; 23.47; Acts 4.21; 11.18; 21.20.
[50] A usage more familiar from the Fourth Gospel, e.g., Jn 8.54; 13.31-32; 16.14; 17.1.
[51] R. W. Wall, 'The Acts of the Apostles', in L. E. Keck (ed.), *Acts–First Corinthians* (NIB, 10; Nashville: Abingdon, 2002), pp. 1–368 (80).
[52] See S. Walton, 'A Tale of Two Perspectives? The Temple in Acts', in T. D. Alexander and S. J. Gathercole (eds.), *Heaven on Earth: The Temple in Biblical Theology* (Carlisle: Paternoster, 2004), pp. 135–49 (138-43).

Exodus	Acts 7
1.5 Now **Joseph** (Ἰωσήφ) was in Egypt. All the <u>people</u> (ψυχαί) from **Jacob** (ἐξ Ἰακώβ) were <u>seventy-five</u> (πέντε καὶ ἑβδομήκοντα).	14 Then **Joseph** (Ἰωσήφ) sent a message inviting his father **Jacob** (Ἰακώβ) to join him, with the whole extended family of <u>seventy-five people</u> (ψυχαῖς ἑβδομήκοντα πέντε).
1.8 Now **another king, who had not known Joseph, came to power over Egypt** Ἀνέστη δὲ βασιλεὺς ἕτερος ἐπ' Αἴγυπτον, ὃς οὐκ ᾔδει τὸν Ἰωσήφ	18 ... until the time when **another king, who had not known Joseph, came to power [over Egypt]** ἄχρι οὗ ἀνέστη βασιλεὺς ἕτερος (ἐπ' Αἴγυπτον) ὃς οὐκ ᾔδει τὸν Ἰωσήφ
1.10 <u>let us deal craftily</u> (κατασοφισώμεθα) with them. 22 Then Pharaoh gave instructions to all his people, 'Every male which is born of the Hebrews, throw in the river; and every female, <u>keep alive</u> (ζωογονεῖτε).	19 This man <u>dealt craftily</u> (κατασοφισάμενος) with our race and compelled [our] ancestors to throw out their infants in order that they might not <u>be kept alive</u> (ζωογονεῖσθαι).
2.2 And she became pregnant and bore a male; when they saw that he was <u>good-looking</u> (ἀστεῖον), they hid him **for three months** (μῆνας τρεῖς)	20 At that very time, Moses was born and he was <u>good-looking</u> (ἀστεῖος) as far as God was concerned. He was brought up **for three months** (μῆνας τρεῖς) in his father's house
General summary of Exod. 2.5-10	21 but when he [sc. Moses] was exposed, Pharaoh's daughter claimed him for herself and brought him up as her own son.
2.11a Now it happened in those many days, when Moses had grown up, he went out to **his compatriots, the descendants of Israel** (τοὺς ἀδελφοὺς αὐτοῦ τοὺς υἱοὺς Ἰσραήλ). (cf. Deut. 24.7; Judg. 20.13)	23 When he was forty years old, it came into his mind to visit **his compatriots, the descendants of Israel** (τοὺς ἀδελφοὺς αὐτοῦ τοὺς υἱοὺς Ἰσραήλ).
2.11b-12 As he considered their hard labour, <u>he saw</u> (ὁρᾷ) an Egyptian striking **a certain** (τινα) Hebrew from his compatriots the sons of Israel; and when he had looked around this way and that, he saw no-one and **after striking the Egyptian** (πατάξας τὸν Αἰγύπτιον), he hid him in the sand	24 <u>When he saw</u> (ἰδών) **a certain one** (τινα) in the process of being treated wrongly, he came to his defence and took vengeance **by striking the Egyptian** (πατάξας τὸν Αἰγύπτιον)

Exodus	Acts 7
2.13 summarised, no clear quotation	26 The next day he appeared as some were fighting and he tried to reconcile them by saying, 'Men, you are brothers: why are you harming each other?'
2.14a But <u>he said</u> (εἶπεν), **'Who put you in charge as a ruler and judge over us? Surely you do not want to kill me in the same way you killed the Egyptian** (Τίς σε κατέστησεν ἄρχοντα καὶ δικαστὴν ἐφ' ἡμῶν; μὴ ἀνελεῖν με σὺ θέλεις, ὃν τρόπον ἀνεῖλες...τὸν Αἰγύπτιον) yesterday?'	27-28 (+ 35) The one who was harming his neighbour pushed him aside, <u>saying</u> (εἰπών), **'Who put you in charge as a judge and ruler over us? Surely you do not want to kill me in the same way you killed the Egyptian?'** (τίς σε κατέστησεν ἄρχοντα καὶ δικαστὴν ἐφ' ἡμῶν; μὴ ἀνελεῖν με σὺ θέλεις ὃν τρόπον ἀνεῖλες ἐχθὲς τὸν Αἰγύπτιον;)
Summary of 2.15-22, with specific echoes: 2.15 **Moses** (Μωυσῆς) withdrew from the presence of Pharaoh and lived **in the land of** <u>Midian</u> (**ἐν γῇ** <u>Μαδιάν</u>) 2.22 The woman became pregnant and bore a son, and Moses named him with the name Gershom, saying, 'I am **an alien** (πάροικος) in a foreign land'. 18.3-4 his <u>two sons</u> (τοὺς <u>δύο υἱοὺς</u> αὐτοῦ)	29 **Moses** (Μωϋσῆς) fled because he said this and became **an alien in the land of** <u>Midian</u> (πάροικος ἐν γῇ Μαδιάμ), where he fathered **two sons** (υἱοὺς δύο).
3.2 **An angel** (ἄγγελος) of the Lord appeared **to him** (αὐτῷ) in <u>flaming fire</u> (**ἐν πυρὶ φλογός**) out of the **bush** (βάτου)	30 When forty years had passed an angel (ἄγγελος) appeared **to him** (αὐτῷ) in the wilderness of Mount Sinai in <u>flaming fire</u> in a **bush** (ἐν φλογὶ πυρὸς[53] βάτου)
Summary of 3.3-4a: Then **Moses** (Μωυσῆς) said, 'As I pass by, <u>I will look</u> (ὄψομαι) at this great **sight** (τὸ δράμα), why the bush is not being consumed. When <u>the Lord</u> (κύριος) saw that he was approaching to look, <u>the Lord</u> (κύριος) called to him out of the bush	31 When **Moses** (ὁ...Μωϋσῆς) <u>saw</u> (ἰδών) this, he was amazed at **the sight** (τὸ δράμα); as he was approaching to look more closely, the voice <u>of the Lord</u> (κυρίου) came.

---

[53] Some Acts mss read πυρὶ φλογός, as LXX, doubtless under LXX influence.

Exodus	Acts 7
3.6 And he said to him, 'I am **the God** (Ἐγώ εἰμι ὁ θεός) <u>of</u> **your** (σου) <u>ancestor</u> (τοῦ πατρός), **God of Abraham and** God **of Isaac and** God **of Jacob** (θεὸς Ἀβραὰμ καὶ θεὸς Ἰσαὰκ καὶ θεὸς Ἰακώβ)'. **Moses** (Μωυσῆς) turned away his face, for he was acting reverently to look down before God.	32 '**I am the God** (ἐγὼ ὁ θεός) **of your** (σου) <u>ancestors</u> (τῶν πατέρων), **the God of Abraham and Isaac and Jacob** (ὁ θεὸς Ἀβραὰμ καὶ Ἰσαὰκ καὶ Ἰακώβ)'. **Moses** (Μωυσῆς) began to tremble and did not dare to look more closely.
3.5, 7, 8, 10 And he **said** (εἶπεν), 'Do not come near here! <u>Take off</u> (λῦσαι) **the sandals** (τὸ ὑπόδημα) **from your feet, for the place** (τῶν ποδῶν σου, ὁ γὰρ τόπος) <u>in</u> (ἐν) **which you are standing is holy ground** (ᾧ σὺ ἕστηκας, γῆ ἁγία ἐστίν)'…**The Lord** (κύριος) **said** (εἶπεν) to Moses, '**I have indeed seen the oppression of my people in Egypt** (Ἰδὼν εἶδον τὴν κάκωσιν τοῦ λαοῦ μου τοῦ ἐν Αἰγύπτῳ) and **I have heard** (ἀκήκοα) **their** (αὐτῶν) outcry on account of their supervisors, for I know their pain; and **I have come down in order to deliver them** (κατέβην ἐξελέσθαι αὐτούς) from the hand of the Egyptians…**so now, come, let me send you** (καὶ νῦν δεῦρο ἀποστείλω σε) <u>to</u> (πρός) Pharoah, the king of <u>Egypt</u> (Αἰγύπτου)	33-34 Then **the Lord** (ὁ κύριος) **said** (εἶπεν) to him, '<u>Take off</u> (λῦσον) **the sandals from your feet, for the place** (ὑπόδημα τῶν ποδῶν σου, ὁ γὰρ τόπος) <u>upon</u> (ἐφ') **which you are standing is holy ground** (ᾧ ἕστηκας γῆ ἁγία ἐστίν). **I have indeed seen the oppression of my people in Egypt** (Ἰδὼν εἶδον τὴν κάκωσιν τοῦ λαοῦ μου τοῦ ἐν Αἰγύπτῳ) and <u>I heard</u> (ἤκουσα) **their** (αὐτῶν) groaning, and **I have come down in order to deliver them** (κατέβην ἐξελέσθαι αὐτούς). So now, **come, let me send you** (καὶ νῦν δεῦρο ἀποστείλω σε) <u>to Egypt</u> (εἰς Αἴγυπτον)
2.14a He said, '**Who put you in charge as a ruler and judge over us?** (Τίς σε κατέστησεν ἄρχοντα καὶ δικαστὴν ἐφ' ἡμῶν;) 3.2a <u>An angel</u> (ἄγγελος) of the Lord <u>appeared</u> (ὤφθη) **to him** (αὐτῷ) in flaming fire <u>out of the bush</u> (ἐκ τοῦ βάτου)	35 (cf. 27) This Moses—the one they rejected, saying, '**Who put you in charge as a ruler and judge?**' (τίς σε κατέστησεν ἄρχοντα καὶ δικαστήν;)— this is the one God sent as ruler and deliverer through the hand of <u>an angel</u> (ἀγγέλου) who <u>appeared</u> (ὀφθέντος) **to him** (αὐτῷ) <u>in the bush</u> (ἐν τῇ βάτῳ).
7.3 But I will harden Pharoah's heart and I will multiply my **signs** (σημεῖα) **and** (καί) wonders in the land of Egypt (τέρατα ἐν γῇ Αἰγύπτῳ). Summary of Exodus 14	36 This is the one who led them out by doing **wonders and signs in the land of Egypt** (τέρατα καὶ σημεῖα ἐν γῇ Αἰγύπτῳ) and at the Red Sea—as well as in the wilderness for forty years.

Exodus	Acts 7
Summary of Exod. 19.1-6; 20.1-17	³⁸ This is the one who was in the congregation in the wilderness with the angel who spoke to him on Mount Sinai—and with our ancestors. He received living words to give to us
³²·¹ When the people saw that Moses delayed to come down from the mountain, the people gather together around **Aaron** (Ἀαρών) and said to him, 'Get up and **make gods for us, who will go before us** (ποίησον ἡμῖν θεούς, οἳ προπορεύσονται ἡμῶν); **for this** person **Moses, who led us out from Egypt** (ὁ γὰρ Μωυσῆς οὗτος ὁ ἄνθρωπος ὃς ἐξήγαγεν ἡμᾶς ἐξ Αἰγύπτου)—**we don't know what** (οὐκ οἴδαμεν, τί) has happened (γέγονεν) **to him** (αὐτῷ)'. ³²·²³ For they said (λέγουσιν) to me (μοι) [*sc.* Aaron], '**Make for us gods, who will go before us** (Ποίησον ἡμῖν θεούς, οἳ προπορεύσονται ἡμῶν); **for this** person **Moses, who led us out from** the land of **Egypt** (ὁ γὰρ Μωυσῆς οὗτος ὁ ἄνθρωπος, ὃς ἐξήγαγεν ἡμᾶς ἐξ γῆς Αἰγύπτου)—**we don't know what** (οὐκ οἴδαμεν, τί) has happened (γέγονεν) **to him** (αὐτῷ)'.	⁴⁰ when they said to Aaron (εἰπόντες τῷ Ἀαρών), '**Make for us gods who will go before us** (ποίησον ἡμῖν θεοὺς οἳ προπορεύσονται ἡμῶν); for this Moses, who led us out from Egypt (ὁ γὰρ Μωϋσῆς οὗτος, ὃς ἐξήγαγεν ἡμᾶς ἐκ γῆς Αἰγύπτου)—**we don't know what** (οὐκ οἴδαμεν τί) happened (ἐγένετο) **to him** (αὐτῷ)!'
Summary of 32.4-6 with a few exact echoes: And he received from **their hands** (τῶν χειρῶν αὐτῶν) and shaped them with an engraving tool and made (ἐποίησεν) them a molten calf (μόσχον) and said...and they offered **a sacrifice** (θυσίαν) of salvation	⁴¹ At that time they made a calf (ἐμοσχοποίησαν), offered **sacrifice** (θυσίαν) to the idol, and began celebrating the works of **their hands** (τῶν χειρῶν αὐτῶν).

Exodus	Acts 7
25.8a (9a Rahlfs-Hanhart) echoes the event: And do for me **according to** (**κατά**) everything which I showed you (πάντα, ὅσα ἐγώ σοι δεικνύω) on the mountain 25.40 See to it that you do **according to the pattern** (**κατὰ τὸν τύπον**) which was shown to you (τὸν δεδειγμένον σοι) on the mountain. 27.21 In the tent **of witness** (ἐν τῇ σκηνῇ τοῦ μαρτυρίου)	44 The tent **of witness** ('Η σκηνὴ τοῦ μαρτυρίου) was with our ancestors in the wilderness just as the one who spoke instructed Moses to make it **according to the pattern** which he had seen (**κατὰ τὸν τύπον** ὃν ἑωράκει)
33.3, 5 For I shall not go up with you because you are a stiff-necked (σκληροτράχηλον) people… You are a stiff-necked (σκληροτράχηλος) people	51 Stiff-necked (Σκληροτράχηλοι) and uncircumcised in hearts and ears—that's you, constantly resisting the Holy Spirit; you are just like your ancestors!

Stephen's speech has the air of 'rewritten Bible', 'a narrative that follows Scripture but includes a substantial amount of supplements and interpretative developments'.[54] It is a form of re-presentation of biblical history or biblical stories that interprets the Bible for the presenter's own setting (and thus some identify the speech as 'historical review'[55]). Like other examples, it is highly selective in order to convey the themes and focus that the speaker/author intends.[56] In the literary setting of Acts, Stephen's speech is a response to the (false) accusations that he speaks against the temple and the law (6.11-14). His speech responds both by answering the accusations and (typically of a soon-to-be martyr[57]) denouncing his judges. Limitations of space forbid a full study of every echo and quotation of Exodus in the speech;[58] what follows identifies some principles and techniques used in the speech's appropriation of Exodus and zeroes in on some particularly pertinent examples.

First, *there is considerable variation in how close Acts' phrasing is to the LXX Exodus text*. In places the correspondence is exact or has only minor variations (vv. 18, 27-28, 35, 33-34, 40), whereas in other places whole stories, or sections of stories, are summarised in broad strokes (vv. 21, 26, 29, 38, 41). A third group

---

[54] E. Schürer, G. Vermes, F. Millar, and M. Goodman, *The History of the Jewish People in the Age of Jesus Christ (175 BC–AD 135)* (4 vols.; Edinburgh: T. & T. Clark, rev. edn, 1973–1986), vol. 3.1, p. 326.
[55] E.g., E. J. Schnabel, *Acts* (ZECNT, 5; Grand Rapids: Zondervan, 2012), p. 362 n. 8.
[56] For discussion of 'rewritten Bible', see P. S. Alexander, 'Retelling the Old Testament', in D. A. Carson and H. G. M. Williamson (eds.), *It is Written: Scripture Citing Scripture: Essays in Honour of Barnabas Lindars* (Cambridge: Cambridge University Press, 1988), pp. 99–121, esp. 116–18.
[57] E.g., *Mart. Pol.* 9.2.
[58] For such discussion, see the forthcoming Word Biblical Commentary on Acts; Marshall, 'Acts', pp. 556–71; and other commentaries.

are passages where the story is being told in Luke's language, but with particular words or phrases—often rare or striking ones—from LXX Exodus used (vv. 30, 32, 44, 51). This variation illustrates how Luke's Stephen is not simply re-telling the stories of Moses, but angling them towards his own focus on Jesus. Thus, the sonorous title of God, 'the God of your ancestors, the God of Abraham, Isaac, and Jacob' (v. 32), is reproduced verbatim, for it is vital to Stephen's argument that the God who exalted Jesus is the ancestral Jewish God.

Second, *the echoes of Exodus are shaped by the speech's focus on God fulfilling the promise to Abraham* (vv. 2-8, esp. 6-7). The speech aims to show that God has fulfilled this promise in Israel's history, and is now fulfilling it in and through Jesus and his followers. Verses 6-7 blend together biblical texts from Genesis and Exodus, notably by combining 'after these things, they shall come out here (μετὰ δὲ ταῦτα ἐξελεύσονται ὧδε) with much baggage' (Gen. 15.14) with 'at the time when you [singular] have brought my people out of Egypt, you [plural] shall worship God on this mountain (λατρεύσετε τῷ θεῷ ἐν τῷ ὄρει τούτῳ)' (Exod. 3.12) to produce 'and after these things, they shall come out and shall worship me in this place' (v. 7). Thus, the true focus of God's promise to Abraham is not the escape from Egypt *per se*, but that the escape enables the people to worship God at a specific location.[59] This forms an interesting counter-point to—even relativization of—God's promise to Abraham of the land (7.3). We might characterize vv. 6-7 as the 'text' for Stephen's 'sermon'; certainly, Stephen introduces Moses with clear reference to the Abrahamic promise (v. 17), providing theological commentary on the story he tells. In Moses' encounter at the burning bush, YHWH is Abraham's God (v. 32). Stephen also names obstacles to God fulfilling his promises: Egypt and its people (vv. 17, 18, 22, 24, 28, 34, 39, 40), Pharoah/the king (vv. 18-19; cf. v. 21), and the people's rejection of Moses (vv. 27-29, 35, 39-41). Stephen's speech should be read, at one level, as telling the story of God fulfilling his promise to Abraham, and the Exodus material echoed and cited serves this end. More than that, the speech asserts that what God is now doing through Jesus and his people is in continuity with God's covenant with Israel—Jesus is the 'prophet like Moses' promised in Scripture (v. 37; Deut. 18.15).

Third, *it is striking to notice which episodes from Moses' life are included in this retelling*, for the retelling is (of necessity) highly selective.

Moses' birth and upbringing are significant (vv. 18-22) and have echoes of Jesus' birth in Luke 2: both are born at times when God's people are under foreign domination (vv. 17-19; Lk. 2.1-2), and both grow in wisdom (v. 22; Lk. 2.52) and enjoy God's favor (v. 20; Lk. 2.52). The episode where Moses kills the Egyptian and is rejected by his own people is given a good deal of airtime (vv. 23-29), preparing for the implication that, just as the people of Moses' day

---

[59] There is debate over whether 'this place' should be understood as Sinai, Moses' location when God spoke the promise in Exod. 3.12, or the Jerusalem temple, which Stephen has been accused of attacking and about which he speaks later (6.11-14; 7.44-50). See respectively F. S. Spencer, *Acts* (Readings; Sheffield: Sheffield Academic, 1997), p. 71; and C. S. Keener, *Acts: An Exegetical Commentary* (4 vols.; Grand Rapids: Baker, 2012-15), vol. 2, pp. 1359-60.

rejected him (v. 35), so now the Jewish leaders with whom Stephen speaks have rejected Jesus (v. 52b).

God's call of Moses at Sinai is central (vv. 30-34), for this is Moses' divine legitimation as he hears God's self-identification (v. 32) and God's commitment to deliver his people through Moses (v. 34). Stephen mentions nothing of the argument between God and Moses which Exod. 3.13–4.17 records, for he is giving attention to parallels between Moses and Jesus, rather than contrasts—Jesus' obedience to God is a key feature of Luke's portrait (e.g. Lk. 3.22; 4.1-14; 18.31-33).

The exodus itself receives only brief mention (v. 36), as does Moses' receiving 'living oracles' at Sinai (v. 38), for Stephen moves quickly on to *the golden calf episode* (vv. 39-42; Exod. 32–34). A striking lexical connection is the use of σκληροτράχηλος ('stiff-necked') in v. 51. This term is found only here in the NT, and in the LXX predominantly in the golden calf story, where God and Moses both use it to describe the people (Exod. 33.3, 5; 34.9; Deut. 9.6, 13).[60] The relevance of the story is that Moses is the obedient leader of Israel who is rejected by the stiff-necked people in favor of Aaron and idolatry; thus, to reject God's chosen leader leads to idolatry. The implication is that the stiff-necked rejection of Jesus by the leaders is hand-in-glove with their making the temple—originally God's good gift to his people—into an idol. Stephen can even use the derogatory term 'hand-made' (χειροποίητος, v. 48; cf. Acts 17.24), a characteristic of idols, for the temple.[61]

Stephen's selectivity is no accident, for at each key time in Moses' life, Stephen is pointing to Jesus and the Jewish leaders' response to him. The vehicle of the speech is Moses' story, but the tenor is Jesus. This leads to our fourth observation on this speech, that there is (again) a strong christological focus in the way Luke reads Exodus. *Moses is a 'type' of Jesus* in two key ways.

First, *Moses is a leader and prophet who speaks for God, but who is rejected.* The fighting Israelites turn on him and ask who made him their 'ruler and judge' (ἄρχοντα καὶ δικαστήν, vv. 27, 35; Exod. 2.14 LXX), even though God intended him as 'ruler and deliverer' (ἄρχοντα καὶ λυτρωτήν, v. 35). The shift from 'judge' to 'deliverer' implies that through Moses God delivers the Israelites from Egypt. Further, at Mt. Sinai, Moses as prophet received 'living oracles' from God (v. 38), but was rejected by the people, who turned to Aaron for leadership instead and engaged in idolatry (vv. 38-42). Jesus has similarly come as ruler and deliverer but been rejected by his own people (vv. 51-52). Jesus is the prophet like Moses announced by God (v. 37) and, like Moses, is rejected.

Second, *Moses performs 'wonders and signs'* (τέρατα καὶ σημεῖα, v. 36) in Egypt and at the Red Sea, a clear reference to the plagues and the exodus (Exod. 7.3 and ch. 14). Peter has earlier spoken of Jesus performing 'wonders and signs'

---

[60] Other LXX uses are Prov. 29.1; Sir. 16.11; Bar. 2.30; Baruch's use is of the people's exile because they are stiff-necked.

[61] LXX Lev. 26.1, 20; Isa. 10.9; 19.1; 31.7; 46.6; Dan. 5.4, 23; 6.27; Jdt. 8.18; Wis. 14.8. See more fully Walton, 'Tale', pp. 138–43; P. W. L. Walker, *Jesus and the Holy City: New Testament Perspectives on Jerusalem* (Grand Rapids: Eerdmans, 1996), pp. 66–68.

(τέρασιν καὶ σημείοις, Acts 2.22), and they are also a feature of the life of the believing communities (2.43; 4.30; 5.12), including by Stephen himself (6.8). 'Wonders and signs' are relatively rare in biblical history and tend to be concentrated on particular periods, of which the exodus and the time of Jesus and the early believers stand out.[62] As Keener notes, '[t]hose resisting Stephen's message should notice the pattern, for Stephen and Jesus worked signs as Moses did'.[63]

In sum, Acts 7 offers a rich re-reading of the Moses stories from Exodus with a strong focus on Christology and its implications for the present situation of Stephen and the believers. Through this speech, Luke moves forward his claim that the believing community is the true, renewed Israel, in continuity with God's covenant people of Scripture. The charges against Stephen are manifestly false, but they are true of the Jewish leaders: they are the ones who rejected Jesus as their ancestors rejected Moses and the prophets; they are the ones who have made the temple into an idol; they are the ones who speak and act against the temple, the Torah and the traditions handed on from Moses (6.13-14). By contrast, Stephen, along with other leaders of the Jesus movement, speaks for God and interprets Scripture rightly, for he reads it through a christological lens.

c. God as Creator in Debate with Paganism (Exodus 20.11 in Acts 14.15; 17.24)

Exod. 20.11, LXX	Acts 14.15	Acts 17.24
ἐν γὰρ ἓξ ἡμέραις **ἐποίησεν κύριος τὸν οὐρανὸν καὶ τὴν γῆν καὶ τὴν θάλασσαν καὶ πάντα τὰ ἐν αὐτοῖς** καὶ κατέπαυσεν τῇ ἡμέρᾳ τῇ ἑβδόμῃ· διὰ τοῦτο εὐλόγησεν κύριος τὴν ἡμέραν τὴν ἑβδόμην καὶ ἡγίασεν αὐτήν. For in six days the Lord **made the sky and the earth and the sea and everything which is in them** and he rested on the seventh day; therefore the Lord blessed the seventh day and set it apart.	εὐαγγελιζόμενοι ὑμᾶς ἀπὸ τούτων τῶν ματαίων ἐπιστρέφειν ἐπὶ θεὸν ζῶντα, ὃς **ἐποίησεν τὸν οὐρανὸν καὶ τὴν γῆν καὶ τὴν θάλασσαν καὶ πάντα τὰ ἐν αὐτοῖς**· [We] bring you good news, to turn from these worthless things to the living God, who **made the sky and the earth and the sea and everything in them.**	ὁ θεὸς ὁ <u>ποιήσας</u> τὸν κόσμον **καὶ πάντα τὰ ἐν** αὐτῷ, οὗτος <u>οὐρανοῦ καὶ γῆς</u> ὑπάρχων <u>κύριος</u> οὐκ ἐν χειροποιήτοις ναοῖς κατοικεῖ The God who <u>made</u> the world **and everything which is in** it, this one, being <u>Lord of sky and earth</u>, does not inhabit hand-made shrines.

---

[62] The other main period of such events is that of Elijah and Elisha (1 Kgs 17–2 Kgs 13).
[63] Keener, *Acts*, vol. 2, p. 1402.

The exact citation of Exod. 20.11 LXX in Acts 14.15 and the clear allusion in Acts 17.24 both come in the setting of Paul engaging with pagans who are misunderstanding—or not understanding—the nature of the God whom Paul proclaims. In Lystra Paul and Barnabas face worshippers of Zeus who assume that they are gods in human form (14.11), probably because of a tradition in the area of a previous visit by Zeus and Hermes, which did not end well because of the inhospitality of most people.[64] In Athens, Paul faces a request for the justification of the Areopagus council's assumption that he wishes to open a temple to Jesus there.[65] In both cases, Paul is explaining a Jewish understanding of the one true God as the only one worthy of worship in order to critique the pagan assumption that there were many gods. There are similarities with other Jewish apologetic, and some philosophical traditions would be sympathetic to Paul's argument here,[66] although Paul's approach is much more openly critical—indeed, blunt—in its rejection of paganism: 'these worthless (ματαίων) things' (14.15), the rejection of shrines and idols (17.24, 29), and the description of paganism as 'superstition' (δεισιδαιμονεστέρους, 17.22) and 'ignorance' (ἀγνοίας, 17.30) show Paul combatively criticizing his hearers' present mistaken understanding in order to move them towards true understanding and worship. God's creative power is one of the two key things that mark YHWH as the one true God, distinct from all else in creation, in the Jewish Scriptures (the other is YHWH's sovereign rule over the universe).[67]

The Exodus context, by contrast, is in the Decalogue, with the claim about creation in six days and God's rest on the seventh day forming the basis for the Sabbath command (20.8-10; cf. similar phrasing about creation in Ps. 145.6 LXX). Acts makes no mention of the six days or the seventh day rest; the appeal to God's creative power is used differently to signal that YHWH is not only 'the living God', but the *only* living God, contrasting with other gods.[68] In this sense, Acts is in line with other Second Temple Jewish sources, which use creation as a key marker of YHWH's 'divine identity', and the relevance of that claim is clear in both pagan Lystra and Athens, a city that was 'a forest of idols' (κατείδωλος, 17.16).[69] Indeed, to claim God as creator is to reject the claim that Paul preaches a new god in Athens—this is the one true God whose creative power stands behind everything that the Athenians can see.[70]

---

[64] Ovid, *Metam.* 8.618-724; for discussion, see C. H. Gempf, 'Mission and Misunderstanding: Paul and Barnabas in Lystra (Acts 14:8-20)', in A. Billington, M. M. B. Turner, and T. Lane (eds.), *Mission and Meaning (Festschrift Peter Cotterell)* (Carlisle: Paternoster, 1995), pp. 56–69 (61–66).

[65] B. W. Winter, 'On Introducing Gods to Athens: An Alternative Reading of Acts 17:18-20', *TynBul* 47 (1996), pp. 71–90.

[66] F. G. Downing, 'Common Ground with Paganism in Luke and in Josephus', *NTS* 28 (1982), pp. 546–59; Keener, *Acts*, vol. 2, pp. 2158–59.

[67] E.g. Isa. 40.25-26, 28; 42.5; 45.7, 12, 18. R. Bauckham, *God Crucified: Monotheism and Christology in the New Testament* (Didsbury Lectures 1996; Carlisle: Paternoster, 1998), pp. 6–16.

[68] C. Breytenbach, 'Zeus und der lebendige Gott: Anmerkungen zu Apostelgeschichte 14:11-17', *NTS* 39 (1993), pp. 396–413 (397).

[69] R. E. Wycherley, 'St Paul at Athens', *JTS* n.s. 19 (1968), pp. 619–21 (619–20).

[70] C. K. Rowe, *World Upside Down: Reading Acts in the Graeco-Roman Age* (Oxford: Oxford University Press, 2009), p. 34.

d. Testing God (Exodus 17.2b in Acts 15.10)

Exod. 17.2b LXX	Acts 15.10
καὶ εἶπεν αὐτοῖς Μωυσῆς Τί λοιδορεῖσθέ μοι, καὶ **τί πειράζετε** κύριον; And Moses said to them, 'Why are you abusing me, and **why are you testing** the Lord?'	νῦν οὖν **τί πειράζετε** τὸν θεὸν ἐπιθεῖναι ζυγὸν ἐπὶ τὸν τράχηλον τῶν μαθητῶν ὃν οὔτε οἱ πατέρες ἡμῶν οὔτε ἡμεῖς ἰσχύσαμεν βαστάσαι; So now, **why are you testing** God by placing a yoke on the neck of the disciples which neither our ancestors nor we have been strong enough to carry?

During the Jerusalem meeting that debates the terms on which gentiles may be admitted to the believing community, Peter speaks to the gathering, drawing on his experience with Cornelius' household (Acts 15.7-9; more fully, 10.1–11.18). From God's welcome of those gentiles by giving them the Spirit in like manner to the first (Jewish) believers, Peter draws the conclusion that those who wish to require gentile believers to be circumcised and keep the Torah are asking something which is 'testing' (πειράζω) God. He uses the image of the Torah as a 'yoke' (v. 10), an image for the Torah found among the rabbis, but there seen positively.[71] By contrast, Peter presents the Torah as a burden too great to bear, even by the Jewish people.

The image of 'testing God' is found elsewhere in Acts (e.g., 5.9) and draws on imagery from Exod. 17.2, where Moses warns the Israelites that, in abusing him because they lack water (17.1), they are pushing God to see how far God will let them go before punishing them. Although their words are directed against Moses, their criticism is against God and demonstrates their lack of trust that God who brought them out of Egypt will continue to sustain them (17.3, 7).

The common theme of the two passages is testing God's patience and generosity. The echo of Exodus is somewhat ironic, since it is the Torah *from Moses* that Peter now says is an unbearable burden for both Jews and Gentiles, and in Exod. 17.2 the people criticize Moses and thereby test God. By contrast, the events in Acts lead the believing community away from Mosaic requirements because *God* does not require them. The same grace and generosity that was seen in God's deliverance of Israel from Egypt is now seen in God's welcome of gentiles by giving them the Spirit.

---

[71] E.g. *m. 'Abot* 3.5: 'From whoever accepts upon himself the yoke of Torah do they remove the yoke of the state and the yoke of hard labor' (Neusner).

e. (Not) Criticizing Your Leader(s) (Exodus 22.27 LXX in Acts 23.5)

Exod. 22.28 (27 Rahlfs-Hanhart) LXX	Acts 23.5
Θεοὺς οὐ κακολογήσεις καὶ <u>ἄρχοντας</u> τοῦ λαοῦ σου <u>οὐ</u> κακῶς ἐρεῖς. You shall not speak badly of gods, and **you shall not speak badly** <u>of leaders</u> **of your people.**	ἔφη τε ὁ Παῦλος· οὐκ ᾔδειν, ἀδελφοί, ὅτι ἐστὶν ἀρχιερεύς· γέγραπται γὰρ ὅτι <u>ἄρχοντα</u> τοῦ λαοῦ σου <u>οὐκ</u> ἐρεῖς κακῶς And Paul said, 'I did not know, brothers, that he was the high priest; for it is written, "**You shall not speak badly** <u>of a leader</u> **of your people**"'.

Uniquely in Acts, the Exodus quotation here is signaled by an introductory formula, 'it is written' (γέγραπται).[72] Luke thus signals to his readers that he wants them to notice that Scripture is being cited here. The quotation is almost identical with the LXX; the only substantial difference is that the plural 'leaders' (ἄρχοντας) is singular (ἄρχοντα), presumably because of the Acts context, which is focused on one particular Jewish leader.

Paul quotes Exod. 22.27 by way of (partial) apology for his harsh words to Ananias the high priest, who orders Paul to be struck for his claim to be a faithful Jew (Acts 23.1-3). On learning that he is the high priest, Paul explains that he did not know Ananias to be high priest and shows that he knows that a leader should be treated with respect. Paul may be speaking ironically, implying that the high priest should not be ordering the striking of a man on trial, for it seems unlikely that he did not know that the high priest would preside at a meeting of the Sanhedrin.[73] That said, the address, 'brothers' (ἀδελφοί), repeated in v. 6, presents Paul as identifying with the group he addresses, and thus, if there is irony present, it is probably not in Luke's presentation of Paul as citing Jewish Scripture as a key control on his behavior. The Paul of Acts is thus a loyal Jew, albeit a messianic Jew, for whom Jewish Scripture is not to be set aside; any impression of that—seen, for example, in the (false) accusation that he brought gentiles into a restricted area of the temple (Acts 21.28; cf. 21.21)—is mistaken. This answer is thus of a piece with Paul's teaching from Scripture in synagogues (e.g., 13.16-41), his discussing the interpretation of Scripture with Jewish people (e.g., 17.2-3, 10-12), his readiness to keep Jewish vows (e.g., 18.18; 21.22-24, 26), and his desire to be present at Jewish festivals (e.g., 20.16).

---

[72] This formula is used elsewhere in Acts when introducing quotations from other biblical books (1.20; 7.42; 13.33; 15.15). Cf. Lk. 2.23; 7.27.

[73] So, e.g., J. Calvin, *The Acts of the Apostles* (2 vols.; Edinburgh: St. Andrew's Press, 1966), ad. loc., citing Augustine in support; contra E. Haenchen, *The Acts of the Apostles* (Oxford: Blackwell, 1971), p. 610. *BegC*, vol. 4, p. 288, suggests that the Mishnaic idea of the high priest presiding over the Sanhedrin may be an anachronism.

4. Conclusion

Luke and Acts appeal to Exodus material to recall foundational events of divine salvation, revelation, and preservation in Israel's history, which highlight the glory and character of YHWH and the nature of his covenant relationship with his people. Luke and Acts appeal on multiple occasions to the abiding authority of the 'written' (γέγραπται) text of Exodus (Lk. 2.23; 7.27; Acts 23.5). Luke does not directly stress the promissory nature of Exodus, though Jesus declares that 'everything written about me in the Law of Moses…must be fulfilled' (Lk. 24.44),[74] which doubtless includes Exodus. At the same time, Stephen's speech presents the events of Israel's exodus from Egypt as the fulfillment of divine promises to the patriarchs (Acts 7.6, 17). Luke and Acts primarily cite and appeal to Exodus as authoritative Scripture with enduring, paradigmatic significance (e.g., Lk. 20.38; Acts 7). Further anticipations of the new exodus deliverance that Jesus 'the Lord' brings can be seen through the reference to Jesus' ἔξοδος (Lk. 9.31), the fusion of Exod. 23.20 and Mal. 3.1 in Lk. 7.27, and Jesus' Sabbath healing and interpretation of the fourth commandment in Lk. 13.12-16, particularly when these passages are read in light of programmatic appeals to new exodus prophecies in the opening chapters of Luke's Gospel (e.g., Lk. 2.25 [Isa. 40.1]; 3.4-6 [Isa. 40.3-5 LXX]).[75]

---

[74] For discussion of Lk. 24, see B. J. Tabb, *After Emmaus: How the Church Fulfills the Mission of Christ* (Wheaton, IL: Crossway, 2021), pp. 21–33.

[75] On the Isaianic new exodus in Luke–Acts, see Pao, *Acts*; Hays, *Echoes of Scripture in the Gospels*, pp. 215–18.

Chapter 5

EXODUS IN JOHN

Andreas J. Köstenberger

As J. Pryor aptly noted, John is the 'evangelist of the covenant people'.[1] Of particular importance for the fourth evangelist is the central redemptive event in Israel's history, the exodus. The exodus theme in John encompasses the figure of John the Baptist, the depiction of Jesus as the signs-working Messiah, the giver of the heavenly manna, and God's Passover lamb, and various other strands of salvation-historical motifs that are carefully woven together in the course of the Fourth Gospel. In what follows, we will trace the unfolding of the exodus theme in John's narrative.[2] As will become evident, 'the identity-defining Exodus narrative hovers constantly in the background of John's story'.[3]

---

* The present article draws on relevant portions in A. J. Köstenberger, 'John', in G. K. Beale and D. A. Carson (eds.), *Commentary on the New Testament Use of the Old Testament* (Grand Rapids: Baker, 2007), pp. 415–512. Used by permission.

[1] J. W. Pryor, *John: Evangelist of the Covenant People* (Downers Grove, IL: InterVarsity, 1992).

[2] The following treatment will focus on the most extensive instances of the exodus motif in John's Gospel. In addition, the following passages may briefly be noted. John 1.12 refers to believers' right to become 'children of God', which builds on the OT characterization of Israel as God's children (Deut. 34.1; cf. Exod. 4.22). John 4.24, with its reference to God being spirit, invokes the law's prohibition for Israel to make idols 'in the form of anything' unlike the surrounding nations (Exod. 20.4). John 9.29 refers to God speaking to Moses, presumably at the occasion of the giving of the Mosaic covenant at Sinai (Exod. 33.11; cf. Num. 12.2-8). John 12.28-29 may invoke the thunder that was part of the theophany at Mt. Sinai (Exod. 19.16, 19). John 17.26 concludes with the words, 'I myself may be in them', which harks back to God coming down to dwell with Israel at the giving of the law at Sinai (Exod. 24.16; 40.34; cf. Exod. 29.45-46; Deut 7.21; 23.14). For more detailed discussions of these passages, see Köstenberger, 'John', pp. 421, 439, 461, 474–75, 499.

[3] R. B. Hays, *Echoes of Scripture in the Gospels* (Waco, TX: Baylor University Press, 2016), p. 301.

1. Prologue (John 1.1-18): Jesus the Climactic Manifestation of God's Glorious Presence

The prologue contains allusions to God's presence in Israel during the exodus[4] and to God's giving of the law through Moses.[5] In these and other cases, the evangelist's primary purpose of adducing OT antecedents is to locate Jesus at the climax of God's self-disclosure to his people. In the past, God was present in the tabernacle and the temple; now he has taken up residence among his people in the Word made flesh.[6] In the past, God made himself known through the law; now he has revealed himself definitively in and through Jesus Christ.[7]

Broadly speaking, therefore, the reference to Jesus taking up residence among God's people, resulting in the manifestation of God's glory in 1.14 (the first occurrence of the term δόξα in this Gospel), harks back to OT references to various manifestations of the presence and glory (כבוד) of God.[8] While many during the Second Temple period deplored the absence of divine revelation due to Israel's apostasy,[9] the fourth evangelist announces that now, in Jesus, God's glory has taken up residence in the midst of his people once again.

In fact, bringing glory to God is said to be Jesus' overriding purpose in this Gospel.[10] As Jesus brings glory to God, glory also accrues to him. This, in turn, continues what was true of Jesus prior to his coming, for glory characterized both his eternal relationship with God and his pre-incarnate state.[11] While on earth, Jesus manifested his glory to his first followers particularly through his messianic signs.[12] As the obedient, dependent Son, Jesus brought glory to the Father throughout his ministry, but supremely by submitting to the cross, which is the place of God's—and Jesus'—ultimate glorification.[13]

---

[4] John 1.14, σκηνόω ('pitched his tent'); cf. Exod. 25.8-9; 33.7; 2 Sam. 7.6; Pss. 15.2; 26.8; 27.4-6; 43.3; 74.7; 84.1; Ezek. 37.27-28.

[5] John 1.17; cf. Exod. 31.18; 34.28. On Moses, see Hays, *Echoes of Scripture in the Gospels*, pp. 291–92.

[6] John 1.14. Tabernacle: Exod. 33.9; 40.34-35; temple: 1 Kgs. 8.10-11. For a discussion of God's 'dwelling' among his people in the OT, see D. A. Carson, *The Gospel According to John* (PNTC; Grand Rapids: Eerdmans, 1991), pp. 127–28. See also G. K. Beale, *The Temple and the Church's Mission: A Biblical Theology of the Dwelling Place of God* (NSBT; Downers Grove, IL: InterVarsity, 2004).

[7] John 1.16-17. For the interpretive issues surrounding the phrase 'grace in return for grace' in 1.16 and its explication in 1.17, see A. J. Köstenberger, *John* (BECNT; Grand Rapids: Baker, 2004), pp. 46–48.

[8] E.g., Exod. 33.22; Num. 14.10; Deut. 5.22; Pss. 26.8; 102.16; Jer. 17.12; Ezek. 10.4. Cf. A. J. Köstenberger, 'What Does It Mean to Be Filled with the Spirit? A Biblical Investigation', *JETS* 40 (1997), pp. 229–40 (230). See also Hays, *Echoes of Scripture in the Gospels*, p. 313, who contends that 1.14 alludes to the tabernacle where God's presence manifested itself to Israel in the wilderness.

[9] See, e.g., 1 Macc. 9.23-27; *t. Sotah* 13.2-4. But see 1QH^a 20.11-12; and cf. J. R. Levison, 'Spirit, Holy', in John J. Collins and D. C. Harlow (eds.), *Eerdmans Dictionary of Early Judaism* (Grand Rapids: Eerdmans, 2010), pp. 1252–54.

[10] John 9.3; 11.4, 40.

[11] See 17.5 and 12.41, respectively.

[12] See, e.g., 2.11; Carson, *John*, p. 128.

[13] Cf. 12.23-33; 13.31-32; 14.13; 17.1, 4-5.

Another significant allusion to the exodus is present in the Johannine depiction of Jesus as 'full of grace and truth', which in all probability harks back to the phrase 'loving-kindness and truth'.[14] In the original context, this joint expression refers to God's covenant faithfulness to his people Israel. The fourth evangelist's message is that this covenant fidelity found ultimate expression in God's sending of his one and only Son.[15]

2. The Book of Signs (John 1.19–12.50): Jesus the Signs-Working Prophet and Messiah

The first half of John's Gospel is given primarily to a narration of Jesus' signs, addressed specifically to the Jews.[16] There are two major OT antecedents: (1) the signs and wonders performed by Moses at the exodus; and (2) prophetic symbolic acts denoting future judgment (e.g., Isa. 20.3). Specific connections between the Johannine signs and the exodus motif will be noted in the discussion below.[17]

a. John 1.23: John the Baptist Inaugurates a New Exodus by Heralding the Coming of the Messiah

The exodus motif—and, in particular, the notion of a new exodus led by the Messiah—is sounded in the evangelist's characterization of John the Baptist as 'the voice crying in the wilderness'.[18] In its Isaianic context, the reference is part of the opening section of the second of four speeches which comprises 40.1-9. By announcing Yahweh's intentions, the passage serves as a prologue that sets the tone for chs. 40–48 and the rest of the book.[19] On the heels of the repeated references to judgment in chs. 1–39, the opening of ch. 40 marks a major shift in orientation, introducing the theme of comfort that represents the *Leitmotif* of the remainder of the book.

---

[14] John 1.14, 17; cf. Exod. 34.6; see also 33.18-19. H. Mowvley, 'John 1^{14-18} in the Light of Exodus 33^7–34^{35}', *ExpTim* 95 (1984), pp. 135–37 (137); L. J. Kuyper, 'Grace and Truth: An Old Testament Description of God and Its Use in the Johannine Gospel', *Int* 18 (1964), pp. 3–13 (3–10); cf. Pss. 25.10; 26.3; 40.10; Prov. 16.6; see also Ps. 83.12 LXX = Ps. 84.11.

[15] John 1.14, 18; cf. 3:16, 18; see also the reference to the giving of the law in 1.17. On the expression μονογενής, see esp. G. Pendrick, 'Μονογενής', *NTS* 41 (1995), pp. 587–600; P. Winter, 'Μονογενής παρὰ Πατρός', *ZRGG* 5 (1953), pp. 335–65 (336); see also D. Moody, 'God's Only Son: The Translation of John 3:16 in the Revised Standard Version', *JBL* 72 (1953), pp. 213–19.

[16] See esp. 12.37; 20.30-31. See A. J. Köstenberger, *A Theology of John's Gospel and Letters* (BTNT; Grand Rapids: Zondervan, 2009), pp. 323–35; Köstenberger, 'The Seventh Johannine Sign: A Study in John's Christology', *BBR* 5 (1995), pp. 87–103, who argues for the temple clearing (2.13-22) as the seventh Johannine sign.

[17] See esp. the discussion of the feeding of the multitude and Jesus as the 'bread from heaven' in ch. 6.

[18] John 1.23, citing Isa. 40.3.

[19] J. Blenkinsopp, *Isaiah 40–55* (AB, 19A; New York: Doubleday, 2002), p. 179; J. D. W. Watts, *Isaiah* (WBC, 25; Waco, TX: Word, 1987), p. 79; J. N. Oswalt, *The Book of Isaiah 40–66* (NICOT; Grand Rapids: Eerdmans, 1998), p. 49.

The precise identity of the voice itself is unspecified, yet the context makes clear that the reference is to a human messenger.[20] In light of the fact that several features of 40.1-11 are reminiscent of 6.1-13, it is likely that v. 3 does not describe a 'new call of a new person' but 'an expansion and adaptation of the single Isaiah's original call'.[21] The lack of specificity regarding the messenger's identity focuses attention on his actual message.[22]

The Hebrew allows for the readings 'a voice crying' or 'the voice of one crying'; the LXX (followed by the NT writers) adopts the latter. Also, the Hebrew reads, 'A voice crying, "*In the wilderness* prepare the way of the LORD"', while the LXX (again followed by the NT writers) has, 'A voice crying *in the wilderness*, "Prepare the way of the LORD"'.[23] In the Hebrew, taking 'in the wilderness' with what follows preserves the parallelism, while in the NT, reading 'in the wilderness' in conjunction with the 'voice crying' adapts Isaiah's message to the person of John the Baptist.[24]

Another important part of the voice's message is that Yahweh will come to his people *through the wilderness*, a notion most likely grounded in Sinai traditions.[25] The desert is also a fitting figure for the desolate condition of God's people.[26] Just as the voice remains unidentified, no addressees are explicitly stated. Most likely, they are 'my people' (cf. v. 1), that is, captive Jacob/Israel.[27] No longer is Israel referred to as 'this people' (6.9; 8.6); once again, covenant language is used.[28] The message to God's people is that they are to prepare Yahweh's path in the wilderness and make straight in the desert a highway for their God. This was customary procedure for preparing for a visiting dignitary.[29] The prophet Ezekiel had depicted Yahweh as abandoning Jerusalem (chs. 9–11); now Yahweh will return to take up residence in his city once again, calling for 'monstrous preparation, including a *highway*'.[30]

How are God's people to prepare the way for his return? While again not explicitly stated, the answer most likely is, 'by way of repentance'.[31] If Yahweh is to return, his people must get ready for his coming by repenting of their sins that caused them to be led into exile. This is borne out by the Baptist's message,

---

[20] E. J. Young, *The Book of Isaiah* (NICOT; 3 vols.; Grand Rapids: Eerdmans, 1972), p. 3:26.
[21] Oswalt, *Isaiah*, p. 48.
[22] Oswalt, *Isaiah*, p. 51. This is captured well by the Baptist's words, 'He must increase, but I must decrease' (3.30).
[23] K. Snodgrass, 'Streams of Tradition Emerging from Isaiah 40:1-5 and Their Adaptation in the New Testament', *JSNT* 8 (1980), pp. 24–45.
[24] This does not necessarily mean that the LXX and the NT writers have changed the original meaning. If Yahweh's path is to be prepared *in the wilderness*, it makes perfect sense for the voice to cry *in the wilderness* to call for such preparations.
[25] Cf. Hab. 3.3. Oswalt, *Isaiah*, p. 52.
[26] Young, *Isaiah*, p. 3:29 n. 15.
[27] Cf. Isa. 40.12–44.12. Watts, *Isaiah*, p. 79.
[28] Exod. 6.7; 19.5; Lev. 26.12; Deut. 26.17-18, etc.; Oswalt, *Isaiah*, p. 2:49.
[29] J. A. Motyer, *The Prophecy of Isaiah* (Downers Grove, IL: InterVarsity, 1993), p. 300.
[30] Watts, *Isaiah*, p. 79 (emphasis original); see Isa. 35.8-10; cf. 35.1.
[31] Young, *Isaiah*, p. 3:28.

'Bear fruit in keeping with repentance' (Mt. 3.8). As Isa. 40.1-2 makes clear, God's ultimate purpose for his people is not judgment but salvation, life rather than death.[32]

Yet comfort for God's people is grounded not in anything they do but solely in 'the activity of the Lord, his coming into the sphere of human activity…the revelation of him in human sight'.[33] The purpose for these preparations is the revelation of God's glory,[34] not merely to Israel and Judah but to all of humanity (40.5; cf. 60.1-3). This harks back to the original exodus, where God's glory was manifested universally as well (Exod. 16.10; 24.16-18; 33.18; 40.34). The prediction that all humanity will witness Yahweh's triumphant return to his lowly people is part of the prophetic defiance of current political realities.[35]

Later on, Isaiah also speaks of the coming 'Servant' (esp. 52.13–53.12) who will provide even greater deliverance,[36] to be consummated in the new heavens and the new earth (chs. 65–66). Similar to other prophetic writings, Isaiah's vision draws heavily on exodus typology.[37] In fact, 'the intensity and fullness of Exodus symbolism in Isaiah 40–55 is unique'.[38] The Messiah's redemption will usher in a new exodus at which God's glory will be revealed.[39]

As 40.3, in the context of the entire book of Isaiah, makes clear, God's people—conceived of more broadly than Israel—will be prepared for Yahweh's coming by a prophetic voice. According to the Baptist, as well as the fourth evangelist, the Baptist is that voice. Several elements of the original context of 40.3 resonate with its use in Jn 1.23: (1) the wilderness as the site of prophetic activity;[40] (2) the focus on the message rather than the messenger; (3) the future revelation of God's glory through his visible coming and bringing of salvation, not merely to Israel but to all humanity; and (4) the need for repentance in preparation for the Lord's coming.

Isaiah 40.3 thus invokes the larger exodus motif, including the themes of salvation and God's glory. The use of this passage in Jn 1.23 therefore suggests that the Baptist's salvation-historical role is that of 'the herald of a new exodus, announcing that God is about to redeem his people from captivity, as he had in the days of Moses'.[41] In accordance with Isaiah's prophecy, the Baptist called God's people to repentance in preparation for the coming Servant.[42]

---

[32] Cf. the fourth evangelist's words in 3.17-18 and Jesus' words in 12.47.
[33] Oswalt, *Isaiah*, p. 50.
[34] This is one of the 'ruling concepts' of all of Isaiah; cf. Oswalt, *Isaiah*, p. 52.
[35] Cf. Isa. 49.26; 66.16, 23-24; Blenkinsopp, *Isaiah 40–55*, p. 183.
[36] Oswalt, *Isaiah*, p. 51.
[37] E.g., Jer. 2.6-7; 7.22, 25; 11.4, 7; Hos. 2.16-17; 11.1; 12.10, 14; 13.4-5; Amos 2.9-10; 3.1-2; 9.7; Mic. 6.4; see also Isa. 10.24, 26; 11.16-18.
[38] Watts, *Isaiah*, p. 81.
[39] Young, *Isaiah*, p. 3:30 n. 18.
[40] Köstenberger, *John*, pp. 62–63.
[41] C. S. Keener, *The IVP Bible Background Commentary: New Testament* (Downers Grove, IL: InterVarsity, 2nd edn, 2014), p. 251.
[42] Carson, *John*, p. 144.

b. John 1.29, 36: John the Baptist refers to Jesus as 'the lamb of God who takes away the sin of the world'

In narrating Jesus' baptism, the fourth evangelist focuses on John's declaration concerning Jesus.[43] He is 'the' lamb (ἀμνός) of God, that is, the lamb par excellence. What is more, he is the lamb 'of God', God's provision who 'takes away the sin of the world'. The use of αἴρω ('take away') carries with it the implication of 'bearing off', 'getting rid of', or 'carrying away' (2.16; 5.8-12; 10.18), in association with the Hebrew כפר, which suggests the idea of sins being 'wiped away'.[44] In the OT sacrificial system, the shed blood of the substitute provided atonement, appeasing God's wrath and covering sins (cf. 1 Jn 2.2; 4.10). The Baptist is likely thinking of Isa. 53.7, where the servant is referred to as a lamb (LXX: ἀμνός). However, it is quite possible that he is speaking better than he knows, a device the evangelist uses elsewhere (e.g., 11.49-51). The evangelist's inclusion of this statement places it into the wider context of his passion narrative where Jesus is demonstrated to be the climactic fulfillment of the yearly paschal lamb (cf. Exod. 12), whose bones must not be broken (19.36; cf. 19.14).[45]

Moreover, as God's lamb, Jesus' death will not only address the sins of Israel, but of the entire world (cf. 1.10). There was no expectation within first-century Judaism of a Messiah who would suffer for Jews and Gentiles alike. The evangelist, however, is clear that Jesus came to save the entire world (3.17; 1 Jn 2:2) and is not only the Savior of Israel, but of the world (4.42; 1 Jn 4.14). The NT's depiction of Jesus as 'the lamb of God' culminates in Revelation, where Jesus is the 'lamb who was slain' who returns in universal triumph.[46] Here again, the evangelist's use of Exodus is one of typological fulfilment, with Jesus as the climactic fulfillment of the type.

c. John 3.14: Jesus is the Typological Fulfillment of the Bronze Serpent in the Wilderness; Believing Looking at the Lifted-Up Son of Man Results in the Reception of Eternal Life

The exodus motif continues with Jesus' allusion to Moses lifting up the serpent in the wilderness. The reference is plainly to Num. 21.8-9, where God is shown to send poisonous snakes to judge rebellious Israel. When Moses intercedes for his people, God provides salvation in the form of a raised bronze serpent, so that 'when anyone was bitten by a snake and looked at the bronze snake, he lived' (21.9). Yet the primary analogy in the present passage is not that of the raised bronze serpent and the lifted-up Son of Man. Rather, the focus is on the people's response and its result: looking at the bronze serpent results in the restoration

---

[43] The following discussion is adapted from Köstenberger, *John*, pp. 66–68. On the Passover motif, see further the discussion of 19.24, 36 below.
[44] G. L. Borchert, *John* (NAC, 25A; Nashville: Broadman & Holman, 1996), pp. 135–36.
[45] G. M. Burge, *The Gospel of John* (NIVAC; Grand Rapids: Zondervan, 2000), pp. 73–74; C. K. Barrett, *The Gospel According to St. John* (Philadelphia: Westminster, 2nd edn, 1978), p. 176. For alternative proposals, see Köstenberger, *John*, pp. 66–67 and p. 66 n. 36.
[46] Rev. 5.6, 9, 12; 7.17; 12.11; 13.8; 17.14; 19.7, 9; 21.22-23; 22.1-3.

of people's physical lives while looking in faith at the Son of Man issues in their reception of eternal life.[47] As in the case of wilderness Israel, however, it is ultimately not a person's faith but the God in whom that faith is placed who is the source of salvation.[48]

In addition, a second, slightly more subtle, connection between the Numbers account and Jesus' words to Nicodemus emerges as well. Just as the Israelites' unbelief in the wilderness was deserving of divine judgment and required salvation—to be attained by looking at God's means of deliverance—so Nicodemus is in danger of incurring divine judgment by failing to recognize God's revelation in his one and only Son. Thus, it is not only the trusting gaze at the God-appointed means of salvation that is parallel but also the predicament necessitating the divine remedy. Contrary to their own self-understanding, Nicodemus and his fellow Sanhedrin members—not to mention other Jews and the readers of John's Gospel—are not objective, neutral judges of the merits or demerits of Jesus' claims. Rather, they are called to render a verdict that will either allow them to pass from death to life (5.24) and from God's wrath to his favor (3.36) or confirm the verdict of death upon them (3.19-21).

Yet another important connection between the Johannine source text in the book of Numbers and its appropriation in the context of Jesus' conversation with Nicodemus represents the theme of life—new *physical* life in the case of the original wilderness incident, new *spiritual* life in the case of believers in the crucified Jesus. Significantly, the affirmation in 3.15 'that everyone who believes may in him have eternal life' constitutes the first reference to 'eternal life' in this Gospel.[49] The probable meaning of the expression 'eternal life' is 'the life of the age to come', that is, resurrection life, which, according to John, can already be experienced in the here and now (e.g., 10.10). This life, however, is found only 'in him' (3.15).[50] The eternal life entered by the new, spiritual birth is therefore none other than that of the preexistent Word become flesh in Jesus who has life in himself and is himself the resurrection and the life.[51]

In the flow of discourse, Jesus moves from a prophetic reference to being born from above by water and spirit (3.5; cf. Ezek. 36.25–26) to an OT narrative passage, the account of the bronze serpent in the wilderness (Num. 21.4-9), which served as the divinely appointed means of new—*physical*—life to the people of Israel. Correspondingly, Jesus presents himself as the means of new *spiritual* life—eternal life—for those who become God's children by looking at the lifted-up Son of Man in faith (3.14-15; cf. 1.12).

---

[47] Cf. 3.15-18; Barrett, *Gospel According to St. John*, p. 214; cf. Carson, *John*, p. 202.
[48] Cf. Wis. 16.6-7.
[49] See later 3.16, 36; 4.14, 36; 5.24, 39; 6.27, 40, 47, 54, 68; 10.28; 12.25, 50; 17.2, 3; and the reference to 'life in his name' in 20.31, which, in turn, by way of *inclusio*, corresponds to 1.12.
[50] Explicating and harking back to the prologue: 1.4.
[51] 5.26; 11.25; Carson, *John*, pp. 202–3.

Just as the new birth—the entrance into eternal life—is grounded in the 'lifting up' of God's Son (3.14-15), this 'lifting up' is grounded in God's love.[52] In theological adaptation of the language of Isa. 52.13 LXX (ὑψωθήσεται),[53] the expression 'lifted up' (ὑψωθῆναι) has a double meaning here and elsewhere in John's Gospel, referring both to the literal lifting up of the bronze serpent in the wilderness and to Jesus' lifting up on the cross.[54] The latter, for its part, took place both literally in crucifixion and figuratively in the exaltation Jesus received from God as a result of his obedient submission to his will in pursuit of his mission.[55]

What is more, not only does John's use of the verb ὑψόω in a dual sense draw on Isaianic terminology, but already in Isaiah is 'lifting up' linked with 'being glorified', and this, significantly, in the context of the figure of the suffering Servant of the LORD.[56] What the fourth evangelist discerns in this source text, then, is that *Jesus' crucifixion and exaltation are not discrete steps that are realized successively (as one might surmise from reading the Synoptics) but rather that Jesus' crucifixion constitutes at the same time his exaltation by marking the culmination of his messianic mission as the heaven-sent Word and obedient Son of the Father*. Thus, according to the fourth evangelist, Jesus' death is not a moment of ignominy and shame but an event that brings glory not only to God, Jesus' sender (12.28; 17.1, 4), but also to the Son who completed his mission in perfect obedience to the Father's will (12.23; 17.1). The cross thus becomes the way by which Jesus returns to the glory he possessed with the Father before the world began (17.5, 24; cf. 13.1; 16.28).

While the dual meaning of the term 'lifted up' was veiled to Nicodemus, and may have eluded some of the Gospel's first-time readers, the expression's import is gradually revealed in the course of the remaining narrative.[57] In effect, therefore, John's use of ὑψόω here and later in his narrative is akin to the Synoptic parables in that the term 'both intimates and also obscures what is to come'.[58] Nevertheless, Nicodemus, on the basis of the analogy from Numbers, is called 'to turn to Jesus for new birth in much the same way as the ancient Israelites were

---

[52] 3.16; Carson, *John*, p. 204. For a study of Jn 3.16, see A. J. Köstenberger, 'Lifting Up the Son of Man and God's Love for the World: John 3:16 in Its Historical, Literary, and Theological Contexts', in A. J. Köstenberger and R. W. Yarbrough (eds.), *Understanding the Times: New Testament Studies in the 21st Century* (Wheaton, IL: Crossway, 2011), pp. 141–59.

[53] E.g., C. H. Dodd, *The Interpretation of the Fourth Gospel* (Cambridge: Cambridge University Press, 1953), p. 247.

[54] 8.28; 12.32, 34.

[55] H. N. Ridderbos, *The Gospel of John* (trans. J. Vriend; Grand Rapids: Eerdmans, 1997), pp. 136–37; see esp. the *inclusio* between 4.34 and 17.4 and Jesus' final cry at the cross, 'It is finished!', in 19.30. In addition, John may have established the connection between the term ὑψόω and crucifixion on the basis of the Aramaic expression זְקַף ('to lift up', 'to crucify'; Carson, *John*, p. 201, with reference to G. Bertram, 'ὕψος', in *TDNT*, pp. 8:610–11 [610], who cites 1QS 7.11).

[56] Cf. Isa. 52.13–53.12; see esp. 52.13 LXX; Carson, *John*, p. 201.

[57] See the other Johannine 'lifted up sayings' in 8.28; 12.32, 34; cf. G. C. Nicholson, *Death as Departure: The Johannine Descent–Ascent Schema* (SBLDS, 63; Chico, CA: Scholars Press, 1983), pp. 75–144; A. J. Köstenberger, 'Jesus as Rabbi in the Fourth Gospel', *BBR* 8 (1998), pp. 97–128 (126–28).

[58] Bertram, *TDNT*, p. 8:610.

commanded to turn to the bronze snake for new life. Only when Nicodemus saw Jesus on the cross, or perhaps only in still later reflection on the cross, would it become clear that the 'lifting up'/exaltation of Jesus' served as the life-giving analogue of the raised-up serpent in the wilderness.[59] Thus there is an aspect of Jesus' saying that calls for Nicodemus' immediate attention and action while the fuller appreciation of Jesus' message awaits a later time at which Jesus' prophetic words will be realized and can be interpreted with the benefit of hindsight.

In addition, the fact that the double meaning of 'lifted up' is original to neither Jesus nor John but found already in Isaiah would—indeed, should—have enabled Nicodemus to grasp at least the broad contours of Jesus' pronouncement that he must be 'lifted up'—that is, *physically elevated* as well as *spiritually exalted*—even if he was unable to discern that Jesus' physical 'lifting up' would take place on a cross, a truth veiled even to Jesus' closest followers.[60]

The fourth evangelist's inclusion of Jesus' Numbers reference is part of a comprehensive exodus or Moses/exodus typology that pervades the entire Gospel. It includes not only the above-mentioned references to Jesus in relation to the giving of the law through Moses in the prologue and to the Baptist as the prophetic forerunner of Jesus but also Jesus' signs which hark back to Moses' signs and wonders at the exodus,[61] the Johannine references to the Prophet envisaged in Deuteronomy 18 (1.45; 6.14; 7.40) and to Moses writing about Jesus and testifying about him (5.45-47), the feeding of the multitude and the portrayal of Jesus as the 'bread from heaven' (ch. 6), and the farewell discourse (chs. 13–17), which is largely patterned after Moses' parting words to the Israelites in the book of Deuteronomy.

d. John 6.20: Jesus' Walking on the Water Harks Back to Manifestations of God's Presence during the Exodus

The Johannine account of Jesus' walking on the water in 6.16-24 may echo Job 9.8 LXX where God is depicted as walking on the waters.[62] Jesus' words to the disciples in 6.20, 'It is I; do not be afraid', likewise suggest an OT background. Apart from the plain meaning of the words as conveying Jesus' self-identification, there may be overtones of epiphany ('I am' is God's name in the OT; see Exod. 3.14), especially in light of the fact that Jesus is walking on water. The statement may also allude to Ps. 77.16, 19, which refers to God's manifestation to Israel during the exodus.[63]

---

[59] Carson, *John*, p. 202.
[60] Cf. Mk 8.31-33; 9.30-32; 10.32-45 pars.; see also Jn 6.60, 66; 12.23-26, 33.
[61] Jesus' reference to 'signs and wonders' in 4.48 may constitute an echo of the 'signs and wonders' performed by Moses at the exodus. See A. J. Köstenberger, *The Missions of Jesus and the Disciples According to the Fourth Gospel* (Grand Rapids: Eerdmans, 1998), pp. 58–59, esp. n. 43. Cf. Mt. 24.24 par.; cf. 2 Thess. 2.9, where 'signs and wonders' are said to be performed by false messiahs and prophets.
[62] Note also the parallel wording in Mk 6.48 ('passing by') and Job 9.11; cf. C. S. Keener, *The Gospel of John* (Peabody, PA: Hendrickson, 2003), p. 673.
[63] E.g., G. R. Beasley-Murray, *John* (WBC, 36; Waco, TX: Word, 2nd edn, 1999), pp. 89–90.

e. John 6: Jesus' Body is the Typological Fulfillment of the Manna in the Wilderness

The feeding of the multitude (6.1-15), recorded in all four Gospels and one of the Johannine signs (6.26, 30), provides the occasion for Jesus' extended interchange with the crowds (6.25-58), which at some point transitions into his instruction in the synagogue at Capernaum (cf. 6.59). People's immediate reaction to the miraculous multiplication of the loaves and fishes was to recognize Jesus as the Prophet referred to by Moses (6.14; cf. Deut. 18.15, 18) and to try to compel Jesus to be their king (6.15). Jesus withdraws but is eventually found by the crowds (6.25) who engage him in further discussion.

In the ensuing interchange, Jesus chides them for their failure to look beyond the feeding miracle to its 'signs' character that reveals Jesus' messianic identity (6.26-27; cf. 20.30-31). When they ask Jesus regarding the works God requires (6.28), he responds that the only work they must perform is that of believing in 'the one God has sent' (6.29).[64] The crowd promptly demands a sign that would warrant belief, oblivious to the fact that Jesus had just furnished such proof in form of the multiplication of the loaves (6.30).

At this point, people invoke the experience of Israel's wilderness generation at the exodus: 'Our ancestors ate the manna in the wilderness; as it is written, "He gave them bread from heaven to eat"' (6.31).[65] In other words, people contend, '*Moses* provided our forefathers with manna; what are *you* going to do for us?'[66] Of course, the contention is dripping with irony, for as the reader knows, Jesus is greater than Moses (1.17; 5.45-47). In the ensuing interchange, Jesus proceeds to point out that in his ministry the prophetic vision is fulfilled that in the last days God's people will all be taught by God (6.45; cf. Isa. 54.13).[67]

The statement, 'He gave them bread from heaven to eat', seems to be derived from several OT passages.[68] Perhaps most relevant as a potential background is the reference to the giving of manna in Ps. 78.23-24,[69] where it is part of a recital of wilderness events during the exodus (vv. 12-39). Verses 12-16 speak of God's gracious and wondrous deeds, while vv. 17-20 recount Israel's rebellion[70]

---

[64] S. Grindheim, 'The Work of God or of Human Beings: John 6:29', *JETS* 59 (2016), pp. 63–66.
[65] See Ps. 78.24b; cf. Num. 11.7-9 and the discussion below.
[66] On Moses in the Fourth Gospel, see T. F. Glasson, *Moses in the Fourth Gospel* (SBT, 40; London: SCM, 1963); W. A. Meeks, *The Prophet-King: Moses Traditions and the Johannine Christology* (NovTSup, 14; Leiden: Brill, 1967); M.-E. Boismard, *Moses or Jesus: An Essay in Johannine Christology* (trans. B. T. Viviano; Minneapolis: Fortress, 1993), pp. 1–68; S. Harstine, *Moses as a Character in the Fourth Gospel: A Study of Ancient Reading Techniques* (JSNTSup, 229; Sheffield: Sheffield Academic, 2002). More broadly, see J. Lierman, *The New Testament Moses: Christian Perceptions of Moses and Israel in the Setting of Jewish Religion* (WUNT, 2/173; Tübingen: Mohr Siebeck, 2004).
[67] See Köstenberger, 'John', pp. 648–50, and the discussion below.
[68] See especially Exod. 16.4, 15; Pss. 78.23-24; 105.40; Carson, *John*, p. 286; H. Gunkel, *Die Psalmen* (Göttingen: Vandenhoeck & Ruprecht, 5th edn, 1968), p. 344.
[69] M. J. J. Menken, 'The Provenance and Meaning of the Old Testament Quotation in John 6:31', *NovT* 30 (1988), pp. 39–56 (47–54).
[70] Balanced in ten statements each; cf. A. F. Campbell, 'Psalm 78: A Contribution to the Theology of Tenth Century Israel', *CBQ* 41 (1979), pp. 51–79 (54–55); cited in M. A. Tate, *Psalms 51–100* (WBC, 20; Dallas: Word, 1990), p. 290.

and vv. 21-22 describe God's wrath kindled by the Israelites' lack of trust in his saving power.

Nevertheless, as vv. 23-31 indicate, God still 'rained' (vv. 24, 27) down manna, 'the grain of heaven', as well as meat, on the Israelites. Interestingly, in this section God's gracious provision is intermingled with his judgment on the unbelieving Israelites.[71] Because the wilderness generation 'tested God' (vv. 18, 41, 56), provoking him and rebelling against him, he struck them at the very moment at which they were feeding on the food they had craved (vv. 29-31; cf. Num. 11.33-34). This draws a stark contrast between the goodness and longsuffering nature of God and the ingratitude and unbelief of his people. Psalm 78 continues to recount subsequent events in Israel's history and concludes with a reference to David, the shepherd and servant of God, and the people of Israel.

The divine provision of manna for wilderness Israel is further celebrated in several later OT passages. In addition to Ps. 78.24, important instances include Ps. 105.40 ('gave them bread from heaven in abundance') and Neh. 9.15 ('You gave them bread from heaven for their hunger'). Several Second Temple Jewish works were looking forward to a time when God would again provide manna for his people.[72]

The reference to Ps. 78.24b in Jn 6.31 is closely aligned with the LXX, except that the word φαγεῖν ('to eat') comes at the end rather than the beginning of the line and the phrase ἐκ τοῦ ('from the') is added, the latter most likely owing to the influence of Exod. 16.4.[73] The reason for the addition of ἐκ τοῦ is probably Christological: for John, Jesus is not merely the 'bread *of* heaven', he is the 'bread *from* heaven', underscoring Jesus' provenance from God.[74]

The crowds' statement that God 'gave them bread from heaven to eat' is part of the Johannine misunderstanding theme. While Jesus had just performed an amazing feat, feeding the crowds (6.1-15), people are demanding evidence regarding Jesus' messianic calling which he had just provided. This shows that they failed to discern the true significance of this Johannine sign, as is duly noted by Jesus (6.26). In this way, they were perpetrating the wilderness generation's pattern of unbelief in the face of signs performed by God's servants.

One further element of misunderstanding pertains to the reference to the 'he' (i.e., the implied subject of ἔδωκεν) in the quotation in 6.31. The crowd attributes the provision of manna to Moses, yet as Jesus points out, the person providing the manna in the wilderness was ultimately not Moses but God (6.32), the very God who had now sent Jesus as 'the bread of God...who comes down from heaven and gives life to the world' (6.33).[75] In the ensuing interchange,

---

[71] Tate, *Psalms 51–100*, p. 291.
[72] Wis. 16.20; *Sib. Or. Frag.* 3.49; 2 Bar. 29.8; cf. Philo, *Leg. All.* 3.169–76; *Det. Pot. Ins.* 118; *Rer. Div. Her.* 79, 191; *Mut. Nom.* 259-60; Menken, 'Provenance and Meaning', pp. 39–56.
[73] See the discussions in M. Daly-Denton, *David in the Fourth Gospel: The Johannine Reception of the Psalms* (AGJU, 47; Leiden: Brill, 2004), p. 134; Menken, 'Provenance and Meaning', pp. 52–54.
[74] Cf. 8.42, 47: ἐκ τοῦ θεοῦ; see also 3.13, 31 *et passim*; Menken, 'Provenance and Meaning', p. 53.
[75] See the discussion in Menken, 'Provenance and Meaning', pp. 55–65.

the connection between Jesus' present-day interrogators and the unbelieving wilderness generation is further unpacked (see, e.g., 6.41, 44, 61).

The present chapter is connected with the exodus account in at least three ways: (1) the Passover motif; (2) the depiction of Jesus as the prophet like Moses; and (3) the expectation that God will again provide manna in the messianic age.[76] The implied contrast is between Moses and Jesus.[77] There is also continuity between the wilderness generation and the Israelites in Jesus' day. As in 3.14, an event during Israel's wilderness wanderings at the exodus is shown to anticipate typologically God's provision of salvation in and through Jesus.[78] Also as in 3.14, the typology entails an element of escalation: while the manna in the wilderness had Israel as its recipient, God's gift of Jesus is universal in scope and extends beyond believing Israelites also to believing Gentiles.[79]

An 'I am saying', a 'sign', and two OT quotations combine to highlight Israel's obduracy at this juncture of Jesus' ministry (see esp. 6.60-71). The feeding of the multitude is presented as one of Jesus' messianic signs that typologically fulfills, in an escalated manner, God's signs and wonders performed through Moses at the exodus and meets with rejection just as Moses did (cf. 12.37-40).

Jesus' words in 6.32, 'Not Moses...but my Father', as mentioned, exhort the Jews to see God behind Moses as the true provider of the heavenly bread, whereby 'bread from heaven/of God' in vv. 32-33 points to Jesus' heavenly origin.[80] With regard to the phrase 'gives life to the world' in v. 33, rabbinic teaching depicted the giving of the law at Sinai in similar terms: 'the earth trembled when he gave life to the world' (*Exod. Rab.* 29.9). In the present passage, the same function is said to be fulfilled by Jesus (cf. 5.39).

In light of the Jews' largely negative response to his message, Jesus points out that, while his ministry fulfills the prophetic vision that one day—now here—all people will be taught by God, this applies only to those who are drawn by the Father, the sender of Jesus (6.44), and who subsequently come to believe in him as Messiah. This explains Jewish unbelief in Jesus (the subject of further OT substantiation in 12.38-41) while at the same time affirming God's hand upon Jesus and his mission.

Beyond this, the exposition of Isa. 54.13 in Jn 6.45b-46 may also refer back to the theophany at Sinai by invoking two of its central features, positively hearing (v. 45) and negatively seeing (v. 46).[81] While 'hearing' is an important aspect of Sinai,[82] 'seeing' is not; for no one can see God and live (Exod. 33.20). John 6.46,

---

[76] Ridderbos, *Gospel of John*, p. 226; L. Morris, *The Gospel According to John* (Grand Rapids: Eerdmans, 1971), p. 321; Beasley-Murray, *John*, p. 91.
[77] Ridderbos, *Gospel of John*, pp. 226–27.
[78] Barrett, *Gospel According to St. John*, p. 290.
[79] E.g., 10.16; 11.51-52; 12.32; Carson, *John*, p. 287; A. J. Köstenberger, 'Jesus the Good Shepherd Who Will Also Bring Other Sheep (John 10:16): The Old Testament Background of a Familiar Metaphor', *BBR* 12 (2002), pp. 67–96.
[80] Cf. 3.13, 31; Ridderbos, *Gospel of John*, p. 228.
[81] P. Borgen, *Bread from Heaven: An Exegetical Study of the Concept of Manna in the Gospel of John and the Writings of Philo* (NovTSup, 10; Leiden: Brill, 1965), p. 150.
[82] E.g., Deut. 4.12; 5.24; 18.16; Sir. 17.13; 45.5; *Mek. Exod.* 19.2.

in turn, harks back to 1.18, which is part of the concluding section of the prologue and interprets the theophany at Sinai narrated in Exodus 33–34 (1.14-18).[83]

The Jews' fighting among themselves (6.52) resembles their striving with Moses and God during the exodus.[84] Although later rabbinic teaching speaks (figuratively) of 'eating the Messiah',[85] Jesus' repeated references to people 'eating' his flesh and 'drinking' his blood in 6.50-51, 53-58 seem to militate against the scriptural injunctions against the drinking of blood and the eating of meat containing blood in the Mosaic law.[86] Jesus' insistence in 6.55, harking back to 6.27 and 6.32, that his flesh and blood are real—that is, spiritual—food and drink points to the eschatological, typological fulfillment of the Hebrew Scriptures in the Messiah.

f. John 7.19, 22: Jesus' Appeal to the Law of Moses and His Authority over the Law

The question, 'Has not Moses given you the law?' refers to the great event in Israel's history subsequent to the exodus at which God constituted Israel as a nation. Later in the Fourth Gospel, the Pharisees call themselves 'disciples of Moses' (9.28). Yet Jesus' contemporaries are trying to kill him; this hardly is in keeping with the law of Moses that proscribed murder (Exod. 20.13).

The reference in 7.22 to circumcision being given by Moses, yet ultimately the patriarchs, refers back to Gen. 17.9-14 (Abraham) and Exod. 12.44, 48-49; Lev. 12.3 (Moses). In the ensuing argument 'from the lesser to the greater' (cf. 5.47), Jesus points to the commonly acknowledged dilemma that arose when the Sabbath commandment conflicted with the stipulation, also in the law, that a boy must be circumcised on the eighth day (7.21-23).

g. John 7.31: The Expectation of a Miracle-Working Messiah like Moses

Chapter 7 contains several messianic expectations, the second of which is voiced in v. 31: 'The Christ, when he comes, will not perform more signs than he has done, will he?' There is little direct evidence in the OT that the Messiah will perform miracles, though this may be implied from the fact that the Jews expected a prophet like Moses (Deut. 18.15, 18), who, as mentioned, performed miraculous signs at the exodus (Exod. 7–11). In any case, it would have been natural for people to wonder upon witnessing Jesus' miracles whether or not he was the Messiah.[87]

---

[83] A. J. Köstenberger, *Encountering John* (EBS; Grand Rapids: Baker, 2nd edn, 2013), p. 42; see also Jn 5.37 in the context of 5.37-47; cf. Borgen, *Bread from Heaven*, pp. 151–54.

[84] Exod. 17.2; Num. 20.3; see Beasley-Murray, *John*, p. 94; Borchert, *John*, p. 271; R. Schnackenburg, *Gospel According to St. John* (3 vols.; London: Burns & Oates, 1968, 1980, 1982), p. 2:60.

[85] *b. Sanh.* 99a; see C. H. Talbert, *Reading John* (Reading the New Testament; New York: Crossroad, 1992), p. 138.

[86] See Gen. 9.4; Lev. 17.10-14; Deut. 12.16; C. R. Koester, *Symbolism in the Fourth Gospel* (Minneapolis: Fortress, 2nd edn, 2003), pp. 102–4. 'Flesh and blood' is a Hebrew idiom referring to the whole person (cf. Mt. 16.17; 1 Cor. 15.50; Gal. 1.16; Eph. 6.12; Heb. 2.14).

[87] See Mk 13.22; cf. Deut. 13.1-3; see Meeks, *Prophet-King*, pp. 162–64.

h. John 8.12: The Messiah Will Have Followers as Israel Followed the Pillar of Fire during the Exodus

At 8.12, Jesus asserts that those who follow him will never 'walk in darkness but will have the light of life'. This assertion may echo the 'following' motif, which is also found in the exodus narrative, where the Israelites are said to follow the pillar of fire.[88]

i. John 8.24, 28, 58: Jesus Is Identified with the 'I Am' Who Revealed Himself to Moses in the Wilderness

There may be a hint of deity in Jesus' 'I am' statements in 8.24 and 28,[89] recalling passages such as Isa. 43.10.[90] The OT background of Jesus' statement 'If you don't believe that I am [the one I claim to be]' in 8.24 (cf. 8.28, 58) appears to be Exod. 3.13-14 via Isaiah 40–55.[91] Anyone other than God who appropriated this designation was held to be guilty of blasphemy and subject to his wrath (Isa. 47.8-9; Zeph. 2.15).

The statement, 'Before Abraham came into being, I am' (8.58; see Ps. 90.2), startlingly culminates earlier occurrences of 'I am' in this chapter.[92] The claim contrasts Abraham—who experienced a natural human birth—with Jesus who existed from eternity and was the Word made flesh.[93] Once again, Jesus' language echoes God's self-identification to Moses in Exod. 3.14.[94] Thus Jesus does not merely claim preexistence—or he could have said, 'Before Abraham was born, I *was*'—but deity.[95]

j. John 10.3-4: Jesus is the Greater Successor of Moses, the True Joshua

The references to the shepherd leading out his sheep until he has brought out all his own and to him going on ahead of his sheep may involve an allusion to Num. 27.15-18,[96] a possible typological passage alluding to Christ.[97] In that passage, Moses prays for a future figure who will lead God's people and bring them in,

---

[88] Beasley-Murray, *John*, pp. 128–29; for Qumran and Second Temple parallels see Köstenberger, 'Jesus the Good Shepherd', pp. 67–96 (82).
[89] See Köstenberger, *Encountering John*, pp. 247–48.
[90] Morris, *Gospel According to John*, p. 393 n. 25; D. M. Ball, *'I Am' in John's Gospel: Literary Function, Background and Theological Implications* (JSNTSup, 124; Sheffield: Sheffield Academic, 1996), p. 186.
[91] So Carson, *John*, pp. 343–44; Beasley-Murray, *John*, pp. 130–31; Schnackenburg, *Gospel According to St. John*, p. 2:200; see esp. Isa. 41.4; 43.10, 13, 25; 46.4; 48.12; cf. Deut. 32.39.
[92] I.e., 8.24, 28; E. D. Freed, 'Who or What Was before Abraham in John 8:58?', *JSNT* 17 (1983), pp. 52–59.
[93] Ridderbos, *Gospel of John*, pp. 322–23.
[94] Cf. Isa. 43.10, 13; Ball, *'I Am'*, pp. 195–96; Schnackenburg, *Gospel According to St. John*, p. 2:224; Burge, *Gospel of John*, p. 263.
[95] S. Motyer, *Your Father the Devil? A New Approach to John and 'the Jews'* (PBM; Carlisle: Paternoster, 1997), p. 159; note the reaction in 8.59.
[96] See esp. Num. 27.17; see also Ps. 80.1 and Ezek. 34.13.
[97] Carson, *John*, p. 383; cf. Barrett, *Gospel According to St. John*, p. 369; contra Schnackenburg, *Gospel According to St. John*, p. 2:293; F. J. Moloney, *The Gospel of John* (Collegeville, MN: Liturgical, 1998), p. 308.

'so the LORD's people will not be like sheep without a shepherd' (Num. 27.17).[98] The following verse mentions Joshua (Greek: Ἰησοῦς, 'Jesus') as that successor (Num. 27.18; cf. Heb. 4.8-10). Israel's exodus from Egypt is occasionally portrayed in terms of a flock being led by its shepherd.[99] Prophetic literature holds out similar visions of end-time deliverance for God's people (e.g., Mic. 2.12-13).

k. John 12.13: The Messianic King Enters the Holy City Inaugurating the New Exodus

The term 'Hosanna!' occurs most famously in the Hallel (Pss. 113–118), a series of psalms sung each morning by the temple choir during various Jewish festivals.[100] At such occasions, everyone would wave their לולב (a bouquet of willow, myrtle, and palm branches)[101] when the choir reached the 'Hosanna!' in Ps. 118.25 (*m. Sukkah* 3.9). The psalm may have taken on end-time significance in the post-exilic period, with people anticipating a new exodus at which Yahweh would deliver his people through the Messiah.[102]

In the present passage, Jesus is portrayed as the prototypical worshiper who comes to Jerusalem to render proper worship and in turn is hailed by worshipers as Israel's king. In the context of Ps. 118.22 and its NT usage,[103] the fourth evangelist here appropriates Ps. 118.26 on the basis of his hermeneutical axiom that Jesus is the messianic king and Son of David in fulfillment of OT prophecy. Possibly, the new exodus and replacement themes resonate in this passage as well.[104]

l. John 12.37-40: Jewish Unbelief in Moses' Day Anticipates Jewish Unbelief in Jesus the Messiah

The evangelist's indictment in the conclusion to the 'Book of Signs' that 'even though he [Jesus] had performed such great signs before them, they did not believe in him' (12.37) establishes a link between the Jews' failure to believe in Jesus' day and the unbelief displayed by the wilderness generation. Just as that generation of Israelites had witnessed God's mighty acts performed through Moses at the exodus,[105] the Jews in Jesus' day had witnessed a series of startling

---

[98] The passage is applied to Jesus in Mt. 9.36.
[99] I.e., God, by the hand of Moses and Aaron; Ps. 77.20; Isa. 63.11, 14; cf. Ps. 78.52.
[100] Cf. *m. Pesah.* 5.7; 9.3; 10.7.
[101] *b. Sukkah* 37b; cf. Josephus, *Ant.* 3.245.
[102] A. C. Brunson, *Psalm 118 in the Gospel of John: An Intertextual Study of the New Exodus Pattern in the Theology of John* (WUNT, 2/158; Tübingen: Mohr Siebeck, 2003), Chapter 2, esp. 63 n. 181, following N. T. Wright, *The New Testament and the People of God* (COQG, 1; Minneapolis: Fortress, 1992), pp. 269–72 *et passim*.
[103] B. Lindars, *New Testament Apologetic* (London: SCM, 1961), pp. 169–85.
[104] Brunson, *Psalm 118*, ch. 4. Brunson suggests other possible allusions to Ps. 118 elsewhere in John's Gospel (8.56; 10.7-10, 24-25; 11.41-42; cf. Brunson, *Psalm 118*, Chapter 10).
[105] Deut. 29.2-4; see the use of σημεῖα in Exod. 10.1-2; Num. 14.11, 22; Deut. 4.34; 6.22; 29.3; 34.11; Carson, *John*, p. 447; Ridderbos, *Gospel of John*, p. 444; R. E. Brown, *The Gospel According to John XIII–XXI* (AB, 29B; Garden City, NY: Doubleday, 1970), p. 485.

displays of Jesus' messianic authority. The Johannine signs culminate in the raising of Lazarus, which foreshadows Jesus' own resurrection and presents him as the resurrection and the life. Yet, similar to their Israelite counterparts in the wilderness, Jesus' contemporaries responded with 'grumbling'[106] and unbelief (12.39) rather than faith.[107]

The evangelist follows his indictment of Jewish unbelief in the Messiah with a quotation of Isa. 53.1. The verse immediately preceding this passage, that is, 52.15, asserts that those who had not been told of the Servant would see and understand what they had not previously heard.[108] In the context of 53.1, the prophetic message and the revelation of God's power[109] entail the Servant's vicarious sacrifice and subsequent exaltation.[110] Conversely, the Jews' failure to believe in Jesus' day is shown to be part of the trajectory of Jewish unbelief throughout Israel's history, reaching back at least as far as the unbelief of the wilderness generation which had witnessed God's mighty acts displayed through Moses at the exodus.[111]

In v. 40, the evangelist then cites Isa. 6.10, which likewise harks back to Israel's unbelief during the exodus.[112] Deuteronomy 29.2-4 is particularly instructive in this regard:

> You have seen all that the LORD did before your eyes in the land of Egypt, to Pharaoh and to all his servants and to all his land, the great trials which your eyes saw, the signs, and those great wonders; but to this day the LORD has not given you a mind to understand, or eyes to see, or ears to hear.

Thus the evangelist, by citing Isa. 6.10, does not merely refer to that passage but taps into a trajectory that spans all the way from Israel's beginnings as a nation under Moses through the prophetic period to Jesus' day. People's unbelieving response to God's revelation mediated through Moses, Isaiah, and Jesus is part of a typological web that connects God's people throughout salvation history and portrays human resistance to divine revelation in the face of God's provision of redemption along an escalating continuum.

---

[106] 6.41, 61; cf. Exod. 17.3; Num. 11.1; 14.27, 29; 17.6, 20.
[107] Note the use of πιστεύω in Isa. 53.1 and Jn 12.37 *et passim*; B. G. Schuchard, *Scripture within Scripture: The Interrelationship of Form and Function in the Explicit Old Testament Citations in the Gospel of John* (SBLDS, 133; Atlanta: Scholars Press, 1992), p. 89.
[108] Paul cites this passage as support for his belief that this passage was fulfilled in his apostolic preaching of the gospel to the Gentiles (Rom. 15.20-21).
[109] In the OT, 'arm of the Lord' frequently serves as a figurative expression for God's power, including in the exodus narrative; see Exod. 6.1, 6; 15.16; 32.11; Deut. 3.24; 4.34; 5.15; 6.21; 7.8, 19; 9.26, 29; 11.2; 26.8; Isa. 40.10; 48.14; 51.5, 9; 52.10; 63.5; cf. Lk. 1.51.
[110] See esp. 52.13; Oswalt, *Isaiah*, p. 381 n. 85.
[111] Carson, *John*, p. 447; Ridderbos, *Gospel of John*, p. 444; R. E. Brown, *Gospel According to John I–XII* (AB, 29A; Garden City, NY: Doubleday, 1966), pp. 485–86.
[112] C. A. Evans, *To See and Not Perceive: Isaiah 6:9–10 in Early Jewish and Christian Interpretation* (JSOTSup, 64; Sheffield: JSOT, 1989), pp. 134–35.

3. The Book of Exaltation (John 13.1–21.25): Jesus the Exalted, Glorified Son Who Leads His Commissioned Messianic Community

a. Farewell Discourse (John 13–17): The Messiah's Farewell according to the Pattern of Moses' Parting Instructions in the Book of Deuteronomy

The parallels between the Johannine farewell discourse and covenant language in Moses' parting Deuteronomic instructions are underscored by the preponderance of the five major verb themes of Exodus 33–34 and Deuteronomy ('love', 'obey', 'live', 'know', and 'see') in the Johannine discourse, particularly 14.15-24.[113] The similarities between the Johannine and the Deuteronomic farewell discourses indicate that the fourth evangelist casts Jesus as the new Moses who institutes a new covenant with his disciples (cf. the 'new commandment' in 13.34-35). Just as Moses was prevented by death from leading God's people into the promised land, so Jesus will be separated from his followers, albeit only temporarily. Yet in contrast to Moses, Jesus, as the new Joshua, entered heaven itself as our forerunner.[114] In Johannine parlance, Jesus will go to prepare a place for his disciples (14.2-3) and be glorified in the Father's presence with the glory he had with him before the world began (17.5).

b. Passion Narrative (John 18–19, esp. 19.24, 36): Jesus as the Passover Lamb Who Delivers God's People from Their Bondage to Sin

The final two OT fulfillment quotations, both of which are associated with Jesus' crucifixion, culminate and complete the Passover theme in John's Gospel.[115] As Stanley Porter observes, 'Thus, in the death of Jesus, as climactically defined by the Old Testament quotations, the Old Testament fulfillment motif and the Passover theme converge'.[116]

---

[113] See A. Lacomara, 'Deuteronomy and the Farewell Discourse (Jn 13:31–16:33)', *CBQ* 36 (1974), pp. 65–84; Pryor, *Evangelist*, esp. pp. 160, 166, 216 n. 8; E. J. Malatesta, *Interiority and Covenant: A Study of EINAI EN and MENEIN EN in the First Letter of Saint John* (AnBib, 69; Rome: Biblical Institute, 1978), pp. 42–77.

[114] See the discussion of 10.3-4 above. Cf. Heb. 4.8, 14; 6.20; 12.2.

[115] It is sometimes argued that John, in contrast with the Synoptics, places the crucifixion at the time when the Passover offerings were being sacrificed in order to heighten Passover symbolism (Barrett, *Gospel According to St. John*, pp. 48–51; cf. Brown, *Gospel According to John XIII–XXI*, pp. 555–56, who suggests the Synoptic chronology is wrong). However, this is unlikely (see Köstenberger, *John*, p. 400 n. 1, with further bibliographic references; A. J. Köstenberger, 'Diversity and Unity in the New Testament', in S. J. Hafemann [eds.], *Biblical Theology: Retrospect and Prospect* [Downers Grove, IL: InterVarsity, 2002], pp. 144–58 [147–48]), especially in light of the common use of 'day of preparation' to refer to the day preceding the Sabbath (see ibid., pp. 524, 537–38, 551). In any case, John's Passover typology in no way depends on such an alleged shift in time or calendar.

[116] S. E. Porter, 'Can Traditional Exegesis Enlighten Literary Analysis of the Fourth Gospel? An Examination of the Old Testament Fulfillment Motif and the Passover Theme', in C. A. Evans and W. R. Stegner (eds), *The Gospels and the Scriptures of Israel* (JSNTSup, 104; Sheffield: Sheffield Academic, 1994), pp. 396–428; repr. as Chapter 8 in *John, His Gospel, and Jesus: In Pursuit of the Johannine Voice* (Grand Rapids: Eerdmans, 2015). See also Köstenberger, *Theology of John's*

When the soldiers come to Jesus and see that he is already dead, they do not break his legs but one of them pierces his side with a spear, and at once blood and water come out (19.24).[117] The flow of blood and water indicates that Jesus died as a full human being.[118] The evangelist may also be alluding to Exodus 17, especially v. 6: 'Strike the rock, and water will come out of it for the people to drink'.[119] An allusion to the Passover may also be in view,[120] consisting of (1) the hyssop (19.29); (2) the unbroken bones (19.33, 36); and (3) the mingled blood (19.34).[121] If so, the evangelist may bear witness to all three events that cast Jesus as the Passover lamb.

Two sets of Scripture converge in 19.36: (1) Ps. 34.20, affirming God's care for the righteous man: 'He protects all his bones, not one of them will be broken'; and (2) Exod. 12.46 and Num. 9.12, specifying that no bone of the Passover lamb may be broken.[122] The fusion between the exodus narrative and the Psalms passage serves to recast the crucifixion 'as a saving event rather than an ignominious defeat'.[123] Apparently, 'in Jewish thought disfiguration was an obstacle to resurrection', which may further explain why the evangelist takes pains to stress that no bone was broken.[124]

The reference to bones not being broken in Exod. 12.46 comes in the context of requirements for Passover observance. No bone of the sacrificial animal must be broken, among other reasons, as a symbol of the unity of the worshiping family and of the entire covenant community.[125] This passage forms the conclusion of the exodus narrative that began with references to people's bondage in Egypt and Moses' call in chs. 1–4. The command of Exod. 12.46 is reiterated in Num. 9.12.[126]

Psalm 34, a Davidic psalm, constitutes a (slightly irregular) acrostic poem centered on the assurance that the LORD will deliver the righteous (see esp. vv. 19-22). The requirement that none of the bones of the Passover lamb be broken was observed in Judaism. Belief in God's protection of the righteous is

---

Gospel, pp. 414–20; and P. M. Hoskins, *That Scripture Might Be Fulfilled: Typology and the Death of Christ* (Longwood, FL: Xulon, 2009).

[117] Regarding Jesus' legs not being broken, see on 19.36 below.
[118] See *Lev. Rab.* 15.2 on Lev. 13.2; cf. 1 Jn 5.6-8.
[119] Cf. Num. 20.11; Carson, *John*, p. 624.
[120] *m. Pesah.* 5.5-8; cf. *m. 'Ohal.* 3.5.
[121] Barrett, *Gospel According to St. John*, p. 557; Burge, *Gospel of John*, p. 532.
[122] Applied to Jesus in 1 Cor. 5.7 and 1 Pet. 1.19; cf. Brown, *The Gospel According to John XIII–XXI*, pp. 952–53; Moloney, *Gospel of John*, p. 509. On the phenomenon of composite texts, see the essays in S. A. Adams and S. M. Ehorn, *Composite Citations in Antiquity*. Vol. 1, *Jewish, Graeco-Roman, and Early Christian Uses* (LNTS, 525; London: Bloomsbury T&T Clark, 2016).
[123] Hays, *Echoes of Scripture in the Gospels*, p. 317. See his entire discussion of the Passover motif in John on pp. 316–18.
[124] D. Daube, *The New Testament and Rabbinic Judaism* (London: Athlone, 1956), pp. 325–29; cf. A. Scheiber, 'Ihr sollt kein Bein dran zerbrechen', *VT* 13 (1963), pp. 95–97.
[125] J. I. Durham, *Exodus* (WBC, 3; Waco, TX: Word, 1987), p. 173; W. H. C. Propp, *Exodus 1–18* (AB, 2; New York: Doubleday, 1999), p. 418.
[126] R. de Vaux, *Studies in Old Testament Sacrifice* (trans. J. Bourke and R. Potter; Cardiff: University of Wales Press, 1964), pp. 9–10, cited in T. R. Ashley, *The Book of Numbers* (NICOT; Grand Rapids: Eerdmans, 1993), p. 180 n. 9.

amply attested in Jewish biblical and extra-biblical literature. The presupposed identification of the Passover lamb (Exod. 12.46; Num. 9.12) with the righteous sufferer (Ps. 34.20) is attested as well.[127]

The only difference between Exod. 12.46 (cf. 12.10 LXX) and Num. 9.12 is that the verb form in the former passage is in the second (συντρίψετε) and in the latter in the third person plural (συντρίψουσιν). There are three differences between these texts and the citation in Jn 19.36: (1) the omission of the initial καί; (2) the omission of the preposition ἀπό;[128] and (3) the verbal form, which is a third person singular passive rather than a second or third person plural active in the Pentateuchal texts. In this regard, it is interesting to note that the LXX version of Ps. 34.20 (Ps. 33.21 LXX) features the exact same verb form as Jn 19.36, namely συντριβήσεται. This makes it likely that Ps. 33.21 LXX is the source for the verbal form in John's quotation. Thus, is it most likely that the evangelist's OT quote represents a combination of Exod. 12.46/Num. 9.12 and Ps. 34.20.[129]

By this third of four fulfillment citations, the evangelist underscores the pattern of fulfillment characteristic of Jesus' death. This authenticates Jesus' claim of his messianic identity. In the present instance, a powerful link is established between Jesus' sacrificial death and the Passover, which commemorated the Israelites' deliverance from bondage in Egypt (Exod. 12.46; Num. 9.12). This marks out Jesus as the 'lamb of God' who takes away the sins of the world (1.29, 36) in keeping with the Baptist's witness. This pattern of typology is also part and parcel of the Johannine replacement theme, according to which Jesus fulfills the symbolism inherent in a variety of Jewish festivals and institutions. Also, Jesus, in keeping with Davidic typology, is presented as a righteous man who is preserved by God in keeping with the assurance expressed by God's servants in the past (Ps. 34.20).

The present OT reference constitutes an instance of a typological use of Scripture whereby Jesus is shown to fulfill Passover symbolism. This taps into one of the most powerful symbols of Jewish national identity and connects Jesus' death with God's deliverance of his people from bondage in Egypt. According to the fourth evangelist, just as God delivered Israel from bondage through the exodus, he provided redemption from sin through Jesus' vicarious death. This Passover symbolism, in turn, is applied to God's preservation of the righteous sufferer, signaling that both motifs converge in Jesus, who was both God's perfect Passover lamb and the paradigmatic Davidic righteous sufferer.

---

[127] See references in M. J. J. Menken, *Old Testament Quotations in the Fourth Gospel: Studies in Textual Form* (CBET, 15; Kampen: Kok, 1996), pp. 160–64, with special attention on *Jub.* 49.13; see also Daube, *New Testament and Rabbinic Judaism*, 309; Schuchard, *Scripture Within Scripture*, p. 139.

[128] Presumably owing to the influence of the psalm verse; cf. Menken, *Old Testament Quotations*, p. 152.

[129] See esp. C. H. Williams, 'Composite Citations in the Gospel of John', in S. A. Adams and S. M. Ehorn (eds.), *Composite Citations in Antiquity*. Vol. 2, *New Testament Uses* (LNTS; Bloomsbury T&T Clark, 2018), pp. 94–127 (115–18).

4. Conclusion

John, the 'evangelist of the covenant people', makes a vital contribution to the exodus theme in the NT. The evangelist uses the OT, including the exodus theme, to demonstrate that Jesus is the climax of God's self-disclosure to his people. God's presence in the Tabernacle and revelation in the law have been surpassed in his definitive revelation and presence in his 'one-of-a-kind' Son (1.14). His grace given in the law has culminated in the fullness of grace found in Jesus (1.16-17).

The Baptist, in the wilderness, was the harbinger of the new and greater exodus led by Jesus, the messianic king (1.23; 12.13). The physical life that was found by looking to the bronze serpent points to the provision of spiritual life by trusting in the lifted-up Son of Man (3.14-15). Like Israel in the wilderness who was judged for her unbelief, Nicodemus and his compatriots are under the threat of divine judgment unless they look to the lifted-up Son of Man in faith (3.14-15).

Moses, who performed signs and wonders and provided manna in the wilderness, is eclipsed by one who works greater signs and who provided true, spiritual life for both Jews and Gentiles. By performing these signs, Jesus demonstrates that he is not simply a prophet like Moses, but the fulfillment of the prophetic hope. His signs are a testimony that he is the Messiah (ch. 6; 7.31).[130] The grumbling and rejection of the wilderness generation corresponds to the opposition and rejection of the far greater gift and disclosure of God in the Son by the Jewish authorities (6.41-71; 12.37-40). The similarities in language between the Farewell Discourse and Exodus 33–34 and Deuteronomy further demonstrate that Jesus is the typological fulfillment of Moses. Jesus enters into a new covenant with his new messianic community and goes ahead of his people as the new Joshua to prepare a place for them (13.34-35; 14.2-3, 15-24).

Finally, in Jesus' death the Baptist's contention that Jesus is the 'lamb of God' who removes the world's sin finds its climactic fulfillment (1.29, 36). Jesus is not only the paradigmatic righteous sufferer, but the final paschal offering. The hyssop and mingled blood, and especially his unbroken bones, all affirm this role (19.29, 33-36). But in his fulfillment and replacement of the Passover, the Messiah's blood delivers not merely from earthly slavery but provides redemption from the bondage of sin and death.

The evangelist's portrayal of the Baptist as a 'voice in the wilderness' and of Jesus as the signs-working Messiah converge in presenting Jesus' mission as leading God's people on a new exodus through the death and resurrection of the messianic shepherd-teacher-king. Not only is Jesus the greater Moses, who instructs the community prior to his earthly departure, he is also God's Passover lamb whose sacrifice becomes the way of salvation for all those who put their trust in him and identify with him. In all of this the fourth evangelist discerns God's fingerprint across the pages of Israel's history, despite the rejection by and obduracy of God's people, which culminates in the suffering Servant who is also the Son of the Father, the king of the Jews, and the Savior of the world.

---

[130] See Köstenberger, *Theology of John's Gospel*, pp. 318–19.

As Richard Hays poignantly states, 'For John the Evangelist, therefore, all of Israel's Scripture is a figural web woven with latent prefigurations of the One without whom not one thing came into being'.[131] Reading Scripture (and John's Gospel, in particular) figurally—that is, with a view toward discerning God's fingerprint across the pages of Israel's history—is thus an 'essential means of discerning the anticipatory traces of God the Word in his self-revelation to the world'.[132] Not only does this kind of reading unearth John's underlying hermeneutical approach—grounding Jesus' earthly life in his external preexistence and rooting his revelatory and redemptive work in Yahweh's self-manifestation and mighty acts of deliverance in Israel's history—it also grasps the underlying unity of God and his purposes while at the same time comprehending that God's work came to decisive culmination and fulfillment in the finished cross-work and glorious exaltation of the Son.

---

[131] Hays, *Echoes of Scripture in the Gospels*, p. 344.
[132] Hays, *Echoes of Scripture in the Gospels*, p. 345.

Chapter 6

EXODUS IN THE PAULINE LETTERS

David M. Westfall

1. Introduction

Interpreters have long acknowledged the importance that Israel's exodus from slavery in Egypt holds for our understanding of the apostle Paul's thought-world and for the interpretation of his writings.[1] It is therefore curious that Paul quotes from Exodus so rarely in his undisputed writings—a mere four times (1 Cor. 10.7; 2 Cor. 8.15; Rom. 9.15, 17), with two further references to the ten commandments paralleled in Deuteronomy (Rom. 7.7; 13.9).[2] Given that one can point to other scriptural texts (particularly in Isaiah) as a clear source of exodus material for Paul, one might be tempted to think that the *book* of Exodus is relatively insignificant to the apostle, merely providing the background of a story whose importance largely transcends this textual origin.

Such a conclusion would be mistaken. Paul's undisputed writings are informed not only by the exodus story in broad terms, but also exhibit his detailed familiarity with the text of Exodus itself, particularly in the Corinthian correspondence and in Romans 9–11. This is reflected not least in his use of the golden calf

---

[1] See, e.g., A. J. Roberts and A. Wilson, *Echoes of Exodus: Tracing Themes of Redemption through Scripture* (Wheaton: Crossway, 2018), pp. 142–48; B. D. Estelle, *Echoes of Exodus: Tracing a Biblical Motif* (Downers Grove, IL: InterVarsity, 2018), pp. 263–85; C. S. Works, *The Church in the Wilderness: Paul's Use of Exodus Traditions in 1 Corinthians* (WUNT, 2/379; Tübingen: Mohr Siebeck, 2014); D. L. Smith, 'The Uses of "New Exodus" in New Testament Scholarship: Preparing a Way through the Wilderness', *CBR* 14 (2016), pp. 207–43; S. C. Keesmaat, *Paul and His Story: (Re)Interpreting the Exodus Tradition* (LNTS, 181; Sheffield: Sheffield Academic, 1999); W. D. Davies, 'Paul and the New Exodus', in C. A. Evans and S. Talmon (eds.), *The Quest for Context and Meaning: Studies in Biblical Intertextuality in Honor of James A. Sanders* (Leiden: Brill, 1997), pp. 443–63.

[2] Hickling makes a similar observation, though I would dispute his claim that Paul alludes to the book of Exodus only four times. C. J. A. Hickling, 'Paul's Use of Exodus in the Corinthian Correspondence', in R. Bieringer (ed.), *The Corinthian Correspondence* (Leuven: Peeters, 1996), pp. 367–76 (367).

narrative of Exodus 32–34, a pericope that shaped his understanding of his own apostolic vocation, of the rejection of his gospel by many of his fellow Jews, and of the hope that remains for their future through the mercies of God. In what follows, I concern myself primarily with Paul's deliberate uses of the text of Exodus by way of citation and allusion,[3] while also providing a summary overview of how broader themes and narrative patterns in Exodus influence Paul's undisputed writings.

2. Galatians

Paul's most explicit use of Exodus in Galatians serves a decidedly negative purpose, substantiating his claim that God's promise to Abraham drastically relativizes the Torah's place in God's redemptive economy. Now, in light of the promise's fulfilment in Israel's Messiah,[4] the boundary-marking role of Torah-observance has reached its point of divinely planned eschatological obsolescence.[5] Nevertheless, this should not be allowed to obscure the fact that, for Paul, the eschatological events concerned in the promise's fulfilment also find their figural antecedent in the story of Exodus.[6]

The only unambiguous allusion to the text of Exodus in Galatians appears in 3.17, where Paul juxtaposes the covenant (διαθήκη)[7] with Abraham 'previ-

---

[3] These categories (together with that of 'echo') are drawn with slight modification from R. B. Hays, *Echoes of Scripture in the Letters of Paul* (New Haven, CT: Yale University Press, 1989), pp. 14–33. Since Hays' seminal work, there has been a growing tendency among scholars to deny that authorial intent is a necessary condition for allusion, but I agree with Porter that this is a category mistake. See S. E. Porter, 'Allusions and Echoes', in S. E. Porter and C. D. Stanley (eds.), *As It Is Written: Studying Paul's Use of Scripture* (Atlanta: Society of Biblical Literature, 2008), pp. 29–40. Unlike Porter, however, I do not regard authorial intent as a *sine qua non* of scriptural echo, since an echo (as we normally mean the word) is primarily an acoustic effect of sound's interaction with its *environment*, which constitutes the echo as such by virtue of its own inherent properties and not only the intentionality of the sound's origin (if any). In this way the language of echo aptly conveys the basic insight of Julia Kristeva, Roland Barthes, and others, as summarized by Hays, *Echoes*, p. 15: 'All discourse…is necessarily intertextual in the sense that its conditions of intelligibility are given by and in relation to a previously given body of discourse'. Thus, while the following argument mainly concerns quotation and allusion (and so Paul's deliberate intent), I leave open the possibility that some allusions might more appropriately be categorized as unintended echoes, *without* thereby denying that they may be 'good' readings of Paul's letters.

[4] On Paul's use of messiah-language, see M. V. Novenson, *Christ among the Messiahs: Christ Language in Paul and Messiah Language in Ancient Judaism* (Oxford: Oxford University Press, 2012).

[5] This need not imply that Paul regards continued Torah observance among Jews as problematic; it is simply to say that such observance is no longer to be deemed coextensive with God's covenant people, which now includes Gentiles alongside Jews.

[6] In this discussion, I employ the language of 'figural' rather than 'typological' correspondences in order to withhold judgment concerning how this phenomenon in Paul relates to later instances of 'typology' in church tradition. See S. DiMattei, 'Biblical Narratives', in Porter and Stanley (eds.), *As It Is Written*, pp. 59–93.

[7] Hahn notes the serious difficulties with reading διαθήκη here as 'testament', though it remains a popular view among current interpreters. Even if this reading is accepted, however, it can hardly be denied that Paul is playing with the covenantal overtones of διαθήκη in this passage. S. W. Hahn, 'Covenant, Oath, and the Aqedah: Διαθήκη in Galatians 3:15-18', *CBQ* 67 (2005), pp. 79–100 (80–83).

ously ratified by God' and 'the law that came about after four hundred and thirty years' (ὁ μετὰ τετρακόσια καὶ τριάκοντα ἔτη γεγονὼς νόμος).[8] Here Paul's allusion to Exod. 12.40 is somewhat imprecise, since the 430 years refer to the span of Israel's sojourn in Egypt, and not to the time that elapsed between God's initial dealings with Abraham and the establishment of the covenant at Sinai. Nonetheless, the point is made: the law came long after the promise and so, Paul reasons, cannot be seen to supplement or modify it (cf. Gal. 3.15). Not only that, but it was 'ordered through angels (δι' ἀγγέλων) in the hand of a mediator' (i.e., Moses at Sinai),[9] placing its historical role in contrast with the oneness of God, who unilaterally promises and fulfills, thereby making the recipient of his promise 'an heir through God (διὰ θεοῦ)' (Gal. 3.19; 4.7).

Here a reader of the Pentateuch should detect no small irony, given that the promise 'spoken to Abraham' (ἐρρέθη πρὸς Ἀβράμ) in LXX Gen. 15.13, to which Paul alludes in 3.16 and in which Abraham's διαθήκη with God consisted, concerns *precisely* what will happen at the end of the four centuries to which Paul then refers![10] For Paul, however, the exodus event is but the prefigurement of what God is doing in his own time for those who belong to Israel's Messiah, Abraham's singular 'seed' (Gal. 3.16). He redeems his people from slavery to the law's curse and receives the promised inheritance (κληρονομία) on their behalf, an inheritance that is not limited to Canaan, but consists in the new creation as a whole: even the ends of the earth shall be their possession through him (3.13, 18).[11] Paul's 'eschatological contemporising'[12] of Genesis necessarily exerts hermeneutical pressure on his handling of Exodus, since it can no longer straightforwardly recount the fulfilment of the promise to Abraham *in toto*. This hermeneutical pressure and the resulting tension with the 'original' meaning of Exodus is especially discernible in Galatians 4 which, despite its lack of overt textual references, rehearses the narrative pattern of Exodus. Following a period of slavery (4.3), the Messiah comes to bring redemption at the divinely appointed time (4.4-5), granting his people full sonship and the divine presence, as well as the expectation of a coming inheritance (4.6-7).[13]

---

[8] All translations offered in the following are my own. The critical edition of the LXX used in the following is J. W. Wevers, with the help of U. Quast, *Septuaginta: Vetus Testamentum Graecum Auctoritate Academiae Scientiarum Gottingensis editum, vol. II, 1 – Exodus* (Göttingen: Vandenhoeck & Ruprecht, 1991).

[9] The presence of angels at Sinai finds OT attestation only in Deut. 33.2. This understanding was widespread in Second Temple Judaism, however, and is attested elsewhere in the NT as well: see Acts 7.53; Heb. 2.2; *Jub.* 1.27-29; Philo, *Somn.* 1.140-44; Josephus, *Ant.* 15.134-37.

[10] Cf. Gen. 15.3-8, 13-18.

[11] See E. McCaulley, *Sharing in the Son's Inheritance: Davidic Messianism and Paul's Worldwide Interpretation of the Abrahamic Land Promise in Galatians* (LNTS, 608; London: Bloomsbury T&T Clark, 2019); cf. Ps. 2.8. As McCaulley shows, Paul's understanding of the singular 'seed' as heir to the promise (the focus of considerable debate among exegetes) reflects his attentiveness to Isaac's role in Gen. 17.1-21 as the singular recipient of the land promise, which he also reads in connection with the promises concerning David's seed in 2 Sam. 7.12-14 and Ps. 2.7-8 (see pp. 146–54).

[12] I draw this language from DiMattei, 'Biblical Narratives', pp. 77–88.

[13] So, e.g., J. M. Scott, *Adoption as Sons of God: An Exegetical Investigation into the Background of* ΥΙΟΘΕΣΙΑ *in the Pauline Corpus* (WUNT, 2/48; Tübingen: Mohr Siebeck, 1992), pp. 121–86;

But as Paul makes clear in 4.21-31, taking up Torah observance as a condition of eschatological life (as the Galatians are being tempted to do) effectively sets the clock back, placing those who do so into the state of slavery under the 'covenant' (διαθήκη) established between God and Israel at 'Mount Sinai…in Arabia' (4.24-25). Paul's appropriation of the exodus story thus turns a central theme of its source material on its head: whereas in Exodus, God's covenant with Israel at Sinai is the sequel to Israel's redemption *from* slavery, the narrative goal toward which they journey *out* of their servitude, in Paul's implied narrative Sinai represents the narrative point of entry *into* slavery of a new kind.[14] The covenant 'from Mount Sinai' (allegorically represented by Hagar) is a covenant 'that bears [children] into slavery' (εἰς δουλείαν γεννῶσα), into the condition of servitude and confinement that Paul has attributed to the period of Israel's minority (in parallel with the Galatian's former condition) in the preceding argument (Gal. 3.22-25; 4.1-9). On the other hand, the heirs of the new covenant—that is to say, of the Abrahamic covenant fulfilled in Israel's Messiah—have received what the exodus ostensibly provided for Israel in fulfillment of the promises to Abraham (freedom, full sonship, an inheritance), but which the Sinai covenant temporarily put beyond Israel's reach.[15]

3. The Corinthian Correspondence

Paul's use of Exodus in the Corinthian correspondence reflects many of the same hermeneutical tendencies noted above in Galatians. Unlike Galatians, however, Paul's writings to the church in Corinth engage in greater detail with the actual text of Exodus, which plays an admonitory as well as apologetic role in his arguments. His uses of Exodus are not purely *ad hoc*, however, and reflect with even greater clarity his belief that God's eschatological deliverance of his people in Israel's Messiah corresponds directly to his past dealings with their ancestors. Additionally, and in ways that anticipate his use of Exodus in Romans, Paul draws on the narrative of the golden calf in order to make sense of his Jewish contemporaries' unbelieving response to the gospel.

S. J. Hafemann, 'Paul and the Exile of Israel in Galatians 3–4', in J. M. Scott (ed.), *Exile: Old Testament, Jewish, and Christian Conceptions* (JSJSup, 56; Leiden: Brill, 1997), pp. 329-71.

[14] This contrast is weakened somewhat by the observation that, both in Exodus and in Galatians, the liberation that the people of God experience entails a *transfer* of servitude from Pharaoh (or in Paul's case, sin) to the God of Israel. Cf. Gal. 5.13. In Exodus (MT), this is reflected in the use of the same language to describe Israel's condition under Pharaoh as under YHWH (with a cultic sense predominating in the latter case, reflected in the LXX use of λατρεύω); so Exod. 1.13-14; 3.12; 4.23; 5.18; 6.5; 7.16, 26; 8.16; 9.1, 13; 10.3, 7-8, 11, 24, 26; 12.31; 14.5, 12; cf. 13.5; 20.5; 21.2, 6; 23.24-25, 33.

[15] M. Thiessen, *Paul and the Gentile Problem* (New York: Oxford University Press, 2016), pp. 74–101, argues that Paul's allegory in 4.21-31 refers to two different evangelistic missions to the Gentiles rather than to the old and new covenants. This understanding is unlikely in view of the fact that (1) Paul's explicit reference to two *covenants* (διαθήκαι), one of them 'from Sinai in Arabia', most naturally refers to those already mentioned in Gal. 3, and (2) other themes present in his argument (slavery, promise, Abrahamic sonship, inheritance) similarly point back to this discussion.

a. 1 Corinthians 5

The first direct intertextual reference to Exodus in the Corinthian correspondence appears in 1 Corinthians 5, as an allusion rather than a direct citation. Here Paul draws on the imagery of the Passover and festival of unleavened bread in order to address the community's arrogant and boastful attitude concerning one member's illicit sexual relationship with his stepmother, which he compares to the fermenting effect of leaven (ζύμη) on the whole batch of dough (i.e., the community). In 5.6-8, he develops this imagery into a theologically pregnant assertion about how the achievement of Israel's Messiah determines the ethical reality of his Corinthian assembly. Because 'our Passover has been sacrificed, namely Messiah' (τὸ πάσχα ἡμῶν ἐτύθη Χριστός), the Corinthians must (1) cleanse out the old leaven, which Paul eventually identifies with the ethical qualities of 'depravity' (κακία) and 'baseness' (πονηρία), and (2) celebrate the festival of unleavened bread with the qualities of 'sincerity' (εἰλικρίνεια) and 'truth' (ἀλήθεια).[16]

Paul's Passover and leaven imagery finds its textual basis in Exodus 12 and 13, where Israel is commanded to remove anything leavened from their homes (Exod. 12.15, 19; 13.3, 7) and to 'sacrifice' or 'slaughter' the Passover (θύσατε τὸ πάσχα, 12.21; cf. 12.27). Nevertheless, his assertions in this case do not require a knowledge of the text *per se*, but only of the Passover traditions and rituals as practiced by Paul's and the Corinthians' Jewish contemporaries. The *institution* of 'the Passover', which itself depends on the book of Exodus, could thus be called the primary 'intertext' to Paul's statement, in keeping with Kristeva's definition of the term.[17] Moreover, the ethical character of Paul's appropriation of this institution, while not unique to the apostle, is not based on the Exodus narrative itself, which merely associates the unleavened bread with the speed and urgency of Israel's departure from Egypt.[18]

---

[16] Given that Paul's admonition to the Corinthians includes the instruction in 5.11 '[not] to eat with such a person' as the one whom they are to expel (τῷ τοιούτῳ μηδὲ συνεσθίειν), it is possible that Paul's use of these Passover allusions arises naturally out of the community's practice of the Lord's Supper, reflected in 11.17-34. Several commentators have argued that the addition of μηδέ (usually rendered 'not even') suggests that Paul's instruction most likely refers to eating of any kind (e.g. A. C. Thiselton, *The First Epistle to the Corinthians* [NIGTC; Grand Rapids: Eerdmans, 2000], p. 415). But the negative disjunctive particle (continuing the negation from the preceding μή) does not necessarily function to intensify Paul's instruction, and can simply be rendered as 'nor to eat with such a person'. In favor of a reference to the communal meal, moreover, are the verbal parallels (κρίνω and various prefixes) between Paul's discussion of the propriety of judging insiders versus outsiders to the community in 5.12-13 and his warnings concerning judgment in the context of the Lord's Supper in 11.31-34 (which involves a similar insider/outsider contrast).

[17] See the survey of this concept's history in S. Alkier, 'Intertextuality and the Semiotics of Biblical Texts', in R. B. Hays, S. Alkier, and L. A. Huizenga (eds.), *Reading the Bible Intertextually* (Waco, TX: Baylor University Press, 2009), pp. 3–21 (4–7).

[18] Philo associates leaven with pride, arrogance and sensuality, but unleavened bread with constancy and prudence (*Queast. in Ex.* 1.15; 2.14; *Spec. Laws* 1.293). Leaven is not permitted in the sacrificial system, perhaps with the implication that it causes what is offered to appear as more than it really is (Exod. 23.18; Lev. 2.11; 6.17). In the NT, leaven imagery is employed in both positive (Mt. 13.33; Lk. 13.21) and negative senses (Mt. 16.6, 11-12; Mk. 8.15; Lk. 12.1; Gal. 5.9).

What is noteworthy in Paul's argument is not only what it says, but what it assumes: the slaughtered Passover lamb prefigures Israel's slain Messiah, whose death institutes a festival of unleavened bread that coincides with the remainder of the present age (since its observance consists in the community's ethics on an ongoing basis). Though Paul does not develop this image further, the association tells us a great deal about how he understood the death of the Messiah, whose shed blood brings liberation from slavery and constitutes the recipients of Paul's letter as the redeemed people of God.[19]

b. 1 Corinthians 10

Though it contains only one direct quotation, 1 Cor. 10.1-11 alludes at length to the book of Exodus. Whereas Paul's reference to the Passover and festival of unleavened bread in ch. 5 relies mainly on knowledge of one of Israel's sacred institutions (albeit attested in Exodus), his argument here presupposes a more extensive knowledge of the book of Exodus itself. The admonitory purposes to which Paul puts this text rely on a christocentric reading strategy that enables him to establish a remarkable degree of continuity between the exodus generation and the Corinthians.

The opening four verses of 1 Corinthians 10 summarize the events of Exodus up to the Sinai pericope:

> For I do not wish you to be ignorant, brothers, that our fathers (πατέρες) were all under the cloud (ὑπὸ τὴν νεφέλην) and all passed through the sea, and all underwent baptism into Moses (εἰς τὸν Μωϋσῆν ἐβαπτίσαντο)[20] in the cloud and in the sea, and all ate the same spiritual food and drank the same spiritual drink. For they were drinking from the spiritual rock that followed them, and the rock was the Messiah.

Paul alludes to the theophanic cloud that guided and protected Israel on their journey (Exod. 13.21-22; 14.19-20, 24), to their passage through the waters of the Red Sea (Exod. 14), and to their reception of the manna (Exod. 16) and the water from the rock (Exod. 17) in the wilderness. His recounting of this narrative clearly comes filtered through his own theological presuppositions: the language of baptism 'into Moses' mirrors language used elsewhere in 1 Corinthians, as well as in Romans and Galatians.[21] Similarly the reference to the 'spiritual food

---

[19] The extent to which the Passover is associated with cultic atonement in Paul's day is uncertain, though 2 Chron. 30.15-17 and Ezek. 45.18-25 draw this connection.

[20] The rendering 'underwent baptism' is taken from W. F. Orr and J. A. Walther, *I Corinthians: A New Translation with Introduction and Commentary* (AB, 32; New Haven, CT: Yale University Press, 1976), p. 245. The MS evidence is divided between the middle ἐβαπτίσαντο ($\mathfrak{P}^{46c}$ B K L P 1175. 1241. 1739. 1881 m; Or) and the passive ἐβαπτίσθησαν (ℵ A C D F G Ψ 33. 81. 104. 365. 630. 1505. 2464 latt). Given that a change from the latter to the former is more likely than the reverse, the middle reading may be preferable; so Thiselton, *Corinthians*, p. 722.

[21] Cf. Rom. 6.3; 1 Cor. 1.13-17; 13.13; Gal. 3.27. The statement equally sounds a note of discontinuity, however, since Paul could have said that the Israelites also were baptized into the *Messiah*, in keeping with the christological focus of his other statements in the passage. Based on Paul's

and drink' that the ancestors received is intended to liken their experience to that of the Corinthians: baptized into the Messiah, they share in the food and drink of the Lord's Supper, the Passover meal of the new covenant (1 Cor. 11.23-26).[22] Meanwhile, Paul's claim that 'the rock was the Messiah' simultaneously reflects the same christologically oriented way of reading the scriptures and his indebtedness to Second Temple traditions that understood the rocks that Moses struck to provide Israel with water in Exodus 17 and Numbers 20 to be one and the same.[23]

In vv. 5-11, Paul's reading of the Pentateuchal narrative attains its rhetorical objective. He explains that, despite Israel's common share in his redemptive work,

> God was not pleased with the majority of them, for they were laid low in the wilderness. But these things happened as patterns (τύποι) for us, so that we would not be desirers of evil, as they were. Do not be idolaters as some of them were, as it is written: 'The people sat down to eat and to drink and rose up to play' (ἐκάθισεν ὁ λαὸς φαγεῖν καὶ πιεῖν καὶ ἀνέστησαν παίζειν). And let us not commit sexual immorality either, as some of them did and fell, twenty-three thousand in a single day. And let us not put the Messiah to the test, as some of them did and were destroyed by the serpents. And do not grumble, just as some of them did and were destroyed by the destroyer. But these things happened to those people as a pattern (τυπικῶς), and were written down for our admonition, on whom the end of the ages has come.

Paul's warnings allude to several episodes in Exodus and Numbers. Pride of place is given to Israel's idolatry in the golden calf incident, to which Paul refers with an exact quotation from LXX Exod. 32.6. Even this quotation functions more like an allusion, however, given that its connection to idolatry would be evident only to someone familiar with the context. Paul apparently was confident enough of the Corinthians' knowledge of the scriptures (or at least of this passage) to assume that they would understand the reference. The other allusions that follow come mainly from the book of Numbers.[24] Nevertheless, these episodes of 'testing' and 'grumbling' are also anticipated in the portions of Exodus to which Paul's preceding remarks in 10.1-4 refer.[25]

---

references elsewhere (esp. Gal. 3.27 in the context of the argument that precedes it), it is best to understand this language as indicating their initiation into the covenantal relation to God that Moses mediated through the giving of the law.

22. Cf. similar language in Exod. 24.8.
23. Cf. Exod. 17.1-7; Num. 20.2-13; refs. to YHWH as a 'rock' in Deut. 32.4, 15, 18, 30, 31. This tradition is attested in, e.g., Ps.-Philo, *LAB* 10.7; 11.15; 20.8; *Tg.Onq* Num. 21.16-20. Philo allegorizes the rock as 'the wisdom of God' (*Leg. All.* 2.21). For discussion of these traditions and their import for understanding 1 Cor. 10.4, see P. Enns, 'The "Moveable Well" in 1 Cor 10:4: An Extrabiblical Tradition in an Apostolic Text', *BBR* 6 (1996), pp. 23–38.
24. Cf. Num. 16.41-50; 21.4-9; 25.1-9; also Ps. 106.18.
25. Cf. Exod. 15.24; 16.2, 7-8; 17.2-3, 7. Additionally, it is possible that Paul has combined the number slain by the Levites in Exod. 32.28 following the sin of the golden calf (3,000) with the number recorded in Num. 25.9. See D. E. Garland, *1 Corinthians* (BECNT; Grand Rapids: Baker, 2003), pp. 462–63.

Here too Paul's reading of the scriptures is reconfigured around God's new revelation in the Messiah: it was the Messiah *himself* whom Israel 'tested' in the wilderness, an identification that reflects the early Christian movement's inclusion of Jesus within the divine identity.[26] This repeated identification of the Messiah with Israel's God serves the purpose of establishing continuity between the Corinthians and their Israelite 'ancestors' (!) as much as Paul's assimilation of the exodus generation's experiences to the Corinthians' own practices and institutions. Such a degree of continuity arguably would not be necessary were it Paul's purpose merely to provide a negative example for the Corinthians to avoid. Rather, the degree of association between the two groups presses us to conclude that, although Paul uses exodus traditions here for admonitory purposes, this rests on deeper assumptions regarding this story's significance. It is the story of the *same* people to whom Paul is now writing, who have always belonged to the same Messiah and Lord.[27]

c. 2 Corinthians 3

In 2 Corinthians 3, Paul again deals with the narrative of Exodus at some length, now focusing his attention on the aftermath of Israel's idolatry in the golden calf incident.[28] Here the tone is apologetic, rather than admonitory. Moreover, the dissimilarities and discontinuities between the experience of the wilderness generation and that of the Corinthians stand out, in contrast with 1 Corinthians 10. This owes to the polemical nature of Paul's argument: the story of Moses and Israel in Exodus serves as a foil for Paul's ministry to God's people under the new covenant, the superiority of which is demonstrated by way of multiple contrasts, drawn not least from the book of Exodus.[29]

---

[26] See the essays in R. Bauckham, *Jesus and the God of Israel: God Crucified and Other Studies on the New Testament's Christology of Divine Identity* (Grand Rapids: Eerdmans, 2008); also C. Tilling, *Paul's Divine Christology* (Grand Rapids: Eerdmans, 2012); D. B. Capes, *The Divine Christ: Paul, the Lord Jesus, and the Scriptures of Israel* (Grand Rapids: Baker, 2018). Κύριον is read in ℵ B C P 33. 104. 326. 365. 1175. 2464 sy^{hmg}; the reading Χριστόν, which nearly all recent commentators accept, is supported by 𝔓^{46} D F G K L Ψ 630. 1241. 1505. 1739. 1881 𝔐 latt sy co; Ir^{lat} Or^{1739mg}. The latter is to be deemed more likely, given its early attestation (esp. in 𝔓^{46}) and the fact that a change to κύριον can easily be explained as an attempt to harmonize Paul's statement with the texts that it evokes (cf. LXX Num. 21.5-6; Deut. 6.16; Ps. 77.18 [78.18]).

[27] Contrast this with *Barn.* 4.6-14, which uses the golden calf story to dissociate its audience from Israel, who are said to have lost their covenant with God through this sin.

[28] This study assumes the textual unity and authenticity of 2 Cor. 3, though these have been challenged in various ways on form-critical grounds. Recently see, e.g., W. O. Walker, '2 Corinthians 3:7-18 as a Non-Pauline Interpolation', *JSPL* 3 (2013), pp. 195–217. I agree with Linda Belleville that such conjecture 'overlooks the extent to which Paul's terminology and ideology can be accounted for on the basis of Septuagintal and extrabiblical dependence, and the degree to which his style is attributable to the haggadic character of his sources and method'. L. L. Belleville, 'Tradition or Creation? Paul's Use of the Exodus 34 Tradition in 2 Corinthians 3.7-18', in C. A. Evans (ed.), *Paul and the Scriptures of Israel* (Sheffield: Sheffield Academic, 1993), pp. 165–86 (168).

[29] Nonetheless, Paul's use of Exodus in 1 Corinthians as well as the fundamental importance of this same pericope in Rom. 9–11 (see below) indicate that Paul does not make use of this scripture only because his putative opponents do. Here one must beware of the dangers of excessive mirror-reading, as helpfully considered (with reference to Galatians) by J. M. G. Barclay, 'Mirror-Reading a Polemical Letter: Galatians as a Test Case', *JSNT* 31 (1987), pp. 73–93.

In response to his critics' demand that he carry letters of recommendation, Paul insists that the Corinthians are themselves a letter inscribed on his and his associates' hearts, ever available to be read by anyone who should question their credentials (2 Cor. 3.2). Paul then pivots the discussion, complicating the metaphor in the process: the 'letter' (ἐπιστολή) in question is 'written not with ink but with the Spirit of the living God, not on stone tablets but on tablets of fleshly hearts'. Paul's statement compactly alludes to at least three texts simultaneously, combining the description of the law in Exod. 31.18 as 'stone tablets written with the finger of God (πλάκας λιθίνας γεγραμμένας τῷ δακτύλῳ τοῦ θεοῦ)'[30] with the respective predictions of Jeremiah and Ezekiel that God will renew his covenant with Israel by inscribing his law on their heart and by replacing their heart of stone with a heart of flesh that is receptive to his Spirit (LXX Jer. 38.33; Ezek. 11.19; 36.26-27).

The awkwardness of this transition—contending that the letter is not written on stone has little to do with the demand for letters—reflects Paul's rhetorical strategy: rather than meeting his opponents' objection concerning letters of recommendation head-on, he wishes to re-orient their whole perception of the significance of his ministry, portraying himself (like Moses) as one whom God has made sufficient (ἱκανός) for the exercise of his ministry—possibly an allusion to the burning bush narrative (cf. Exod. 4.10-12)[31]—and yet whose ministry also far surpasses that of Moses (2 Cor. 3.4-5). The remainder of 2 Corinthians 3 is devoted to laying out the contrast between these ministries and their effects. Whereas the ministry of Moses is a ministry of the death-dealing letter that brings condemnation and offers only limited access to a lesser, ineffective glory, Paul's ministry is a ministry of the life-giving Spirit of God that brings righteousness and offers universal access among God's people to the greater, transformative glory now revealed in the Messiah (3.7-18).

While a broader array of evidence in the Pentateuch (not least those episodes in Numbers to which he refers in 1 Cor. 10) could be seen to underlie some of Paul's assertions, the three direct allusions to Exodus in 3.7-18 make it obvious that he primarily has in mind Moses' interactions with the people of Israel following the golden calf incident (Exod. 34.29-35). In this pericope, after forty days and nights on the mountain fasting and writing down the words of the covenant once again as he was instructed, Moses returns to the people without realizing 'that the appearance of the skin of his face had been glorified (δεδόξασται)' through his encounter with God (34.29; cf. 34.30, 35). Aaron and all the elders are afraid to approach him, and from then on, Moses would reveal his appearance to the people of Israel only temporarily, while issuing the commands that the Lord gave on Mount Sinai (34.30-33). In this way, Moses' earlier request in 33.16-18 is partially granted: because God is 'glorified in him' before the people, it is known

---

[30] Cf. similar language in LXX Exod. 31.18; 32.15-16; 34.1, 4, 28-29; also LXX Deut. 4.13; 5.22; 9.9-11; 10.1-2. Paul's statement is slightly closer to the Greek of LXX Exod. 31.18 than to Deut. 9.10 (instrumental dative without the preposition ἐν).

[31] See C. K. Stockhausen, *Moses' Veil and the Glory of the New Covenant: The Exegetical Substructure of II Cor. 3,1–4,6* (AnBib, 116; Rome: Pontificio Istituto Biblico, 1989), pp. 82–85.

that Moses has found favor with him. Otherwise, he placed a veil (κάλυμμα) over his face, but would remove it 'whenever [he] entered in before the Lord to speak to him' (34.34).

In Paul's hands, this episode becomes emblematic of the old covenant's inferiority to the new. In 2 Cor. 3.7 and 3.13, he describes the Israelites' inability to 'stare' or 'look intently' (ἀτενίζω) at the reflection of God's glory in Moses' face, although the reasons that Paul gives are distinct in each case: in the former, because of the intensity of the glory itself; in the latter, because Moses veiled it. In both instances, he describes this glory as καταργούμενος—a word whose translation is disputed in this case, but is probably best understood in the sense of 'being rendered inoperative'.[32] If this is correct, Paul's language matter-of-factly indicates the veil's function of preventing the glory of Moses' face from having a certain effect on its viewers (in Paul's words, 'the outcome [τέλος] of what was being rendered ineffective', 3.13), though Exodus does not explicitly tell us what this is. Assuming the consistency of these two statements (in which case 'what was being rendered ineffective' in 3.13 is 'the glory of [Moses'] face' in 3.7), the 'outcome' in question most naturally refers to what Paul describes in 3.18: the *transformation* of those who, like Moses, contemplate the glory of the Lord with unveiled faces and are changed into the same glorified image—that of the Messiah, the image of God, whose face reflects God's glory (cf. 4.4, 6).

This is possible, Paul says, because 'whenever one turns to the Lord, the veil is removed' (3.16). Here Paul refers to LXX Exod. 34.34, with significant modification:

2 Cor. 3.16   ἡνίκα δὲ ἐὰν <u>ἐπιστρέψῃ πρὸς κύριον</u>, <u>περιαιρεῖται</u> τὸ κάλυμμα

Exod. 34.34   ἡνίκα δ' ἂν <u>εἰσεπορεύετο</u> Μωυσῆς <u>ἔναντι κυρίου</u> λαλεῖν αὐτῷ, <u>περιῃρεῖτο</u> τὸ κάλυμμα ἕως τοῦ ἐκπορεύεσθαι

The imagery of Moses' encounter with the Lord thus becomes a pattern for conversion, but a pattern by way of contrast as well as comparison.[33] In both cases the veil is removed, but what Moses himself removes in Exodus '*is* removed' (περιαιρεῖται) by God in 2 Corinthians, and removed from the party that was formerly being prevented from seeing it (Israel). Moreover, whereas Exod. 34.34 describes Moses' repeated and temporary entries into the tent of meeting (ἡνίκα

---

[32] So G. H. Guthrie, *2 Corinthians* (BECNT; Grand Rapids: Baker, 2015), pp. 211–12, 219–22. The more common reading understands καταργούμενος as 'fading' (so, e.g., Belleville, 'Tradition or Creation?'; R. P. Martin, *2 Corinthians* [WBC, 40; Grand Rapids: Zondervan, 2014], p. 204). Despite its popularity, however, this reading is entirely without lexical warrant; see S. J. Hafemann, *Paul, Moses, and the History of Israel: The Letter/Spirit Contrast and the Argument from Scripture in 2 Corinthians 3* (WUNT, 2/81; Tübingen: Mohr Siebeck, 1995), pp. 301–9 (noting also his survey of extrabiblical traditions concerning Moses' face on pp. 287–98).

[33] It is possible that Paul's statement is still referring to Moses, but it is nonetheless clear (whether by direct statement or implication) that Paul uses this 'turning' to describe what happens to the veil at conversion. So C. Wolff, *Der zweite Brief des Paulus an die Korinther* (THKNT, 8; Berlin: Evangelische Verlagsanstalt, 1989), p. 75: 'Was damals Mose tat, das weist auf die Bekehrung der Israeliten hin'.

δ' ἂν εἰσεπορεύετο...ἕως τοῦ ἐκπορεύεσθαι),[34] Paul describes a more decisive event of 'turning' (ἐπιστρέφω) to the Lord, the indeterminacy of which owes to the conditionality of the action (i.e., will a person repent?) rather than to its temporary nature. In his emphasis on 'turning' and his use of a different prepositional phrase to describe the action, Paul may be drawing on the language of LXX Exod. 32.31 (ὑπέστρεψεν δὲ Μωυσῆς πρὸς κύριον), which describes Moses' action of returning to the Lord following the revelation of Israel's idolatry with the golden calf.[35] If this is so, Paul's language suggests the idea of a repentant Israel finally attaining what was available only to Moses under the old covenant, and attaining it permanently.

d. 2 Corinthians 8

The last overt use of the text of Exodus in 2 Corinthians appears in the midst of Paul's discussion of generosity and the relief of the saints in Jerusalem in chs. 8 and 9. Enjoining them, in view of their present abundance, to share their wealth with those in need, in 8.15 Paul quotes LXX Exod. 16.18 as support: 'the one with much did not have too much, and the one with little did not have too little' (ὁ τὸ πολὺ οὐκ ἐπλεόνασεν, καὶ ὁ τὸ ὀλίγον οὐκ ἠλαττόνησεν).[36] The setting for this statement in Exodus is in the wilderness immediately after Israel's deliverance at the Red Sea, when the people become hungry and complain to Moses and then receive God's gracious provision of manna. The text that Paul quotes describes the result of their obedience to Moses' instructions: each person has exactly the right amount, regardless of whether he gathered much or little. But for those who keep leftovers until the next morning, the manna breeds worms and gives a foul odour (16.19-20).

Interpreters generally suppose that Paul's point in using this text mainly concerns *equality*: the Corinthians should not have too much, nor the saints in Jerusalem too little.[37] While this is undeniably part of Paul's intent, Hays is probably right in arguing that the citation's purpose has mainly to do with *dependence* on God's provision.[38] The Corinthians' excess of wealth should be treated as something that may be freely given up in order to provide what others lack, since the accumulation of such excess is not fitting for God's eschatological people in the 'wilderness', who trust in the sufficiency of his provision rather than their own capacity. As Exod. 16.4 makes clear, the point of this provision is not merely to promote equality (nor even, for that matter, to satisfy the Israelites' hunger), but to test their willingness to trust and obey God by gathering *only*

---

[34] Cf. also LXX Exod. 33.8-9.
[35] Cf. similar language in connection with divine presence in Exod. 4.18; 16.10; 32.15; 34.31.
[36] LXX: οὐκ ἐπλεόνασεν ὁ τὸ πολύ, καὶ ὁ τὸ ἔλαττον οὐκ ἠλαττόνησεν. Paul's quotation differs slightly from the LXX in word order, and reads 'little' (ὀλίγον) rather than 'less' (ἥλαττον), the latter corresponding more closely to the accompanying verb. Paul is closer to the MT, however, which reads והממעיט לא החסיר.
[37] So e.g., Martin, *2 Corinthians*, p. 445; Wolff, *Korinther*, p. 174. Philo makes use of Exod. 16 in a discussion of equality in *Rer. Div. Her.* 191.
[38] Hays, *Echoes*, p. 90.

enough for the day (and for the Sabbath day as well, at the end of each week). Moses reiterates this instruction in 16.16: the people are to gather only an amount appropriate for the number of persons in their tents. Understood thus, Paul's use of Exod. 16.18 reflects a careful attentiveness to his source material.

4. Romans

Paul's use of Exodus in his letter to the Romans reflects the same characteristics noted above: a broad influence at the thematic level, coupled with the use of quotations that, while infrequent, reflect a detailed knowledge of the text from which they are drawn. The former is apparent in Romans 1–8, which, with one partial exception,[39] does not quote Exodus (and will be dealt with here only briefly). The latter is especially evident in Romans 9–11, for which the book of Exodus plays a more centrally formative role than is normally recognized.[40]

a. Romans 1–8

Although Paul does not engage directly with the text of Exodus in Romans 1–8, one can nonetheless follow a fairly continuous argumentative thread through these chapters by noting their intertextual relationships with the book.[41] Though there remains uncertainty in some cases as to whether one encounters deliberate allusion or unintended intertextual echo, on the whole the cumulative weight of evidence that the story of Exodus informs and shapes Paul's account in these chapters of God's dealings with Israel and the nations through the Messiah is impressive. Since others have dealt with these themes in greater detail than is possible here, it will be sufficient to provide a summary overview.

Central to the argument of Romans 1–8 is the theme of eschatological glory, which God bestows on his people through the death and resurrection of the Messiah.[42] Paul's introduction of this theme in 1.23, where he says that humanity 'exchanged the glory of the incorruptible God for the likeness of an image', alludes to the description of Israel's idolatry at Sinai in the episode of the golden calf in LXX Ps. 105.20, thereby hinting at the direction of Paul's argument ('both

---

[39] Rom. 7.7, which quotes the tenth commandment of the Decalogue (οὐκ ἐπιθυμήσεις) as recorded in Exod. 20.17 and Deut. 5.21.
[40] The Decalogue reappears in Rom. 13.9, but will not be discussed here, since the ordering follows Deuteronomy more closely.
[41] See esp. Keesmaat, *Paul and His Story*; N. T. Wright, *Pauline Perspectives: Essays on Paul, 1978–2013* (Minneapolis: Fortress, 2013); N. T. Wright, 'God Put Jesus Forth: Reflections on Romans 3:24-26', in D. M. Gurtner, G. Macaskill, and J. T. Pennington (eds.), *In the Fullness of Time: Essays on Christology, Creation and Eschatology in Honor of Richard Bauckham* (Grand Rapids: Eerdmans, 2016), pp. 135–61.
[42] Cf. Rom. 1.23; 2.7, 10; 3.7, 23; 4.20; 5.2; 6.4; 8.18, 21. For a recent discussion of this theme, see H. Goranson Jacob, *Conformed to the Image of His Son: Reconsidering Paul's Theology of Glory in Romans* (Downers Grove, IL: InterVarsity, 2018). It is unnecessary, in my view, to follow Jacob in driving a sharp wedge between glory as God's own attribute, which serves as a metonymy for his presence, and as a descriptor of the exalted status of his adopted image-bearers. The latter ought to imply the former, as their rule by its very nature mediates the divine presence to creation.

Jews and Hellenes are under sin', 3.9). This theme is retrieved and resolved in 3.23-25, where Paul describes Israel's Messiah as God's gracious solution to humanity's forfeiture[43] of his glory: they are 'justified through the redemption (ἀπολύτρωσις) that is in Messiah Jesus, whom God set forth as a mercy seat (ἱλαστήριον) through faith, by means of his blood...' (3.24-25a).[44] This nexus of themes—divine glory, redemption and a mercy seat cleansed with sacrificial blood—draws together the broad narrative movements of Exodus (an act of deliverance from slavery and the provision of a cultic apparatus that enables God to reside in the midst of his people) into a single compact description of the person of the Messiah, in whom they find their eschatological realization.[45]

The resulting eschatological hope, already anticipated in believers' reception of the Spirit through the Messiah's death and resurrection, becomes a key theme in Paul's argument in the remainder of Romans 4–8, again with significant allusion to the story of Exodus. In the Messiah, God's people are brought out of slavery to sin and death through the waters of baptism (6.1-6, 14-22; 7.6, 14, 24-25; 8.1-2, 15, 21-23), although the resulting freedom (as in Exodus) can also be described with the language of servitude (6.18-19; 7.6). As in Galatians, this freedom also entails release from the law, though Paul is more careful here to stress that sin, rather than the law itself, is the enslaving agent (7.7, 12-14). Paul's use of the tenth commandment in Rom. 7.7-11 (cf. LXX Exod. 20.17; Deut. 5.21) may have the narrative of Exodus in mind: like Israel at Sinai, the would-be observer of Torah who formerly lived in freedom apart from the law finds that the law's arrival brings sin and death.[46] Liberation from this slavery,

---

[43] Given the backward reference of Rom. 3.23 to 1.23, it is unlikely that ὑστερέω is to be understood in the sense of 'fall short' (as it is normally translated); rather, Paul describes sinful humanity's 'lack' of the glory of God because, as in Rom. 1.23 and LXX Ps. 105.20, they have traded away their glory through idolatry. Cf. the historical parallels in M. Wolter, *Der Brief an die Römer (Teilband 1: Röm 1–8)* (EKKNT, 6/1; Neukirchen-Vluyn: Neukirchener Verlag, 2014), p. 252.

[44] For the reading of ἱλαστήριον in Rom. 3.25 as 'mercy seat', see D. P. Bailey, 'Jesus as the Mercy Seat: The Semantics and Theology of Paul's Use of *Hilasterion* in Romans 3:25', *TynBul* 51 (2000), pp. 155–58 (summarizing his 1999 dissertation); D. Stökl ben Ezra, *The Impact of Yom Kippur on Early Christianity: The Day of Atonement from Second Temple Judaism to the Fifth Century* (WUNT 2/163; Tübingen: Mohr Siebeck, 2003), pp. 198–201; Wright, 'God Put Jesus Forth'. As I have argued elsewhere, Paul is referring here to the crucified-*and-raised* Jesus as the mercy seat, because he (like the mercy seat) is the locus of God's glory among God's people. D. M. Westfall, 'Substitution and Participation in the Writings of Paul: A Study of Four Texts' (Ph.D. diss, University of St Andrews, 2018), pp. 49–60; D. M. Westfall, '"Thine Be the Glory": Christ the Mercy Seat in Romans 3:25' (paper presented at the St Andrews Symposium for Biblical and Early Christian Studies, St Andrews, Scotland, 5 June 2018).

[45] Wright, 'God Put Jesus Forth', p. 148. It is also possible that the theme of divine righteousness should enter into consideration here as well; cf. LXX Exod. 15.13: 'by your righteousness (τῇ δικαιοσύνῃ σου) you have led this your people, whom you have redeemed (ὃν ἐλυτρώσω), having called [them] by your might into your holy habitation'. So D. P. Bailey, 'Jesus as the Mercy Seat: The Semantics and Theology of Paul's Use of *Hilasterion* in Romans 3:25' (Ph.D. diss., University of Cambridge, 1999), pp. 177–217.

[46] The meaning of Rom. 7 is of course highly controversial, and it is not my intention to enter into debate concerning the various interpretative options here. I follow the majority in thinking that Paul's discourse is not intended to describe the normal experience of those led by the Spirit. See the different views in, e.g., E. Wasserman, *The Death of the Soul in Romans 7: Sin, Death, and the Law in Light of Hellenistic Moral Psychology* (WUNT, 2/256; Tübingen: Mohr Siebeck, 2008); J. D. G. Dunn, 'Rom 7:14-25 in the Theology of Paul', *TZ* 31 (1975), pp. 257–73; M. Croasmun, *The*

as again in Galatians, bestows sonship, and with it, the promise of a (worldwide) land-inheritance, toward which believers are 'led' by the presence of God (4.13; 8.14-17). At the same time, their present state of expectation can be compared to that of Israel in Egypt: they 'groan' (στενάζω) and 'cry out' (κράζω) to God as they await the completion of their adoption in the 'redemption' (ἀπολύτρωσις) of their body (8.19, 23).[47]

b. Romans 9–11

Paul's argument concerning God's righteousness in Romans 9–11 draws on two episodes from Exodus which, in their respective emphases on God's twin actions of showing mercy and hardening, form a thematic *inclusio* with the end of ch. 11.[48] Far from being insignificant, then, the book of Exodus—particularly the golden calf narrative of chs. 32–34—gives Paul the canvas on which to paint his sobering analysis of Israel's spiritual condition as well as his hope for their future.[49]

Paul's explicit quotations of Exodus appear in close succession. Having asserted in 9.6-13 that God's free promise rather than fleshly descent has always been constitutive of Israel's identity, Paul answers the logical objection in 9.14-18 in diatribe style:

> What, then, shall we say? There is not unrighteousness with God, is there? Certainly not! For to Moses he says 'I will have mercy on whom I have mercy, and compassion on whom I have compassion'. Consequently it does not belong to the one who wills or who runs, but to God who has mercy. For the scripture says to Pharaoh, 'For this purpose I have raised you up: that I may demonstrate my power in you and that my name may be proclaimed in all the world'. So then, on whom he will, he has mercy, and whom he will, he hardens.

Emergence of Sin: The Cosmic Tyrant in Romans (New York: Oxford University Press, 2017); N. T. Wright, *Paul and the Faithfulness of God* (COQG, 4; Minneapolis: Fortress, 2013), pp. 892–902. In my opinion it is at least plausible to regard Israel's experience at Sinai as one background to Paul's argument at this point. Even if this is not Paul's intent, however, the text's placement in the midst of an extended argument with recurring allusion to Exodus warrants the detection of such intertextual echoes.

[47] Cf. Exod. 2.23-25.

[48] Noted by E. Lohse, *Der Brief an die Römer* (KEK, 4; Göttingen: Vandenhoeck & Ruprecht, 2003), p. 266; N. T. Wright, 'The Letter to the Romans: Introduction, Commentary, and Reflections', in L. E. Keck (ed.), *The New Interpreter's Bible*, vol. 10 (Nashville: Abingdon, 2002), pp. 10:393–770 (638–39); R. Jewett, *Romans: A Commentary* (Hermeneia; Minneapolis: Fortress, 2007), p. 710.

[49] See also the analysis in J. M. G. Barclay, '"I will have mercy on whom I have mercy": The Golden Calf and Divine Mercy in Romans 9–11 and Second Temple Judaism', *EC* 1 (2010), pp. 82–106, whose thesis that Rom. 9–11 is 'an interpretative extension of the theological dynamics of Exodus 32–34' (p. 83) finds further support in the argument given here. It is also worth noting that some of Israel's privileges that Paul identifies in 9.4-5 (esp. υἱοθεσία and νομοθεσία) allude to events in Exodus; cf. Exod. 4.22; 19.1-9; Hos. 11.1. Moreover, many have heard an echo of Moses' request to be blotted out if YHWH will not forgive Israel in Paul's prayer/wish to be ἀνάθεμα for the sake of his kinsman (Rom. 9.3). So, e.g., J. D. G. Dunn, *Romans 9–16* (WBC, 38B; Dallas: Word Books, 1988), p. 532.

While the first quote matches LXX Exod. 33.19 exactly (ἐλεήσω ὃν ἂν ἐλεῶ, καὶ οἰκτιρήσω ὃν ἂν οἰκτίρω), the second quote differs from LXX Exod. 9.16 in at least one substantial respect:

Rom. 9.17: <u>εἰς αὐτὸ τοῦτο ἐξήγειρά σε ὅπως</u> ἐνδείξωμαι ἐν σοὶ τὴν <u>δύναμίν</u> μου καὶ ὅπως διαγγελῇ τὸ ὄνομά μου ἐν πάσῃ τῇ γῇ

LXX Exod. 9.16: <u>ἕνεκεν τούτου διετηρήθης, ἵνα</u> ἐνδείξωμαι ἐν σοὶ τὴν <u>ἰσχύν</u> μου, καὶ ὅπως διαγγελῇ τὸ ὄνομά μου ἐν πάσῃ τῇ γῇ

MT Exod. 9.16: ואולם בעבור זאת העמדתיך בעבור הראתך את כחי ולמען ספר שמי בכל הארץ:

The reading ἐξήγειρα in Romans and διετηρήθης in the LXX (a 'divine passive') constitute two viable interpretations of the *hiphil* verb העמדתיך, which literally says 'I have caused you to stand'. Whereas the LXX translator understands this in the sense of preservation,[50] Paul's citation takes it in the sense of 'setting up' what was not there before.[51] This rendering accords with Paul's argumentative aims in the chapter, which center around God's sovereign prerogative to order creation to his glory.[52] Read thus, the second quote from Exodus in Romans 9 intensifies the theological claim of the first: whereas in 9.15 Paul uses Exod. 33.19 to deny that human volition or exertion can condition God's mercy, in 9.17 he uses Exod. 9.16 to affirm the opposite: *God's* discriminating mercy conditions *human* agency.

Paul's conclusion shows clearly that he is reading Exod. 9.16 with an attentiveness to its narrative context, where Pharaoh's 'hardening', to which Paul is alluding (but which does not appear in the quote) is a key theme.[53] Paul's inference broadens the action's scope. God's dealings with Pharaoh show that he hardens and shows mercy to 'whom he will'—that is, whom*ever* he will, whether Jews or Gentiles. Accordingly, the very people whose liberation came through the hardening of Pharaoh's heart find themselves hardened in order that others, Gentile pagans, would be saved (Rom. 9.22-24). Paul spends the rest of Romans 9–10 legitimating this claim through an extended argument from scripture. But this still leaves his main problem unresolved: what of God's promises to Israel? Is his historical people merely a disposable tool that he uses to save Gentiles and will soon discard, now that their purpose has been achieved?

The answer Paul finally gives to this question reveals his equal attentiveness to the narrative context of his other citation, Exod. 33.19. This background is vital for understanding the climax of Paul's argument in Rom. 11.25-32, where the

---

[50] Cf. 1 Kgs. 15.4; Prov. 29.4; 2 Chron. 9.8.
[51] Cf. Judg. 16.25; 2 Chron. 23.10, 19; Ps. 148.6 (MT 149.6).
[52] So Jewett, *Romans*, pp. 584–85. Jewett regards the change from ἰσχύν to δύναμιν as rhetorically significant, in that it relates Exod. 9.16 to the thesis of the letter concerning the gospel as God's δύναμις (Rom. 1.16-17). Similarly he notes the verbal link of ἐνδείξωμαι to 3.25.
[53] Cf. Exod. 4.21; 7.3, 22; 8.15; 9.12, 35; 10.1, 20, 27; 11.10; 13.15; 14.4, 17.

themes of mercy and hardening introduced through the two Exodus quotations in ch. 9 reappear in a tightly woven cord that draws together the threads of the whole argument in these chapters.[54] In 11.25-27, Paul summarizes the 'mystery' (μυστήριον) into which he has been peering: 'A hardening has happened to part of Israel (πώρωσις ἀπὸ μέρους τῷ Ἰσραὴλ γέγονεν)[55] until the time when (ἄχρι οὗ) the fulness of the Gentiles enters in, and so (οὕτως)[56] all Israel will be saved'. In 11.30-32, Paul puts this in terms of divine mercy, again mirroring his use of Exodus in ch. 9:

> For just as you once were disobedient to God, but now have been shown mercy (ἠλεήθητε) because of the disobedience of these ones [Israel], so also these ones [Israel] have been disobedient because of the mercy shown to you,[57] so that they themselves may [now][58] be shown mercy (ἐλεηθῶσιν) also. For God has imprisoned all in disobedience, so that he may have mercy (ἐλεήσῃ) on all.

Through the chain of events set off by Israel's disobedience to the gospel, God's mercy ultimately reaches Israel again, carrying the Gentiles along in its wake. This will take place in the manner that Paul has just described in 11.26-27, which contains a composite citation that inserts LXX Isa. 27.9 into 59.20-21a (with some further modification) and thereby links the hope of Israel's future deliverance with covenant renewal and the forgiveness of sins: 'as it is written, "The deliverer will come from Zion; he will turn away acts of ungodliness (ἀσεβείας) from Jacob. And this is my covenant with them (αὕτη αὐτοῖς ἡ παρ' ἐμοῦ διαθήκη), when I take away their sins (ὅταν ἀφέλωμαι τὰς ἁμαρτίας αὐτῶν)"'.

---

[54] Rom. 11.25-32 remains a notorious *crux interpretum*. I am persuaded by the traditional (and still, it seems, majority) interpretation that Paul expects a general corporate repentance on the part of hardened Israel once the addition of Gentiles has reached a 'critical mass'. See esp. J. K. Goodrich, 'Until the Fullness of the Gentiles Comes In: A Critical Review of Recent Scholarship on the Salvation of "All Israel" (Romans 11:26)', *JSPL* 6 (2016), pp. 5–32; J. M. Scott, '"And Then All Israel Will Be Saved" (Rom 11:26)', in J. M. Scott (ed.), *Restoration: Old Testament, Jewish, & Christian Perspectives* (Leiden: Brill, 2001), pp. 489–526. The question of whether or not Paul presupposes a *Sonderweg* available to Israel lies beyond my purposes, though I am not myself persuaded by this interpretation, and am puzzled by the implication of some critics that the traditional view necessarily amounts to a version of this (see discussion in Goodrich, 'Critical Review', pp. 22–24). For a critical evaluation of the *Sonderweg* reading, see M. G. Vanlaningham, *Christ, the Savior of Israel: An Evaluation of the Dual Covenant and* Sonderweg *Interpretations of Paul's Letters* (Edition Israelogie, 5; Berlin: Peter Lang, 2012).

[55] The prepositional phrase ἀπὸ μέρους can be used both adverbially and adjectivally (cf. both uses in Rom. 15.15 and 15.24). The translation given here is deemed likely in view of Paul's similar division of Israel in Rom. 11.7 ('what Israel seeks, this it did not find: the elect obtained [it] but the rest were hardened').

[56] The adverb οὕτως may be understood in a modal, temporal, or logical sense. In any case, Paul is referring to a salvific act involving 'all Israel' that will be completed in the future.

[57] Dunn and others argue on structural grounds that the phrase τῷ ὑμετέρῳ ἐλέει should be taken with the preceding ἠπείθησαν rather than the ἵνα that follows. Dunn, *Romans 9–16*, p. 688.

[58] νῦν is omitted in 𝔓46 and some western and Byzantine MSS, but attested in א and B. On the relevance of this textual decision for current debates, see Goodrich, 'Critical Review', p. 26.

The rationale for this textual fusion and its use in the argument at this point has proven rather obscure, and some have argued that the combination of these texts must predate Paul.[59] Whether there is any merit to such a conjecture or not, I think that the reason for its use here becomes readily apparent when one bears in mind that Paul's conclusion to the argument in this section is drawing together the narrative themes introduced near the beginning of his argument with his citations from Exodus, particularly 33.19.[60] God's assertion of his own unconditioned freedom in showing mercy comes in the midst of the golden calf narrative, in response to Moses' request to be given a revelation of God's glory so that he may know with confidence that God will not abandon his people on account of their apostasy but will personally bring them to the promised land. In response, God reveals himself to Moses in 34.6-7 as 'the God who shows compassion and mercy (οἰκτίρμων καὶ ἐλεήμων): patient and very merciful (πολυέλεος) and truthful and keeping righteousness and doing mercy (ποιῶν ἔλεος) to thousands, *taking away lawless deeds and unrighteous acts and sins* (ἀφαιρῶν ἀνομίας καὶ ἀδικίας καὶ ἁμαρτίας)'. Moses' response to this theophany in 34.9 repeats the same language, pleading that God will 'take away' Israel's 'sins' (ἀφελεῖς σὺ τὰς ἁμαρτίας ... ἡμῶν), to which YHWH immediately responds in 34.10 *by reestablishing the covenant* before Moses (ἐγὼ τίθημί σοι διαθήκην), promising to act gloriously in the sight of his people and of the nations among whom they come to dwell.

Given the strength of these parallels and Paul's overt and careful use of the narrative from which they come, it is probable that the underlying logic of Paul's textual choices in Rom. 11.26-27 originates in the narrative to which his citation in 9.15 has already pointed us: Exodus 32–34.[61] If this reasoning is correct, it indicates that the two explicit citations from Exodus in Romans 9 represent more than two miscellaneous episodes from Israel's history intended merely to illustrate a general principle. Rather, for Paul, the story of Israel at Sinai is the paradigmatic tale of Israel's apostasy and restoration, from which he derives hope both for his kinsmen according to the flesh and for all the nations.

---

[59] So, e.g., C. D. Stanley, '"The Redeemer Will Come ἐκ Σιων": Romans 11.26-27 Revisited', in Evans and Sanders (eds.), *Paul and the Scriptures of Israel*, pp. 118–42. The occurrence of parallel demonstrative clauses ('this is…') and of Ἰακώβ in both texts are often noted as possible reasons (e.g., Jewett, *Romans*, p. 705), though this still does not fully explain Paul's decision to employ this composite citation in the present argument. It is also possible that Paul's citation deliberately revisits texts that appear earlier in the catena of Rom. 3.10-18, in which case there is a higher likelihood that its formulation originates with Paul himself. So M. Reasoner, '"Promised Beforehand Through His Prophets in the Holy Scriptures": Composite Citations in Romans', in S. A. Adams and S. M. Ehorn (eds.), *Composite Citations in Antiquity*. Vol. 2, *New Testament Uses* (LNTS, 593; London: Bloomsbury T&T Clark, 2018), pp. 128–58 (148–50).

[60] So Barclay, 'Divine Mercy in Romans 9–11', pp. 82–83, 97–106.

[61] Seifrid notes how the language of taking away sins 'recalls…the Lord's self-revelation to Moses (Exod. 34:5-8)', but misses the link between this descriptor and the re-establishment of the διαθήκη in the very next verses (34.9-10). M. A. Seifrid, 'Romans', in G. K. Beale and D. A. Carson (eds.), *Commentary on the New Testament Use of the Old Testament* (Grand Rapids: Baker, 2007), pp. 607–94 (676).

5. Conclusion

The influence of the book of Exodus is discernible at numerous points in the undisputed writings of Paul the Apostle, despite the relative sparsity of quotations from this book in comparison with others. Though it was not among his most frequently invoked texts, Exodus played a deeply formative role in Paul's theological imagination, providing him with a narrative pattern for understanding God's new act of eschatological redemption in Israel's Messiah and the situation of his people in the last days of the present evil age. This is evident in the first half of Romans and most explicitly in the Corinthian correspondence, where Paul repeatedly grounds his arguments on the assumption that his converts are participants in the eschatological fulfillment of ancient Israel's prefigurative story, beneficiaries of a new act of redemption through the same Lord who accompanied their Israelite 'ancestors' out of Egypt and through the wilderness toward their inheritance. In some instances—this is especially true when Paul's argumentation concerns the law and covenant delivered at Sinai, as in Galatians—Paul's figural readings of Exodus turn some of this book's main themes on their head. Thus, in Galatians, Sinai is Israel's point of entry *into* slavery, from which God's new act of redemption in the Messiah in fulfillment of the promise to Abraham must free them. His use of texts is nonetheless attentive to the larger literary context in which they appear, in ways that usually have bearing on his argument. As his reflections in 2 Corinthians 3 and Romans 9–11 show, the golden calf narrative in particular played a deeply formative role in Paul's imagination: it was chiefly in conversation with this text that he sought to make sense of his kinsmen's hostility toward his gospel and to find hope for their future in the purposes of God.

Chapter 7

EXODUS IN THE DISPUTED PAULINE LETTERS

Seth M. Ehorn

This chapter examines the use of Exodus and exodus traditions in the disputed Pauline letters. For present purposes the label 'disputed' serves only to delineate the corpus and does not reflect a value judgment on the authenticity of any or all of the disputed Pauline letters.[1] The corpus of disputed Pauline letters includes Ephesians, Colossians, 2 Thessalonians, and the Pastoral Letters (1–2 Timothy, Titus). Each of these letters presents its own challenge and, accordingly, each letter (or grouping of letters) will be treated separately. Because there are no quotations or allusions to Exodus in 2 Thessalonians, that letter is not discussed in this chapter.

Before turning to the data of the disputed letters, a few brief definitions are in order.[2] A text may be considered a *quotation* when an author provides linguistic signs that indicate that literary borrowing has occurred. Typically, this is accompanied by a formula of introduction (e.g., καθὼς γέγραπται, γάρ) or a noticeable break in the syntactical flow of the passage. However, as Steve Moyise notes, 'if the text is particularly well known, it is possible to introduce it without

---

[1] The vexing problems associated with Pauline authorship of the 'disputed' letters are well-known and need not deter the present investigation. For the sake of simplicity and to avoid distraction, I will refer to 'the author' throughout this essay. For recent (and, at times, opposing) conclusions on authorship of several of the disputed letters, see the studies by D. A. Campbell, *Framing Paul: An Epistolary Biography* (Grand Rapids: Eerdmans, 2014), and B. D. Ehrman, *Forgery and Counterforgery: The Use of Literary Deceit in Early Christian Polemics* (New York: Oxford University Press, 2012). For challenges to some of the scholarly assumptions about authorship, see recently P. Foster, 'Who Wrote 2 Thessalonians? A Fresh Look at an Old Problem', *JSNT* 35 (2012), pp. 150–75.

[2] Definitions of 'quotations', 'allusions', and 'echoes' are debated in the scholarly literature. See especially S. E. Porter, 'Allusions and Echoes', in S. E. Porter and C. D. Stanley (eds.), *As It Is Written: Studying Paul's Use of Scripture* (SBLSymS, 50; Atlanta: Society of Biblical Literature, 2008), pp. 29–40, for a discussion of some of the prospects and pitfalls of these terms.

any marker at all'.³ Because Exodus is well-known, especially the Decalogue, Moyise's observation is important for recognizing the quotation of Exod. 20.12 in Eph. 6.2-3. For the purposes of this chapter, an *allusion* is 'a figure of speech that makes indirect extratextual references'.⁴ Such indirect extratextual references may include texts, people, events, or objects and, in my view, are intentional. Most of the 'uses' of Exodus and exodus tradition in the disputed Pauline letters fall under the category of allusion, especially allusions that evoke themes or characters ultimately derived from Exodus.

1. Ephesians

There are several places where the author uses exodus tradition and even quotes an Exodus text in the letter to the Ephesians. Some of these appear at the level of thematic parallels. For example, the language of God 'choosing' a people (e.g., ἐξελέξατο ἡμᾶς, 1.4) certainly resonates with texts from Exodus (e.g., 19.5-6) and Isaiah (e.g., Isa. 14.1; 44.1-2; 49.7). The language of 'adoption' (υἱοθεσία, 1.5), 'redemption' (ἀπολύτρωσις, 1.7, 24), and 'inheritance' (κληρόω cf. κληρονομία, 1.11), all appear in the opening prayer of Eph. 1.3-14 and generally correspond to an Exodus-pattern, even if the precise terminology differs (for more detail on a similar pattern of language, see below on Col. 1.12-14). Additionally, Eph. 4.30 warns readers 'do not grieve the Holy Spirit of God' (μὴ λυπεῖτε τὸ πνεῦμα τὸ ἅγιον τοῦ θεοῦ), which may be an allusion to Isa. 63.10, a passage that recalls Israel's exodus and God's act of deliverance through the sea (cf. Isa. 53.11-14).⁵ As the following examples illustrate, a quotation and (possible) allusions to Exodus and/or later exodus traditions can be found in Ephesians. However, the author appears more concerned to draw upon Exodus for instruction than to map the symbolic world of his readers/listeners onto the book of Exodus itself.

a. Quotation of Psalm 68(67).19 (Exodus Tradition?) in Ephesians 4.8

It might seem odd to consider the quotation of Ps. 68(67).19 in Eph. 4.8 in a volume titled *Exodus in the New Testament*, but the well-known complications of the text require an examination of the possible relationship between this text and a later targumic tradition connected with Moses' giving of Torah on Mount Sinai—i.e., traditions directly associated with Exodus (19.3; 24.1-2; etc.).⁶

---

³ S. Moyise, 'Quotations', in Porter and Stanley (eds.), *As It Is Written*, pp. 15–28 (15).
⁴ Porter, 'Allusions and Echoes', p. 30.
⁵ As commentators often note, Eph. 4.30 is closer to the Hebrew, 'they grieved his Holy Spirit' (ועצבו את רוח קדשו), rather than the Greek, 'and they *provoked* his Holy Spirit' (καὶ παρώξυναν τὸ πνεῦμα τὸ ἅγιον αὐτοῦ), and the Göttingen edition of Exodus lists no variants here. On this passage, see A. T. Lincoln, *Ephesians* (WBC, 42; Dallas: Word, 1990), p. 306.
⁶ Another approach is taken by D. Starling, 'Ephesians and the Hermeneutics of the New Exodus', in R. M. Fox (ed.), *Reverberations of the Exodus in Scripture* (Eugene, OR: Pickwick, 2014), pp. 139–59 (152–54), who argues the psalm itself is replete with Exodus imagery and is interpreted typologically within a New Exodus framework. Yet, it is not clear why Exodus imagery in Ps. 68 should be interpreted as *New* Exodus imagery.

Thorsten Moritz acknowledged this very fact in his essay in *The Psalms and the New Testament* by stating that '[w]hen an Old Testament verse or fragment becomes so embedded in the exegetical tradition...that people become virtually unaware of the original text and co-text, any subsequent use of that fragment may well be a reflection of such later reflection, rather than the original text itself'.[7]

The possible relationship between Ephesians and Targum Psalms can be seen by comparing the texts. Following Stec's edition of Targum Psalms, the English translation of Tg. Ps. 68.19 uses *italics* 'to indicate what is additional in TgPss as compared with the MT, and to indicate what changes TgPss has made to the sense of MT'.[8] In this table (and those that follow) the first two columns use **bold** to express verbatim agreement, ***bold italics*** express near verbatim agreement, and underlining highlights the significant word(s) under discussion.

Ps. 67.19, LXX	*Eph. 4.8*	*Tg. Ps. 68.19*
ἀνέβης εἰς ὕψος, ᾐχμαλώτευσας αἰχμαλωσίαν, <u>ἔλαβες</u> **δόματα ἐν ἀνθρώπῳ,** καὶ γὰρ ἀπειθοῦντες τοῦ κατασκηνῶσαι. κύριος ὁ θεὸς εὐλογητός,	διὸ λέγει· ***ἀναβὰς εἰς ὕψος ᾐχμαλώτευσεν αἰχμαλωσίαν,*** <u>ἔδωκεν</u> **δόματα τοῖς ἀνθρώποις.**	סליקתא לרקיע משה נבייא שביתא שבייתא אלפתא פיתגמי אוריתא <u>יהבתא</u> להון מתנן לבני־נשא וברם סרבניא די מתגיירין תייבין בתתובא שרת עליהון שכינת יקרא דיהוה אלהים:
You ascended **on** ***high; you led captive captivity;*** <u>you received</u> **gifts** *by a person*, indeed, when they were disobedient to encamp. The Lord God be blessed;	Therefore it says, '***When he ascended*** **on high** ***he took captive captivity;*** <u>he gave</u> **gifts** *to humanity*'.	You ascended to the *firmament, O prophet Moses*, you took captives, *you taught the words of the Torah*, <u>you gave</u> them as gifts *to the sons of man*; even among the rebellious *who are converted and repent* does *the Shekinah of the glory of the* LORD *God dwell*.

The curious agreement of the verb 'give' has suggested to many that Eph. 4.8 has a closer relationship with Tg. Ps. 68.19 than it does with known Greek (or Hebrew)

---

[7] T. Moritz, 'The Psalms in Ephesians and Colossians', in S. Moyise and M. J. J. Menken (eds.), *The Psalms in the New Testament: The New Testament and the Scriptures of Israel* (London: T&T Clark, 2004), pp. 181–95 (181–82).
[8] D. M. Stec, *The Targum of Psalms: Translated, with a Critical Introduction, Apparatus, and Notes* (ArBib, 16; London: T&T Clark, 2004), p. 23.

versions of the Psalm.⁹ The majority of Ephesians scholars even posit a relationship between the two traditions.¹⁰ Representative is Ernest Best, who argues that 'to suppose two independent thinkers altered the verb in the Psalm in the same way at or about the same time and one replaced Yahweh with Christ and the other introduced Moses is hard to credit'.¹¹ Reflecting the majority interpretive opinion, Best posits that Eph. 4.8 and Targum Psalms have some sort of relationship—either direct or indirect—and this relationship flows in a particular direction with Ephesians dependent on a prior tradition that is also represented in the targum.¹² Craig Evans agrees, claiming that 'although at one time it was thought that the author of Ephesians intentionally misquoted Ps 68:19, we now recognize that he has followed an interpretive tradition akin to the Aramaic version'.¹³

This relationship with Ephesians comes with interpretive baggage. Indeed, it is freighted with meaning that gets imported into Ephesians. For example, Jean-Noël Aletti argues

> Il serait donc erroné de dire qu' Ep 4,8 christologise purement et simplement les affirmations théologiques du Psaume: l'intermédiare mosaïque, tel qu'il apparaît dans les traditions juives d'alors, ne doit être ni ignoré ni oublié.¹⁴

This connection with a 'Mosaic intermediary' allegedly appears in a polemical context where 'Christ is better than Moses' or 'grace is better than law'.¹⁵ In a significant study on the passage, Moritz states that 'the change of wording in Eph. 4.8 looks more like a parody on rabbinic appropriations of the Psalm than an authoritative quotation of Scripture'.¹⁶ Are these polemical connections

---

⁹ See S. M. Ehorn, 'The Use of Psalm 68(67).19 in Ephesians 4.8: A History of Research', *CBR* 12 (2013), pp. 96–120.

¹⁰ Here I side-step the issue of dating Targum Psalms. See B. Chilton, 'Greek Testament, Aramaic Targums, and Questions of Comparison', *AS* 11 (2013), pp. 225–51 (225), who rightly notes that '[t]wo unsupported assumptions have hampered comparison of the Targumim with the New Testament. One assumption presumes the Targumim are pre-Christian; the other presumes that they are too late to be of relevance to the exegesis of the New Testament.' Dating issues have led to an impasse in this discussion about Eph. 4.8.

¹¹ E. Best, *A Critical and Exegetical Commentary on Ephesians* (ICC; Edinburgh: T&T Clark, 1998), p. 381; cf. G. B. Caird, 'The Descent of Christ in Ephesians 4, 7–11', in F. L. Cross (ed.), *Studia Evangelica II. Papers Presented to the Second International Congress on New Testament Studies held at Christ Church Oxford, 1961* (Berlin: Akademie-Verlag, 1964), pp. 535–45 (541); W. H. Harris, III, *The Descent of Christ: Ephesians 4:7-11 and Traditional Hebrew Imagery* (AGJU, 32; Leiden: Brill, 1996);

¹² Only a few recent interpreters suggest Ephesians may have influenced Targum Psalms. See S. E. Fowl, *Ephesians: A Commentary* (NTL; Louisville: Westminster John Knox, 2012), p. 137; F. Thielman, *Ephesians* (BECNT; Grand Rapids: Baker, 2010), p. 267.

¹³ C. A. Evans, 'Praise and Prophecy in the Psalter and in the New Testament', in P. W. Flint and P. D. Miller, Jr. (eds.), *The Book of Psalms: Composition and Reception* (VTSup, 99; Leiden: Brill, 2005), pp. 551–79 (577).

¹⁴ J.-N. Aletti, SJ, *Saint Paul Épître aux Éphésiens: Introduction, traduction et commentaire* (ÉBib, 42; Paris: J. Gabalda, 2001), pp. 215–16; cf. T. Moritz, *A Profound Mystery: The Use of the Old Testament in Ephesians* (NovTSup, 85; Leiden: Brill, 1996), pp. 74–76.

¹⁵ See Moritz, *A Profound Mystery*, pp. 74–76; W. H. Harris, III, 'The Ascent and Descent of Christ in Ephesians 4:9–10', *BSac* 151 (1994), pp. 198–214 (212).

¹⁶ Moritz, *A Profound Mystery*, p. 72.

compelling readings that set Eph. 4.8 within its proper interpretive tradition or figments of scholarly imagination?

Now is not the place to unpack this question fully.[17] But, it is worth observing that Best (and many other Ephesians scholars) invoke an argument that sounds a lot like 'parallelomania'. Samuel Sandmel rightly criticized readings like this when he observed that 'two passages may sound the same in splendid isolation from their context, but when seen in context reflect difference rather than similarity'.[18] In the larger context of Targum Psalms there are numerous interpretive additions of the very same type that appear in Tg. Ps. 68.19, making it quite plausible that the targumist could produce independently a reading that is (superficially) similar to Eph. 4.8.

In further support of this point, the linguistic explanation commonly offered for the targum's connection with Eph. 4.8 is weak and, upon closer examination, highly implausible. The usual explanation is that Hebrew לקח ('to receive') was understood as חלק ('to give') by the targumist, perhaps due to metathesis, and then was rendered into Aramaic as יהב ('to give').[19] But in no other place does Targum Psalms render חלק with יהב. A better explanation begins with the verb in our known Hebrew textual tradition (לקח), which, curiously, has another possible translation equivalent in Tg. Ps. 68.19. The verb לקח is probably rendered in the targum by אלף, which has precedent as a translation equivalent elsewhere in Targum Psalms.

Ps. 68.19	Tg. Ps. 68.19
לקחת מתנות באדם	אלפתא פיתגמי אוריתא יהבתא להון מתנן לבני נשא
You received gifts from humanity.	You taught the words of Torah, you gave them as gifts to the sons of man.

The similarities in translation technique are illuminating when compared with Tg. Ps. 49.16:

Ps 49.16	Tg. Ps. 49.16
אך אלהים יפדה נפשי מיד שאול כי יקחני סלה	אמר דוד ברוח נבואה ברם אלהא יפרוק נפשי מן דין גהנם ארום ילפינני אוריתיה לעלמין
But God will ransom my soul from the power of Sheol, for he will receive me. Selah	David said through the spirit of prophecy, 'But God will redeem my soul from the judgment of Gehenna, for he will teach me his Torah'. For ever.

---

[17] For that, see S. M. Ehorn, 'The Citation of Psalm 68(67).19 in Ephesians 4.8 within the Context of Early Christian Uses of the Psalms' (Ph.D. diss., University of Edinburgh, 2015), ch. 5.
[18] S. Sandmel, 'Parallelomania', JBL 81 (1962), pp. 1–13 (2).
[19] E.g., H. St. J. Thackeray, The Relation of St. Paul to Contemporary Jewish Thought (London: Macmillan, 1900), pp. 181–82; R. N. Longenecker, Biblical Exegesis in the Apostolic Period (Grand Rapids: Eerdmans, 2nd edn, 1999), p. 108.

As in Tg. Ps. 49.16, the Hebrew verb לקח appears to be rendered by אלף in Tg. Ps. 68.19. There are additional words added following this, notably 'Torah', which is a characteristic addition throughout Targum Psalms, especially following verbs of 'learning' and 'teaching' (e.g., Tg. Pss. 1.2; 19.8; 51.17; 53.3; 81.11; 121.8; 127.2; 139.2-3; 144.12).[20] There is also an additional clause inserted within Tg. Ps. 68.19 that is, again, characteristic of Targum Psalms.[21] The importance of these data is that they undercut the common linguistic argument that connects Eph. 4.8 with a Mosaic ascent tradition in Tg. Ps. 68.19. The accompanying interpretive freight is also offloaded, allowing the quotation in Eph. 4.8 to be interpreted in other ways. That, however, is a matter for another publication.

b. Allusion to Exodus 29.18 in Ephesians 5.2

The UBS⁵ edition suggests that the phrase εἰς ὀσμὴν εὐωδίας (Eph. 5.2) is an allusion to Exod. 29.18.

Exod. 29.18	Eph. 5.2
καὶ ἀνοίσεις ὅλον τὸν κριὸν ἐπὶ τὸ θυσιαστήριον ὁλοκαύτωμα κυρίῳ **εἰς ὀσμὴν εὐωδίας· θυσίασμα κυρίῳ** ἐστίν.	καὶ περιπατεῖτε ἐν ἀγάπῃ, καθὼς καὶ ὁ Χριστὸς ἠγάπησεν ἡμᾶς καὶ παρέδωκεν ἑαυτὸν ὑπὲρ ἡμῶν προσφορὰν καὶ **θυσίαν τῷ θεῷ εἰς ὀσμὴν εὐωδίας**.
And you shall offer up the whole ram on the altar as a whole burnt offering to the Lord **for a fragrant aroma**. It is *a sacrifice for the Lord*.	That is, walk in love, as also Christ loved us and gave himself up for us, an offering and *sacrifice to God* **for a fragrant aroma**.

This exact collocation occurs three times in Exodus 29 (vv. 18, 25, 41), and may be further supported by the similar terminology in the immediate context. In the context of Exodus, the 'sacrifice' refers to the offering used to set apart priests for cultic service (Exod. 29.1). Given the presence of temple language and imagery in Ephesians (e.g., 2.19-22), this may suggest that Ephesians is drawing upon this Exodus terminology in connection with the consecration of God's people as priests. If this reading is correct, it would further underscore the complexity of the cultic atonement metaphors in the New Testament.[22]

Despite this possibility, other evidence from the LXX versions also suggests that εἰς ὀσμὴν εὐωδίας is too common to pin down to Exodus alone (e.g., LXX Lev. 2.12; 4.31; 8.21; 17.4, 6; Num. 15.7; etc.). In addition to Jewish Scripture, similar statements appear also in the literature from Qumran (e.g., 1QS 8.9; 11Q9

---

[20] On this point, see M. J. Bernstein, 'Torah and its Study in the Targum of Psalms', in Y. Elman and J. S. Gurock (eds.), *Ḥazon Naḥum: Studies in Jewish Law, Thought, and History Presented to Dr. Norman Lamm on the Occasion of his Seventieth Birthday* (Noboken, NJ: Yeshiva University Press, 1997), pp. 39–67.

[21] For more of the data, see Ehorn, 'Ephesians 4.8'.

[22] For more on the metaphors, see S. Finlan, *The Background and Content of Paul's Cultic Atonement Metaphors* (Atlanta: Society of Biblical Literature, 2004).

13.12).²³ Richard Hays' criterion of *volume*, which includes 'how distinctive or prominent is the precursor text within Scripture', should be applied here.²⁴ At best, we can claim that the language of Christ as a 'sacrifice to God for a fragrant aroma' (Eph. 5.2) draws upon a rich tradition of scriptural language used to speak of Israel's cultic practices.²⁵

c. Quotation of Exodus 20.12 in Ephesians 6.2-3

The *Haustafel* or 'household code' in Ephesians develops a common literary *topos* in Greco-Roman literature that was already adopted within Hellenistic Judaism.²⁶ Additionally, although largely adopted from Colossians, it includes several expansions when compared with its source.²⁷ For example, it is noteworthy that this section of the household code is expanded both christologically and with a quotation from the Decalogue. Both of these expansions appear in the comments directed toward children:²⁸

Col. 3.20	Eph. 6.1
Τὰ τέκνα, ὑπακούετε τοῖς γονεῦσιν κατὰ πάντα, τοῦτο γὰρ εὐάρεστόν ἐστιν ἐν κυρίῳ.	Τὰ τέκνα, ὑπακούετε τοῖς γονεῦσιν ὑμῶν ἐν κυρίῳ· τοῦτο γάρ ἐστιν δίκαιον. τίμα τὸν πατέρα σου...
Children, obey your parents in all things, for this is pleasing in the Lord.	Children, obey your parents in the Lord, for this is right. Honor your father...

While maintaining the substance of its Colossian source, the text of Ephesians relocates the christological expansion (ἐν κυρίῳ) into the main clause and replaces εὐάρεστον ('pleasing') with δίκαιον ('right'). As Moritz rightly notes, the latter change in Ephesians contributes to the 'stress on ethical continuity with the Jewish mother religion'.²⁹ This is precisely the place where the author introduces a quotation from Jewish Scripture.

Although Eph. 6.2-3 does not include an introductory formula, it is clear that the words are a citation of Jewish Scripture offered in support of the instruction

---

²³ See H. W. Hoehner, *Ephesians: An Exegetical Commentary* (Grand Rapids: Baker, 2002), pp. 650–51.
²⁴ R. B. Hays, *Echoes of Scripture in the Letters of Paul* (New Haven, CT: Yale University Press, 1989), p. 30. Cf. R. E. Ciampa, 'Scriptural Language and Ideas', in Porter and Stanley (eds.), *As It Is Written*, pp. 41–58 (48).
²⁵ Thielman, *Ephesians*, p. 322, rightly notes that '[t]he curious phrase "for a fragrant aroma" was an OT idiom for God's acceptance of a sacrifice because of the sincerity and wholeheartedness of the worshiper'.
²⁶ G. Sellin, *Der Brief an die Epheser* (KEK, 8; Göttingen: Vandenhoeck & Ruprecht, 2008), pp. 424–33.
²⁷ See M. Gese, *Das Vermächtnis des Apostels: die Rezeption der paulinischen Theologie im Epheserbrief* (WUNT, 2/99; Tübingen: Mohr Siebeck, 1997), pp. 39–53.
²⁸ The text-critical issue of the inclusion of ἐν κυρίῳ in Eph. 6.1 is relevant to this discussion, but the manuscript evidence for its inclusion and the scribal tendencies (e.g., harmonization toward Colossians) suggest that the printed text in NA²⁸ is correct.
²⁹ Moritz, *A Profound Mystery*, p. 176.

that children should obey their parents. The verbs in the citation are singular, creating a break in the syntactical flow from Eph. 6.1, which uses a plural subject (τὰ τέκνα) and a plural verb (ὑπακούετε). Although interpreters generally agree that this is a quotation, some dispute the *Vorlage* of Eph. 6.2-3, positing either Exod. 20.12, Deut. 5.16, or a conflation of the two.[30]

Exod. 20.12, LXX	Eph. 6.2-3	Deut. 5.16, LXX
τίμα τὸν πατέρα σου καὶ τὴν μητέρα,	τίμα τὸν πατέρα σου καὶ τὴν μητέρα, ἥτις ἐστὶν ἐντολὴ πρώτη ἐν ἐπαγγελίᾳ,	τίμα τὸν πατέρα σου καὶ τὴν μητέρα σου, ὃν τρόπον ἐνετείλατό σοι κύριος ὁ θεός σου,
ἵνα εὖ σοι γένηται, καὶ ἵνα μακροχρόνιος γένῃ ἐπὶ τῆς γῆς τῆς ἀγαθῆς, ἧς κύριος ὁ θεός σου δίδωσίν σοι.	³ ἵνα εὖ σοι γένηται καὶ ἔσῃ μακροχρόνιος ἐπὶ τῆς γῆς.	ἵνα εὖ σοι γένηται, καὶ ἵνα μακροχρόνιος γένῃ ἐπὶ τῆς γῆς, ἧς κύριος ὁ θεός σου δίδωσίν σοι.
Honor your father and mother,	**Honor your father and mother**, which is the first command with a promise,	**Honor your father** and **your mother,** as the Lord your God commanded you,
that it may go well with you, **and** that you may be **long-lived on the** good **land** that the Lord your God is giving to you.	³ **that it may go well with you and** you might be **long-lived on the earth.**	**that it may go well with you and** that you may **be long-lived on the land** that the Lord your God is giving to you.

Some observe that the phrase ἵνα εὖ σοι γένηται ('that it may go well with you') in Eph. 6.3 is represented in Deut. 5.16 MT (and 22.7) but not in Exod. 20.12 MT. But, as seen in the table above, this ignores the fact that the phrase occurs in both Exod. 20.12 and Deut. 5.16 in the LXX versions. When this is taken into account, it becomes clear that Eph. 6.2-3 is closer to LXX Exodus than to Deuteronomy. If Deut. 5.16 LXX was the *Vorlage*, further omissions would need to be posited, including the pronoun σου following μητέρα and the entire clause ὃν τρόπον ἐνετείλατό σοι κύριος ὁ θεός σου. Accordingly, it is more likely that Exod. 20.12 LXX is the source of the quotation in Eph. 6.2-3.

---

[30] For a helpful summary of all the textual differences in the command to honor one's parents, see C. Dohmen, *Exodus 19–40* (HThKAT, 5; Freiburg: Herber, 2nd edn, 2012), pp. 99–100.

Regarding the use of ἔση (Eph. 6.3) rather than ἵνα ... γένῃ (Exod. 20.12), several late LXX versions (e.g., 53' [= 53 + 664] 73 646) agree with the unified tradition in Ephesians.[31] The omission of ἵνα in Eph. 6.3 eliminates an unnecessary word because the prior ἵνα may be considered joined by the connective καί (cf. Eph. 6.22). Furthermore, the alternate verb may have been changed for stylistic reasons because the advancing of the verb prior to μακροχρόνιος would have resulted in clumsy Greek: γένηται καὶ γένῃ μακροχρόνιος ἐπὶ τῆς γῆς. Verbal variation seems a plausible explanation for the form of εἰμί. However, because there is no aorist subjunctive form of the verb, it occurs in the future indicative.

Following the command that children obey their parents in Eph. 6.2, the author interjects an interpretive comment that refers to the 'first commandment' (ἐντολὴ πρώτη), which simultaneously serves to point readers back to the Decalogue and introduces an interpretive problem. The two points are related because the quoted words create a tension in their original context. In Exod. 20.4-6, Israel's God promises to 'repay the sins' (ἀποδιδοὺς ἁμαρτίας) and 'do mercy ... to those who love me and keep my ordinances' (ποιῶν ἔλεος ... τοῖς ἀγαπῶσίν με καὶ τοῖς φυλάσσουσιν τὰ προστάγματά μου). How can Exod. 20.12—the fifth commandment—be called the 'first commandment' (ἐντολὴ πρώτη) given with a promise? Dating back to at least the time of Origen (d. 253 CE), interpreters have observed that there is a promise associated with the second commandment (Exod. 20.4-6). Various solutions to this problem have been advanced.[32] Some resolve the tension by interpreting πρώτη with the sense of 'prominence', not unlike the meaning of the word in Mk 12.29.[33] The most compelling explanation is that the commandment to honor one's father and mother is the first to have a specific promise associated with it.[34] Earlier promises in Exod. 20.4-6 are linked causally (γάρ / כִּי) to the preceding commandments, but they serve to explain further God's judgment and are not linked to a specific text. Thus, in Eph. 6.2, the author demonstrates close familiarity with the text and logic of the Decalogue by noting that Exod. 20.12 is the first commandment associated with a specific promise.

Yet, while familiar with the larger contours of the Decalogue, the author also departs from the logic of the commandment in two specific ways. First, in its original context, the command to honor one's parents is best understood as addressing not young children but adults. This understanding of the fifth commandment is supported by early Jewish and later rabbinic interpretive

---

[31] Several manuscripts replace ἵνα...γένῃ with ἵνα...ἔση (e.g., 15 C' 392).
[32] For a survey of five possible views, see Hoehner, *Ephesians*, pp. 790–91; Lincoln, *Ephesians*, p. 404.
[33] W. J. Larkin, *Ephesians* (BHGNT; Waco, TX: Baylor University Press, 2009), p. 146, objects that this 'view attempts to avoid the difficulty of seeing the fifth commandment as the first to contain a promise when the second commandment appears to have one'. But, given that πρῶτος can be used to mean 'first in dignity *or* importance' in certain constructions (cf. *GE*, 1849.C), this criticism is overstated.
[34] Cf. B. Witherington III, *The Letters to Philemon, the Colossians, and the Ephesians: A Socio-Rhetorical Commentary on the Captivity Epistles* (Grand Rapids: Eerdmans, 2007), p. 336; Hoehner, *Ephesians*, pp. 790–91.

traditions.[35] Nevertheless, in the context of Ephesians, it is quite clear that young(er) children are being addressed: 'fathers...*bring up* [your children] in the discipline and instruction of the Lord' (Eph. 6.4).[36] The verb ἐκτρέφω often denotes raising a child or bringing a child up in a certain way of life (3 Kgdms 11.20; 4 Kgdms 10.6; Hos. 9.12; 1 Macc. 6.17; 2 Macc. 7.27). The shift to young(er) children is also suggested by the *Haustafel* context in Ephesians. Thus, the command to honor one's parents has been adapted or, better, redeployed to address the needs of the church(es) and, in particular, the order of the household.

Second, the final part of the quotation is also different from the text of the commandment in Exodus. Rather than the full phrase 'upon the good land that the Lord your God is giving to you (ἐπὶ τῆς γῆς τῆς ἀγαθῆς ἧς κύριος ὁ θεός σου δίδωσίν σοι', Exod. 20.12), Ephesians has the much shorter ἐπὶ τῆς γῆς ('upon the land/ earth'), which is often understood in a general sense rather than as a reference to inheriting the land.[37] As found in the Decalogue, the promise of life in the land is best understood not as personal blessing. Rather,

> [t]he appeal to the promise of the land here, through its qualification that the land is given by God, enlarges the vision beyond that of individual and his family in the sense that Israel as God's people is being addressed. In doing so, the commandment is firmly linked back to the beginning of the Decalogue with its statement about the fundamental relationship between YHWH and Israel.[38]

The fifth commandment is not alone in promising a long life and linking this, in some way, to obedience or wise living (cf. Deut. 22.7; 1 Kgdms 29.28; Ps. 91.16). This dynamic receives extended attention in Sir. 3.1-16, which begins 'listen to me, your father, children, and do thusly in order that you might be kept safe' (Ἐμοῦ τοῦ πατρὸς ἀκούσατε, τέκνα, καὶ οὕτως ποιήσατε, ἵνα σωθῆτε, 3.1).

Turning back to Ephesians, some suggest that living a long life 'upon the land/ earth' is incompatible with the (undisputed) Pauline letters because Paul expected that the world as he knew it was coming to an end.[39] From this perspective, reference to a long life reflects non-Pauline eschatology. But there are other ways to understand the text. One of Philo's quotations of Exod. 20.12 omits any reference to life 'in the land' and, instead, emphasizes a long life:

---

[35] On this point, see the discussion in S. Safrai and M. Stern, *Compendia Rerum Iudaicarum ad Novum Testamentum: The Jewish People in the First Century II* (Leiden: Brill, 1976), p. 771; C. Dohmen, 'Decalogue', in T. B. Dozeman, C. A. Evans, and J. N. Lohr (eds.), *The Book of Exodus: Composition, Reception, and Interpretation* (VTSup, 164; Leiden: Brill, 2014), pp. 193–219 (199).

[36] See Moritz, *A Profound Mystery*, p. 169.

[37] See Moritz, *A Profound Mystery*, p. 174.

[38] Dohmen, 'Decalgoue', p. 199.

[39] On this point, see Lincoln, *Ephesians*, p. 406; J. D. G. Dunn, *Theology of the Apostle Paul*, p. 313; also see E. P. Sanders, 'Did Paul's Theology Develop?', in J. R. Wagner, C. K. Rowe, and A. K. Grieb (eds.), *The Word Leaps the Gap: Essays on Scripture and Theology in Honor of Richard B. Hays* (Grand Rapids: Eerdmans, 2008), pp. 325–50 (338–41).

παρηγόρησεν εἰπών· τίμα πατέρα καὶ μητέρα, ἵνα εὖ σοι γένηται καὶ ἵνα μακροχρόνιος γένῃ.

He gave encouragement saying, 'Honour your father and mother, that it may be well with you and that your time may be long'. (*Spec. Leg.* 2.261)

Philo's quotation certainly takes the prize for clarity if, as some suggest, Eph. 6.2 is also speaking only about living a long life rather than a long life 'in the [particular] land'. In context, Philo makes it clear that 'long life' (μακροχρόνιος) refers to immortality (*Spec. Leg.* 2.262). But the context of Ephesians provides no such clarification and, notably, retains the reference to 'the land/earth' (τῆς γῆς) from Exodus. For Philo, this forms part of a larger pattern of his quotations from the Decalogue. For example, in a quotation of another commandment, Philo again shortens the text:

οὐκ ἐπιθυμήσεις.

You shall not desire. (*Spec. Leg.* 4.78; cf. *Dec.* 142-143, 173)

This abbreviated text, not attested in any known manuscripts of LXX Exodus, generalizes the meaning of the tenth commandment: 'You shall not desire *your neighbor's wife*' (Exod. 20.17). Here, as in Exod. 20.12 above, the omission of part of the text in Philo's quotation is not incidental. Rather, it forms the basis for Philo's subsequent discussion of the problem with 'desire' (ἐπιθυμία) in *De specialibus legibus*, which should probably be understood as a representative summary of Torah (cf. Rom. 7.7).[40] That is, he examines the root problem of ἐπιθυμία rather than a particular expression of it.

Philo's tendency to generalize these texts may be helpful for reading Ephesians, but it does not prove that the author of Ephesians reads these texts in the same way. What we can say is that the author of Ephesians is in good company finding ongoing significance in the Decalogue and, in particular, in the fifth commandment. Like at least one of his Jewish contemporaries, the author does not find the particularity of 'the land *that God gave to you*' useful when addressing his audience(s). The quotation in Eph. 6.1-2 is shortened because the fuller text does not serve his needs in a context where household relationships are under discussion. Without the adjectival modifier and additional relative clause, Ephesians applies the quotation more generally, expressing the desire that those who obey the command 'may live a long life upon the earth [ἔσῃ μακροχρόνιος ἐπὶ τῆς γῆς]' (Eph. 6.3) rather than the more specific reference to the promised land in Exod. 20.12.[41]

---

[40] See H. Svebakken, *Philo of Alexandria's Exposition of the Tenth Commandment* (SPhiloM, 6; Atlanta: Society of Biblical Literature, 2012).

[41] Space does not permit a discussion of Mk 10.17-22 (and parallels), where a man approached Jesus and asked, 'what must I do to inherit eternal life?' (τί ποιήσω ἵνα ζωὴν αἰώνιον κληρονομήσω, Mk 10.17). Jesus' response quotes the sixth, seventh, eighth, ninth, and fifth commandments, respectively.

Before turning to another use of Exodus in the disputed Pauline letters, this quotation provides some opportunity for reflection on intertextual methodology. A few interpreters argue that an 'exodus framework' should be understood in Eph. 6.2-3.[42] According to this way of thinking, even when an author omits wording from a quotation, that omitted content should be understood (i.e., filled in) by the reader/hearer and used by the interpreter. David Starling makes this argument explicitly in reference to Eph. 6.2:

> [T]here is no need for the promise about 'life in the land' to be turned into a promise about 'life on the earth'; 'the land' is still 'the land', but the readers are expected to know that the promise being quoted is a word addressed to Israel at Mt. Sinai and the corresponding promise for them—as the new exodus community—is a promise about life in the eschatological kingdom in which they have obtained an inheritance through Christ.[43]

If the author of Ephesians had wanted readers to make interpretive associations (implicatures), he could accomplish this by making sure he left linguistic signs (explicatures) to ensure that readers bridged the gap correctly. This is all the more important when there are *omissions* in a biblical quotation. In his work on citation techniques, Christopher Stanley observes that

> the most common motive for adapting the wording of a quotation is to ensure that it communicates the precise point that the later author wanted to make in adducing the text. Every adaptive technique encountered thus far is pressed into service at one time or another to help draw out the 'correct' meaning of a given quotation. Omissions remove materials that might cause problems for a later interpretation or that otherwise fail to advance the author's argument.[44]

In light of Stanley's conclusions about citation techniques, Starling's hermeneutical approach to Eph. 6.2 must be rejected. The omission of wording from the Exodus quotation helps to clarify the meaning of the text in its new rhetorical setting and, significantly, there is additional evidence that other Jewish and early Christian authors made a similar interpretive move with this and other commandments from the Decalogue (cf. Rom. 7.7).[45]

---

[42] This methodology follows the suggestion by N. T. Wright, articulated, for example, in *Paul: In Fresh Perspective* (Minneapolis: Fortress, 2009), p. 8: 'Jewish literature from the Bible to the present day is soaked in certain controlling stories, such as those of Abraham, of the Exodus, and of exile and return, so that a small allusion to one of these within a Jewish source is usually a safe indication that we should understand the whole narrative to be at least hovering in the background'.

[43] Starling, 'Hermeneutics', p. 158; cf. H. Schlier, *Der Brief an die Epheser* (Düsseldorf: Patmos-Verlag, 1957), p. 282, who spiritualizes the meaning of 'long life'.

[44] C. D. Stanley, *Paul and the Language of Scripture: Citation Technique in the Pauline Epistles and Contemporary Literature* (SNTSMS, 74; Cambridge: Cambridge University Press, 1992), p. 347.

[45] On the potential problem(s) of filling in the gap of altered quotations, see S. A. Adams and S. M. Ehorn, 'Composite Citations: A Conclusion', in S. A. Adams and S. M. Ehorn (eds.), *Composite Citations in Antiquity*. Vol. 2, *New Testament Uses* (LNTS, 593; London: Bloomsbury T&T Clark, 2018), pp. 209–49 (232–33).

2. *Colossians: Exodus Motif in Colossians 1.12-14*

It is widely acknowledged that there are no quotations from Jewish Scripture in Colossians.[46] However, in the wake of Richard Hays' *Echoes of Scripture in the Letters of Paul*,[47] several scholars have explored possible echoes and allusions within the letter drawing from (and, at times, building upon) Hays' methodology.[48] This section will explore a possible exodus motif in Col. 1.12-14.[49]

At the end of the thanksgiving section of the letter, the author of Colossians includes a prayer report (1.9-14) that is packed with scriptural echoes that push the attentive reader back to the Jewish Scriptures. Reference to the 'image' (εἰκών) and 'firstborn of all creation' (πρωτότοκος πάσης κτίσεως) in 1.15 would likely evoke the book of Genesis. And, for present purposes, a cluster of language in 1.12-14 may constitute an allusion to an 'exodus motif'.[50] It is hard to disagree with the broad thematic correspondences produced, for example, by Beetham. Here I summarize some of Beetham's argument in chart form.[51]

Exodus Motif	*Colossians*
Israelites delivered from Egypt	Believers *delivered* (ἐρρύσατο) from the domain of darkness (1.13)
God brought Israelites to a new land	God transferred believers into the kingdom of his Son (1.13)
God redeemed Israel from slavery	God secured *redemption* (ἀπολύτρωσιν) of believers (1.14)
God gave the Israelites an inheritance	God allotted believers the *inheritance* (τὴν μερίδα τοῦ κλήρου) of light (1.12)

---

[46] E.g., G. K. Beale, 'Colossians', in G. K. Beale and D. A. Carson (eds.), *Commentary on the New Testament Use of the Old Testament* (Grand Rapids: Baker, 2007), pp. 841–70 (841).
[47] Hays, *Echoes of Scripture in the Letters of Paul*.
[48] G. D. Fee, 'Old Testament Intertextuality in Colossians: Reflections on Pauline Christology and Gentile Inclusion in God's Story', in S.-W. Son (ed.), *History and Exegesis: New Testament Essays in Honor of E. Earle Ellis for his 80th Birthday* (London: T&T Clark, 2006), pp. 201–22; Beale, 'Colossians'; C. A. Beetham, *Echoes of Scripture in the Letter of Paul to the Colossians* (BIS, 96; Leiden: Brill, 2008).
[49] For purposes of conciseness, the scriptural background of Col. 1.9-10 is not discussed in this section. Although Beale ('Commentary', pp. 846–48) argues that Exod. 31.3 and 35.31-32 are strong contenders for the background, Beetham (*Echoes of Scripture*, pp. 61–79) argues that Isa. 11 is a better candidate.
[50] In addition to Fee, Beale, and Beetham, see G. E. Cannon, *The Use of Traditional Materials in Colossians* (Macon, GA: Mercer University Press, 1983), pp. 17–19.
[51] Beetham, *Echoes of Scripture*, pp. 81–95. Other commentators also discuss this motif: e.g., E. Lohmeyer, *Die Brief an die Philipper, und die Kolosser und an Philemon* (KEK, 9; Göttingen: Vandenhoeck & Ruprecht, 1930), p. 39; R. Hoppe, *Epheserbrief, Kolosserbrief* (SKKNT, 10; Stuttgart: Katholisches Bibelwerk, 1987), p. 111; J. D. G. Dunn, *The Epistles to the Colossians and Philemon* (NIGTC; Grand Rapids: Eerdmans, 1996), pp. 75–77.

In addition to the thematic parallels, some of the language of Colossians is reminiscent of Exod. 6.6-8, which is a summary of words that Moses must speak to the enslaved Israelites:

> Say therefore to the Israelites, 'I am the LORD, and I will free you from the burdens of the Egyptians and *deliver* [ῥύομαι] you from slavery to them. I will *redeem* [λυτρόω] you with an outstretched arm and with mighty acts of judgment. ⁷ I will take you as my people, and I will be your God. You shall know that I am the LORD your God, who has freed you from the burdens of the Egyptians. ⁸ I will bring you into the land that I swore to give to Abraham, Isaac, and Jacob; I will give it to you for a *possession* [κλῆρος]. I am the LORD.'

These correspondences are interesting and suggestive. Indeed, the narrative pattern of the motif and some of the specific terminology help to establish the connection between Exodus and Colossians. Nevertheless, it is hard to assess to what extent the similarities represent reflection on Exodus alone. Beetham goes on to suggest that the author 'probably is echoing not only the ancient exodus, but *that initial event and its subsequent interpretive tradition*'.⁵² The linguistic data bear this out. The verb ῥύομαι (cf. Col. 1.13) is used to refer to the exodus only four times (out of over 200 uses) in the LXX (Exod. 5.23; 6.6; 14.30; Ps. 22.4).⁵³ The language of 'inheritance' (εἰς τὴν μερίδα τοῦ κλήρου) recalls the promise to Abraham (Gen. 13.14-17) and its subsequent renewal (e.g., Num. 26.52-56; Josh. 19.19) and, yet, in the context of Colossians its meaning is transformed. Whereas the 'inheritance' in Jewish Scripture referred to the land of promise, in Colossians the inheritance is understood 'in the [realm of] light' (ἐν τῷ φωτί, 1.12).⁵⁴ In the context of Colossians 1, ἐν τῷ φωτί parallels 'the kingdom of the Son' (εἰς τὴν βασιλείαν τοῦ υἱοῦ, 1.13), which suggests that the inheritance that believers attain is directly linked with the Son's kingdom and inheritance.

Judging by the density of 'redemption' language employed in the LXX, it might be wise also to link this language in Colossians more closely with exilic redemption rather than Exodus proper. Nevertheless, because the Exodus itself plays a paradigmatic role in Israel's story, it is possible that Colossians links the major redemptive events from Israel's Scripture in broad strokes.⁵⁵

Given the significance of the exodus event, it is not surprising that later readers understood their own struggles and triumphs through the lens of Exodus. This includes not merely the linguistic resources that authors could appropriate

---

[52] Beetham, *Echoes of Scripture in Colossians*, p. 94 (emphasis original).
[53] On this point, see D. J. Moo, *The Letters to the Colossians and to Philemon* (PNTC; Grand Rapids: Eerdmans, 2008), p. 103 n. 94.
[54] Here the phrase ἐν τῷ φωτί ('in the light') is taken in contrast with σκότος ('darkness') in 1.13 and 'it denotes the environment of the inheritance' (F. F. Bruce, *The Epistles to the Colossians, to Philemon, and to the Ephesians* [NICNT; Grand Rapids: Eerdmans, 1984], p. 50).
[55] Following Moo, *Colossians*, p. 103.

into their own writings, but the typological or figural framework(s) that could help them articulate the patterns they observed in their own experiences. As the closing lines of the thanksgiving section demonstrate, remembering Israel's God as a rescuer and his Son as a redeemer help situate these two figures within a larger, scriptural storyline that spans back to Exodus.

3. The Pastoral Letters: Exodus Tradition (cf. Exodus 7.8-13) in 2 Timothy 3.8-9

The following discussion of the Pastoral Letters overlooks several places that may have broad correspondences with Exodus or an exodus motif, but which cannot be pinned down easily to a specific text or tradition. For example, the laying of hands on elders (2 Tim. 1.6) certainly resembles when Moses laid hands on Joshua (Num. 27.18-23), but this practice is also developed in subsequent Judaism as well.[56] Likewise, the doxology in 1 Tim. 6.16 has some similarities with Exod. 33.20, but it is difficult to isolate influence to Exodus alone and, thus, speak of its 'use' in 1 Tim. 6.16. The language of 'a special people' (λαὸν περιούσιον) in Tit. 2.14 appears also multiple times in Exodus (19.5; 23.22) and Deuteronomy (7.6; 14.2; 26.18) to describe God's obedient people. The author appears to appropriate this Israelite term and applies it to both Jewish and Gentile believers. We are left, then, with the fascinating reference to exodus tradition in 2 Tim. 3.8-9.

Second Timothy 3 begins by introducing an eschatological framework: 'in the last days difficult times will come' (ἐν ἐσχάταις ἡμέραις ἐνστήσονται καιροὶ χαλεποί, 3.1). After describing many vices of humankind in general (3.1-5) and exhorting readers/hearers to avoid certain people who ensnare women (3.6a), the author compares his own opponents to Jannes and Jambres:

> ὃν τρόπον δὲ Ἰάννης καὶ Ἰαμβρῆς ἀντέστησαν Μωϋσεῖ, οὕτως καὶ οὗτοι ἀνθίστανται τῇ ἀληθείᾳ, ἄνθρωποι κατεφθαρμένοι τὸν νοῦν, ἀδόκιμοι περὶ τὴν πίστιν. ⁹ ἀλλ' οὐ προκόψουσιν ἐπὶ πλεῖον· ἡ γὰρ ἄνοια αὐτῶν ἔκδηλος ἔσται πᾶσιν, ὡς καὶ ἡ ἐκείνων ἐγένετο.

> As Jannes and Jambres opposed Moses, so also these people oppose the truth—men of corrupt mind and counterfeit faith. ⁹ But they will not advance much, because their folly will be manifest to all, as also was the [folly] of them. (2 Tim. 3.8-9)

Mention of Jannes, Jambres, and Moses in 2 Tim. 3.8 clearly evokes the exodus story, particularly Exod. 7.8-13, where Moses and Aaron perform miracles at God's command. Specifically, God's servants throw their staffs down on the ground and turn them into serpents. According to Exod. 7.11-12, Pharaoh's magicians perform the same feat of prestidigitation. Both the Hebrew and Greek

---

[56] See the discussion in E. Lohse, 'χείρ', in *TDNT*, 9:424–34 (429).

texts of Exodus seem to imply more than two magicians—which is, possibly, confirmed by Philo's version of the story, which includes many magicians (*Vit. Mos.* 1.92). The performance ends abruptly when Aaron's staff swallows up the other staffs, yet, without achieving the desired goal: Pharaoh's heart remains hardened. Despite this context, it is interesting that in 2 Timothy, and in some other early sources, they are not referred to as magicians. Indeed, their identity and connection with the exodus narrative will need to be considered carefully and we will need to consider the rich extra-biblical history of the exodus story and their place within it.

The names 'Jannes and Jambres' are not included in Exodus itself, but are found in a number of other Jewish (CD-A 5.17-19; Tg. Ps.-J. Exod. 1.15; 7.11; Num. 22.22; *Exod. Rab.* 9.7; *b. Menaḥ* 85a; *Tanḥ., Ki Tisa* 19 on Exod. 32; *LAB* 47.1),[57] Christian (*Acts Pil.* 5.1; Origen, *Comm. Matt.* 23.37; 29.9; *Cels.* 4.51; Numenius cf. Eusebius, *Praep. Ev.* 9.8), and Greco-Roman writings (Pliny the Elder, *Nat.* 30.2.11; Apuleius, *Apol.* 90.6). This wide distribution of references suggests that the brothers—who are not always (both) named in the sources and whose names are sometimes spelled differently—were reasonably well known in antiquity. This likely explains why the author of 2 Timothy introduces Jannes and Jambres with very little explanation.

Having judged that Jannes and Jambres were probably known to the earliest readers of 2 Timothy, we must now ask: how are Jannes and Jambres used in the argument of 2 Tim. 3.8-9? Ben Witherington suggests that this story represents a *typological* reading strategy, which is 'based on an assumption about salvation history that earlier events are precursors and prefigurements of later events'.[58] He goes on to suggest the possibility that Timothy and, perhaps, Paul (the named sender and recipient of the Pastoral Letters) should be seen as (a) Moses figure(s) in opposition to the opponents. Conversely, the author may simply be evoking recognizable figures in order to make a point—namely, just as Jannes and Jambres opposed Moses, so also certain people oppose the truth now. This explanation is *analogical*. In this vein, Luke Timothy Johnson observes that the Egyptian magicians mimic Aaron's trick of turning the staff into a serpent (Exod. 7.12) as well as Moses' trick of turning the Nile's water into blood (Exod. 7.22). But, curiously, they do not reappear later in Exodus during other confrontations and wonder-working. Based on this Johnson suggests that '[p]erhaps this is one way in which they anticipate Paul's assurance concerning the current opponents: "They will not progress much further" (3:9)'.[59] While both readings are attractive, the explicit linguistic feature that begins 2 Tim. 3.8—ὃν τρόπον ('in the manner in which = [just] as')—makes better sense with the analogical reading.[60] However,

---

[57] M. McNamara, *Targum and Testament Revisited: Aramaic Paraphrase of the Hebrew Bible* (Grand Rapids: Eerdmans, 2nd edn, 2010), p. 236.

[58] B. Witherington, III, *Letters and Homilies for Hellenized Christians*. Vol. 1, *A Socio-Rhetorical Commentary on Titus, 1–2 Timothy, and 1–3 John* (Downers Grove, IL: InterVarsity, 2006), p. 354.

[59] L. T. Johnson, *The First and Second Letters to Timothy: A New Translation with Introduction and Commentary* (AB, 35A; New York: Doubleday, 2001), p. 408.

[60] BDAG, 1016.1, s.v., τρόπος.

it is interesting that the reception history of this story provides some basis for thinking that Jannes and Jambres were thought to be with the Israelites for a longer period of time (see just below).

Finally, given that Jannes and Jambres are compared with (some of) the opponents in 2 Timothy, it is likely that their description as 'corrupted in mind' (κατεφθαρμένοι τὸν νοῦν) should be read against the twin themes of 'knowledge' (e.g., γνῶσις, ἐπιγινώσκω) and 'ignorance' (e.g., ἄνοια, ἀνόητος, μωρός) in the Pastoral Letters, where the language of 'stupidity' is characteristically employed to refer to people who have left behind Christianity (e.g., 1 Tim. 1.6, 13; 4.3, 7; 6.4, 5; 2 Tim. 2.25; 3.8; Tit. 1.10; 3.3).[61] The implication of this is that Jannes and Jambres should be thought of *as insiders* (rather than outsiders) and now they are to be considered apostates.[62] This reading finds support in the *Damascus Document*, which states that 'Belial...raised up Jannes and his brother' (CD-A 5.18-19) after noting that 'Belial will be set loose *amidst Israel* [בישראל]' (CD-A 4.12-13).[63] Pliny's *Natural History*, which includes a reference to Jannes, might also support this: 'There is yet another branch of magic, derived from Moses, Jannes, Lotapes, and the Jews...' (*Nat. Hist.* 30.2.11).[64] In a footnote accompanying the LCL text of Pliny, the editor writes that 'Jannes was not a Hebrew but an Egyptian magician', but this is stated by the editor *precisely because* Pliny's text seems to imply the opposite. This idea takes an interesting turn in latter rabbinic literature, where Jannes and Jambres are described as Egyptians who escaped Egypt *with the Israelites* and they are blamed for the golden calf incident (*Tanḥ., Ki Tisa* 19 on Exod. 32). The late dating for the compiling of *Midrash Tanḥuma* (ca. 800 CE) does not permit any firm conclusions here, but it is interesting to see the similar pattern of Jannes of Jambres *alongside/with* Israel for a sustained period of time rather than a relatively isolated incident in Egypt.[65]

The complex web of associations with 'Jannes and Jambres' that is evoked in 2 Tim. 3.8-9 is sticky. While clearly referencing Moses and, presumably Exod. 7.8-13, the evocation also seems to presuppose a wider interpretive tradition that names Moses' opponents and, in all likelihood, places them alongside or with Israel for a period of time. Here it is not Scripture alone, but interpreted Scripture that informs the author's argument, his rebuke of the opponents, and the resulting encouragement for readers of 2 Timothy.

---

[61] So J. Tromp, 'Jannes and Jambres (2 Timothy 3,8-9)' in A. Graupner (ed.), *Moses in Biblical and Extra-Biblical Traditions* (BZAW, 372; Berlin: de Gruyter, 2007), pp. 211–26 (224–25).

[62] Tromp, 'Jannes and Jambres', p. 225.

[63] Here I depart from the translation by F. G. Martínez and E. J. C. Tigchelaar, *The Dead Sea Scrolls: Study Edition* (2 vols.; Leiden: Brill, 1999), p. 1:556, because the collocation of ב + שלח (in the *piel*) has the sense 'to let loose *into*' rather than 'to let loose *against*' (cf. *DCH* 8:383–84).

[64] See W. H. S. Jones, *Pliny, Natural History 28–32* (LCL, 418; Cambridge, MA: Harvard University Press, 1963).

[65] A. Pietersma, 'Yohanah and his brother', in L. H. Shiffmann and J. C. VanderKam (eds.), *Encyclopedia of the Dead Sea Scrolls*, vol. 2 (Oxford: Oxford University Press, 2000), pp. 1000–1001, also posits that they might be apostate Israelites.

4. Conclusion

Several themes that emerged in this study are worth drawing attention to and exploring further. First, it is commonly asserted that Ephesians (as well as the other disputed Pauline letters) generally relies more heavily upon Jewish or Christian liturgical traditions than Jewish Scripture. This seems to be true in some instances. For example, Eph. 5.14 is hymnic in nature and, perhaps, reflects a liturgical composition that had already combined Isa. 26.19 and 60.1-2.[66] Many scholars also conclude that the quotation in Eph. 4.8 is also derived from a traditional source rather than Scripture itself (although this was disputed above). However, the quotation of Exod. 20.12 in Eph. 6.2-3 provides evidence that the author knew the Decalogue intricately, describing the fifth commandment as 'the first commandment with a promise'. Here, as elsewhere, the author undergirds his ethical arguments by an appeal to Torah, drawing out its ongoing significance for Pauline churches. Likewise, in the Pastoral Letters the author claims that 'all Scripture is inspired by God and is useful for teaching, reproof, correction, and training in righteousness' (2 Tim. 3.16). Although the Pastoral Letters contain only limited explicit references to Scripture, the author's overt statement that *all* Scripture is useful coheres with this perspective in Ephesians. The author(s) demonstrate(s) great interest and, at times, deep familiarity with the texts and traditions that are cited.

Second, traditions related to exodus play a significant role in the interpretation of several passages in the disputed Pauline letters. For example, although the tradition was ultimately rejected in the discussion above, many scholars interpret Eph. 4.8 in light of a Mosaic ascent tradition (e.g., Tg. Ps. 68.19). Similarly, the mention of Jannes and Jambres in 2 Tim. 3.8-9 clearly reflects a growing tradition of reflection on these figures that builds from the book of Exodus itself. The fact that the author mentions them without any explanation also suggests that this tradition was known to the readers of 2 Timothy. This underscores that the ongoing reception of biblical traditions (and not just the 'original' texts) must be brought to bear on the question of the use of Scripture in the New Testament.

Finally, in contrast with the undisputed Pauline letters, Dibelius and Conzelmann claim that '[t]here is no typology of the wilderness generation in the Pastoral Epistles'.[67] If the *Hauptebriefe* (or Hebrews) are taken as the standard of a wilderness typology (e.g., 1 Cor. 10.1-11; 2 Cor. 3.7-13; Heb. 3.7–4.11), then this statement is almost certainly true. Nevertheless, the curious reference to Jannes and Jambres in 2 Tim. 3.8-9 certainly evokes the exodus timeline and the comparison with the opponents of 2 Timothy, if only for a fleeting moment, is certainly suggestive. In the context of Exod. 7.8-13 there can be no mention of the wilderness generation, of course. But, the other exodus traditions that speak

---

[66] Moritz, *A Profound Mystery*, pp. 97–116; A. T. Lincoln, 'The Use of the OT in Ephesians', *JSNT* 14 (1982), pp. 16–57 (18).

[67] M. Dibelius and H. Conzelmann, *The Pastoral Epistles: A Commentary on the Pastoral Epistles* (Hermeneia; Philadelphia: Fortress, 1972), p. 117.

explicitly of Jannes and Jambres sometimes place these two figures within the wider narrative of Exodus. In any event, the mention of the brothers in 2 Timothy coheres well with the Pauline statement that 'these things happened to [the Israelites] to serve as an example, and they were written to instruct us' (1 Cor. 10.11).

Chapter 8

EXODUS IN HEBREWS

David M. Moffitt

1. Introduction

The Epistle to the Hebrews arguably quotes explicitly from a Greek version of Exodus only two times. Hebrews 8.5 reproduces Exod. 25.40 LXX with minor variations, while Heb. 9.20 more loosely cites Exod. 24.8b LXX.[1] Additionally, however, Hebrews contains numerous echoes and allusions to stories, passages and motifs found in Exodus. To note only a few examples, Heb. 11.22 refers to the exodus; Heb. 11.23-28 summarizes and interprets Exod. 2.1-15 and Exodus 12; Heb. 11.29 recalls Exod. 14.21-31; and Heb. 12.18-19 draws on Exod. 19.12-13. The presence of this pentateuchal book at these and other points in Hebrews is well known, and the author's extended reflection on the generation of Israelites who left Egypt and were led into the wilderness naturally calls up the exodus. Not many, however, have focused sustained attention on the various roles the book of Exodus plays in the author's theological reasoning.[2] By way of

---

[1] I discuss these quotations in more detail in §2 below.
[2] Of course, commentators engage with the exodus tradition in Hebrews largely in terms of the wilderness wandering assumed to be so important for Hebrews. The short study of R. C. Oudersluys highlights the contrasts set up by the eschatological wilderness wandering and the author's call not to turn back as key ways that Hebrews uses the exodus narrative to subvert the cult of the Mosaic covenant ('Exodus in the Letter to the Hebrews', in J. I Cook [ed.], *Grace Upon Grace: Essays in Honor of Lester J. Kuyper* [Grand Rapids: Eerdmans, 1975], pp. 143–52). P. C. B. Andriessen explores some of the ways the opening chapters of Hebrews draw on the exodus themes especially of liberation ('La Teneur Judéo-Chrétienne de He 1 6 et II 14B-III 2', *NovT* 18 [1976], pp. 293–313). More recently, Gabriella Gelardini has explored the influence of Exodus (esp. chs. 32–33) in Hebrews (see several of her essays in *Deciphering the Worlds of Hebrews: Collected Essays*, NovTSup, 184 [Leiden: Brill, 2021]) B. C. Shin offers a biblical theology of certain new exodus themes in Hebrews (*New Exodus in Hebrews* [ANTS; London: Apostolos, 2016]). In my view Shin's work is hobbled somewhat by the argument that Hebrews conflates Passover and Yom Kippur, though several important themes linked with the exodus narrative are noted.

contrast, Deuteronomy has tended to receive more sustained attention in recent times.³

This brief study cannot fully address all the ways that Exodus is in play in Hebrews. I highlight instead some of the most important ways that the author of Hebrews draws upon the book of Exodus and the larger exodus tradition in his brief 'word of exhortation' (Heb. 13.22). I look first at the two clear citations of Exodus noted above, turning second to explore ways that Exodus and the exodus narrative inform larger themes in Hebrews. Rather than offer a granular account of all the possible echoes of and allusions to Exodus (though several of these will necessarily be mentioned), I unpack three specific ways that Exodus functions in the theological reasoning of this text.

First, Exodus provides narrative elements that help to structure the main contours of the author's argument, particularly in the first four chapters of Hebrews. The author's exodus-generation metaphor, which serves to shape the identity of the intended audience as those who have been freed from bondage and are now in the wilderness waiting to receive their inheritance, draws heavily from the narrative of the exodus.⁴ Second, Exodus provides material that influences the author's belief in the existence of significant heavenly realities, especially the heavenly tabernacle. As such, certain passages of the book serve as biblical evidence for the author's cosmological commitments. Exodus thereby offers the author biblical material that informs, albeit dialogically, his reflection on Jesus' death, inauguration of the new covenant, and ascension through the heavens into the heavenly tabernacle where he serves as high priest. Third, Exodus not only functions as a source from which the author draws, but also as a source that he feels some freedom to adapt for moral and theological illustration. This is evident at various points throughout Hebrews, but is especially clear in 11.23-29 and 12.18-24.

One caveat should be noted at the outset of this study. I do not intend to imply that an identification of a possible allusion to the exodus event or of the

---

³ The importance of Deuteronomy in Hebrews has been convincingly demonstrated by David M. Allen (see esp. his *Deuteronomy and Exhortation: A Study in Narrative Re-Presentation* [WUNT, 2/238; Tübingen: Mohr Siebeck, 2008]; and 'More than Just Numbers: Deuteronomic Influence in Hebrews 3:7–4:11', *TynBul* 58 [2007], pp. 129–49). More recently see M. H. Kibbe, *Godly Fear or Ungodly Failure? Hebrews 12 and the Sinai Theophanies* (BZNW, 216; Berlin: De Gruyter, 2016). Kibbe dedicates a section of his volume to the role of Exodus, though he does not see it playing as significant or positive a role as here argued (see esp. pp. 112–20). G. J. Steyn's essay, 'Deuteronomy in Hebrews', in S. Moyise and M. J. J. Menken (eds.), *Deuteronomy in the New Testament* (LNTS, 358; London: T&T Clark, 2007], pp. 152–68) discusses the citations of Deuteronomy in Hebrews, but also helpfully lays out some of the major motifs in Hebrews that have especially interesting points of contact with Deuteronomy.

⁴ I have explored aspects of this idea in a handful of other publications. See especially D. M. Moffitt, 'Wilderness Identity and Pentateuchal Narrative: Distinguishing between Jesus' Inauguration and Maintenance of the New Covenant in Hebrews', in K. M. Hockey, M. N. Pierce, and F. Watson (eds.), *Muted Voices of the New Testament: Readings in the Catholic Epistles and Hebrews* (LNTS, 565; London: Bloomsbury T&T Clark, 2017), pp. 153–71; and, Moffitt, 'Perseverance, Purity, and Identity: Exploring Hebrews' Eschatological Worldview, Ethics, and In-Group Bias', in J. Kok, T. Nicklas, D. T. Roth, and C. M. Hays (ed.), *Sensitivity to Outsiders: Exploring the Dynamic Relationship between Mission and Ethics in the New Testament and Early Christianity* (WUNT, 2/364; Tübingen: Mohr Siebeck, 2014), pp. 357–81.

use of language and themes that recall or come from the book of Exodus necessarily exclude allusions to or the influence of other biblical texts on the author. The author does not always bind himself to one source, even with respect to his depiction of the exodus and subsequent wilderness journey of those liberated from slavery. He can and does at points draw from and conflate different biblical accounts of these events.[5] He simply assumes the reality of the exodus and wilderness journey and conflates depictions of these events from throughout the Pentateuch, among other texts, when reflecting on them. Thus, the author does not always approach biblical texts atomistically, but can draw freely from them in a way that suggests an assumption of coherence and harmony among differing accounts.[6] God, as he says at the very beginning of his discourse and repeatedly illustrates throughout, speaks in Scripture. He takes these words as authoritative and revelatory. Moreover, not only do his interpretive moves at times betray his knowledge of extra-biblical traditions (e.g., he appears in Heb. 2.2 to know the tradition of angels giving the law), his exegesis of these texts can also take him well beyond the explicit details of any of the biblical passages that serve as his primary sources (e.g., Heb. 11.19, 27). The author's biblical and theological insights are complex and profound. I take this complexity as a given. I nevertheless seek here to unpack the peculiar influence of Exodus on the homily even though this narrow focus requires at times a certain reduction and simplification of the author's labrynthine engagement with Scripture.[7]

2. Hebrews' Explicit Quotations of Exodus

a. Hebrews 8.5b and Exodus 25.40 LXX

Assuming LXX Exodus is best represented by the critical text of the Göttingen *Septuaginta* volume,[8] the differences between Heb. 8.5 and Exod. 25.40 LXX are

---

[5] For example, his depiction of Moses and the people at the foot of Mount Sinai in Heb. 12.18-21 is a pastiche that freely draws from elements of the Sinai account in Exod. 19 (see the command to stone even animals who touch the mountain in Exod. 19.13 LXX) and the two Horeb accounts in Deut. 4 and 9 (see especially Moses' expression of fear in Deut. 9.19 LXX). For a more complete discussion of this kind of phenomenon in Hebrews, see S. E. Docherty, 'Composite Citations and Conflation of Scriptural Narratives in Hebrews', in S. A. Adams and S. M. Ehorn (eds.), *Composite Citations in Antiquity*. Vol. 2, *New Testament Uses* (LNTS, 593; London: Bloomsbury T&T Clark, 2018), pp. 190–208,

[6] Susan E. Docherty has ably demonstrated the wide variety of ways that the author, in keeping with the sophistication of late-Second Temple Jewish exegesis, can engage with Scripture (*The Use of the Old Testament in Hebrews: A Case Study in Early Jewish Bible Interpretation* [WUNT, 2/260; Tübingen: Mohr Siebeck, 2009]).

[7] The rich web of inner-biblical connections in Hebrews is one way in which the epistle is very much at home in late-Second Temple Jewish interpretation. The point is well illustrated by David Flusser who, in his brief study of Heb. 3–4 and Ps. 95 in the light of Jewish interpretive traditions, uncovers some of the 'mycelium' or 'network of exegetical tissues' present in both rabbinic reflection on Ps. 95 and Heb. 3–4 ('"Today if You will Listen to His Voice": Creative Jewish Exegesis in Hebrews 3–4', in B. Uffenheimer and H. G. Reventlow [eds.], *Creative Biblical Exegesis: Christian and Jewish Hermeneutics Through the Centuries* [JSOTSup, 59; Sheffield: JSOT, 1988], pp. 55–62, here 59).

[8] Steyn has recently demonstrated afresh the validity of this conclusion (G. J. Steyn, *A Quest for the Assumed LXX Vorlage of the Explicit Quotations in Hebrews* [FRLANT, 235; Göttingen:

minor. The differences are illustrated below by italicizing the variants in Hebrews relative to LXX.

Exod. 25.40, LXX	Heb. 8.5b
ὅρα ποιήσεις κατὰ τὸν τύπον τὸν δεδειγμένον σοι ἐν τῷ ὄρει	ὅρα...ποιήσεις *πάντα* κατὰ τὸν τύπον τὸν *δειχθέντα* σοι ἐν τῷ ὄρει[10]
See that you make [these things] according to the pattern that has been shown to you on the mountain[9]	See...that you make *everything* according to the pattern that *was* shown to you on the mountain

As this side-by-side comparison shows, the differences consist in the textual plus in Hebrews of the direct object πάντα after ποιήσεις and the occurrence in Hebrews of the aorist passive participle of δείκνυμι (δειχθέντα) instead of the perfect passive form of the verb (δεδειγμένον) attested in LXX.

The textual plus of πάντα in Hebrews probably represents the author's local manuscript/*Vorlage*. Evidence for this supposition comes from Philo (*Leg. All.* 3.102), who independently attests πάντα as the object of ποιήσεις in a citation of Exod. 25.40.[11] This suggests that manuscripts containing πάντα (or at least common interpretive traditions that took the word as a given) were in circulation.

Apart from Hebrews itself, support for δειχθέντα in the LXX-manuscript tradition is late.[12] These manuscripts likely reflect the influence of Hebrews on the transmission of LXX Exodus.[13] This does not by itself prove that that author's local manuscript read something other than δειχθέντα, but given the evidence available, it seems most likely that his *Vorlage* contained the perfect participle, which he then changed to the aorist.[14]

If this is correct, then one can reasonably inquire into the potential rationale for the alteration. The effect of the aorist is felt mainly in the contrast (δέ) that follows in Heb. 8.6 where the author uses a perfect tense verb (τετύχεν) with reference to Jesus' perpetual heavenly ministry. The interplay of δείκνυμι and τυγχάνω in this part of his discourse, in terms of the semantics of both the lexemes and their tense forms, correlates well with the presumed superiority of the current ministry of Jesus. Jesus has *now obtained* (νυνὶ δὲ...τετύχεν) a better ministry than that of Moses. Jesus, that is, is now in the state of having a ministry that is superior to

---

Vandenhoeck & Ruprecht, 2011], p. 241).
[9] All translations are my own.
[10] The phrase γάρ φησιν in Heb. 8.5 is the author's postpositive introduction to the citation and has therefore been replaced here with ellipses.
[11] See especially the detailed discussion in Steyn, *Quest*, esp. pp. 242–45. It should be noted that Philo's citation of the verse differs from that of Hebrews. On the point under discussion, Philo transposes the order of the verb and its direct object relative to Hebrews. His citation of the phrase in question reads: πάντα ποιήσεις. He also locates the phrase at the end of Exod. 25.40, not, as in LXX and Hebrews, at the beginning of the verse.
[12] O-767-15 f s 126-128 426 799. Though the verb is misspelled, MSS 130 and 376 also appear to support the aorist form.
[13] So J. W. Wevers, *Notes on the Greek Text of Exodus* (SCS, 30; Atlanta: Scholars Press, 1990), p. 410.
[14] Many interpreters draw this conclusion (see, e.g., Steyn, *Quest*, pp. 243, 245).

that of Moses not least because Moses was only shown (δειχθέντα) the heavenly tabernacle when he sojourned on the mountain, while Jesus has now entered that reality and obtained the ministry that gives him perpetual access to the Father (see esp. 8.1-4). Thus, the shift between the aorist tense form with reference to Moses to the perfect tense form with reference to Jesus aligns well with the author's larger argument that the τύπος shown to Moses belongs to the superior ministry that Jesus is now in the state of having obtained and is presently performing, partly by virtue of his entry into and perpetual intercession in the very structure that Moses only saw (see 4.14-16; 7.25; 8.1-2; 9.1-11, 24-26).

b. Hebrews 9.20 and Exodus 24.8b LXX

The relationship between Heb. 9.20 and Exod. 24.8b LXX proves less clear than that of Heb. 8.5b and Exod. 25.40 LXX. The relevant sections of the two texts are again compared below with *italics* highlighting the points where Hebrews diverges from LXX.

Exod. 24.8b, LXX	Heb. 9.20
Ἰδοὺ τὸ αἷμα τῆς διαθήκης ἧς διέθετο κύριος πρὸς ὑμᾶς	τοῦτο τὸ αἷμα τῆς διαθήκης ἧς ἐνετείλατο πρὸς ὑμᾶς ὁ θεός
Behold, the blood of the covenant that the Lord made with you	This is the blood of the covenant that God enjoined on you

This comparison shows the degree of difference between LXX and Hebrews, which is greater than was evident in Heb. 8.5. To summarize: Hebrews (1) reads τοῦτο where LXX reads ἰδού, (2) uses a different finite verb in the relative clause (ἐντέλλομαι rather than διατίθημι), and (3) both transposes the location of the subject of the relative clause in relation to the prepositional phrase and uses a different lexeme with reference to God (ὁ θεός rather than the anarthrous κύριος in LXX).[15]

Commentators puzzle over these differences and offer a variety of solutions. Many think that the author intentionally changes ἰδού to τοῦτο in order to allude to Jesus' words at the institution of the eucharist.[16] Some argue that Hebrews alters διέθετο to ἐνετείλατο due to a desire to stress that the Mosaic covenant was

---

[15] Steyn argues that the number of variations between Heb. 9.20 and Exod. 24.8 LXX suggest that Hebrews does not technically qualify as a citation of the verse but rather counts more loosely as a reference to it (*Quest*, pp. 178–82).

[16] K. J. Thomas suggests that τοῦτο 'appears to be a deliberate change to echo the words of Jesus at the Last Supper' ('The Old Testament Citations in Hebrews', *NTS* 11 [1965], pp. 303–25, here 313). See also P. Ellingworth, *The Epistle to the Hebrews: A Commentary on the Greek Text* (NIGTC; Grand Rapids: Eerdmans, 1993), p. 469, who points to several older commentators that take the same view. Among more recent commentaries, see K. Backhaus, *Der Hebräerbrief* (RNT; Regensburg: Friedrich Pustet, 2009), pp. 231–32; J. W. Kleinig, *Hebrews* (ConcC; St. Louis: Concordia, 2017), p. 443; J. Massonet, *L'épître aux Hébreux* (Commentaire Biblique: Nouveau Testament, 15; Paris: Cerf, 2016), p. 248. So also Steyn, *Quest*, pp. 274–75.

one of commands or laws in contrast with the new covenant.¹⁷ Harold Attridge suggests that the author may have changed the verb to reserve διατίθημι for the new covenant.¹⁸ The use of θεός instead of κύριος is assumed by many to be an intentional change in order to distinguish the Father, often identified in Hebrews as θεός, from Jesus, several times called κύριος.¹⁹

It is clear that Hebrews works freely with the larger narrative of Exodus 24 in this section of the homily.²⁰ This does not, however, necessarily imply that the author has only loosely cited Exod. 24.8b, changing elements to fit his theological presuppositions. Steyn nevertheless favors the view that the number of changes in Heb. 9.20 relative to LXX points to this being a paraphrase of the verse from the author's memory rather than a proper citation.²¹

Yet, the author introduces Exod. 24.8b with the participle λέγων. It may be significant that he uses this participle elsewhere to put citations of Scripture into the mouths of various speakers (see 2.6, 12; 12.26; cf. 4.7).²² A few pieces of evidence may also indicate that alternate versions of this verse were circulating. There is some evidence from Philo to suggest that he knew a version of Exod. 24.8b that contained ἐντέλλομαι instead of διατίθημι (see *Quaest. in Exod.* 2.36, though the original Greek is lacking). Septuagint manuscripts in the *x* group²³ agree with Hebrews in attesting both ἐνετείλατο and πρὸς ὑμᾶς ὁ θεός, but these are late minuscules whose readings are likely due to the influence of Hebrews. More interesting is the Aramaic version of Exod. 24.8b in Targum Onqelos, which has Moses say, 'Behold, this is (דין הא) the blood…'.²⁴ Whatever the source of this reading, it conflates the reading in LXX/MT and the reading attested here in Hebrews. Curiously, the same conflation occurs in most of the later *f* group of Septuagint manuscripts.²⁵ The reading of *Onqelos* may be a coincidence, but one wonders if the targum points to a Hebrew text form that did contain a demonstrative pronoun. At the very least, the targum appears to show that some interpretive traditions felt the need to place emphasis on the blood, as the reading in Hebrews also does. As for θεός, the use of the word to render the Tetragrammaton is well attested. Hebrews, moreover, is hardly consistent in identifying the Father as θεός and Jesus as κύριος (see, e.g., 1.8 where the Son is referred to as θεός by way of a scriptural citation, and 7.21; 8.8-11; 10.16,

---

[17] So, for example, Thomas, 'Old Testament Citations', pp. 313–14; Massonet, *Hébreux*, p. 248.

[18] H. W. Attridge, *The Epistle to the Hebrews: A Commentary on the Epistle to the Hebrews* (Hermeneia; Philadelphia: Fortress, 1989), p. 257.

[19] E.g., Ellingworth, *Hebrews*, p. 470; Kleinig, *Hebrews*, p. 443; Massonet, *Hébreux*, p. 248; Steyn, *Quest*, p. 278.

[20] For a helpful and compact discussion of the main differences between Hebrews and Exod. 24, see esp. L. T. Johnson, *Hebrews: A Commentary* (NTL; Louisville: Westminster John Knox, 2006), pp. 241–42.

[21] Steyn, *Quest*, pp. 278–79.

[22] Steyn also notes this fact (*Quest*, p. 279).

[23] The *x* group consists of minuscules 71, 527 (ab 288) and 619.

[24] See the text in A. Sperber (ed.), *The Bible in Aramaic: Based on Old Manuscripts and Printed Texts, Volumes I–III* (Leiden: Brill, 2004), p. 1109.

[25] The *f* group consists of minuscules 53, 56, 129, 246, and 664. In this case, the original reading of 56 does not support the variant.

30; 12.5-6 for instances where κύριος refers to the Father). The argument that the author has altered his *Vorlage* to read θεός to avoid confusion is, therefore, tenuous.

While the preceding evidence is meager and does not definitively prove the existence of an alternate version of Exod. 24.8b, the assessment of George Howard on Hebrews' version of this verse is worth noting. Howard comments, 'There is a possible Hebrew influence here since [Hebrews] quotes Ex. xxiv 8 fairly accurately but in words different from the LXX'.[26] There is something to this observation. In my view, while it is not impossible that the author offers here his own translation from a Hebrew text as Howard's comment implies, the supposition that the author has a Greek *Vorlage*/local manuscript that contains a translation of a Hebrew text which differs here from LXX seems plausible. Howard is in any case right that the rendering in Hebrews does not look like an unreasonable translation of something like Exod. 24.8b MT, though it clearly differs from LXX. If it is the case that Hebrews knows a version other than LXX, then arguments about why Hebrews has changed LXX are far less persuasive.

3. Aspects of Exodus' Narrative in Hebrews 1–4

In the opening chapter of Hebrews the author's discussion of the 'Son' (υἱός) invokes concepts and language evocative of the larger exodus narrative found in Exodus. Attentive and biblically literate auditors can already detect echoes of the exodus story in Heb. 1.6, which describes God 'leading' (εἰσαγεῖν) his 'firstborn son' (πρωτότοκος) into 'the inhabitable world' (εἰς τὴν οἰκουμένην). This descriptive language, which depicts Jesus' entrance into the eschatological inheritance promised to God's people (see Heb. 2.5),[27] uses terms and phrasing that recall God's act of delivering Israel from Egypt. Thus, Exod. 4.22 LXX describes Israel as God's 'firstborn son' (υἱὸς πρωτότοκός μου Ἰσραήλ). God performs this deliverance in order to 'lead' (εἰσαγεῖν, Exod. 3.8; 13.5, 11; 15.17; 23.20) Israel into the promised land of their inheritance, which Exod. 16.35 LXX describes as 'an inhabitable land' (εἰς γῆν οἰκουμένην).[28]

Those who hear echoes of Exodus in Hebrews 1 are likely to prick up their ears even more when in Heb. 2.2 the author appears to allude to a Jewish interpretative tradition of the Sinai events that identifies angels as the ones who gave the law to Moses.[29] Furthermore, when the author speaks in Heb. 2.4 of God performing 'signs (σημεῖα) and wonders (τέρατα) and various powers, and distributions of the Holy Spirit', astute listeners may well recall the fact that the collocation of the plural terms 'signs' (σημεῖα) and 'wonders' (τέρατα) first occurs in the Pentateuch in Exod. 7.3 LXX. The terms refer here specifically to the mighty

---

[26] G. Howard, 'Hebrews and the Old Testament Quotations', *NovT* 10 (1968), pp. 208–16, here 215.
[27] For my detailed argumentation defending this interpretation and critiquing others, see D. M. Moffitt, *Atonement and the Logic of Resurrection in the Epistle to the Hebrews* (NovTSup, 141; Leiden: Brill, 2011), pp. 53–118.
[28] See Andriessen, 'La Teneur', esp. pp. 295–300; Allen, *Deuteronomy and Exhortation*, p. 150.
[29] This tradition is evident in *Jubilees* where the angel of the presence speaks with Moses on the mountain, as well as in Acts 7.38 and Gal. 3.19.

works God did in the course of liberating his people from their enslavement in Egypt. The plausibility that the author of Hebrews intends to recall the exodus at Heb. 2.4 only increases in light of the fact that the collocation of the terms 'signs' and 'wonders' throughout Exodus generally refers to these miraculous acts (see Exod. 7.9; 11.9-10). In fact, while the collocation does not always in Septuagintal parlance recall the events of the exodus (e.g., Deut. 28.46; Ps. 64.9; Wis. 8.8; Isa. 8.18; 20.3), God's mighty works during the exodus are by far the most common referent of the collocation of 'signs and wonders' in Septuagint Greek (see Deut. 4.3; 6.22; 11.3; 26.8; 29.2; 34.11; Pss. 77.43; 104.27; 134.9; Wis. 10.16; Jer. 39.20-21; Bar. 2.11; see also the similar phrase in extra-biblical texts such as *Jub.* 48.4, 12 and *LAB* 9.7; as well as the collocation in Acts 7.36).[30]

The strongest evidence, however, that the author intends to refer to the exodus comes when he explicitly encourages his readers to imagine their current situation in terms of the exodus generation's liberation from enslavement and initial wilderness journey towards their promised inheritance. The comparison in Hebrews 3–4 of his readers with the very generation of Israelites who were liberated from slavery in Egypt and led to the edge of the inheritance promised to them by God makes good sense when seen within the matrix of echoes of Exodus and the exodus events embedded in Hebrews 1–2. In fact, the larger narrative arc of the exodus tradition provides much of the underlying plotline the author uses to shape and inform the imagination of his readers, whom he exhorts not to waver in their confession about Jesus.

The major contours of this narrative arc begin to emerge in Heb. 2.14-18 where the writer speaks about Jesus' death as an act that liberates Abraham's seed from the enslaving power of the fear of death and that defeats the Devil, the one who wields this power.[31] The imagery of the Devil holding God's people in bondage and being defeated by Jesus, whose death delivers them from their enslavement, alludes to Exodus. This language particularly recalls the story of Moses performing the first Passover.[32] Within the larger context of Hebrews

---

[30] See also Allen, *Deuteronomy and Exhortation*, p. 142; and Kibbe, *Godly Fear*, p. 124.

[31] As I hinted above, the narrative of God leading his firstborn Son into the coming world seems itself to follow a new exodus pattern. Jesus' faithfulness in his life and death, which issues in his resurrection and entrance into the promised inheritance, functions in part as a moral and eschatological paradigm in the homily. For an exploration of these dynamics in Hebrews, see M. C. Easter, *The Faith and Faithfulness of Jesus in Hebrews* (SNTSMS, 160; Cambridge: Cambridge University Press, 2014).

[32] A few commentators recognize this. For example, Johnson suspects a connection between the slaughter of the Passover lamb and the exodus with Jesus' death and the liberation of his people (*Hebrews*, p. 303). P. E. Hughes briefly notes the possibility of a link between Heb. 11.28 and 2.14-16 (*A Commentary on the Epistle to the Hebrews* [NICNT; Grand Rapids: Eerdmans, 1977], pp. 500–501). J. Dunnill has a more robust account of Passover in Hebrews, arguing that it is a substantial motif throughout the epistle's argument (*Covenant and Sacrifice in the Letter to the Hebrews* [SNTSMS, 75; Cambridge: Cambridge University Press, 1993], esp. pp. 127–28, 154–55, and 159 [cf. 107]). Many, however, think Passover is not significant for Hebrews. For example, Attridge states, 'Hebrews does not make explicit any symbolic or typological significance of [the Passover]' (*Hebrews*, p. 343). See also P. M. Eisenbaum, *The Jewish Heroes of Christian History: Hebrews 11 in Literary Context* (SBLDS, 156; Atlanta: Scholars Press, 1997), p. 171; and C. R. Koester, *Hebrews: A New Translation with Introduction and Commentary* (AB, 36; New York: Doubleday, 2001), p. 504.

the logic of these verses appears to presuppose an implicit comparison between Jesus' death and Moses' act of applying the blood of the Passover lambs to the doors and lintels of the Israelite houses.

This is not to say that the allusion is direct. Rather, the resonances are heard most clearly when amplified by other Jewish interpretive traditions about Exodus that predate Hebrews. The rewriting of Genesis and the first half of Exodus known as *Jubilees* offers some particularly illuminating parallels, especially around its interpretation of Exod. 12.23, which speaks of the Destroyer striking the firstborn during the night of the first Passover. In Heb. 11.28 the author refers clearly to the first Passover by way of an allusion to Exod. 12.23.

Exodus presents Moses' direction about and performance of the Passover as essential to protecting the Israelite firstborn from 'the Destroyer' (ὁ ὀλεθρεύων, Exod. 12.23 LXX) and to liberating the nation from their bondage to Pharaoh. In Heb. 11.28, the author alludes to Exod. 12.23 when he explicitly affirms that Moses' use of the Passover blood protected God's people from 'the Destroyer' (ὁ ὀλοθρεύων). The evidence of *Jubilees* demonstrates that some Second Temple Jews understood Exod. 12.23 to mean that a malevolent angel, known in *Jubilees* as Prince Mastemah, was involved in striking down the firstborn during that first Passover (see esp. *Jub.* 48.4–49.6).[33] Given that Mastemah is identified throughout *Jubilees* with the Satan figure/destroyer who accuses God's people (see *Jub.* 10.17; 17.16-17; 23.29; cf. Job 1.6-12; 2.1-6), it follows that some Jews understood Exod. 12.23 in terms of Moses' liberation of the Israelites not just from Pharaoh, but also from the satanic power controlling him and keeping the people in slavery.

In light of (1) the existence of this sort of interpretation of the one-off reference to the Destroyer in Exodus, and (2) Hebrews' obvious knowledge and acceptance of the claim in Exod. 12.23 that the Passover blood prevented the Destroyer from striking the Israelites (see Heb. 11.28), it makes good sense to understand Hebrews' claim that Jesus' death defeated the Devil and liberated God's people from the fear of death in terms of Passover and the exodus. This is not to claim that the author of Hebrews knows *Jubilees*. Whether or not he had read *Jubilees*, the kind of interpretation of Exod. 12.23 that *Jubilees* attests sheds helpful light on the underlying logic of aspects of Hebrews, particularly in view of the theme of liberation from spiritual bondage actually present in Heb. 2.15.[34] To put the point differently, given the author's comment about the Destroyer in Heb. 11.28, it is hardly a stretch to conclude that Jesus' defeat of the Devil and liberation of Abraham's descendants from the fear of death itself in Heb. 2.14-16 intends to recall the account in Exodus of Moses' role in protecting Abraham's descendants from the Destroyer and liberating them from their bondage at the first Passover.[35]

---

[33] Specifically, Prince Mastemah's minions do the smiting according to *Jubilees*.

[34] This curious reference in Exodus to a destroyer in Exod. 12.23 seems to have sparked substantial exegetical reflection. The influence of this interpretive tradition continues to reverberate even among modern Christians who assume that it was the angel of death who passed over the Israelites.

[35] I argue the point in detail in D. M. Moffitt, 'Modelled on Moses: Jesus' Death, Passover, and the Defeat of the Devil in the Epistle to the Hebrews', in M. Sommer, E. Eynikel, V. Niederhofer, and

If this is correct, then the narrative sweep of the Son's incarnation is being presented in terms that recall Moses, Passover, the exodus, and the ultimate consummation of the God's promises to give his people an enduring inheritance.

The actual progression of the homily lends further plausibility to this interpretation for, shortly after linking Jesus' death with the event that liberates Abraham's seed from enslavement, the author turns in Heb. 3.1-6 to compare Jesus and Moses. Even more tellingly, he engages in Heb. 3.7–4.13 in an extended comparison of his present readers with the very generation of Israelites whom Moses protected from the Destroyer, liberated from Egypt and led into the wilderness.[36] The possible allusions to Exodus detailed above in Hebrews' language about the Son entering his promised inheritance in Hebrews 1, the author's reference in Heb. 2.2 to angels giving the law at Sinai, his likely echo in Heb. 2.4 of the 'signs and wonders' performed by God before and throughout the exodus, his discussion of Jesus' death in Heb. 2.14-16 as the event that defeated the Devil and released Abraham's seed from bondage, and his subsequent comparison of Moses and Jesus (Heb. 3.1-6) all suggest that Exodus plays a foundational role in giving narrative form and shape to the author's theological reflection on what Jesus has done for God's people. The exodus provides the plotline for that reflection. Hebrews' comparison in 3.7–4.11 between the generation in the wilderness and those whom he addresses in the present fits this plotline remarkably well. If (1) the author intends in Heb. 2.14-18 to illuminate something of the salvific role of Jesus' death by viewing it through the lens of the first Passover and Moses' work of liberating God's people from the Destroyer, as well as from their slavery in Egypt; and (2) he intends further to locate his readers within the broader narrative of Exodus, then the comparison he draws in Heb. 3.7–4.11 between the current audience and the very Israelites whom Moses led out of Egypt follows naturally from his preceding discussion.

In sum, the homilist's correlation of the present time and people with the time and people depicted in Exodus imaginatively positions his audience in a place similar to those who were liberated from Egypt according to the unfolding plotline of Exodus—recently liberated from slavery and now in the wilderness, looking forward to their promised inheritance. The author's comparison between

---

E. Hernitscheck (eds.), *Mosebilder: Gedanken zur Rezeption einer literarischen Figur im Frühjudentum, frühen Christentum und der römisch-hellenistischen Literatur* (WUNT, 1/390; Tübingen: Mohr Siebeck, 2017), pp. 279-97.

[36] One might object that the mere mention of Moses is sufficient to trigger the author's turn to the generation who was led into the wilderness. The presence of the motif of liberation from an enslaving power already highlighted in Heb. 2, however, suggests that the author's turn to Moses in 3.1-6 already follows naturally from ideas with which he works in Heb. 2. The author's movement from Jesus as the one who defeated the Devil and liberated God's people, to a consideration of Moses, and then to a discussion of the very generation of Israelites whom Moses liberated from Egypt is, in other words, not likely to be coincidental. This progression roughly follows that of the exodus and the first Passover, key aspects from the narrative of Exodus. The extended analogy that the author draws in 3.7–4.11 between the audience's current situation and that of Israel just after the exodus—having journeyed in the wilderness to the edge of the inheritance God has promised them—makes good sense on the hypothesis that the author works with an underlying exodus analogy.

the newly freed Israelites in the wilderness and the audience is a natural next step in the analogy when one recognizes that he works with the general progression of the narrative in Exodus. Thus, the homilist draws upon Exodus throughout Hebrews 2–4 not only to inform his reflection on what Jesus has done, but also to help his listeners to imagine their present situation in terms analogous to those of the people led by Moses out of their bondage, into the wilderness and, more importantly, about to receive the inheritance God has promised them. All of this, it should be noted, coheres well with the discussion in Hebrews 1 of the firstborn Son's entrance into the promised inheritance. Indeed, the Son in Hebrews is not only the effective agent of this new exodus—a new and greater Moses who performs a new and greater Passover/exodus—he is also the first of God's many sons to have successfully gone through the experience of death and liberation from the one who holds death's power. His narrative—his life, death, resurrection and ascension—itself traces the arc of the exodus analogy and provides thereby the illustration of God's liberation and the ultimate salvation intended for those who hold fast to their confession about Jesus. This is not, however, the full extent of our author's use of Exodus.

4. Exodus, the New Covenant, and Jesus' Service in the Heavenly Tabernacle

Although the homilist's defense of the legitimacy of Jesus' high-priestly office in Hebrews 5–7 does not explicitly draw on Exodus or the larger exodus narrative in the ways or to the extent that his progression of points in Hebrews 1–4 does, he has hardly left Exodus behind as he continues to reflect on Christ's person, work and people in the rest of his sermon. In Hebrews 8 his citation of Jer. 38.31-35 LXX brings the events surrounding the exodus back into consideration. The new covenant promised in Jeremiah is explicitly compared and contrasted with the covenant God made with Israel and Judah when he brought them out of Egypt (Heb. 8.9; Jer. 38.32 LXX). Fully in keeping with the exodus-shaped narrative explored above, the author here appeals to Jeremiah to show that the new covenant God has made with his people through Jesus is patterned on the very one he made with them through Moses when he brought them out of Egypt. Even as the new covenant differs markedly from that earlier covenant (Heb. 8.9; Jer. 38.32 LXX), the two are inextricably linked by the author's analogical reflection on the new covenant in the light of the old.[37] That is to say, the existence, logic and to some degree significance of the new are firmly rooted in those of the old, even organically connected with them. As, then, God freed his people from slavery, brought them out Egypt and made a covenant with them through Moses, so now, in these last days, he has freed them from slavery to the Devil, brought them out of their bondage to the fear of death and made a new covenant—indeed, *the promised* new covenant—with them through Jesus.

---

[37] So also Kibbe, *Godly Fear*, pp. 118–20.

The author's discussion of the tabernacle's structure and accoutrement in Heb. 9.1-5 further accords with this pattern, as do his references in 9.19-20 to the events of the inauguration of the Mosaic covenant and the tabernacle. In fact, as explored above, the author's most explicit references to Exodus occur in the larger context of his discussion of the new covenant and the heavenly tabernacle. His use of the narrative of Exodus, particularly his interest in Exodus' account of the people's time in the wilderness after their liberation continues to help him explain Jesus' person and work. Jesus, like Moses before him, is now the one who mediates the new, determinative covenant. As the one appointed high priest within this new and better covenant, the author naturally continues to draw from Exodus to inform his understanding of how and where Jesus ministers on behalf of his people. To put the point differently, the citation of Exod. 25.40 in Heb. 8.5, coupled with the confession that Jesus has 'passed through the heavens' (Heb. 4.14) and entered the heavenly tabernacle where he now ministers for his people (Heb. 8.1-4; see also 7.25), enables the author to look to the wilderness tabernacle's structure, which is detailed in Exodus, as informative for the layout and structure of the place that Jesus has entered when he passed through the heavens.[38] Exodus not only grounds his exodus-generation metaphor, certain details in the book also underwrite in significant ways his analogical reasoning about Jesus' person and work. Hebrews, moreover, appears to read this part of Exodus in terms of certain other cosmological commitments that take the heavenly reality Moses saw to be a structure located in the heavens. Jesus' ascension through the heavens allows him to enter this structure and engage in his high-priestly ministry there.

Thus, Heb. 8.5 provides a biblical foundation and some warrant for the discussion in Hebrews 9, wherein the pattern of the wilderness tabernacle is used to explain aspects of where Jesus has gone and presently ministers. Because Moses made the old covenant tabernacle in accord with what he saw on the mountain, the textual depiction of that tabernacle can be used as a kind of map to understand where Jesus has gone since he has entered the very heavenly structure that Moses saw and upon which he based the design of the earthly model.

While not as cosmologically loaded, the reference to Jeremiah's new-covenant prophecy in Heb. 8.8-12 and the citation of Exod. 24.8 in Heb. 9.20 show a similar commitment to take seriously the pattern of the Mosaic covenant's inauguration when reflecting on that of the new covenant. The author works with the text in a way that appears to assume both that God himself promised a new covenant, but also that since the Mosaic covenant was inaugurated in a particular way, as Exod. 24.8 is taken to indicate, so the new covenant must be inaugurated in a similar fashion. Following the narrative progression of Exodus, in which the inauguration of the old covenant provides the presumed context within which the

---

[38] For my detailed argumentation of these points, see D. M. Moffitt, 'Serving in the Tabernacle in Heaven: Sacred Space, Jesus's High-Priestly Sacrifice, and Hebrews' Analogical Theology', in G. Gelardini and H. W. Attridge (eds.), *Hebrews in Contexts* (AJEC, 91; Leiden: Brill, 2016), pp. 259–79. Steyn also points out the importance of Exod. 25 for Jewish and early Christian reflection on the heavenly sanctuary (*Quest*, pp. 237–40).

heavenly tabernacle is revealed to Moses and within which the earthly tabernacle can thereby be set up and used, the author of Hebrews locates the inauguration of the new covenant prior to the inaugural entrance into and ongoing ministry of Jesus in the heavenly tabernacle. The nature of the relationship of covenant and tabernacle service in Exodus, therefore, helps one better understand the argument and logic of Hebrews' depiction of Jesus' entrance and ministry in the heavenly tabernacle after his death and resurrection.

According to the book of Exodus, one of the reasons for the exodus was to enable God's people to meet with him and to serve/worship him (e.g., Exod. 4.23; 7.16; 8.1; 9.1; 10.3, 26; 12.31). The fact that the inauguration of that first covenant preceded the building and inauguration of the tabernacle and service of worship within it suggests that a kind of institution of a place for service, followed by the ongoing maintenance of that service and the relationship it implies is presupposed in Hebrews. God's relationship and prior covenants with the patriarchs clearly indicate that his commitment to Israel precedes the Passover, the exodus, and the Mosaic covenant. Exodus itself affirms that the Passover, the exodus, and the people's reception of an inheritance are themselves realities predicated on God's covenant with Abraham (e.g., Exod. 2.24; 3.16; 6.7-8; 32.12-13; 33.1). Nevertheless, the latter events hold a special place in establishing and defining God's relationship with his people.

The author of Hebrews clearly thinks in a similar way, as his lengthy citation of Jer. 38.31-34 LXX demonstrates. Of note, then, is the inauguration of and ongoing worshipping relationship implied in the details of Exodus. The close correlation of covenant and tabernacle evident in Hebrews 8–9, in other words, follows the pattern of Exodus. Moses first inaugurates the covenant and the tabernacle, then God's people can meet with him and serve him there. In a similar way, Jesus first inaugurates the new covenant and service in the heavenly tabernacle, then approaches God's presence in that heavenly space to perform his service there, opening the way for God's people to enter and serve him there too.

If the pattern just identified is correct, then one can see how Hebrews maps the death, resurrection, and ascension of Jesus onto the events of the exodus/ covenant inauguration, the inauguration of the priesthood and tabernacle, and the ongoing work of worship and covenant maintenance the priests performed within that sacred space. This implies further that the author thinks sequentially through various moments of the incarnation and sees within them particular ways in which they contribute to the larger goal of saving God's people. Hebrews, in other words, does not reduce the means of salvation only to the event of Jesus' death on the cross, but sees instead a variety of ways in which particular events that constitute the story of the incarnate Son ultimately issue in God's people receiving the salvation promised to them so long ago. Exodus provides some of the key categories and concepts used by the author to develop his analogical reflection on the salvific work of the Son.[39] Specifically, the author's use of

---

[39] As a corollary, this sort of account also helps explain the author's polyvalent use of the language of 'blood' in Hebrews. Blood language is used by the author with reference to the rituals Moses performed to inaugurate the covenant (esp. Heb. 9.15-20) and with reference to the sacrificial

Exodus helps to clarify that Jesus' death is a new Passover moment that defeats the one who holds the power of death, simultaneously liberating his people from their slavery and inaugurating the promised new covenant relationship between God and his people. Jesus' death is, therefore, the new Passover/new covenant inaugurating event.[40] In his resurrection, he is appointed to the role of high priest of this new covenant coming into possession of the indestructible life that qualifies him to serve in the heavenly priesthood and elevates him above all the angels. In his ascension, Jesus presents his Yom Kippur offering and begins his ministry of intercession on behalf of his followers.

5. Moses, Exodus, Sinai, and Zion

The preceding discussion suggests that Exodus exercises significant influence on the author's conception of Jesus' salvific work and the identity the author wants to inculcate in his audience precisely to the extent that this text provides a pattern for how God liberated his people, inaugurated his covenant with them, and then commanded Moses to construct the tabernacle as a means for God and his people to dwell close together within the context of that covenant. The discussion of the new covenant and the tabernacle in Hebrews 8–9 shows that the author's reflection is shaped by, even at points normed by aspects of Exodus in important ways.

Hebrews does not, however, slavishly follow Exodus or the exodus narrative. The author, a bit like one sees in other Second Temple texts that rewrite Scripture such as *Jubilees*, feels the freedom to interpret Exodus. His engagement with Exodus is dialogical, working at times from Exodus forwards and at times from his viewpoint as one who confesses Jesus as the Christ backwards. In Hebrews we find Christology both under construction in light of Exodus (and numerous other Old Testament texts) and informing ways that Exodus (and numerous other Old Testament texts) can now be read afresh. The relationship between Scripture and Christology runs in both directions.

Something of this dynamic can already be seen in the Hebrews 3–4, where, from the perspective of God's speaking through the Son in 'these last days' (1.2), Hebrews calls its auditors to consider what the exodus generation truly lost when they refused to enter God's rest. For Hebrews, that generation did not just miss out on obtaining the land of Canaan, which Joshua later led the people into, they

---

rituals that effect purification and forgiveness (i.e., sacrificial atonement along the lines depicted in Leviticus, e.g., Heb. 9.12-14, 24-26; 13.11-12). In the former case the author connects blood closely with death as he identifies Jesus' death with the inaugural events of the old covenant (here he conflates Passover and the rituals of Exod. 24, as arguably Jer. 31 presupposes). The latter use of blood language focuses attention on the sacrificial acts of presenting the offering of life to God. The thing that binds these distinct moments together in the case of the new covenant is the person of Jesus himself. The very one who died is the one who rose, who became the great high priest, who ascended through the heavens, and who entered the heavenly tabernacle in order to offer himself to the Father and to intercede even now on behalf of his siblings.

[40] As discussed in the preceding note, the close conceptual connection between Passover and covenant inauguration is presumed in Jer. 31.32.

and those who came later missed out on obtaining the fullness of God's promised rest.

Hebrews 11.23-29 also illustrates the author's freedom to read Exodus in the light of Jesus. Here the author retells the story of Moses from Exodus in a highly condensed form. When he comments that Moses was willing to turn away from the treasures of Egypt and endure abuse on account of Christ because he looked ahead to the reward (11.26), he clearly introduces into Exodus his convictions about the truth of Jesus' identity as the eternal Son who guarantees that the fullness of God's promised inheritance will come to his people. This reading appears to rely on the conviction that the author stated at the outset of his homily, the same God who spoke in the past in the prophets now speaks through Jesus, the Son. Moses, and indeed all those who illustrate faith in Hebrews 11, are counted among the people of God who will all be made perfect together because of Jesus (11.39-40).

The author's comparison in Heb. 12.18-24 between the 'congregation of the firstborn' who have come to Mount Zion and the events of God's giving the law at Mount Sinai further highlights both the role of Exodus in the homily and the ways in which Hebrews uses Exodus creatively. The debates over the referent of the phrase 'congregation of the firstborn' are well known.[41] To the arguments put forward by Helyer and many modern commentators[42] that the author intends to refer to his audience with this language, I would add the following: if Exodus has been in play in the homily in the ways I have argued, then the identification of the 'congregation of the firstborn' around Mount Zion, in contrast to the liberated Israelites around Mount Sinai, would naturally recall the claims and narrative progression of Hebrews 2–4. That is to say, the use of 'firstborn' language in Hebrews 12 aligns well with the author's previous encouragement of the auditors to imagine their liberation from the Devil and their bondage to the power of death in terms of the exodus narrative, particularly given this narrative's depiction of the protection of the firstborn from the Destroyer at the first Passover and the subsequent liberation of that generation from bondage.[43] If the connection between this narrative and the audience is valid, then all who belong to the congregation addressed by the homily can rightly see analogies between themselves and the firstborn who were protected by the use of the Passover blood when Moses led the people out of Egypt. All in this congregation, including Jesus himself, the great high priest who is the firstborn Son who leads them in worship, have been liberated from death and the Devil.

Another observation is germane. Clearly the narrative underlying the exodus generation metaphor, particularly as this is played out with reference to the congregation of the firstborn in Hebrews 12, overlaps with Deuteronomy.[44]

---

[41] See the discussion of the term and engagement with various views in L. R. Helyer's detailed article, 'The *Prōtotokos* Title in Hebrews', *SBT* 6 (1976), pp. 3–28, here esp. 12–16.

[42] Helyer, '*Prōtotokos*', pp. 14–16. See also, e.g., Attridge, *Hebrews*, p. 375; W. L. Lane, *Hebrews 9–13* (WBC, 47B; Dallas: Word, 1991), pp. 468–29; Koester, *Hebrews*, p. 545.

[43] Helyer rightly suspects this sort of connection given the new exodus idea in play in Hebrews ('*Prōtotokos*', p. 16).

[44] See esp. the discussion of this verse in Allen, *Deuteronomy and Exhortation*, pp. 139–40.

Deuteronomy plays a significant role in Hebrews' argument.[45] This overlap, particularly the comparison of the two mountains, marks an element of the author's creative interaction with Exodus. Yet, Exodus still has a particular role to play, for unlike Deuteronomy, Hebrews does not envision those whom Jesus has liberated and led into the wilderness as being at the end of something like Israel's forty years of wandering. The author constructs a metaphor of God's people in the wilderness that crucially locates them at a point *prior* to a Kadesh-Barnea-like event. They are, as it were, at the first opportunity to receive the inheritance.[46] To put the point differently, Hebrews forecloses on any hope of a Deutero-Christos moment analogous to Deuteronomy's post-forty-years setting. To find oneself wandering as Israel did for forty years would mean for this author that one has fallen away/failed the test and, like Esau, has lost the inheritance.

This latter point is important just to the extent that modern Hebrews' scholarship has at times overplayed the idea of God's people 'wandering' or engaged in 'pilgrimage'.[47] While the appeal to the motif of journeying has some merit,[48] the location of God's people in the author's exodus generation metaphor suggests a subtle qualification is in order. Those liberated by Jesus' death are not in a state of wandering until Jesus leads them into their inheritance. Rather, the author exhorts them not to fall prey to the same mistake that Israel made at Kadesh-Barnea, the rebellion that resulted in the bodies of many of those liberated from Egypt falling in the wilderness (Heb. 4.16-19). Hebrews clearly draws from Deuteronomy, but the metaphor that the author uses to develop so much of his exhortation locates the audience much earlier in the pentateuchal story. As in Exodus, they are in a Sinai-like position, from which they have not and should not move. Yet, as in Deuteronomy, they are at the same time about to receive their inheritance, having seen in some sense what it will mean for them if they turn away in unbelief. They stand, as it were, both at the end of Exodus and the beginning of Numbers and at the end of Deuteronomy.[49] They know from the Pentateuch how the story

---

[45] See n. 3 above for a few of the recent studies that focus on this fact.

[46] M. Thiessen rightly emphasizes this point ('Hebrews and the End of Exodus', *NovT* 49 [2007], pp. 353–69).

[47] As is well known, the case for this as the central theme of Hebrews was powerfully argued by Ernst Käsemann.

[48] Throughout Hebrews there are passages that call for the auditors to move forward. These tend to correlate with their current access into the heavenly holy of holies where Jesus presently is (e.g., 4.16; 10.19-22; 12.22-24), and even trace the pattern of Jesus' ascension. The eschatological hope of Hebrews to inherit salvation and the unshakable kingdom, however, tends to be correlated with language of reception of something and/or someone coming to the auditors (e.g., 2.5; 6.5; 9.28; 10.25, 37; 11.10, 13-16, 39-40; 12.28; 13.14). The primary exceptions to this pattern are the discussion of rest in Heb. 3–4 (though much here depends on whether the rest is now accessible or a strictly eschatological reality), and the theme of perfection (see esp. 6.1). Hebrews, in other words, works generally with a concept of being able to approach God in worship in heavenly space now (forward motion), while also making it clear that the fullness of the eschatological inheritance is something that is going to come to the congregation, and thus something for which they must faithfully wait.

[49] Allen's conclusion that Hebrews 'does not just use Deuteronomy; it becomes a new Deuteronomy' (*Deuteronomy and Exhortation*, p. 225) has much to commend it. But the importance of Exodus and the distinction between waiting and wandering should not be downplayed. Here one comes up against the complexity of Hebrews' interaction with Scripture.

will play out for them if they choose to behave in the same way that the firstborn of the exodus generation did. This complex engagement with the pentateuchal narrative helps to explain why, for this author, God's people are not being led into the promised land by their Joshua, but are instead waiting for their Joshua, who has gone ahead of them into the inheritance, but will return to them in order to bring back with him the salvation they hope to inherit (Heb. 9.28; cf. 1.14).[50] This is also why the parenetic heart of Hebrews beats with the call to persevere and remain faithful while they wait. For Hebrews, there will not be, because there cannot be, a Deuteronomy-like moment in this story.[51]

6. Conclusion

The preceding argument surveys some of the most significant ways that Exodus serves to contribute to the pentateuchally shaped narrative that grounds the author's exodus-generation metaphor, a metaphor he develops as he exhorts his readers to hold fast to their confession about Jesus. This metaphor presents followers of Jesus as a new wilderness generation who must endure struggles and tests while they wait for their new Moses, even their new Joshua, to bring their salvation to them when he returns, both, as it were, coming down from the mountain and coming back from the land. Explicit citation of Exodus does not feature prominently in Hebrews, but the preceding arguments show that the book nonetheless serves as one of the author's most significant intertexts. Not only does this book of the Pentateuch provide him with the essential elements of an overarching narrative consisting of Passover and liberation, covenant inauguration, wilderness period prior to receiving the promised inheritance, and ongoing worship of God at a holy mountain, the central events narrated in Exodus also provide a rich vein of images, language, and motifs that he mines throughout his homily.

Two final points are worthy of reflection. First, there are many different elements to the work of the Son in Hebrews. The author's use of the exodus narrative enables him to highlight some of the different ways in which the Son's life, death, resurrection, ascension, heavenly session at the right hand of the Father, and return to his waiting people each contribute to the larger goal of their salvation—the reception of the unshakable inheritance. Importantly, however, no one event in this sequence is the unifying or central element. The cross, for example, is not the sole focus of the author, for Jesus' death is not itself the

---

[50] O. Hofius argues this point well, writing, '[D]ie Gemeinde [ist] nicht als das zum Himmel wandernde, wohl aber als das auf die Heilsvollendung wartende Gottesvolk gesehen, und der Verfasser will dieses Volk...mit aller Dringlichkeit dazu aufrufen, die Erwartung nicht preiszugeben, der allein die Erfüllung verheißen ist' (*Katapausis: Die Vorstellung vom endzeitlichen Ruheort im Hebräerbrief* [WUNT, 1/11; Tübingen: Mohr Siebeck, 1970], p. 150).

[51] The author's rigorous perspective on the impossibility of restoration should one abandon the community parallels God's harsh judgment of the exodus generation in Ps. 95, but also works by way of logic that would require the re-crucifixion of the resurrected and ascended Jesus, something that by virtue of the author's concept of Jesus' resurrection (a resurrection to indestructible life) is impossible. That is, the events that make up the story of the Son's incarnation cannot be repeated.

unifying soteriological aspect of the incarnation. Rather, Jesus himself, his very person, unifies all these elements. It is for Hebrews Jesus himself, the Son who became incarnate and has returned to his Father in his resurrected humanity, who is central to salvation. The work of salvation is unified, in other words, by the very one who can now be seen both to have liberated his people and presently to be interceding for them—Jesus.

Second, however, if the arguments advanced here are more or less correct, then an important implication for reflection on Jesus' atoning work follows. The author's use of Exodus to emphasize the liberating/Passover and covenant inaugurating effect of Jesus' death, together with his equally important emphasis on the subsequent high-priestly work of Jesus in the Father's presence in the heavenly holy of holies (a more Leviticus-oriented emphasis), allows the conclusion that the author of Hebrews both distinguished between the roles and importance of Passover (associated with Jesus' death) and Yom Kippur (associated with Jesus' ascension), while also holding these two salvific elements together in the very narrative and person of the incarnate Son of God.

Chapter 9

EXODUS IN THE GENERAL LETTERS

Katie Marcar

1. Introduction

The relative sparsity of quotations from and allusions to the book of Exodus or to exodus traditions more broadly in the General Letters affords the opportunity for a detailed look at the references that do occur. In this study, a quotation is defined as a passage that reproduces a portion of text with a great degree of verbal similarity and minimal contextual modification; it may be signalled with a quotation formula or term (such as γάρ), but need not be.[1] In many cases, it seems that quotations are intended to be recognized as such by the text's intended audience.[2]

By contrast, allusions may reproduce portions of a source text, but tend to be woven more seamlessly into their context. Porter identifies three important elements of allusions: their intentionality, reference to shared knowledge, and their function.[3] In order for an allusion to be present, an author must have consciously intended it, even if it was not recognized by his recipient. Allusions also draw on a shared pool of knowledge that should make it possible for the recipient to recognize the intended reference. Finally, Porter writes that the purpose of an allusion 'is to draw the earlier person, text, or event into the present

---

[1] S. Moyise, 'Quotations', in S. E. Porter and C. D. Stanley (eds.), *As It Is Written: Studying Paul's Use of Scripture* (SBLSymS, 50; Atlanta: Society of Biblical Literature, 2008), pp. 15–28 (15–16).
[2] The degree to which an intended audience aligns with the actual audience is unclear. See C. D. Stanley, 'Paul's "Use" of Scripture: Why the Audience Matters', in Porter and Stanley (eds.), *As It Is Written*, pp. 125–55.
[3] S. E. Porter, 'Allusions and Echoes', in Porter and Stanley (eds.), *As It Is Written*, pp. 29–40 (35–36).

text as a means of addressing a particular literary problem'.[4] Importantly, what this means is that the allusion must *do* something; it is not merely decorative.

However, in this investigation, it is not always possible to determine whether an allusion is present. Specifically, it is not always possible to determine whether a proposed correspondence with a text was intended by the author and therefore qualifies as an allusion. In some instances, his text may allow such a correspondence, but claims about the author's intentions must remain tentative. In these cases, functions of an allusion will be proposed, but with the qualification that the status of the allusion is unclear. Methodologically, an elegant and coherent interpretation of an allusion's function may contribute to the arguments in favor of its recognition as an allusion.

2. James

James contains only one possible quotation of Exodus in a reference to the Decalogue (Exod. 20.13-15 in Jas 2.11), and two proposed allusions (Exod. 20.5 in Jas 4.5 and the statement of divine self-disclosure in Exod. 34.6 in Jas 5.11). James 4.5 is most likely a reference to the now-lost book of *Eldad and Modad*. The references to the Decalogue and the statement of divine self-disclosure may demonstrate familiarity with traditional Jewish teaching in general rather than knowledge of the book of Exodus *per se*. James may have known these passages from Exodus, or he may have internalized them from Jewish or Christian teaching. These two options are not mutually exclusive.

a. Prohibitions Against Adultery and Murder: The Decalogue in James 2.11

In Jas 2.11, the author invokes the Decalogue's prohibitions against adultery and murder to support his argument against favoritism. Textually, it is unclear whether he is quoting from Exod. 20.13-15 or Deut. 5.17-18. Given the prominence of the Decalogue for both Christians and Jews in this period, it is possible, and perhaps likely, that the author did not need to quote directly from either source and reproduced the text as he knew it from oral tradition and Christian teaching.[5] These prohibitions fit into the author's larger argument against favoritism by illustrating how keeping the whole law means keeping all of its parts.

---

[4] Porter, 'Allusions and Echoes', p. 36.
[5] In the NT, see Mt. 19.18; Mk 10.19; Lk. 18.20; Rom. 13.9; cf. Mt. 5.21, 27. The Decalogue is also well represented Second Temple Jewish literature, a noteworthy example is its inclusion in the Qumran teffilin. For a good overview and bibliography, see H. Najman, 'Decalogue', in J. J. Collins and D. C. Harlow (eds.), *The Eerdmans Dictionary of Eary Judaism* (Grand Rapids: Eerdmans, 2010), pp. 526–28. Also see the sources cited in nn. 7-8 below.

Table 10.1. *Comparison of James 2.11, Exodus 20.13-15, and Deuteronomy 5.17-19*

Jas 2.11, NT	Exod. 20.13-15, OG	Deut. 5.17-19, OG	Exod. 20.13-14, MT
ὁ γὰρ εἰπών, Μὴ μοιχεύσῃς, εἶπεν καί, Μὴ φονεύσῃς· εἰ δὲ οὐ μοιχεύεις, φονεύεις δέ, γέγονας παραβάτης νόμου.	οὐ μοιχεύσεις. οὐ κλέψεις. οὐ φονεύσεις.	οὐ μοιχεύσεις. οὐ φονεύσεις. οὐ κλέψεις.	לא תרצח לא תנאף

Two textual issues are present, the tense of the verbs and the order of the commandments. The first is minor, but the latter is potentially more significant. First, the tenses of the prohibitions in James do not exactly reproduce the Old Greek (OG). In James, the prohibitions are formed with aorist subjunctives, compared to the future indicatives of the OG. In this regard, other New Testament quotations of the Decalogue sometimes agree with the OG and sometimes with James.[6]

The second and more interesting issue is the order of the commandments. James, along with the OG Deuteronomy, the Nash papyrus and other witnesses, has the ordering of adultery (A), murder (M), and theft (T; hence, A M T).[7] In contrast, the MT, Samaritan Pentateuch, and some other witnesses have murder, adultery, and theft (M A T).[8] Finally, the OG version of Exodus has the order adultery, theft, and murder (A T M). It is clear that the order of these commandments was somewhat fluid. For this reason, it is difficult to determine the significance of this variation in James. One possible conclusion could be that the author was using the version of the Decalogue as recorded in OG Deuteronomy rather than OG Exodus. However, it is also possible that the author was quoting the commandments from memory or paraphrasing.[9]

Adultery and murder are clear examples of transgressions of the law. For the author of James, the 'whole law' (ὅλον τὸν νόμον) is a unity: to transgress one part

---

[6] Mt. 19.18 and Rom. 13.9 (Lk. 18.20 in D) have future verbs, while Lk. 18.20 and Mk 10.19 have aorist subjunctives.

[7] This order is also found in Lk. 18.20, Rom. 13.9; Philo, *Dec.* 51, 121-137, 168-171; *Rer. Div. Her.* 173. In *Spec. Leg.* 3.8, Philo refers to the prohibition against adultery as the first commandment on the second table, making it the sixth commandment. In *LAB* 11.10-11, adultery and murder are followed by prohibitions against false witnessing and coveting. In a longer list of transgressions, see *Barn.* 20.1. For more, see D. Flusser, '"Do not commit adultery", "Do not murder"', *Text* 4 (1964), pp. 220–24.

[8] This order is found in the MT, Mt. 19.18, Mk 10.19, the Samaritan Pentateuch, Josephus, *Ant.* 3.91-92, 4QDtn, 4QDPhyl^b, 4QDPhyl^g, 4QDPhyl^j. Matthew 5.21-22 and 5.27-28 discuss murder and adultery, respectively. For more see S. A. White, 'The All Souls Deuteronomy and the Deacalogue', *JBL* 109 (1990), pp. 193–206, esp. pp. 202–203.

[9] D. C. Allison Jr., *James* (ICC; London: Bloomsbury, 2013), p. 415; D. A. Carson, 'James', in G. K. Beale and D. A. Carson (eds.), *Commentary on the New Testament Use of the Old Testament* (Baker: Grand Rapids, 2007), pp. 997–1014 (1002).

is to transgress against the whole (Jas 2.10). Those who do not commit adultery but do murder are transgressors (Jas 2.11b). This fits into the author's larger argument against favoritism based on wealth (Jas 2.1-7).

Instead of showing favoritism to the rich, the author calls his readers to love their neighbors as themselves (Jas 2.8; Lev. 19.18b).[10] The command to love in Lev. 19.18 is established by God, 'You shall love your neighbor as yourself: I am the LORD'.[11] Just as those who murder are transgressors of the whole law, those who show partiality to the wealthy transgress the law because they have failed to love their neighbors, the poor.

James draws attention to the character of God when he reminds his recipients of the one who spoke these prohibitions. In Jas 2.11, the author says, 'For the one who said (ὁ γὰρ εἰπών), "You shall not commit adultery", also said (εἶπεν καί), "You shall not murder"'. Biblical narrative, as well as later Jewish tradition, maintained that God literally uttered the Decalogue.[12] It is likely that 'the one who said' in Jas 2.11 refers to God. This is supported by the fact that in James, biblical quotations are elsewhere always introduced with present verbs (2.23; 4.5, 6). It is therefore likely that the author has adapted his style here specifically to invoke the divine origin of the law as the source of its authority.[13] The unity of God sustains the unity of the law. In conclusion, the author uses the prohibitions against adultery and murder from the Decalogue to explain how any infraction of the law compromises the integrity of the whole. Believers are called to keep the whole law, which is summarized by the command to love one's neighbor as oneself, without regard for wealth or status.

b. A (Very) Debatable Allusion: Jas 4.5 and Exod. 20.5

Though Jas 4.5 appeals to 'the scripture' (ἡ γραφή), a precise reference for this quotation has evaded scholars. Textual difficulties further obscure the problematic content of the verse. Allison concedes that '[t]his is one of the most challenging lines in early Christian literature. It is of uncertain sense and uncertain origin.'[14]

Though the editors of the UBS[5] cite Jas 4.5 as an allusion to Exod. 20.5, this is unlikely. There is no significant shared vocabulary between Jas 4.5 and Exod. 20.5 OG. Instead, some scholars have argued convincingly that James quotes here from the now-lost book of *Eldad and Modad*.[15]

---

[10] For Lev. 19.18 elsewhere in the NT, see Mk 12.31; Lk.10.27; Rom. 13.8-10; Gal. 5.14. For more on the command to love, see Allison, *James*, pp. 402–403.

[11] Unless otherwise stated, quotations from the NT and OT are taken from the NRSV.

[12] Both Exodus and Deuteronomy say that God orally gave the law (Exod. 20.1; Deut. 5.4, 22; 18.16); Allison, *James*, pp. 414–15.

[13] Allison, *James*, p. 414.

[14] Allison, *James*, p. 611.

[15] D. C. Allison Jr., 'Eldad and Modad', *JSP* 21 (2011), pp. 99–131 (99); R. Bauckham, 'The Spirit of God in Us Loathes Envy: James 4:5', in G. N. Stanton *et al.* (eds.), *The Holy Spirit and Christian Origins: Essays in Honor of James D. G. Dunn* (Grand Rapids: Eerdmans, 2004), pp. 270–81. For a summary of earlier proponents of the influence *Eldad and Modad* on early Christian literature and the reception of this theory in scholarship, see Allison, 'Eldad and Modad', pp. 107–19.

This lost text probably expanded the narrative of Num. 11.24-29, the only place where Eldad and Modad appear in the Hebrew scriptures.[16] Allison and others have marshalled a substantial body of evidence to support James' use of this text. Though lost, fragments of this work can be pieced together from *The Shepherd of Hermas*, which explicitly quotes *Eldad and Modad* (*Vis.* 2.3.4), and from two quotations of a source in *1–2 Clement* which is probably *Eldad and Modad* (*1 Clem.* 23.3; *2 Clem.* 11.2).[17] With these citations, along with evidence gathered from Jewish and early Christian traditions, especially interpretations of Numbers 11, there is sufficient evidence to justify the attribution of this Jacobean reference to *Eldad and Modad*. Furthermore, these points of correspondence occur not just in Jas 4.5, but also in other elements in James 4, which strongly suggests that the influence of *Eldad and Modad* extends beyond the explicit citation in v. 5.[18]

Several of the main points of correspondence are as follow. First, James 4.5 and Num. 11.24-29 share the themes of jealousy and the divine bestowal of the spirit.[19] It is nearly certain that a work like *Eldad and Modad* would have been anchored by the narrative in Num. 11.24-29, the only biblical reference to its titular characters.[20] Second, in rabbinic tradition, Eldad and Modad are rewarded for their humility.[21] This theme aligns with the quotation of Prov. 3.34 against pride in Jas 4.6 (cf. 4.10) and probably also the reference to grace in Jas 4.6.[22] Third, Jas 4.8 is very close to the quotation of *Eldad and Modad* in *Hermas* (*Vis.* 2.3.4).[23] Other correspondences exist, though the necessarily detailed process of excavating the clues embedded in existent texts requires more space than the present context affords. Allison summarizes, 'James concerns himself with desire, jealousy, "the spirit", speaking against others, the humble being exalted, the giving of grace, and God drawing near to the saints, all of which were part and parcel of the lore surrounding Eldad and Modad'.[24] The combined weight of this evidence supports the conclusion that Jas 4.5 is a reference to the now-lost book of *Eldad and Modad*, not a reference to Exod. 20.5 or any other text now part of the Christian canon.

c. A Possible Verbal Echo of Divine Self-disclosure: James 5.11 and Exodus 34.6

When James encourages his readers to show endurance like Job in Jas 5.11, he reminds them that 'the Lord is compassionate and merciful' (πολύσπλαγχνός ἐστιν

---

[16] Allison, 'Eldad and Modad', pp. 99–100, 116.
[17] Allison, 'Eldad and Modad', pp.101–12.
[18] Allison, 'Eldad and Modad', pp. 112–26.
[19] Allison, 'Eldad and Modad', pp. 113, 120.
[20] Allison, 'Eldad and Modad', p. 116.
[21] Allison, 'Eldad and Modad', pp. 113, 120–21.
[22] Allison, 'Eldad and Modad', pp. 113–14, 122–23. As Allison observes, Cyril of Jerusalem, Cyril of Alexandria, and Theodoret of Cyrus all identify Eldad and Modad as the recipients of divine grace.
[23] Compare Jas 4.5a, ἐγγίσατε τῷ θεῷ καὶ ἐγγιεῖ ὑμῖν, with *Vis.* 2.3.4b, ἐγγὺς κύριος τοῖς ἐπιστρεφομένοις. Allison, 'Eldad and Modad', pp. 101–6, 113.
[24] Allison, 'Eldad and Modad', p. 124.

ὁ κύριος καὶ οἰκτίρμων). There may be an allusion to the statement of divine self-disclosure in Exod. 34.6 where God describes himself as 'merciful and gracious' (οἰκτίρμων καὶ ἐλεήμων).

Table 10.2. *Comparison of James 5.11 and Exodus 34.6*

Jas 5.11, NT	Exod. 34.6, OG	Exod. 34.6, MT
ἰδοὺ μακαρίζομεν τοὺς ὑπομείναντας· τὴν ὑπομονὴν Ἰὼβ ἠκούσατε, καὶ τὸ τέλος κυρίου εἴδετε, ὅτι πολύσπλαγχνός ἐστιν ὁ κύριος καὶ οἰκτίρμων.	καὶ παρῆλθεν κύριος πρὸ προσώπου αὐτοῦ καὶ ἐκάλεσεν Κύριος ὁ θεὸς οἰκτίρμων καὶ ἐλεήμων, μακρόθυμος καὶ πολυέλεος καὶ ἀληθινός	ויעבר יהוה על פניו ויקרא יהוה יהוה אל רחום וחנון ארך אפים ורב חסד ואמת

The significance of this statement in Exod. 34.6 is already evident within the Hebrew scriptures, where it is clearly alluded to on eight occasions (Num. 14.18; Neh. 9.17; Pss. 86.15; 103.8; Joel 2.13; Jon. 4.2; Nah. 1.3).[25] The reverberations of this language are widely felt elsewhere in Jewish literature.[26] Therefore, rather than quoting directly from Exod. 34.6, James may have drawn from the wealth of Jewish tradition on the character of God. While Exod. 34.6 may be the seed from which this tradition originally grew, it has expanded well beyond its initial starting point, establishing an important place in Jewish theology. James could therefore reflect on the character of God using language of, or very similar to, the well-known statement in Exod. 34.6 without necessarily quoting it intentionally or alluding to it directly.

3. 1 Peter

a. Scripture and Hermeneutics in 1 Peter

Of all of the General Letters, 1 Peter makes the greatest use of Exodus tradition.[27] However, the author's use of Exodus is part of a larger hermeneutical strategy in which the scriptures and narrative of Israel are appropriated for the church through Christ (cf. 1 Pet. 1.10-12).[28] The Petrine author began from the

---

[25] R. C. Dentan, 'The Literary Affinities of Exodus XXXIV 6f', *VT* 13 (1963), pp. 34–51.
[26] See also 2 Chron. 30.9; Pss. 25.6; 40.11; 51.1; Hos. 2.19; Lam. 3.22; 1 Macc. 3.44; *Jos. Asen.* 11.10; *T. Jud.* 19.3. Cf. 1QH 19.29; 4Q511 frag. 52, 54-55, 57-59; *LAB* 19.8; *4 Ezra* 7.132-33; *2 Bar.* 77.7; *Apoc. Abr.* 17.10, as listed in Allison, *James*, p. 720.
[27] For example, see M. H. Scharlemann, 'Exodus Ethics: Part One: 1 Peter 1:13-16', *ConJ* 2, no. 4 (1976), pp. 165–70; P. E. Deterding, 'Exodus Motifs in First Peter', *ConJ* 7, no. 2 (1981), pp. 58–65; N. K. Gupta, 'A Spiritual House of Royal Priests, Chosen and Honored: The Presence and Function of Cultic Imagery in 1 Peter', *PRSt* 36 (2009), pp. 61–76; A. M. Mbuvi, *Temple, Exile and Identity in 1 Peter* (LNTS, 345; London: T&T Clark, 2007).
[28] P. J. Achtemeier, *1 Peter: A Commentary on First Peter* (Minneapolis: Fortress, 1996), p. 69; P. T. Egan, *Ecclesiology and the Scriptural Narrative of 1 Peter* (Eugene, OR: Pickwick, 2016), pp. 2, 53–55; L. Doering, '"You are a Chosen Stock...": The Use of Israel Epithets for the Addressees in First Peter', in Y. Furstenberg (ed.), *Jewish and Christian Communal Identities in the Roman World* (Leiden: Brill, 2016), pp. 243–76.

assumption that scripture is about Christ. He then used this christological focus to demonstrate to his recipients that, through Christ, the story of Israel had also become their story.[29]

As Achtemeier and others have noted, the relationship of the church to ethnic Israel is never addressed in the letter.[30] Rather, the language and tradition of Israel 'pass without remainder' to the new people of God.[31] For the author of 1 Peter, those who believe are the people of God. The author therefore drew from a great diversity of scriptural traditions, including the Pentateuchal narratives, the prophecies of Isaiah, and the Psalms to show his recipients how they participate in this narrative. Exodus traditions, therefore, were one source among many for the Petrine author.

The Petrine author deployed this Christian ecclesiocentric hermeneutic through the letter's abundant quotations, allusions, and echoes of scripture. Many direct quotations are signaled with an introductory formula or term, while more allusive references are woven seamlessly into the fabric of the letter.[32] The author's skill as an exegete and rhetorician contrasts with the scholarly task of unraveling this theological tapestry. Similarly, one of the complicating factors for this study is the embeddedness of Exodus material already within Jewish literature, and later, early Christian teaching. This polyvalence contributes to the complexity of these themes in 1 Peter. Namely, the author of 1 Peter did not use the Exodus material in isolation. Rather, he drew deeply from the biblical corpus to construct Christian identity from the appellations, narratives, and theology of the Hebrew scriptures as mediated through early Jewish and Christian tradition.

b. 1 Peter, Diaspora Letters and Exodus Traditions

Before proceeding, one very important observation must be made: namely, that for the Petrine author, believers were currently living in a type of Christian 'diaspora', and would continue to do so for the foreseeable future. As Lutz Doering has shown, 1 Peter exhibits many of the characteristics of Jewish diaspora letters.[33] The letter is addressed 'to the exiles of the Dispersion' (παρεπιδήμοις διασπορᾶς, 1.1), refers to believers as 'aliens and exiles' (παροίκους καὶ παρεπιδήμους, 2.11), and concludes with greetings from 'She who is Babylon' (my translation, 5.13, ἡ ἐν Βαβυλῶνι). However, one of the key motifs in the reception of the Exodus tradition was the departure from Egypt and the return to and conquest of the land.[34]

---

[29] For more thorough exploration of this hermeneutic, see Egan, *Ecclesiology and the Scriptural Narrative of 1 Peter*, esp. pp. 54–56. See also J. R. Michaels, *1 Peter* (WBC, 49; Waco, TX: Word, 1988), pp. xlix–li.

[30] Achtemeier, *1 Peter*, p. 69; Michaels, *1 Peter*, pp. xlix–li, liv–lv.

[31] Achtemeier, *1 Peter*, p. 69.

[32] K. Marcar, 'The Quotations of Isaiah in 1 Peter: A Text-Critical Analysis', *TC: A Journal of Biblical Textual Criticism* 21 (2016), pp. 1–22.

[33] L. Doering, *Ancient Jewish Letters and the Beginnings of Christian Epistolography* (WUNT, 1/298; Tübingen: Mohr Siebeck, 2012), pp. 429–79.

[34] M. Fishbane, *Biblical Text and Texture: A Literary Reading of Selected Texts* (Oxford: Oneworld, 1979), pp. 121–40.

Later, Exodus imagery and language was applied to situations of foreign dominance and Babylonian exile.³⁵ Therefore, what for many is the defining act of Exodus, the liberation from domination and return from exile, is palpably absent from 1 Peter. While Exodus themes are used in 1 Peter, their significance must be moderated by the letter's diaspora frame.

(1) For Obedience and For Sprinkling: 1 Peter 1.2 and Exodus 24.8

The first possible reference to Exodus traditions occurs early in the letter's second verse when the author addresses his recipients as destined 'for obedience and sprinkling with the blood of Christ' (εἰς ὑπακοὴν καὶ ῥαντισμὸν αἵματος Ἰησοῦ Χριστοῦ).³⁶ The author is here drawing on the covenant ratification ceremony in Exodus 24.³⁷ After Moses reported God's words to the people, they gave their formal assent to the covenant (24.3). This assent is sealed with burnt offerings and peace offerings (24.5), followed by a public reading from the book of the covenant, at which time the people affirm again, 'All that the LORD has spoken we will do, and we will be obedient' (Exod. 24.7b).

Table 10.3. *Comparison of 1 Peter 1.2, Exodus 24.7, and Exodus 29.20*

1 Pet. 1.2	Exod. 24.7, OG	Exod. 24.7, MT
κατὰ πρόγνωσιν θεοῦ πατρός, ἐν ἁγιασμῷ πνεύματος, εἰς ὑπακοὴν καὶ ῥαντισμὸν αἵματος Ἰησοῦ Χριστοῦ· χάρις ὑμῖν καὶ εἰρήνη πληθυνθείη.	λαβὼν δὲ Μωϋσῆς τὸ αἷμα κατεσκέδασεν τοῦ λαοῦ καὶ εἶπεν Ἰδοὺ τὸ αἷμα τῆς διαθήκης, ἧς διέθετο κύριος πρὸς ὑμᾶς περὶ πάντων τῶν λόγων τούτων.	ויקח משה את־הדם ויזרק על־העם ויאמר הנה דם־ הברית אשר כרת יהוה עמכם על כל־הדברים האלה
	Exod. 29.20, OG	*Exod. 29.20, MT*
	καὶ σφάξεις αὐτὸν καὶ λήμψῃ τοῦ αἵματος αὐτοῦ καὶ ἐπιθήσεις ἐπὶ τὸν λοβὸν τοῦ ὠτὸς Ααρων τοῦ δεξιοῦ....	ושחטת את־האיל ולקחת מדמו ונתתה על־תנוך אזן אהרן

---

[35] Mic. 7.14-15; Isa. 11.11-16; 19.19-25; 43.16-21; 48.20-21; 51.9-11; Jer. 16.14-15; 23.7-8; Ezek. 20.33-38, analyzed in Fishbane, *Text and Texture*, pp. 125–40.

[36] Author's translation. Commentators disagree over whether this εἰς clause should be interpreted as telic or causal. With the majority, I agree that it is telic: believers are elected for obedience and sprinkling with the blood of Christ. See Achtemeier, *1 Peter*, pp. 87–88; Michaels, *1 Peter*, pp. 11–12; R. Feldmeier, *The First Letter of Peter: A Commentary on the Greek Text* (Waco, TX: Baylor University Press, 2008), p. 58; Doering 'Chosen Stock', pp. 249–50.

[37] Achtemeier, *1 Peter*, p. 88; J. H. Elliott, *1 Peter: A New Translation with Introduction and Commentary* (AB, 37B; New Haven: Yale University Press, 2000), p. 320; Feldmeier, *First Peter*, pp. 58–59; K. H. Jobes, *1 Peter* (Grand Rapids: Baker Academic, 2005), pp. 72; D. A. Carson, '1 Peter', in Beale and Carson (eds.), *Commentary on the New Testament Use of the Old Testament*, pp. 1015–45 (1016–17).

Some of the blood was sprinkled on the altar; the remaining blood was sprinkled on the people, 'And Moses took the blood and threw it upon the people, and said, "Behold the blood of the covenant which the LORD has made with you in accordance with all these words"' (Exod. 24.8; cf. v. 3). In both Exodus 24 and 1 Peter, obedience and sprinkling are linked together in the formation of God's people.

Recently, Nijay Gupta and Lutz Doering have suggested that another reference may also be in view.[38] Doering notes that the verb in 1 Pet. 1.2, ῥαντίζω, differs from the verb in Exod. 24.7, κατασκεδάννυμι. Further, there is only one other passage in the Greek scriptures where ῥαντίζω appears, namely the consecration of priests in Exod. 29.20-21. Following Doering, this may be a *tertium comparationis*, in which the sprinkling of the people and the sprinkling of the priests are both held together. Furthermore, the sanctification of the people and of the priests may anticipate the Petrine author's development of these themes in 2.5 and 2.9 where the identity of believers is constructed in both corporate and priestly terms. This intriguing possibility suggests a theologically complex polyvalency in 1 Peter in which the author blends the language of Passover and priestly consecration to describe Christian identity.

(2) Girding Up the Loins of the Mind: A Possible Allusion in 1 Peter 1.13 to Exodus 12.11

The Petrine author may faintly echo the words of Exod. 12.11 in 1 Pet. 1.13 when he exhorts believers to 'therefore gird up the loins of your mind' (Διὸ ἀναζωσάμενοι τὰς ὀσφύας τῆς διανοίας ὑμῶν).[39] Exodus 12.11 explains how the Israelites are to eat the Passover, 'with your loins girded' (αἱ ὀσφύες ὑμῶν περιεζωσμέναι). Due to differences in the verbs, it is difficult to tell if it is a reference to the Passover (Exod. 12.11), to the Jesus tradition in Lk. 12.35 (identical to LXX Exod. 12.11), or a general use of a common expression (cf. Eph. 6.14). Many commentators see an allusion to the Passover here.[40] Achtemeier, however, is not convinced because the Petrine language was sufficiently common to be a general use of language and not an allusion.[41]

---

[38] Gupta, 'Cultic Imagery in 1 Peter', p. 65; L. Doering, 'Gottes Volk: Die Adressaten als "Israel" im Ersten Pestrusbrief', in D. du Toit (ed.), *Bedrängnis und Identität: Studien zu Situation, Kommunikation und Theologie des 1. Petrusbriefes* (BZNW, 200; Berlin: de Gruyter, 2013), pp. 81–113 (90–91); Doering, 'Chosen Stock', p. 250. Earlier, Sieffert suggested that the sprinkling of priests in Lev. 8.30 and the purification of the leper in Lev. 14.1-7 together with the covenant ceremony in Exod. 24 should all be understood as forms of sanctification, see E. L. Sieffert, 'Die Heilsbedeutung des Leidens und Sterbens Christi nach dem ersten Brief des Petrus', *JDT* 20 (1875), pp. 371–440.

[39] My translation. The aorist participle ἀναζωσάμενοι derives its force from the imperative ἐλπίσατε later in the verse. However, as Achtemeier has noted, it is less of an imperative 'than it is a description of the kind of people who can benefit from such an imperative, namely, those who are ready for disciplined effort'. Achtemeier, *1 Peter*, p. 118. See also Jobes, *1 Peter*, pp. 110–11, 120.

[40] For example, the following scholars recognize a paschal allusion here, Elliott, *1 Peter*, p. 365; Gupta, 'Cultic Imagery in 1 Peter', pp. 66–67; Deterding, 'Exodus Motifs', p. 62.

[41] Achtemeier is more sceptical and does not see an allusion to Exodus here, see Achtemeier, *1 Peter*, p. 118.

However, as Elliott notes, the likelihood of a Passover allusion here may be strengthened by the author's use of Passover and Exodus material later in 1.17-19 and 2.4-10.[42] If it is an allusion, then it is best, with Elliott, to note that the author is intentionally using the Passover as a metaphor for believers' state of mind (τῆς διανοίας ὑμῶν).[43] Believers may be encouraged to have this state of mind, but their existence remains one firmly grounded in the diaspora. In conclusion, it seems best, with Jobes, to allow for the possibility of an allusion here, but that this connection should not be unduly stressed.[44]

(3) A Spotless Lamb of Redemption: 1 Peter 1.17-19, Isaiah 52.3, and Exodus Traditions

In 1 Pet. 1.17, the author reminds his audience to 'live in reverent fear during the time of your exile' (ἐν φόβῳ τὸν τῆς παροικίας ὑμῶν χρόνον ἀναστράφητε). This reference to sojourning is another iteration of the diaspora trope.

Several strands of tradition, if they are present, are tightly woven together in 1.17-19, namely, Exodus, Isaianic tradition and early Christian teaching. In some places, these threads can be neatly unraveled, while in others this is more difficult. Indeed, it seems that some of these strands lie in the eye of the beholder: if, following the Gospels, Christ described his death as a ransom (Mk 10.45; Mt. 20.28), using Exodus language, and this language then became one of the standard ways of articulating the significance of his death by early Christians (1 Cor. 5.7; Jn 19.36), to what degree does this later usage of language still invoke the Exodus context from which it originated?

The author reminds believers that 'you were ransomed (ἐλυτρώθητε) ...not with perishable things, such as silver or gold (ἀργυρίῳ ἢ χρυσίῳ), but with the precious blood of Christ, like that of a lamb without defect or blemish (ὡς ἀμνοῦ ἀμώμου καὶ ἀσπίλου Χριστοῦ)' (1.18-19). The verb λυτρόω has the basic meaning 'free by paying a ransom, redeem'.[45] Similarly, its paronym, λύτρον, means 'price of release, ransom'.[46] While this word group occurred in a number of contexts, such as the freeing of prisoners of war, the manumission of slaves, and legal contexts in Greco-Roman and Jewish literature, it was often used in the context of God's redemption of Israel from bondage in Egypt.[47] In this context, the price is not usually mentioned.[48] One notable exception is Isa. 52.3-4:

> For thus says the LORD: 'You were sold for nothing, and you shall be redeemed without money' (MT: ולא בכסף תגאלו; LXX: οὐ μετὰ ἀργυρίου λυτρωθήσεσθε). For thus says the LORD GOD: Long ago, my people went

---

[42] Elliott, *1 Peter*, p. 356.
[43] Elliott, *1 Peter*, p. 356.
[44] Jobes, *1 Peter*, pp. 110–11.
[45] BDAG, p. 606.
[46] BDAG, p. 605.
[47] Exod. 6.6; 15.13; Deut. 7.8; 9.26; 15.15; 21.8; 2 Kgdms 7.23, cf. Isa. 44.22-23; 45.13; 51.11; 52.3. Cf. F. Büchsel, 'λυτρόω, λύτρον', in *TDNT*, pp. 4:340–51; Achtemeier, *1 Peter*, p. 127; Elliott, *1 Peter*, p. 369.
[48] Achtemeier, *1 Peter*, p. 127.

down into Egypt to reside there as aliens (MT: לגור; LXX: παροικῆσαι), and the Assyrian, too, has oppressed them without cause.

Whereas Isaiah declares that Israel was not redeemed with money (ἀργύριον), the author of 1 Peter instead declares that believers have been redeemed not with silver or gold (ἀργύριον), but with the blood of Christ. In Isaiah, Israel sojourned in Egypt where she was oppressed. However, believers in 1 Peter are to understand themselves as redeemed with the blood of Christ, but as still living in exile as resident aliens and sojourners.

In 1 Pet. 1.19, the passage explains that believers were redeemed with the blood of Christ, 'like that of a lamb without defect or blemish' (ὡς ἀμνοῦ ἀμώμου καὶ ἀσπίλου Χριστοῦ). Elsewhere in the New Testament, Christ is identified as a lamb.[49] Later, in 1 Pet. 2.22-25, the author weaves together references to Isaiah 53 to describe the work of Christ in terms of the Isaianic suffering servant.[50] Though the Petrine author does not quote Isa. 53.7, in which the servant is identified as a lamb (MT: שה; LXX: πρόβατον) and a sheep (MT: רחל; LXX: ἀμνός), he alludes to Isa. 53.7 in 2.23 and also alludes to Isa. 53.6 in 2.25, the immediately preceding verse, in which he likens believers to straying sheep. The close proximity of these references (1 Pet. 1.18/Isa. 52.3 and 1 Pet. 2.23/Isa. 53.7 and 1 Pet. 2.25/Isa. 53.6) has led some commentators to interpret the lamb in 1 Pet. 1.19 as the lamb of Isa. 53.7.[51]

Many commentators also see a reference to the Passover in 1 Pet. 1.19.[52] However, the language of 1 Pet. 1.19 does not replicate the Passover instructions in Exodus 12. Indeed, both the noun (ἀμνός and πρόβατον) and the qualifier (ἄμωμος and τέλειος) are different.

Table 10.4. *Comparison of 1 Peter 1.19, Exodus 12.5, and Isaiah 53.7*

1 Pet. 1.19	Exod. 12.5, LXX	Isa. 53.7, LXX
ὡς ἀμνοῦ ἀμώμου καὶ ἀσπίλου	πρόβατον τέλειον	ὡς ἀμνός
	Exod. 12.5, MT	Isa. 53.7, MT
	שה תמים	כשה

While this tempers the likelihood of an explicit quotation, it nevertheless allows for polyvalent allusions here that combine several traditions. The allusion to the

---

[49] For example, Jn 1.29, 36; Acts 8.32-35.
[50] Jobes, *1 Peter*, pp. 191–200; S. Moyise, 'Isaiah in 1 Peter', in S. Moyise and M. Menken (eds.), *Isaiah in the New Testament* (London: T&T Clark, 2005; repr. 2007), pp. 175–88 (182–84).
[51] Elliott, *1 Peter*, pp. 373–74. With nuance, Michaels, *1 Peter*, p. 65. Unlike Achtemeier, who calls this association 'possible' but the lack of further corroborating evidence makes it 'questionable'; Achtemeier, *1 Peter*, p. 129.
[52] Deterding, 'Exodus Motifs', p. 59; Gupta, 'Cultic Imagery in 1 Peter', pp. 69–70; Egan, *Ecclesiology and the Scriptural Narrative of 1 Peter*, pp. 82–83. Contrast Achtemeier, *1 Peter*, pp. 128–29, who concludes that the primary reference here is not to Passover, but to the sacrificial system in general.

Passover tradition is a sturdy possibility, given extra weight by the reference to the ransom in v. 18. However, the reference in v. 19 to the 'lamb without defect or blemish' more clearly echoes the Pentateuchal cultic traditions that state that sacrifices should be blameless.[53] In several places, the term ἀμνός is qualified as ἄμωμος.[54] For example, Lev. 14.10 includes among the required offerings for the cleansing of a leper 'two male ewe lambs without blemish' (MT: שני כבשים תמימים; LXX: δύο ἀμνοὺς ἐνιαυσίους ἀμώμους).

In conclusion, the language of 1 Pet. 1.19 is influenced primarily by the Jewish sacrificial system (thus, Achtemeier and Michaels). However, the author's language does allow for more allusive echoes to the Passover and to the Isaianic suffering servant to be lying just below the surface of the text.

(4) A Holy Priesthood: 1 Peter 2.5 and Exodus 19.6

First Peter 2.4-10 forms a discrete section, a fitting and majestic climax to the first half of the letter. As Elliott has shown, vv. 4-5 introduce the two sections that follow (vv. 6-8 and 9-10).[55] The Petrine author begins this unit by naming the themes, vocabulary, and characters he will discuss in vv. 6-10. In 1 Pet. 2.5, the author makes his first reference to Exod. 19.6 when he calls believers a 'holy priesthood'. The use of the term ἱεράτευμα anticipates the fuller development of Exod. 19.6 in 2.9 where God's people are called a 'royal priesthood' (βασίλειον ἱεράτευμα).

Table 10.5. *Comparison of 1 Peter 2.5 and Exodus 19.6*

1 Pet. 2.5, NT	Exod. 19.6, OG	Exod. 19.6, MT
καὶ αὐτοὶ ὡς λίθοι ζῶντες οἰκοδομεῖσθε οἶκος πνευματικὸς εἰς ἱεράτευμα ἅγιον, ἀνενέγκαι πνευματικὰς θυσίας εὐπροσδέκτους θεῷ διὰ Ἰησοῦ Χριστοῦ.	ὑμεῖς δὲ ἔσεσθέ μοι βασίλειον ἱεράτευμα καὶ ἔθνος ἅγιον. ταῦτα τὰ ῥήματα ἐρεῖς τοῖς υἱοῖς Ισραηλ.	ואתם תהיו לי ממלכת כהנים וגוי קדוש אלה הדברים אשר תדבר אל בני ישראל

Notably, the author applies the language of priesthood to all believers. The adjective ἅγιος recalls the letter's earlier command to be holy as God is holy (1 Pet. 1.15-16; cf. Lev. 19.1). All believers are to understand themselves as God's holy, priestly people, and to live accordingly. This language functions to bestow honor on believers who were facing ostracism and prejudice from their neighbors. Like Christ, their cornerstone and exemplar par excellence, believers may face rejection and scorn from the world, but they will be honored before God.

---

[53] Michaels, *1 Peter*, p. 66; Achtemeier, *1 Peter*, pp. 128–29; Elliott, *1 Peter*, p. 374.
[54] LXX Exod. 29.38; Lev. 14.10; 23.18; Num. 6.14; 28.3; 29.1. LXX Exod. 29.38 specifies that the lamb must be blameless, while the Hebrew text does not.
[55] Elliott, *1 Peter*, pp. 407–408.

c. A Royal Priesthood: 1 Peter 2.9 and Exodus 19.5-6

First Peter 2.9-10 is the theological crescendo of the letter. After the introduction in vv. 4-5, the author elaborates on the effect of Christ on those who do not believe in him (vv. 6-8). He does this with an assortment of scriptural quotations (Isa. 28.16, Ps. 118.22, and Isa. 8.14-15). In vv. 9-10, the author turns to the identity of those who do believe. In a similar fashion, he marshals an impressive array of scriptural texts to describe believers' honored identity with epithets taken from Israel's history and scriptures.

In 1 Pet. 2.9-10, the author weaves together quotations and allusions to Exod. 19.6, Isa. 43.20-21, and Hos. 2.25 to describe Christian identity using epithets for Israel. In v. 9, he uses four titles in quick succession, 'a chosen race, a royal priesthood, holy nation, God's own people'. The first and last of these titles are drawn from Isa. 43.20-21, while the middle two come from Exod. 19.6 (cf. LXX Exod. 23.22).[56]

Table 10.6. *Comparison of 1 Peter 2.9, Exodus 19.5-6, Exodus 23.22, and Isaiah 43.20-21*

1 Pet. 2.9, NT	*Exod. 19.5-6, OG*	*Exod. 19.5-6, MT*
Ὑμεῖς δὲ γένος ἐκλεκτόν, βασίλειον ἱεράτευμα, ἔθνος ἅγιον, λαὸς εἰς περιποίησιν, ὅπως τὰς ἀρετὰς ἐξαγγείλητε τοῦ ἐκ σκότους ὑμᾶς καλέσαντος εἰς τὸ θαυμαστὸν αὐτοῦ φῶς·	καὶ νῦν ἐὰν ἀκοῇ ἀκούσητε τῆς ἐμῆς φωνῆς καὶ φυλάξητε τὴν διαθήκην μου, ἔσεσθέ μοι **λαὸς περιούσιος** ἀπὸ πάντων τῶν ἐθνῶν· ἐμὴ γάρ ἐστιν πᾶσα ἡ γῆ· ὑμεῖς δὲ ἔσεσθέ μοι **βασίλειον ἱεράτευμα καὶ ἔθνος ἅγιον.**	ועתה אם שמוע תשמעו בקלי ושמרתם את בריתי והייתם לי סגלה מכל העמים כי לי כל הארץ: ואתם תהיו לי ממלכת כהנים וגוי קדוש אלה הדברים אשר תדבר אל בני ישראל
	Exod. 23.22, OG	*Exod. 23.22, MT*
	ἐὰν ἀκοῇ ἀκούσητε τῆς ἐμῆς φωνῆς καὶ ποιήσῃς πάντα, ὅσα ἂν ἐντείλωμαί σοι, καὶ φυλάξητε τὴν διαθήκην μου, ἔσεσθέ μοι **λαὸς περιούσιος** ἀπὸ πάντων τῶν ἐθνῶν· ἐμὴ γάρ ἐστιν πᾶσα ἡ γῆ, ὑμεῖς δὲ ἔσεσθέ μοι **βασίλειον ἱεράτευμα καὶ ἔθνος ἅγιον.**	כי אם שמע תשמע בקלו ועשית כל אשר אדבר ואיבתי את איביך וצרתי את צרריך

---

[56] Achtemeier, *1 Peter*, p. 163; Michaels, *1 Peter*, p. 107; Elliott, *1 Peter*, p. 435.

	Isa. 43.20-21, OG	Isa. 43.20-21, MT
	εὐλογήσει με τὰ θηρία τοῦ ἀγροῦ, σειρῆνες καὶ θυγατέρες στρουθῶν, ὅτι ἔδωκα ἐν τῇ ἐρήμῳ ὕδωρ καὶ ποταμοὺς ἐν τῇ ἀνύδρῳ ποτίσαι **τὸ γένος μου τὸ ἐκλεκτόν, λαόν μου, ὃν περιεποιησάμην τὰς ἀρετάς μου** διηγεῖσθαι.	תכבדני חית השדה תנים ובנות יענה כי נתתי במדבר מים נהרות בישימן להשקות עמי בחירי: עם זו יצרתי לי תהלתי יספרו:

The pair of phrases from Exod. 19.6, ἔθνος ἅγιον and βασίλειον ἱεράτευμα, nicely complements one another and highlight the two themes of holiness and priesthood. The phrase ἔθνος ἅγιον highlights the theme of holiness and believers' relationship with God, while the complementary βασίλειον ἱεράτευμα relates believers to God and gestures towards their priestly role in wider society.

The phrase βασίλειον ἱεράτευμα has an interesting history.[57] In its Greek form in 1 Peter and the OG (Exod. 19.6; 23.22), it is composed of the noun ἱεράτευμα and the adjective βασίλειος.[58] As such, it is rendered 'royal priesthood'. By contrast, the Hebrew phrase is composed of two nouns in the construct state and means 'kingdom of priests'.

The phrase occurs at a significant place in the Exodus narrative. After delivering his people out of slavery in Egypt, God brought them to Mt. Sinai to establish his covenant. Exodus 19.1 signals the remembrance of these events, 'On the third new moon after the people of Israel had gone forth out of the land of Egypt...'. Through the events of the Exodus, God has chosen a new people for himself who were called to corporate holiness according to his own character. God's holiness therefore defines the holy character of his people, a theme clearly voiced in 1 Pet. 1.16-17.[59]

---

[57] Quotations and allusions to Exod. 19.6 may include 2 Macc. 2.17; *Jub.* 16.18; 33.20; Philo, *Abr.* 56; *Sobr.* 66, and possibly Rev. 1.6 and 5.10. More allusive references include 1Q21, Greek frag. of *T. Levi* 11.4-6, ln. 67 and Rev. 20.6. For a more detailed discussion, see J. H. Elliott, *The Elect and the Holy: An Exegetical Examination of 1 Peter 2:4-10 and the Phrase* Βασίλειον ἱεράτευμα (NovTSup, 12; Leiden: Brill, 1966), pp. 63–128.

[58] Elliott took βασίλειον ἱεράτευμα as two substantives, 'a royal residence, a priestly community' based on the appearance of two substantives in many quotations and allusions to Exod. 19.6 in Jewish and early Christian literature; Elliott, *The Elect and the Holy*, pp. 120–28. However, he has not convinced others. One of the chief arguments against Elliott's position is the fact that v. 9 is composed of a series of nouns modified by adjectives, which indicates that this is probably how βασίλειον ἱεράτευμα is to be taken. For more on this, see Achtemeier, *1 Peter*, pp. 164–65; Michaels, *1 Peter*, pp. 108–109.

[59] T. B. Dozeman, *Commentary on Exodus* (Grand Rapids: Eerdmans, 2009), pp. 445–46, cf. pp. 411–15.

Israel's priestly nature also has an outward dimension. In a mysterious way, Israel as a nation holds a priestly identity in relation to the rest of the world.[60] This may already be seen in Isa. 61.6, where other nations call Israel 'priests of the Lord', and Ezek. 20.41, where God manifests his holiness to Israel in the sight of all the nations.[61] Both of these aspects, corporate holiness and priestly orientation, have resonance with 1 Peter. As shown above, the theme of corporate holiness runs throughout 1 Peter (esp. 1.15-16). Furthermore, one of the purposes of a holy, priestly identity, as v. 9 explains, is to proclaim the deeds of God, an inherently missional activity.[62]

First Peter, in its own way, has taken up Israel's epithets and deployed them in the service of Christian identity. However, unlike the Israelites, 1 Peter continues to address believers as those living in a type of spiritual exile based on their Christian identity. Writing to a mostly Gentile audience, the author used these terms of Israelite identity to forge a new Christian identity. The scriptures and narratives of Israel, interpreted through the work of Christ, are now what defines the life and identity of believers as God's royal priesthood and holy nation.

4. 2 Peter and Jude

In Jude and 2 Peter, Exodus material is used only once, in Jude 5. Though 2 Peter reworks much of Jude, this reference to the Exodus is not taken up.[63] In 2 Pet. 2.1-10, the author chooses his biblical examples, such as the wicked angels, Noah and Lot to illustrate that 'the Lord knows how to rescue the godly from trial, and to keep the unrighteous under punishment until the day of judgment' (2.9).[64] While Noah and Lot are encouraging examples of those who steadfastly lived a righteous life in the face of adversity, the example of the wilderness generation, whom God saved but later destroyed, hardly suits this motivational purpose. It seems likely that, for this reason, the example of the wilderness generation was not incorporated into 2 Peter. Within Jude, this example serves a very different purpose.

In Jude 5-7, the author provides three biblical examples of those who were once favored or privileged, or at least prosperous, who ultimately faced judgment and destruction: the wilderness generation, the fallen angels, and the cities of

---

[60] Dozeman, *Commentary on Exodus*, pp. 445–46; B. S. Childs, *The Book of Exodus: A Critical, Theological Commentary* (OTL; Philadelphia: Westminster, 1974), p. 367.

[61] Dozeman, *Commentary on Exodus*, p. 446.

[62] Gupta, 'Cultic Imagery in 1 Peter', p. 74. The letter also stresses believers' responsibility to live honorable lives among their unbelieving neighbours so that their behavior may be a witness. For example, see 1 Pet. 2.12; 3.1-2, 15-16.

[63] In good company, I work from the standpoint that 2 Peter is dependent on Jude. See R. Bauckham, *Jude, 2 Peter* (WBC, 50; Grand Rapids: Zondervan, 1983), pp. 8, 141–43; T. Wasserman, *The Epistle of Jude: Its Text and Transmission* (ConBNT, 43; Stockholm, Sweden: Almqvist & Wiksell International, 2006), pp. 73–98; P. H. Davids, *The Letters of 2 Peter and Jude* (PNTC; Grand Rapids: Eerdmans, 2006), pp. 136–43; J. H. Neyrey, *2 Peter, Jude* (AB, 37C; New Haven, CT: Doubleday, 1993), pp. 121–22.

[64] Bauckham, *Jude, 2 Peter*, pp. 246–47; Wasserman, *Epistle of Jude*, pp. 82–85.

Sodom and Gomorrah.⁶⁵ In Jude, these examples function as warnings against false teachers and counter-examples for right Christian behavior (cf. Jude 4). Similar lists of sinners who face divine judgement are found throughout Jewish literature.⁶⁶ Unlike Jude, most of these Jewish lists are given in chronological order, a peculiarity Jude shares only with the *Testament of Naphtali*.⁶⁷

As Tommy Wasserman has said, Jude 5 'is one of the textually most difficult passages in Jude, and in the whole NT'.⁶⁸ As such, it has received a great deal of scholarly attention.⁶⁹ The two most significant textual questions in this verse (among others!) are the placement and meaning of ἅπαξ and the subject of ἀπώλεσεν. These questions will be examined first because they have great bearing on the verse's theological claims.

First, should ἅπαξ modify εἰδότας, or come after the ὅτι clause and modify σώσας? The textual evidence is evenly divided, though Wasserman judges the textual evidence supporting ἅπαξ as an adverb modifying εἰδότας as slightly better.⁷⁰ Either way, ἅπαξ modifies a past participle. As Hafemann observes, the predominant, though not exclusive, meaning of ἅπαξ in this construction is 'once for all' in a definitive and ultimate sense.⁷¹ This seems to be the best understanding of the term with either reading.

On external and internal grounds, Hafemann has recently argued that ἅπαξ should be taken with σώσας. He rightly argues that Jude 5 must be read against the background of Numbers 14, because this is the only place in the Exodus narrative where God intends to destroy the Israelites (καὶ ἀπολῶ αὐτούς; LXX Num. 14.12) for their unbelief (οὐ πιστεύουσίν μοι; Num. 14.11; cf. 14.22-23, 27-28, 33-35).⁷² Based on the strong set of structural, linguistic, and theological parallels between Numbers 14 and Exodus 32–34, Hafemann then argues that the ἅπαξ event is

---

⁶⁵ In Gen. 13.10-11, Lot sees that the Jordan valley was well-watered 'like the garden of the LORD, like the land of Egypt'.
⁶⁶ Sir. 16.7-10; CD 2.17–3.12; 3 Macc. 2.4-7; *T. Napht.* 3.4-5; *m. Sanh.* 10.3, see Bauckham, *Jude, 2 Peter*, pp. 46–47.
⁶⁷ In *T. Naphthali*, Sodom is mentioned before the Watchers; Bauckham, *Jude, 2 Peter*, p. 46.
⁶⁸ Wasserman, *Epistle of Jude*, p. 255.
⁶⁹ M. Black, 'Critical and Exegetical Notes on Three New Testament Texts: Hebrews 6:11, Jude 5, James 1:27', in W. Eltester *et al.* (eds.), *Apophoreta: Festschrift für Ernst Haenchen zu seinem siebzigsten Geburtstag* (Berlin: A. Töpelmann, 1964), pp. 39–45; A. P. Wikgren, 'Some problems in Jude 5', in B. L. Daniels and M. J. Suggs (eds.), *Studies in History and Text of the New Testament in Honor of Kenneth Willis Clark* (Salt Lake City: University of Utah Press, 1967), pp. 147–52; C. D. Osburn, 'The Text of Jude 5', *Bib* 62 (1981), pp. 107–115; J. Fossum, 'Kyrios Jesus as the Angel of the Lord in Jude 5–7', *NTS* 33 (1987), pp. 226–43; P. F. Bartholomä, 'Did Jesus Save the People out of Egypt? A Re-examination of a Textual Problem in Jude 5', *NovT* 50 (2008), pp. 143–58; S. J. Hafemann, 'God's Salvation "Once and for All" in Jude 5 and the Covenant Argumentation of 2 Peter 1:3-11: Confirming One's Election in the CE', in K.-W. Niebuhr and R. W. Wall (eds.), *The Catholic Epistles and Apostolic Tradition: A New Perspective on James to Jude* (Waco, TX: Baylor, 2009), pp. 331–42.
⁷⁰ For ἅπαξ modifying σώσας, Wasserman lists: 01 04* 044 88 323 424C 442 630 665 1409 1505 1611 1845 1852V 1739T 1881 2138 2200 *al* L:T K:SB S:HPh. For ἅπαξ modifying εἰδότας, 𝔓⁷² 02 03 04C2V 0251 33 81 307 436 453 623 808 1067 1875 *al* 𝔐 Cyr PsOec L:V, Wasserman, *Epistle of Jude*, pp. 258–260.
⁷¹ See also Jude 3. Hafemann, '"Once for all" in Jude 5', p. 333.
⁷² Hafemann, '"Once for all" in Jude 5', pp. 331–37. Also, Bauckham, *Jude, 2 Peter*, pp. 49–50.

God's restoration of the covenant after the golden calf incident in Exodus 32–34.[73] This solution has an elegant coherence. Other commentators identify the referent of the first event in Jude 5 more globally as the larger narrative of Israel's deliverance from Egypt and the second as Israel's failure in Numbers 14.[74]

The alternative reading takes ἅπαξ with εἰδότας. With Bauckham, the first half of the verse can be translated, 'Now I should like to remind you, though you have been informed of all things once and for all, that…'.[75] This prepares the way for the author's list of biblical examples.

Second, what is the subject of ἀπώλεσεν? Wasserman lists the various readings:[76]

κυριος 01 44 1875 *al*
ο κυριος 18 35 307 326 424* 431 436 453 630 808 1505 1611 1836 1837 2138 2200 2495 𝔐 PsOec
(ο) κυριος **S**:H
ιησους 02 03 33C 81 323 424C 665 1739 *pc* Cyr **K**:S
ο ιησους 88 915
(ο) ιησους **L**:V
κυριος ιησους 1735
ο κυριος ιησους L241 L591 L1178
ο θεος 04C2V 442 621 623 1845 *pc* **L**:TV^mss **S**:Ph
θεος κυριος P72

The problem is that (ο) ιησους has the strongest manuscript support.[77] However, this reading is regarded by many commentators as virtually impossible because it would be the only place in the New Testament where the pre-existent Christ is identified as Jesus, an option most find highly unlikely.[78] However, (ο) ιησους has found recent advocates and is the reading printed in the *ECM*.[79] In 1 Cor. 10.4, Paul identifies the pre-existent Christ (ὁ Χριστός) as the rock that follows Israel in the wilderness (cf. 1 Cor. 10.9; Heb. 11.26 and Jn 8.58), which may suggest that such direct articulations of Jesus' pre-existence were possible.[80]

Though some have appealed to a Joshua-Jesus typology to explain the appearance of (ο) ιησους, this explanation does not solve the problem since Joshua does not destroy the unbelievers (v. 5b) or keep the angels in chains (v. 6).[81] However, this typology became popular in the second century and may account

---

[73] Hafemann, '"Once for all" in Jude 5', pp. 336–37.
[74] Bauckham, *Jude, 2 Peter*, pp. 49–50; Davids, *The Letters of 2 Peter and Jude*, pp. 47–48.
[75] Bauckham, *Jude, 2 Peter*, pp. 42–43.
[76] Wasserman, *Epistle of Jude*, p. 262.
[77] B. Metzger, *A Textual Commentary on the Greek New Testament* (London: United Bible Societies, 1971), p. 657; Wasserman, *Epistle of Jude*, pp. 262–63; Osburn, 'Jude 5', pp. 111–15.
[78] Wasserman, *Epistle of Jude*, pp. 263–66; Bauckham, *Jude, 2 Peter*, pp. 43, 49; Davids, *The Letters of 2 Peter and Jude*, pp. 47–48.
[79] Osburn, 'Jude 5', pp. 107–115; Bartholomä, 'Textual Problem', pp. 143–58; Neyrey, *2 Peter, Jude*, pp. 61–62.
[80] Other later examples from early Christianity include Justin, *Dial.* 120.3 See Osburn, 'Jude 5', pp. 112–13; Bartholomä, 'Textual Problem', pp. 154–56.
[81] This typology goes back at least as far as Jerome, contra *Jov.* 1 (cf. Acts 7.45; Heb. 4.8). Osburn, 'Jude 5', pp. 111–12; Bauckham, *Jude, 2 Peter*, p. 43.

for the change from (ο) κυριος to (ο) ιησους by a scribe who missed its pitfalls.[82] Therefore, if (ο) κυριος is accepted as the original, then there are clear ways to explain how the other readings developed.[83] Subsequent scribes may have sought to clarify the term's inherent ambiguity or highlight typological correspondences. It is also possible that some of the textual variants arose over confusion regarding a *nomen sacrum*, $\overline{κc}$ being mistaken for $\overline{ιc}$.[84]

In Jude 5 the exodus tradition establishes a firm historical reference to God's saving action in the past. Just as the wilderness generation, the beneficiaries of God's deliverance, later sinned and faced judgment, so too are believers warned to learn from their example. They must vigilantly guard themselves against false teachers who would lead them in the ways of sin and judgment.

5. Conclusion

In conclusion, the General Letters do not demonstrate a systematic or sustained interest in Exodus or exodus traditions. Rather, the Exodus material reflected in the General Letters seems to reflect the contemporary Jewish and Christian interpretive environment. Hence, the Exodus material that does populate the letters is generally drawn from widely known or particularly influential texts or narratives.

The Exodus material in James demonstrates this well. James has one possible quotation of the Decalogue (Exod. 20.13-15 in Jas 2.11) and a possible allusion to the statement of divine self-disclosure in Exod. 34.6 (Jas 5.11). This chapter also argued that the proposed allusion in Jas 4.5 was in all likelihood not an allusion to Exodus at all but a reference to the now-lost book of *Eldad and Modad*.

First Peter has a wider selection of Exodus references, though these do not demonstrate a special interest in Exodus *per se* as much as an outworking of the author's larger hermeneutical agenda to interpret the Hebrew scriptures in terms of Christ and the church. To this end, the letter gives special attention to texts and narratives that have priestly, sacrificial, or paschal language (thus, the possible allusion to the sprinkling in Exod. 24.8 in 1 Pet. 1.2; the reference to the spotless lamb in 1 Pet. 1.17-19; and the reference to priesthood in 1 Pet. 2.5 and 2.9 drawing on Exod. 19.5-6). Finally, 1 Pet. 1.13 may also be an echo of Exodus tradition.

Jude refers to exodus tradition only once. In Jude 5, Israel's deliverance from Egypt serves as a reminder that while God saved Israel from Egypt, he later destroyed those who did not believe.

These case studies from James, 1 Peter, and Jude illustrate the diversity with which scripture texts and narratives were interpreted in early Christianity. This chapter has also explored how the use of traditional material in the General Letters can fall into the gray areas between quotations and allusions, and between allusions and echoes.

---

[82] For early examples of the Joshua/Jesus typology, see *Barn.* 12.8; Justin, *Dial.* 24.2; 75.12; Clem. Alex., *Paed.* 1.60.3; Bauckham, *Jude, 2 Peter*, p. 43.
[83] Wasserman, *Epistle of Jude*, pp. 262–66; Bauckham, *Jude, 2 Peter*, p. 43.
[84] Metzger, *Textual Commentary*, p. 657; Wasserman, *Epistle of Jude*, pp. 265–66.

Chapter 10

READING EXODUS IN REVELATION

Michelle Fletcher

What is Revelation's relationship with the book of Exodus? Revelation does not behave in a way that makes examination of its relationship with any specific traditions or texts easy. Quite the opposite in fact. This is because, despite Revelation being packed with HB material, it never once quotes a HB text. Its relationship with the HB is far subtler, as it infuses all levels and blends with new textual partners. As a result, an examination of Exodus (or any HB texts) in Revelation is most definitely 'problematic'. Indeed, it goes against the very fabric of the text.

The present study begins by summarizing key scholarly debates on the 'use of the HB' in Revelation, before presenting our chosen approach for examining Exodus. We then move onto our textual studies, which will focus on Exodus-evoking words, phrases, motifs, and structures to facilitate an exploration of the multilevel textual dialogues at work in Revelation. Through this process, we will see how the audience is swept up in a sea of textual experiences as they encounter what is, was, and is to come.

1. Scholarly Trends and Exodus Issues

Revelation's unique use of the HB means that approaches used for other NT books, such as exploring citations, do not adequately explain Revelation's HB relationships. How then will we explore Exodus in Revelation? A summary of methodological shifts reveals the scholarly trends that inform our approach.

Although Revelation's HB resemblance has long attracted scholars,[1] Gregory Beale's 1984 study of Revelation's use of Daniel marks the start of a trend

---

[1] E.g., A. von Schlatter, *Das Alte Testament in der johanneischen Apokalypse.* (Gütersloh: Bertelsmann, 1912); A. M. Farrer, *A Rebirth of Images: The Making of St. John's Apocalypse* (Westminster:

for methodologically focused monographs.² Beale focused on pinpointing HB allusions and HB sources intended by the author. His approach has been influential, with Jon Paulien, Jan Fekkes, and Marko Jauhiainen carrying on the trend of finding allusions and discounting 'erroneous echoes'.³ This seems logical, for if Revelation has no citations, then allusions are the 'next best' textual source. However, these studies have actually revealed, as Fekkes states, that allusions are 'not entirely satisfactory in describing John's method'.⁴ David Mathewson agrees, arguing that Revelation's allusions and echoes are more of a spectrum with 'quieter' voices playing key roles,⁵ and Beate Kowalski shows that studies of linguistic parallels can only go so far as reliance on LXX or MT cannot be confirmed.⁶ What is more, as Paulien admits, focusing on the 'original contexts' of HB allusions has often said more about the HB source texts than Revelation itself.⁷

This has gone hand-in-hand with a recognition of the complexity of Revelation's use of HB sources: they appear on many levels, including verbal, thematic, and structural, and they are blended together, with multiple textual voices frequently heard in a single phrase or image.⁸ Therefore, rather than isolating HB texts and focusing on 'original contexts', methods for reading the interaction of voices within their new contexts have increasingly been sought.⁹ This has meant that, although authorial intent still prevails, reader-response approaches have gained ground as ways of exploring multiple evocations, rather than one 'clearly intended source'.¹⁰ This is reflected in my own work on the HB in Revelation, which focuses on the audience-impact of such multivalency and the interaction

---

Dacre, 1949); R. H. Charles, *A Critical and Exegetical Commentary on the Revelation of St. John* (2 vols.; Edinburgh: T&T Clark, 1920); G. Mussies, *The Morphology of Koine Greek, as Used in The Apocalypse of St. John: A Study in Bilingualism* (Leiden: Brill, 1971).

2. G. K. Beale, *The Use of Daniel in Jewish Apocalyptic Literature and in the Revelation of St. John* (Lanham, MD: University Press of America, 1984). Furthered in G. K. Beale, *John's Use of the Old Testament in Revelation* (JSNTSup, 166; Sheffield: Sheffield Academic, 1998); G. K. Beale, *The Book of Revelation: A Commentary on the Greek Text* (NIGTC; Grand Rapids: Eerdmans, 1999). For post-1980s debates see Chapter 1 of M. Fletcher, *Reading Revelation as Pastiche: Imitating the Past* (LNTS, 571; London: Bloomsbury T&T Clark, 2017).

3. J. Paulien, *Decoding Revelation's Trumpets: Literary Allusions and Interpretation of Revelation 8:7–12* (Berrien Springs: Andrews University Press, 1988); J. Fekkes, *Isaiah and Prophetic Traditions in the Book of Revelation* (Sheffield: JSOT, 1994); M. Jauhiainen, *The Use of Zechariah in Revelation* (WUNT 2/199; Tübingen: Mohr Siebeck, 2005).

4. Fekkes, *Isaiah*, p. 69.

5. D. Mathewson, *A New Heaven and a New Earth: The Meaning and Function of the Old Testament in Revelation 21:1–22:5* (JSNTSup, 238; London: Sheffield Academic, 2003).

6. B. Kowalski, *Die Rezeption des Propheten Ezechiel in der Offenbarung des Johannes* (Stuttgart: Verlag Katholisches Bibelwerk, 2004).

7. Paulien, *Decoding*, p. 431.

8. Beale, *Commentary*, p. 79, notes that '[m]ost of the OT reminiscences are combined into groups. Sometimes four, five, or more OT references are merged into one picture.'

9. E.g., J.-P. Ruiz, *Ezekiel in the Apocalypse: The Transformation of Prophetic Language in Revelation 16,17–19,10* (Frankfurt am Main: Peter Lang, 1989); S. Moyise, *The Old Testament in the Book of Revelation* (JSNTSup, 115; Sheffield: Sheffield Academic, 1995); A. Jack, *Texts Reading Texts, Sacred and Secular* (JSNTSup, 179; Sheffield: Sheffield Academic, 1999); M. Sommer, *Der Tag der Plagen* (WUNT, 2/387; Tübingen: Mohr Siebeck, 2015).

10. E.g., Mathewson, *New Heaven*, p. 24, believes in giving equal weight to the potential uses of the HB and the effect on the interpreter, and Jauhiainen, *Zechariah*, uses a reader-focused mechanism.

of HB voices in their new contexts, both temporal and textual.[11] However, multi-vocal approaches create problems when wanting to focus on the use of a single text in Revelation; if multiple textual evocations are possible, surely reading for just one goes against the fabric of the text (and indeed quite against this author's methods). Therefore, the solution proposed here is to read 'with Exodus', rather than 'for Exodus'. What this means is that Exodus will be used to present a 'flavour' of Revelation's HB saturated fabric, with our focus being how Exodus-evoking elements resonate in their new contexts and how Exodus may not be all that they evoke.[12] The goal is not to show or map how Exodus is used, or list all its potential resonances (the list would cover most of the text),[13] but rather to use Exodus to give a flavour of the complex way the HB resonates in Revelation.

To do this, a variety of textual features will be discussed in the order they appear in Revelation, ranging from loan words to phrases to motifs. Each is selected because it has drawn commentators, ancient and modern, to hear the text of Exodus. The resonances heard by commentators and the readings these effect will be our core focus, thus providing the material to demonstrate the wide-ranging variety of reader responses to potential Exodus material within the text.[14] This allows us to move on from arguments regarding whether something is or is not an 'allusion' to Exodus, to explore instead how scholars have reacted to potential Exodus evocations.[15]

Studies of the use of Exodus in Revelation are limited, despite a repeated attestation to its textual presence. Two of the most in-depth examinations to date are (1) Michael Sommer's *Der Tag der Plagen*, which focuses on the potential use of Exodus 7–11 in Revelation and, (2) HaYoung Son's concise study of the relationship of Revelation 15 with Exodus 15.[16] These volumes alert us to two key issues particularly pertinent to Exodus-specific studies of Revelation. First, because Exodus recounts one of the seminal events in Israelite history, it is absorbed and rewritten in later HB texts. As a result, just because something in Revelation is Exodus-like, it does not mean it is drawing on the book of Exodus; it may be drawing on later re-tellings. Second, references to the exodus as an event (what Son calls 'Exodus traditions') and references to the text of Exodus can be difficult

---

[11] I nuance Moyise's and Mathewson's suggestions that intertextuality offers a methodological solution, as intertextuality itself is not a methodology (despite frequent arguments that it is), nor even a description of specific textual practices, but is instead a way of describing textual relationships. Therefore, while we can state that Revelation is highly intertextual, something more is required to read its composite nature. I argue specific practices of combination and imitation can do this; see Fletcher, *Reading Revelation*.

[12] Reading texts in new locations always alters and this is the same for *any* text. However, this focus on new temporal locations helps to draw our attention away from 'original HB contexts' and 'respect of meaning'.

[13] Indeed, Beale's commentary index references nearly the entire text; Beale, *Commentary*, pp. 1175–76.

[14] Those chosen are some of the most frequently noted, but are not usually considered together.

[15] These will often have been argued to be Exodus allusions by scholars but are here termed 'evocations' to remind us of their more complex nature. The shunning of the term 'allusion' is intentional.

[16] H. Son, *Praising God Beside the Sea: An Intertextual Study of Revelation 15 and Exodus 15* (Eugene, OR: Wipf & Stock, 2017).

to separate (as they are in her study). Therefore, we will read expecting altered traditions, considering how Exodus-originating elements might resonate within first-century interpretative frameworks.[17]

Finally, it is important to note that while the theme and narrative of the exodus/ the new exodus is undeniably infused into Revelation, and many others have done invaluable work on this topic, this will not be our focus.[18] Instead, we will concentrate on specific moments in the text which a number of scholars, ancient and modern, have argued evoke specific parts of the book of Exodus (as opposed to broader themes as in, e.g., Rev. 12), asking what impact they may have on Revelation's audience, past and present (although of course exodus themes are key to remember and will inevitably infuse scholarly readings).

So, we now turn to explore the text, looking at the use of the divine name in Rev. 1.4, manna in Rev. 2.17, the arrival of the Lamb in Revelation 5, the song of Moses in Revelation 15, and the Plagues in Revelation 16. These examples will provide a 'flavour' of the micro to macro way(s) that Revelation evokes, combines, and relocates HB material.

2. Divine Name: Revelation 1.4

After Revelation's initial greetings, the author sends grace and peace from ὁ ὢν καὶ ὁ ἦν καὶ ὁ ἐρχόμενος (Rev. 1.4).[19] This marks Revelation's first major Exodus-sighting, with commentators noting similarity to the LXX rendering of the divine name in Exod. 3.14. It also likely marks the first use of ὁ ὢν by a 'Christian author',[20] making this a stand-out textual moment. However, Revelation's tripartite rendering is somewhat distinct, causing debate about potential sources.

Among treatments of the divine name in Rev. 1.4, Sean McDonough's is one of the most comprehensive, tracing its history from early roots into first-century manifestations.[21] First-century context is essential to him, and so he begins not with HB usage, but with Greek literature. He particularly focuses on concepts of 'Being' related to τὸ ὄν to contextualize Rev. 1.4 within its Hellenistic inheritance because: '[w]hen John used the phrase ὁ ὢν to describe God in Rev. 1.4, he landed himself (wittingly or unwittingly) in the middle of a long and complex philosophical conversation concerning God and Being'.[22] Therefore, central to his discussion is the LXX ἐγώ εἰμι ὁ ὢν (cf. MT אהיה אשר אהיה), which he

---

[17] Even if the textual tradition of Exodus was relatively stable by the time of Revelation, the reception of Exodus is hardly a static or agreed matter.
[18] E.g., A. Boesak, *Comfort and Protest* (Philadelphia: Westminster, 1987); B. K. Blount, *Can I Get a Witness? Reading Revelation through African American Culture* (Louisville: Westminster John Knox, 2005), P. Ricard, *Apocalypse: A People's Commentary on the Book of Revelation* (New York: Orbis, 1998). For important articles and chapters, see Son, *Praising God*, p. xxvii.
[19] Although our focus is the threefold title, its complex textual surroundings should be remembered.
[20] D. E. Aune, *Revelation 1–5* (WBC, 52A; Dallas: Word, 1997), p. 31.
[21] S. M. McDonough, *YHWH at Patmos: Rev. 1:4 in its Hellenistic and Early Jewish Setting* (WUNT, 2/107; Tübingen: Mohr Siebeck, 1999).
[22] McDonough, *YHWH*, p. 11. He examines the tetragrammaton, and the use of YHWH in Jewish literature.

argues is the earliest example of referring to God as ὁ ὤν.²³ Thus, he believes that while translators may have been aware of the philosophical implications of such a rendering (and Philo certainly interprets it this way), the idea of 'ὁ ὤν for a deity was a Jewish innovation'.²⁴ This conclusion may be controversial, but what matters is that ὁ ὤν is definitely hard to separate from LXX Exod. 3.14.²⁵ Therefore, when it appears in the opening lines of Revelation, this evocation is highly likely. Other HB occurrences may also resonate, particularly Jeremiah (1.6; 14.13; 39.17), but even there Exod. 3.14 hovers behind the rendering.

Basically, it is difficult to argue that the first part of Rev. 1.4's threefold formula would not evoke Exod. 3.14, as it did for Andrew of Caesarea: 'through the phrase "who is" the Father is indicated, who spoke to Moses: "I am Who I am [ἐγώ εἰμι ὁ ὤν]"'.²⁶ But what about Revelation's more complex tripartite formulation? Revelation is awash with textual blending and alteration, and this appears to be true even for the divine name: it is not ὁ ὤν, but ὁ ὤν καὶ ὁ ἦν καὶ ὁ ἐρχόμενος. These three elements appear again in Rev. 1.8; 4.8 (transposed) and with a shortened form in Rev. 11.17; 16.5, which David Aune designates as 'perhaps a more traditional form that John expanded'.²⁷ Perhaps, but the first encounter is with the tripartite version, which goes beyond Exod. 3.14.

McDonough points out that nowhere in the HB does ὁ ὤν καὶ ὁ ἦν καὶ ὁ ἐρχόμενος appear; this is the first known textual occurrence of this formulation. So where does it stem from? Aune foregrounds threefold temporal designations for divine figures, such as Pausanias's description of worship at the Sanctuary of Zeus at Dodona: Ζεὺς ἦν, Ζεὺς ἐστίν, Ζεὺς ἔσσεται (*Descr.* 10.12.10), and similar forms can be found in Homer and Hesiod.²⁸ Could this be an influence? Martin McNamara argues not, believing the targums to be the sole sources for Revelation's rendering, with Tg. Ps.-J. Deut. 32.39 closest.²⁹ However, Aune and McDonough argue that dating makes this unlikely, preferring to posit that both Revelation and the targum draw on a common liturgical designation.³⁰

Yet this does not quite explain the addition of ὁ ἐρχόμενος. Beale believes Rev. 1.4's first and last elements reflects this tradition of expanding Exod. 3.14's divine name and resonates with temporal designations from Isaiah.³¹ As a result, he sees ὁ ἐρχόμενος as a clear eschatological reference, which ties into Exodus themes, showing that God will deliver his people 'despite overwhelming odds'.³²

---

²³ McDonough, *YHWH*, p. 131. He includes the Platonic τὸ ὄν, with his earliest references in the first century BCE, arguing that perhaps LXX influenced them (p. 135).
²⁴ McDonough, *YHWH*, p. 135.
²⁵ Evidence that ὁ ὤν was used in the diaspora is found in an inscription from Pergamon: θεὸς κύριος ὁ ὢν εἰς ἀεί; see Aune, *Revelation 1–5*, p. 30.
²⁶ *Commentary on the Apocalypse* 1.4 in W. C. Weinrich, *Revelation* (ACCSNT, 12; Downers Grove, IL: InterVarsity, 2005), p. 3.
²⁷ Aune, *Revelation 1–5*, p. 30.
²⁸ Aune, *Revelation 1–5*, p. 31.
²⁹ M. McNamara, *The New Testament and the Palestinian Targum to the Pentateuch* (Rome: Pontifical Biblical Institute, 1966), p. 112.
³⁰ Aune, *Revelation 1–5*, pp. 32–33; McDonough, *YHWH*, p. 202.
³¹ Isa. 41.4; 43.10; 44.6; 48.12. Beale, *Commentary*, pp. 187–88.
³² Beale, *Commentary*, p. 188.

He too registers the Greek cultic resonances, positing that 'Jewish formulas' were appealed to as 'an apologetic'.[33] McDonough also believes that 'there was likely some Greek influence on the tradition', arguing that 'we cannot exclude the possibility that he [John] employed the tradition in a polemical fashion'.[34] Brian Blount takes these temporal polemics further, hearing strong Greco-Roman undertones in Rev. 1.4's tripartite formulation and arguing that ὁ ὤν combined with other temporal designations 'hijacks' these formulations, and the addition of ὁ ἐρχόμενος provokes by claiming not just that this deity will be, but that he also is coming.[35]

What is more, Aune points out that this use of ὁ ἐρχόμενος stands out grammatically: ὁ ἐσόμενος would be the expected form, as found in Clement of Alexandria.[36] Therefore, both linguistically and conceptually ὁ ἐρχόμενος is attention-grabbing.[37] The standout nature of this divine designation at such an early stage of the text points us forward, as Revelation will culminate in 22.20 with a cry ναί, ἔρχομαι ταχύ. Ἀμήν, ἔρχου κύριε Ἰησοῦ.

So, what does this reveal? First, it is clear that Exod. 3.14 can be heard in the text, traced as the source of the formula, and resonates from a variety of perspectives, despite the additions and alterations. However, this is not all. As McDonough shows, the concept of ὁ ὤν is itself saturated in Greek philosophy, and threefold formulae would have been known to anyone with a knowledge of Homer, Hesiod, or other philosophers. Whether 'John knew' these texts is somewhat irrelevant, for when this phrase was read to a group in Asia minor, it would evoke a range of ways of asking how the world works and who is in charge. What is more, this designation presents a complex interpretative web with each element having a multivalence within the threefold designation. There are, to put it mildly, 'several nuances in play'.[38] It is a phrase that opens up horizons, as Exod. 3.14 resonates, as does the Greek philosophical debates and divine designations, and so too will the narrative of Revelation itself; all woven into this one three-part formula. From these opening lines, there are clear signals that whilst Revelation is evoking the HB, it is speaking into the complexity of the first-century context and resonating with multiple perspectives and traditions. Revelation is not presenting formulations of continuity and unchangeability, regardless of whatever statements the phrase itself may be making about the nature of God; the text itself shows a movement, an alteration, and an indefinability.

---

[33] Beale, *Commentary*, p. 188.
[34] McDonough, *YHWH*, p. 202.
[35] B. K. Blount, *Revelation: A Commentary* (Louisville: Westminster John Knox, 2009), p. 34.
[36] Aune, *Revelation 1–5*, p. 32; H. Kraft, *Die Offenbarung des Johannes* (HNT, 16a; Tübingen: Mohr Siebeck, 1974), p. 31.
[37] Another grammatical anomaly occurs with the nominative rather than genitive occurs after ἀπό. For Beale (*Commentary*, p. 188) this is a 'characteristic solecism' of Revelation, arguing that it enhances the connection to Exod. 3.14.
[38] McDonough, *YHWH*, p. 206.

3. Manna: Revelation 2.17

In the letter to Pergamum, we find a seemingly straightforward reference to the text of Exodus—manna: ᾧ νικῶντι δώσω αὐτῷ τοῦ μάννα τοῦ κεκρυμμένου (Rev. 2.17). Indeed, Beale labels this one of the 'clear Old Testament allusions in the letters'.[39] However, this appearance of manna is a little more complex than it first appears. Manna's textual origins lie in the question in Exod. 16.15: מן הוא, followed by four appearances as מן in the same chapter (Exod. 16.31, 33, 35 [×2]). In the LXX, Exod. 16.15 is literally translated: τί ἐστι τοῦτο, and then the phonetic rendering μαν is used in 16.31.

All other MT occurrences appear outside Exodus in relation to the wilderness wanderings (Num. 11.6, 7, 9; Deut. 8.3, 16; Josh. 5.12 [×2]; Neh. 9.20; Ps. 78.24), and in LXX all use the longer Greek-influenced form μάννα.[40] Therefore, manna becomes part of the wider story of the wilderness wanderings, rather than something specific to Exodus, although (like the divine name) its origins are there. Within this tradition, manna gains a complex interpretative history.

Outside Exodus, manna moves beyond the found-food in the wilderness; Aune shows that synonyms such as 'bread from heaven' (e.g., LXX Neh. 9.15; Ps. 105.40) or 'food of angels' (e.g., LXX Ps. 77.25; Wis. 16.20; *4 Ezra* 1.19) are common, frequently occurring alongside manna itself.[41] The NT absorbs this tradition: twice in John (6.31, 49) referring to the Israelites in the wilderness and to Jesus as the bread of life. He also highlights other Jewish texts that evidence eschatological readings of 'bread from heaven' traditions: manna is connected to the age to come, as in *2 Bar.* 29.8, and also *Sib. Or.* 7.149; *Num. Rab.* 11.2; *Qoh. Rab.* 1.9.[42]

As well as manna in heaven, there is also the tradition of the literal omer of manna placed in the ark (Exod. 16.33), as mentioned in Heb. 9.4. Although the ark's fate was unknown, 2 Macc. 2.4-7 indicates that Jeremiah hid it with the tent and altar in a cave, to be revealed by God at a later time when he gathers his people. In the same vein, *2 Bar.* 6.5-10 has the ground swallow up the ark and temple items until restoration. Therefore, this omer of manna is connected to the tradition of being hidden in the earth until the time of messianic restoration in the future.

All these traditions, originating in Exodus but growing into a complex interpretative history, need to be recalled as we encounter Rev. 2.17. So, one of the key questions is how much is this once-Exodus-originating term bound up in these later layers? Revelation's manna is labelled 'hidden', evoking more than the physical wilderness food. Aune posits three solutions, all bound-up in the discussions above: (1) an eschatological one: it is hidden for those who will enter the age to come; (2) a literal/eschatological one: it is hidden because it is placed in

---

[39] Beale, *Old Testament*, p. 69.
[40] BDAG, pp. 615–16. The Greek τὸ μάννα is likely influenced by ἡ μάννα, 'little grain, granule', also in Josephus, *Ant.* 3.296; 4, 21; *Sib. Or.* 7.149.
[41] Aune, *Revelation 1–5*, p. 189.
[42] Aune, *Revelation 1–5*, p. 189.

a jar before the Lord (possibly even the hidden ark) and will be revealed (by the Messiah in Samaritan tradition); and (3) a heavenly one: manna will be restored in heaven through eternal life. Variations on each of these concepts have their supporters.[43]

Could it be related to the ark's hiding in 2 Macc. 2.4-7? C. J. Hemer thinks so, reading the manna in the ark tradition of Exod. 16.32-34, 2 Macc. 2.4-7, and *2 Bar.* 6.7-10.[44] Beale, Aune, and H. B. Swete also believe that this resonance is there (contra R. H. Charles).[45] Eugene Boring goes further, seeing the loss of the ark and destruction of the temple by the Babylonians as central to the Rev. 2.17 motif, reflecting the longing for the return of the temple for worship. Contextualizing this within the wider text of Revelation, such 'hidden ark' readings are indeed later rewarded, as in Rev. 11.9 the temple opens and the ark is able to be seen.

Boring also hears eucharistic overtones, similar to the bread of heaven of John 6, and Rev. 3.20-21.[46] Andrew of Caesarea concurs, believing that 'the "hidden manna" is "the Bread of Life" which came down from heaven for us and became edible'.[47] Would this evoke such ideas for the ancient audience? Pierre Prigent thinks so,[48] and given Revelation's liturgical content and potential liturgical context, it is surely not incorrect to put such an image into this frame of reference.

Tyconius (c. 370–390 CE) reads allegorically, relating Revelation's manna to Ps. 78.25 (77.25 LXX) and reading it as a reference to 'the uniquely spiritual manna by which [Christ] offers immortality to the faithful',[49] while also speaking of the manna eaten in the wilderness. As already noted, Beale hears hidden ark traditions, believing that the focus is on overcoming pagan idolatry, rewarded with heavenly manna.[50] I. T. Beckwith argues the 'source of the symbol' is the notion of manna hidden until the revealing of the messianic kingdom,[51] with any reference to the 'promise of the eucharist…impossible'.[52]

So, what does this tell us about our possible Exodus evocation? First, like the divine name, manna was not limited to Exodus, although it does have its origins there. Second (following the first), by the time it is used in Rev. 2.17, it has moved through a complex interpretative tradition, with multiple references within HB, Jewish literature, and four NT mentions (including Rev. 2.17). However, unlike

---

[43] Aune, *Revelation 1–5*, p. 189.
[44] C. J. Hemer, *The Letters to the Seven Churches of Asia in Their Local Setting* (JSNTSup, 11; Sheffield: JSOT, 1989), pp. 94–95.
[45] H. B. Swete, *The Apocalypse of St. John* (London: Macmillan, 1906), p. 38; Charles, *Revelation of St. John*, p. 1:65.
[46] M. E. Boring, *Revelation* (Int, 43; Louisville: John Knox, 1989), p. 90.
[47] *Commentary on the Apocalypse* 2.17 in Weinrich, *Revelation*, p. 32.
[48] P. Prigent, *Commentary on the Apocalypse of St. John* (trans. Wendy Pradels; Tübingen: Mohr Siebeck, 2004), p. 177.
[49] *Commentary on the Apocalypse* 2.17 in Weinrich, *Revelation*, p. 32.
[50] Beale, *Commentary*, p. 252. He points out the connection with Balaam in the preceding lines, and the wilderness tradition more generally.
[51] I. T. Beckwith, *The Apocalypse of John: Studies in Introduction, with a Critical and Exegetical Commentary* (New York: Macmillan, 1919), p. 461.
[52] Beckwith, *Apocalypse of John*, p. 416.

the divine name, by the time this Exodus-originating term reaches Revelation, it has become so enamelled with the stages of the wilderness journey and eschatological expectations that Exodus evocations seem but a faint memory. What is more, it is difficult to see underneath the christological readings placed onto the text as scholars seek out its relevance. Yes, perhaps the jar hidden in the ark may be evoked, as Swete argues, but its audience were also likely familiar with the 2 Maccabees traditions, and most probably with the eschatological resonances. This is a motif that if read as a 'clear Old Testament allusion' overlooks what its occurrence in Revelation actually reveals: the distance such distinct terms have travelled by the time they reach Revelation. Revelation's connection of manna and its hidden properties, woven into a liturgically themed text that features the ark appearing in the temple, resonates with multiple traditions, reflecting the complex history of interpretations inherited by its audience.

4. The Lamb: Revelation 5

Encountering these first two supposedly simple Exodus evocations should show that reading 'with Exodus' is revealing the complexity of Revelation's relationship with the HB. Therefore, when the Lamb appears, things are not going to be straightforward.

For many scholars the Lamb is *the* key figure in Revelation, representing Jesus through much of the text.[53] Its stage entrance in Rev. 5.6 is directly preceded by a declaration, ἰδοὺ ἐνίκησεν ὁ λέων ὁ ἐκ τῆς φυλῆς Ἰούδα, ἡ ῥίζα Δαυίδ, and the Christology of this lion/lamb fusion has been, as Christopher Rowland and Judith Kovacs eloquently say, 'explored to the full by interpreters'.[54] Its ovine significance is hotly contested: is it a sacrificial lamb or an eschatological one? Does it have any comparison in the HB? Exodus is often consulted for explanations. But we need to tread carefully. The lamb motif is a common one, and Revelation's Lamb is a particularly multifaceted example, changing roles as the text progresses.[55] Also, as seen with manna, Exodus-originating terms may be uprooted by the time they have been resituated into Revelation. What is more, most early commentators did not hear Exodus, but rather focused on the dual function of Christ as devouring lion through lamb-like death.[56] Nevertheless, when modern scholars seek out inspirational sheep, the book of Exodus, especially Exodus 12, frequently raises its head.

---

[53] From Rev. 5 until Rev. 22.3, it makes multiple appearances.
[54] J. L. Kovacs and C. Rowland, *Revelation: The Apocalypse of Jesus Christ* (BBC; Malden, MA: Blackwell, 2004), p. 70.
[55] For a summary of its roles, including judge, warrior, and shepherd, see T. B. Slater, *Christ and Community: A Socio-Historical Study of Christology of Revelation* (JSNTSup, 178; Sheffield: Sheffield Academic, 1999), pp. 162–208.
[56] Victorinus of Petovium sees the unsealing of the scroll as the unsealing of the testament, and the calf's blood of Exod. 24.8. *Commentary on the Apocalypse* 5.2 in Weinrich, *Revelation*, pp. 77–78.

Specific NT designations of Jesus as a lamb are fewer than might be expected.⁵⁷ There is John the Baptist's repetition of "Ἴδε ὁ ἀμνὸς τοῦ θεοῦ in Jn 1.29, 36. Acts 8.32 compares Jesus to a sheep being led to the slaughter and ὡς ἀμνός before its sheerer, evoking Isa. 53.7. First Peter 1.19 evokes the sacrificial lamb: αἵματι ὡς ἀμνοῦ ἀμώμου; and 1 Cor. 5.7 evokes the Passover lamb: τὸ πάσχα ἡμῶν ἐτύθη.

At no point in Revelation is the Lamb referred to as τὸ πάσχα. Revelation's Lamb is referred to with ἀρνίον.⁵⁸ This alone is enough for some to argue a parallel with Exodus does not exist.⁵⁹ However, let us remember that the Gospel of John also never refers to Jesus with this specific semantic field, yet it is hard to argue that such a comparison is not set up in the text. Therefore, despite semantic surfaces, more attention is warranted.

Some want to sidestep the NT, arguing instead that Revelation directly absorbs Jewish eschatological traditions, and so seek an ovine warrior. Precedents are found in the animal apocalypse of *1 Enoch*, particularly 90.9-13, and *The Testament of Joseph* (19.8-9).⁶⁰ They do offer a pertinent point of comparison in that they both feature warring ovine figures. However, Richard Bauckham believes that these images only go so far in explaining Revelation's Lamb, as none of them are slain/sacrificed.⁶¹ This is a key quality of Revelation 5's Lamb: slain (ἐσφαγμένον).⁶² Frequent references to its blood also occur, and Paul Middleton argues that the idea of the lamb representing Jesus Christ, who has spilt his blood and bought sins by it, is likely drawing on already familiar traditions.⁶³ Such ideas are found in other NT texts, and Bauckham is more emphatic, claiming that 'from the Christian tradition the portrayal of Jesus as Lamb was undoubtedly already familiar'.⁶⁴ A familiar image perhaps; certainly a frame of reference that evokes the realm of lambs and sacrifice, which takes us to the book of Exodus.

However, Loren Johns points out (via Leon Morris) that the Passover sacrifice was either a sheep *or* a goat, with the Hebrew semantic field allowing for an either/or, stated explicitly in Exod. 12.5. He also finds no evidence in extant literature of ἀρνίον referring to the Passover victim. And σφάζω? Johns finds no connection. Therefore, he concludes that Exodus evocations are based on an inappropriate designation for the Passover victim, and are 'mistaken'.⁶⁵ But

---

⁵⁷ For the range of Greek and Hebrew meanings, see L. L. Johns, *The Lamb Christology of the Apocalypse of John: An Investigation into Its Origins and Rhetorical Force* (WUNT, 2/167; Tübingen: Mohr Siebeck, 2003), pp. 22–39.
⁵⁸ Johns' examination of HB, Greco-Roman, NT, and wider usage of lambs reveals the semantic range, and also that the diminutive status is now debated. See Johns, *Lamb Christology*, pp. 22–39.
⁵⁹ Johns (*Lamb Christology*, p. 132) argues that if the Lamb was meant to be the Passover lamb, then the word would appear.
⁶⁰ Other texts cited include Dan. 8. See, e.g., Johns, *Lamb Christology*, pp. 80–98, 135–37.
⁶¹ R. Bauckham, *The Climax of Prophecy: Studies on the Book of Revelation* (Edinburgh: T&T Clark, 1993), pp. 183–84.
⁶² Revelation claims eight out of the ten NT uses of σφάζω.
⁶³ P. Middleton, *The Violence of the Lamb: Martyrs as Agents of Divine Judgement in the Book of Revelation* (LNTS, 586; London: Bloomsbury T&T Clark, 2018).
⁶⁴ Bauckham, *Prophecy*, p. 184.
⁶⁵ Johns, *Lamb Christology*, p. 133; L. Morris, *The Gospel According to John* (Grand Rapids: Eerdmans, 1971).

does this semantic limitation really mean that Revelation does not evoke these concepts?

Jay Smith Casey would argue not. For him, the Exodus evocations of the Lamb are irrefutable: 'John unambiguously points to Jesus' death as that of the new paschal lamb, whose blood marks the redemption of God's people from slavery'.[66] What convinces him is the appearance of another Exodus-evoking phrase in Rev. 5.10—καὶ ἐποίησας αὐτοὺς τῷ θεῷ ἡμῶν βασιλείαν καὶ ἱερεῖς, καὶ βασιλεύσουσιν ἐπὶ τῆς γῆς—which he believes resonates with Exod. 19.6. HaYoung Son concurs with Casey's reasoning. For her, the passage's presentation of a Lamb as slain (5.6, 9) and its blood (5.9) leaves only two options: the daily temple sacrifice or the paschal lamb. But the evocation of Exod. 19.6 confirms the paschal lamb reference. However, Son argues for more than one lamb motif, reading the paschal lamb with eschatological warrior imagery.[67] Thomas Slater reads similarly,[68] as does Bauckham, who sees the fulfilment of Jewish hopes in the messianic conqueror who is a slain lamb, but also cannot avoid the Exodus 12 evocations: 'Doubtless the Lamb is intended to suggest primarily the Passover lamb, for throughout the Apocalypse, and in a passage as close as 5.10, John represents the victory of the Lamb as a new Exodus'.[69] More importantly, he points out that 'he [John] deals with symbols rather than explanations',[70] reminding us not to push semantic studies too far, but to contextualize within the visionary narrative.

So, what does this 'reading with Exodus' tell us about Revelation's Lamb? In our previous section, we saw how manna in a first-century world became somewhat removed from its Exodus-born ancestor. The reverse could be said of the Lamb. While semantic studies may not reveal specific linguistic similarity to Exodus, and may show that the Passover was either a lamb or a goat, this does not mean evocations of Exodus's lambs are absent. Indeed, the majority of readers do find themselves caught up in notions of Passover lambs and sacrifice despite semantic differences. And this is not all that Revelation 5's ovine entrance evokes. As shown, eschatological warriors do not seem completely erroneous, even if this slain example presented in the book of Revelation is a different take on such a warrior, and we should probably not discount resonances of the daily sacrifice either. What is more, we have seen that such an image may well resonate with growing traditions surrounding Jesus' death. And can Exodus 12 be heard? Yes, but along with all these other concepts. Limiting studies to the words of the text of Exodus overlooks the strange image Revelation is presenting: a lamb, an ἀρνίον, standing as if it was slain. It is not an image that demands an either/or

---

[66] J. S. Casey, 'Exodus Typology in the Book of Revelation' (Ph.D. Diss., Southern Baptist Theologgical Seminary, 1981), p. 141.
[67] Son, *Praising God*, p. 82.
[68] Slater, *Christ and Community*, p. 167.
[69] Bauckham, *Prophecy*, p. 184. Also, M. R. Hoffmann, *The Destroyer and the Lamb: The Relationship Between Angelomorphic and Lamb Christology in the Book of Revelation* (WUNT, 2/203; Tübingen: Mohr Siebeck, 2005), p. 117.
[70] Bauckham, *Prophecy*, p. 184.

approach. It is an image, as Slater and Bauckham point out, that is more complex, more visionary. Images such as this evoke multiple textual and conceptual fields, and are something to be entered into, rather than observed from afar while tracing previous terminology. This is not a legal text about sacrifices, but quite a different beast. And as events unfold, this Lamb becomes even more multivalent, furthering each of these conceptual frameworks, Exodus 12 included.

5. The Song of Moses: Revelation 15

In Rev. 15.3 we find those who have conquered the beast singing τὴν ᾠδὴν Μωϋσέως τοῦ δούλου τοῦ θεοῦ καὶ τὴν ᾠδὴν τοῦ ἀρνίου.[71] The announcement has caused scholars to ask if what follows in vv. 3-4 is Moses' song of Exod. 15.1-18. But linguistically, it bears no resemblance.[72] However, as seen above, a lack of linguistic similarity does not mean we should silence such ideas. Exodus may be evoked in other ways. Indeed, explorations reveal some of the complexities of this passage and the multivalence of HB evocations.

Bauckham affirms the lack of explicit Exodus 15 linguistic parallels, but argues that the song is related to Exodus 15 through the medium of *gezerah shawa*. Indeed, he argues for 'very precise allusions to the Old Testament',[73] all of which are intimately associated not only with Exodus 15, but also with one 'key verse' in particular: 15.11. He argues for three main sources: Jer. 10.6-7a, whose context he believes makes it 'peculiarly appropriate';[74] Ps. 86.8-10, which he believes is alluded to near verbatim, bar alterations to smooth translation issues;[75] and Ps. 98.2, again with minor translation variations.[76] Parts not covered by these three 'sources' are labelled as either typical of Revelation's general vocabulary, or as paraphrasing Exod. 15.11, or one of Exod. 15.11's later paraphrasings (e.g., Pss. 86.10; 98.1; 105.5).[77] Therefore, for Bauckham Exodus 15 lies 'beneath the surface',[78] inspiring each of the HB texts chosen, and detectable by anyone using these exegetical methods.

Beale agrees that the words of the song are not from Exodus 15 but still believes in a close affinity. He argues that vv. 3-4 are constructed from subsequent HB interpretations of the Exodus, which 'fill out the framework of the Exodus 15 song of Moses, which is in John's mind'.[79] He is particularly drawn to Deuteronomy, arguing that v. 3 is an allusion to Deut. 28.59-60 LXX,[80] and also

---

[71] This comes after a string of potentially Exodus/exodus-tradition-evoking images, particularly the woman clothed like the sun, and the potential influence on what follows should not be forgotten.
[72] E. Schüssler Fiorenza, *The Book of Revelation: Justice and Judgement* (Minneapolis: Fortress, 1998), p. 135.
[73] Bauckham, *Prophecy*, p. 298.
[74] Bauckham, *Prophecy*, p. 303.
[75] Bauckham, *Prophecy*, p. 303.
[76] Bauckham, *Prophecy*, p. 304.
[77] Bauckham, *Prophecy*, p. 305.
[78] Bauckham, *Prophecy*, p. 297.
[79] Beale, *Commentary*, p. 794.
[80] Beale, *Commentary*, p. 794. Interestingly, he does not note its similarity to v. 1. More on this below.

hearing Deut. 32.4.[81] Psalms 35; 86.9-10; 98.2; 110.2-4 LXX;[82] and Jer. 10.7 are also noted, and he argues that their focus on divine incomparability comes 'from the narrative of the exodus redemption itself'.[83] Therefore, he concludes that 'the use of the OT in vv. 3-4 is not the result of random selection but is guided by the theme of the first exodus and the development of that theme later in the OT...a continuation of the latter-day Red Sea setting'.[84]

Steve Moyise argues that Psalm 86 is most prominent (he counts seventeen parallels) but also hears: '[Pss.] 98, 111, 139, and 145, along with Jer. 10, Deut. 32, a repeated phrase from the book of Amos and possibly Tob. 12'.[85] Therefore, he agrees with Aune's conclusion that the song is a 'pastiche of stereotypical hymnic phrases' familiar from previous HB material, particularly the Psalms.[86] So, how Exodus-related is the song for Moyise? It is conspicuously unrelated. Indeed, he argues against Beale and Bauckham, believing that Exodus 15's non-appearance is intended and so creates a dialogical tension when it is expected, but does not appear.[87] It is not behind or guiding the text, but rather noticeably absent.

Son agrees with Moyise's multiple allusions, but still seeks 'the primary source used in the song of Moses',[88] moving to thematic parallels. She reads Exodus 15 alongside Revelation 15 and compares background, designation, contents, and context. She concludes that 'Exod. 15 shows its strongest influence in Rev. 15.3b-4'.[89] While exact Exodus language may not be present, Son argues that it is a precis of Exodus 15: Rev. 15.3-4 summarizes Exod. 15.4-7, Rev. 15.4a summarizes Exod. 15.14-16, and Rev. 15.4b summarizes Exod. 15.11. Therefore, she concludes that 'the two songs in Rev. 15 and Exod. 15 sing the same things with somewhat different lyrics'.[90]

These readings show the sheer range of HB resonances that Revelation evokes: Deut. 28.59-60; 32.4; Jer. 10.7; Pss. 35; 86.8-10; 98.1; 110.2-4; 145.17; and more. All these are heard by scholars in fewer than two verses. Yet, amidst such polyvalence, all still believe that Exodus 15 is entwined into the song, as a 'hidden' source text (Bauckham and Son), as a framework filled with later retellings (Beale), or by its conspicuous absence (Moyise). Despite no linguistic similarity, Exodus 15 is still the text that hovers over scholarly readings. Why is this?

[81] Beale, *Commentary*, p. 794.
[82] Beale, *Commentary*, p. 798.
[83] Beale, *Commentary*, p. 798.
[84] Beale, *Commentary*, p. 899.
[85] S. Moyise, 'Singing the Song of Moses and the Lamb: John's Dialogical Use of Scripture', *AUSS* 42, no. 2 (2004), pp. 347–60 (350). For a summary, revealing how unspecific claimed HB parallels are, see Son, *Praising God*, pp. 2–3.
[86] D. E. Aune, *Revelation 6–16* (WBC, 52B; Nashville: Thomas Nelson, 1998), p. 874. Moyise prefers 'amalgam', but I argue that 'pastiche' (when understood correctly within literary studies) describes Revelation's textual blending, and so *completely* agree with Aune's claim. See Fletcher, *Reading Revelation*.
[87] Moyise, 'Singing', p. 350, 'He [John] leads his hearers/readers to expect a quotation or at least an allusion to the Song of Moses as recorded in the OT, and then places before them a scriptural song drawn from up to ten different locations'.
[88] Son, *Praising God*, p. 3.
[89] Son, *Praising God*, p. 16.
[90] Son, *Praising God*, p. 88.

The prevalence of Exodus in each reading reveals the subtly interwoven nature of Revelation's HB textual relationships, as in many ways it is neither the song nor its evocations that drive scholars to seek Exodus 15, but rather the surrounding and far less pored-over text.[91] The preceding lines mention plagues, standing beside/on the sea, and conquering, all of which evoke Exodus 15, and this is furthered by mentions of the Lamb, which in this framework seems to be even more embroiled with Exodus evocations.[92] Then, after this run of Exodus-sounding terms, we encounter the announcement of the song of Moses, and potential Exodus 15 evocations are argued to be further enhanced by the desig͟f nation of Moses as τοῦ δούλου τοῦ θεοῦ (Rev. 15.3). This is because directly before the announcement of the song in Exod. 15.1, Moses is referred to as Μωυσῇ τῷ θεράποντι αὐτοῦ (Exod. 14.31).

Therefore, it is the narratival lead-up that brings to the fore Exodus 15, and earlier Exodus-sounding motifs such as the Lamb seem to be affirmed in their connections when embedded in this framework. As a result, when the song commences it is read with one ear on Exodus 15, so much so that Moyise argues expectations are 'dashed' when it does not arrive.[93] But we should not assume that matters are quite so straightforward, as we shall now see. In what follows, some examples will be presented that challenge the potential myopia caused by Exodus 15-focused reading. The point of these examples is not to posit that other readings are wrong, but rather to show what has been overlooked, thereby blurring the lines of the seeming inevitability that all roads lead to Exodus.

First, HB 'sources' have been sought for the song's opening, μεγάλα καὶ θαυμαστὰ τὰ ἔργα σου (Rev. 15.3), but internal evocations seem just as loud with Καὶ εἶδον ἄλλο σημεῖον ἐν τῷ οὐρανῷ μέγα καὶ θαυμαστόν (Rev. 15.1) just two verses before. Bauckham argues for complex rephrasings from Deuteronomy 32, believing that where plagues were not suitable, John replaced them with 'works'. Yet, ironically Rev. 15.1 again offers a linguistic resonance, as plagues are mentioned. Therefore, whilst Son may argue this is a precis of Exodus 15, we can just as easily argue that this is a precis of the previous lines.

Second, Beale notes Dan. 9.4. Theod., κύριε ὁ θεὸς ὁ μέγας καὶ θαυμαστός, in relation to the phrase 'great and marvellous' in Rev. 15.3.[94] But when looking at 'Moses the servant of the Lord' Beale only has eyes for Exod. 14.31. All our four readers do. Yet, there is a linguistically closer parallel: Dan. 9.11 Theod., Μωυσέως δούλου τοῦ θεοῦ (cf. Ian Boxall).[95]

Third, in Deuteronomy 32, which is sometimes argued to contribute to the song in Revelation 15, Moses repeatedly comments on his death. If we follow

---

[91] E.g., Bauckham gives fewer than 20 lines to affirming the Exod. 15 infused nature of the first two verses.
[92] E.g., 'But it is also "the song of the Lamb," because the new exodus is a victory they have won by the blood of the new Passover Lamb' (Bauckham, *Prophecy*, p. 297).
[93] Moyise, 'Singing', p. 335.
[94] Beale, *Commentary*, p. 795.
[95] I. Boxall, *The Revelation of St John* (BNTC; London: Continuum, 2006), p. 219.

this signposting, we reach Deut. 34.10-12's description of the death of Moses, and here we find a string of language similar to Rev. 15.1-4: ἐν πᾶσι τοῖς **σημείοις καὶ τέρασιν**, ὃν ἀπέστειλεν αὐτὸν **κύριος** ποιῆσαι αὐτὰ ἐν γῇ Αἰγύπτῳ Φαραω καὶ **τοῖς θεράπουσιν αὐτοῦ** καὶ πάσῃ τῇ γῇ αὐτοῦ, τὰ **θαυμάσια τὰ μεγάλα** καὶ τὴν χεῖρα τὴν κραταιάν, ἃ ἐποίησεν **Μωυσῆς** ἔναντι παντὸς Ισραηλ. None of the studies mentioned acknowledges this potential parallel, even though it creates a strong polemic.

Finally, Craig Koester draws attention to ὅτι μόνος ὅσιος (Rev. 15.4). He notes that the HB uses ὅσιος for God (e.g., Deut. 32.4; Ps. 145.17) but also draws attention to the fact that in Sardis and Philadelphia 'the god called Holy and Just (*Theos Hosios kai Dikaios*) was a Greco-Roman intermediary between the divine and human world' but 'Revelation, however, ascribes these traits to God alone'.[96]

These examples show a sample of what is overlooked when scholars adopt Exodus-focused lenses. Because of the hovering Exodus presence, other texts such as Deuteronomy 34 are overlooked, and potential linguistic parallels not even noted. The Exodus focus of the first lines may be acknowledged, but their potential linguistic integration into what follows is not given attention, as the focus turns to HB evocations.[97] And this focus on HB texts leads to missing wider Greco-Roman concepts that may also be heard. As with our previous Exodus elements, this is not a case of either/or but a case of many. As we have already seen with the divine name, Revelation throws its readers out into the wider culture, rather than restricting itself to HB-inspired texts only. And as we have already seen with the Lamb, multiple traditions, both Exodus related and not, are evoked by the image. We should hardly expect less here.

6. The Plagues: Revelation 16

In Revelation, the earth experiences the wrath of God in various forms. Three cycles of seven are at the forefront of this devastation: the seven seals (Rev. 6.1–8.1), the seven trumpets (Rev. 8.2–9.21; 11.15-18), and the seven bowl/vials which lead to the 'seven plagues' (Rev. 16).[98] Each cycle seems to echo the previous, growing in intensity, and in Revelation 16 where boils, blood, frogs, darkness, and water-drying events appear in quick succession, the plagues

---

[96] C. R. Koester, *Revelation: A New Translation with Introduction and Commentary* (AB, 38A; New Haven: Yale University Press, 2014), p. 633.

[97] For more on the linguistic connection to what precedes, see P. De Villiers, 'The Composition of Revelation 14:1–15:8: Pastiche or Perfect Pattern?', *Neot* 38, no. 2 (2004), pp. 209–49.

[98] Revelation 16's similarity to the seals and trumpets receives much attention, fuelled by debates about recapitulation. This will not be our focus as discussions tend towards theology rather than textual voices. However, there is a clear link between the cycles. See Sommer, *Der Tag*, pp. 19–27, for some of the key debates about recapitulation in trumpets and bowls. The volume as a whole presents a complex exploration of potential connections between Revelation's cycles. For comparative table of the three cycles/Exodus, see, e.g., Koester, *Revelation*, p. 444; Ricard, *Apocalypse*, pp. 80–82; Boxall, *Revelation*, p. 225.

of Exodus 7–11 cry out to commentators.[99] Indeed, for many this is the most Exodus-evincing section of Revelation.[100]

However, despite this being the place where Exodus is heard by just about everyone, how exactly Exodus is connected to the seven plagues is hotly debated because the plagues of Revelation 16 are not the same as the plagues of Exodus; far from it.[101] These differences have driven scholars to pore over Revelation 16 in order to explain *why* this sequence differs from Exodus, most often with the hope of unveiling the mind of the author and the controlling structure of the text. For our purposes, not focused on authorial intent but rather 'reading with Exodus', observing this fractured relationship between Revelation 16's plagues and those of Exodus provide a fitting final example to demonstrate the altered, cumulative, and potentially unsettling reading experience of Revelation at a structural level.

A number of differences can be observed by a brief comparison between the two texts.[102] Perhaps most obvious is that there are a different number of plagues, with Revelation 16 featuring seven rather than the ten of Exodus.[103] Also, those that do feature are not in the same order as those of Exodus, and have varying content:

Exodus 7–11:   Blood Nile, frogs, gnats, flies, livestock, boils, hail, locusts, darkness, firstborn

Revelation 16:   Sores, blood sea, blood springs, scorching sun, darkness, dry Euphrates, hail

---

[99] Ancient commentators often see this as a tale of the Church, with the plagues read in a spiritual sense. Matthew 24 also plays a strong part in readings. However, Exodus is often present, e.g., 'the nations [are to] receive the same plagues universally, as Egypt once did particularly' (Irenaeus, *Haer.* 4.30.4 in Weinrich, *Revelation*, p. 245); 'That those who are smitten by this hail are moved to blasphemy rather than to repentance reveals the unyielding hardness of their hearts. And so they will be like Pharoah, or rather they will be even more intransigent than he was' (Andrew of Caesarea, *Commentary on the Apocalypse* 16.21 in Weinrich, *Revelation*, p. 264).

[100] E.g., 'We have here a more complete and systematic use of Exodus typology than in any other part of John's book' (G. B. Caird, *The Revelation of St John the Divine* [BNTC, London: A. & C. Black, 2nd edn, 1984], p. 197); 'There have already been striking parallels between several of the trumpet-plagues and the plagues of Egypt... The parallels are even more pronounced in this new sequence of seven bowls, each one of which echoes a particular plague in the Exodus story, though not in the order, and with some repetition' (Boxall, *Revelation*, p. 224); 'Chapter 16 is replete with imagery from the Egyptian plagues' (Rowland and Kovacs, *Revelation*, p. 171); 'the influence of the exodus tradition is strongest on Revelation's bowl visions, where each plague includes an element from the plagues in Egypt' (Koester, *Revelation*, p. 445).

[101] For a detailed linguistic examination of the plagues of Exod. 7–11 and Rev. 16 (and Rev. 1–3), see Sommer, *Der Tag*, pp. 185–213. See also L. Gallus, 'The Exodus Motif in Revelation 15–16: Its Background and Nature', *AUSS*, 46/1 (2008), pp. 21–43 (35–42).

[102] The differences discussed here are far from exhaustive but will effectively indicate the range of alterations.

[103] This numerical shift occurs in later Exodus retellings, with seven plagues mentioned in Ps. 78.43-53 (although not the same plagues as Rev. 16), cf. Koester, *Revelation*, p. 445. Given that it is not an overstatement to say that Revelation is obsessed with sevens, it is perhaps wise to point out that ten plagues at this stage in the text would be far more surprising than seven.

Or to put it another way, as some scholars prefer to argue, different parts of Exodus 7–11 can potentially be heard in different parts of Revelation 16:

Rev. 16.2—Exod. 9.10-11 (Deut. 28.27, 35 also)
Rev. 16.3-4—Exod. 7.7-21
Rev. 16.10—Exod. 10.22
Rev. 16.13—Exod. 8.3-6
Rev. 16.18—Exod. 9.24

The death of the firstborn is strikingly absent from Revelation's plague cycle. Jesus is designated firstborn of the dead in the opening section (Rev. 1.5), but Revelation 16's plagues do not have the culmination of collective human death that happens in the Exodus plagues.[104] What is more, the lack of reference to Egypt and Pharaoh, with action situated at the Euphrates and around the throne of the beast should be noted, pushing Revelation's references into a different geographical and temporal situation.[105]

Revelation 16's streamlined outpouring of destruction is dissimilar from the Exodus account in that it lacks narratival embellishments such as finding water by digging, the dialogue between Moses and Pharaoh, information about the times of day, the threats 'go say to Pharaoh if you do not...' etc. Rather, Revelation 16's short series is more of a list of events, closer to the recalling of the plagues in *Jubilees* 48 and Psalm 78 than the plague-recounting chapters of Exodus.[106]

This list-like arrangement could evoke quite different resonances for a first-century audience. Aune points out that lists of prodigies (*prodigia*) were common in the Greco-Roman world, with events such as those described in Revelation 16 seen as being related to the anger of the gods.[107] Examples include the darkening of the sun and moon (Plutarch *Alex.* 31.4); unusual hail, lightning, and thunderclaps in a clear sky (Cassius Dio, *Hist.* 37.25.2; Appian, *Bell. Civ.* 4.1.4), and earthquakes (Appian, *Bell. Civ.* 1.9.83).[108] Indeed, Koester reads each of the plagues of Revelation 16 in dialogue with these Greco-Roman traditions, revealing pertinent parallels, and thus demonstrating how a mono-view on Exodus can overlook these relevant first-century resonances.[109]

So, what do these brief observations about Revelation 16's plague cycle tell us? We have seen that the differences between Revelation 16 and the plagues of Exodus are multiple and diverse, requiring no complex linguistic comparisons in

---

[104] Farrer, *Rebirth*, pp. 164–15, notes this absence, seeing the 'stroke of death' which was the death of the firstborn in Exodus as reserved 'for the rider on the white horse'. This overlooks the completeness of the seven-fold nature of each cycle of destruction in the text.

[105] This change of situation is key for Ricard, *Apocalypse*, p. 86: 'God's judgment is now being rendered not in Egypt but in the Roman empire'. It should be noted that he reads the trumpets and bowls as deeply interwoven and integral to Revelation's relationship to the exodus.

[106] A similar condensing and intensification can be seen in Rev. 18's trade list. For the effect of these alterations, see Fletcher, *Reading Revelation*, Chapter 6.

[107] Aune, *Revelation 6–16*, pp. 416–19 (416)

[108] Aune, *Revelation 6–16*, p. 417. He argues that these lists were so common that they should be viewed as a 'literary form' embedded in larger genres.

[109] Koester, *Revelation*, pp. 652–56.

order to be noticed. This, coupled with altered frames of reference such as the river-drying action at the Euphrates, makes it difficult to argue that Revelation 16 is a case of Exodus repeating or that Exodus 'controls' what is experienced. The palpable similarity to Exodus heard by commentators is constantly skewed by patently obvious alterations. Such an intense giving and taking of past textual experiences demonstrates how attempts to find a controlling voice in the text of Revelation are destined for failure: however much one textual voice or one part of Israel's history may be invoked, Revelation constantly throws the reader out of any clear sense of 'reliance' and into its own new textual presence, even when parallels seem at their strongest.

The plagues of Revelation 16 also show how the cumulative nature of Revelation's textual fabric works, as HB voices become more multifarious as the narrative progresses. This effect was seen when encountering the song of Moses, where the mentioning of plagues, lamb, sea, and songs pushed us into an Exodus-resounding world. Therefore, by the time the plague series introduced in Rev. 15.1 is finally unleashed, it should come as no surprise that Exodus evocations become louder as listeners become more attuned to its textual presence within the unfolding narrative.[110] Indeed, this growing textual presence helps to explain why Exodus is often heard most resoundingly in the bowl plagues compared to the seven-fold destruction cycles of the trumpets and the seals. The audience is thrown into the world of Exodus through this cumulative building.

Therefore, what Revelation 16 makes clear is that there are undeniable resonances with Exodus, accentuated by the growing weight of evocations. However, these are held in tension with an altered Exodus; different plagues, different targets, different story. To read only for Exodus is to ignore the disquieting sense of difference and distance, and this will only continue as the text marches on. In the next chapter we will be thrust into the wilderness, but not with the wandering Israelites. Rather we will be with John to see Babylon fall and to hear her downfall described in HB prophetic voices such as Jeremiah, Isaiah, and Ezekiel. This too will produce an overwhelming sense of encountering something similar and yet altered, combined, and cumulative.[111] The past of Israel will be there with us, but so will the new situation of 'the now', as Revelation 16's relationship with Exodus 7–11 has demonstrated.

7. Conclusion

The goal of this chapter was neither to map Exodus's use in Revelation nor to argue whether part of the text was or was not 'based on Exodus'. Instead, we set out to read 'with Exodus' as a way of providing a window into the complex interplay of evocations at work in the text, from the macro to the micro. HB

---

[110] It is worth noting that because of this introduction in the preceding chapter, commentators often address the plagues' Exodus likeness prior to the action at the edge of the sea, thus obfuscating how Exodus becomes louder as Rev. 15 and 16 progress, rather than 'the framework' from the start.

[111] For a detailed examination of Rev. 17's complex textual interplay, see Fletcher, *Reading Revelation*, Chapter 5.

original contexts were not the focus, but instead we demonstrated the way these evocations function in their new contexts, both textual and temporal. To facilitate this, a range of readers were brought into dialogue, and this has allowed us to see the ambiguous nature of the 'use of the HB' in Revelation. It has also presented readings with an ear to different potential evocations, including the wider HB, first-century receptions, Greco-Roman concepts, Jesus traditions, and Revelation's narrative. This has allowed us to see how multivalent the most seemingly straightforward Exodus originating terms can be.

Revelation 1.4's ὁ ὢν καὶ ὁ ἦν καὶ ὁ ἐρχόμενος revealed evocations of Exod. 3.14 LXX, but the first-century context means it is also undeniably entangled in philosophical debates concerning God and Being, and perhaps even entering into polemics through the addition of ὁ ἐρχόμενος. Revelation 2.17's manna, a word with clear Exodus origins, demonstrated the traditions it had been absorbed into over the centuries, with its 'hidden' nature resulting in its moorings being loosed. The Lamb is one of Revelation's slipperiest symbols, but its slain appearance in Revelation 5 does thrust readers into paschal reading positions, along with messianic warriors and Jesus traditions. And as we arrive at Revelation 15, where the Lamb stands by the sea, Exodus 15 cannot help but infuse readings of the Song of Moses and the Lamb, although its evocations are caught up in a multivalent text. Finally, we have seen how these cumulative Exodus evocations lead commentators to hear the plagues of Exodus 7–11 in Revelation 16's cycle of destruction, and how, at the same time, at every turn this cycle presents something which is not the same as these past textual traditions.

These five examples have given a taster of the way that Exodus is part of a web of evocations within a text where nothing is quite as it has been seen before and where what is 'expected' increasingly becomes 'the unexpected'. In this framework, it really should not be a surprise when Revelation 15's song is not what has been heard before or if the plague cycle diverges in multiple ways from that of Exodus—nothing else up to that point has been, divine titles included. Therefore, to affirm whether Exodus is or is not the 'source' is a somewhat futile task. Is Exod. 16.15 the 'source' of Revelation's manna? Its origins are certainly there, but temporal connections blur the matter. Revelation 1.4 certainly evokes the divine name of Exod. 3.14, but it is hardly limited to or controlled by this when appearing in a first-century tripartite formulation, where each part brings forth multiple resonances. So too for the Lamb. The lamb(s) of Exodus becomes part of the Lamb of Revelation and to argue against these evocations overlooks how this multifaceted figure functions within the text. Indeed, by the time we are by the edge of the sea singing songs after plagues are spoken of, it is difficult to argue that Exodus 15 cannot be heard, and that the Lamb contributes to this. Yet, Revelation 15 has shown us the pitfalls of allowing one text to monopolize our mind-set. Exodus is not the sole root of the image, but is part of a rich web of concepts working together in the multifaceted scene. And as we encounter Revelation 16's plagues, Exodus seems to scream at its loudest, whilst at the same time the text constantly signals its altered nature. This sequence gives the familiar with one hand while taking away with the other. Revelation's relationship with the text of Exodus reveals how Revelation's evocations are alive with a plurality of reference that opens up interpretative horizons, both textual and temporal, if we only allow them to.

Chapter 11

REVIEW ESSAY:
EXODUS IN THE NEW TESTAMENT

Carmen Joy Imes

The fine essays in this volume examine the full corpus of the New Testament for quotations, allusions, and echoes of the book of Exodus. While each author worked with different New Testament texts and brought to the task a unique set of skills, their discoveries cluster around several common themes.

1. The Indispensability of the Entire Book of Exodus for New Testament Theology

Exodus is best known as the story of Israel's deliverance from Egypt, but it is more than that. As these essays have demonstrated, the book of Exodus furnishes New Testament authors with a rich variety of images and themes, including the circumstances of Moses' birth, God's self-revelation to Moses, the plagues on Egypt, Pharaoh's hard heart, the Passover celebration, worship by the sea, complaints in the wilderness, God's provision of food, the giving of the law, apostasy with the golden calf, the inauguration of covenant, and the building of the tabernacle.

Even where explicit quotations are not present, for some New Testament authors the storyline of Exodus provides the paradigm for understanding Jesus' work of redemption (Brown), Israel's rejections of that work (Westfall), and a warning to believers not to reject it (Moffitt). In some cases an allusion offers an interpretation of or reference to history, while in others the allusion interprets the writer's own day by offering typological correspondences. For example, Brown noted Matthew's 'storied allusions' to the Exodus account, which show Jesus as one who 'inaugurates a return from exile—a new exodus—that promises restoration for the people of Israel and the nations beyond' (Brown, p. 36). By telling Jesus' infancy stories in ways that evoke Moses', Matthew sets up his readers to understand Jesus' work as a new exodus.

2. The Complexity of Allusions to the Exodus Tradition

This observation arises from the previous one. Exodus is important in the New Testament, but it was also important in the development of the rest of the Old Testament canon as well as non-canonical writings. Indeed, Exodus is central to biblical theology. The stories and concepts of Exodus had already undergone significant development prior to the emergence of the New Testament writings. Therefore, the study of Exodus in the New Testament is not simply a matter of locating a source text in Exodus. It is often difficult to know whether an author is drawing on Exodus itself or subsequent texts that cite or develop themes from Exodus (Marcar and Fletcher). Multiple contributors to this volume offer examples where New Testament authors appealed to Exodus *as mediated by other texts* circulating in the first century. An allusion may show the influence of later biblical texts, such as Deuteronomy or Isaiah (Brown, Köstenberger), or the influence of an extra-canonical text such as *Eldad and Modad* (Marcar) or the *Life of Adam and Eve* (among others, Brown).

This complexity takes on even greater proportions when considering the 'bewildering array of textual diversity' among extant manuscripts of Exodus in Hebrew, Aramaic, Greek, and other languages (Longacre). Given this diversity, and the likelihood that only a fraction of ancient manuscripts has survived, certainty is elusive regarding the source of any given reading. When faced with a textual anomaly, the best we can do is conjecture as to its source or motivation.

3. The Challenges and Possibilities for Future Work on Exodus in the New Testament

Gurtner took as his departure point the seminal work of Rikki Watts on Mark's Isaianic new Exodus, showing that Mark's allusions to Exodus are neither all Isaianic nor are they all related to the exodus event itself. Mark's narrative exhibits a wide range of concerns drawn from Exodus—God's self-revelation and covenant chief among them. Gurtner demonstrated this breadth of concerns without diminishing Watts' contribution to the field. As such his essay stands as a model and a reminder that much work remains to be done.

A case in point: while most essays in this volume focused on the *book* of Exodus, Köstenberger construed the exodus more broadly as an *event* that was in some sense repeated with the return from Babylonian exile, and is capable of reiteration in the first century. As a result, Köstenberger's analysis of John spent little time in the text of Exodus, instead relying heavily on Isaianic and other echoes.[1] I wonder whether Gurtner's reassessment of Mark apart from Watts' Isaianic new exodus theme might provide a model for further exploration of allusions to the book of Exodus in John.

---

[1] Köstenberger includes an extended treatment of Isaiah and Numbers, and even a reference to Job, but almost nothing from Exodus. Where he does mention Exodus, I remain skeptical. For example, the 'lamb of God who takes away the sin of the world' seems more likely to allude to the scapegoat ritual in Lev. 16–17 than to Exodus (see Köstenberger, p. 93).

Exodus in the New Testament is not intended to be the final word on the subject, but rather to encourage further exploration. In that vein, I offer two case studies as examples of how this volume has stirred my own thinking. The first, more thematic in nature, interacts with the essays on the Gospels, bringing them in conversation with each other around a single theme. The second case study involves the reexamination of a single text from 1 Peter, illustrating one way in which this volume might stimulate further investigation.

4. Case Study #1: Jesus as a New Moses?

In their own ways, each of the contributors on the Gospels considered whether their Gospel portrays Jesus as a 'new Moses'. Given the symmetry between Moses' childhood and the birth of the Israelite nation, gospel references to similarities between Moses and Jesus may point simultaneously to the ways in which Jesus himself lives out Israel's story. Corporate solidarity is a potential factor in any allusion. Similarities between Moses and Jesus often highlight Jesus' role as a representative Israelite, while simultaneously unveiling his superiority to Moses.

Brown ably demonstrated that Matthew connects the infancies of Jesus and Moses primarily in order to show Jesus as a new Israel, rather than a new Moses (Brown, p. 33). Matthew's 'Jesus as Israel' typology relies in part on Moses' own adumbration of Israel's story, reaching back to Genesis and forward to the rest of Exodus. Gurtner likewise shows how Mark's use of Exodus highlights Jesus not as deliverer but as deity (Gurtner, p. 55).

Tabb and Walton point out that in Luke's account of the transfiguration Jesus announces his own 'exodus', revealing his identity and mission as one who 'shares in the divine glory and accomplishes the divine will' (Tabb and Walton, p. 68). In Acts 7, Stephen's speech highlights similarities between Jesus and Moses. However, Stephen's point is not to say that Jesus is a new Moses, but to expose the pattern of unfaithfulness in God's stiff-necked people. As in generations past, they have rejected their God-appointed leader, in spite of the presence of signs and wonders. By cataloguing examples from the Torah of God's self-revelation outside the land, Stephen relativizes the importance of the temple. By underscoring Aaron's role in the golden calf incident, Stephen calls into question the legitimacy and reliability of the priesthood (Tabb and Walton, p. 82).

Does the Fourth Gospel take a different approach? Köstenberger explicitly claims that 'the fourth evangelist casts Jesus as the new Moses who institutes a new covenant with his disciples' (Köstenberger, p. 104). However, in the few places where Köstenberger engages directly with Exodus, his observations lean away from his conclusion that Jesus is a new Moses. It is the *crowds* who wonder whether Jesus will prove to be a new Moses in Jn 6.31 at the feeding of the 5,000 (Köstenberger, p. 98); Jesus corrects them by claiming to be the bread itself, of 'heavenly origin' (Köstenberger, p. 99), thus bypassing Moses altogether. When Jesus declares, 'I am' (Jn 8.58; 13.19), the gravity of his statement undermines the potential Moses typology; Jesus is claiming *deity* (Köstenberger, p. 101). Köstenberger ends his essay by saying that John elevates Jesus as 'the climax of God's self-disclosure to his people' (Köstenberger, p. 107). Indeed, I agree. The Fourth Gospel presents Jesus as the One for whom Moses served as a witness (Jn 1.45; 5.45-47). Jesus is YHWH, not Moses.[2] The Word was *God* (Jn 1.1).

By showing Jesus as the manna-giver and the manna, the performer and embodiment of signs, the I AM, the one who redefines all Jewish festivals and institutions, the Passover lamb, and the inaugurator of a (re)new(ed) covenant, John presents Jesus as YHWH in the flesh. Echoes of the exodus in John point to Jesus' heavenly provenance, not his resemblance to Moses. If this brief foray is correct, then John joins Mark and Luke in portraying Jesus as the source, rather than simply the conduit, of divine power. Together with Matthew, the four Gospels offer a multi-dimensional portrait of Jesus as representative of both Israel and God.

5. Case Study #2: The Source of Allusion in 1 Peter 2.9

A second case study, this from a particular text in 1 Peter, further illustrates the indispensability of Exodus for New Testament theology and the rich rewards that come by attending closely to the complexity of these allusions.[3] It is not intended as a critique of Marcar's essay as much as an invitation for more exploration on the part of readers and contributors alike.

As Marcar notes, 'what for many is the defining act of Exodus, the liberation from domination and return from exile, is palpably absent from 1 Peter' (Marcar, p. 171). Instead, 1 Peter focuses on the constitution and mission of the people of God in order to bolster the community's perseverance under suffering as they follow Christ's example. Marcar rightly calls 1 Pet. 2.9-10 the 'theological crescendo of the letter' (Marcar, p. 176). The dense concentration of OT allusions—at least nine passages in just two verses—is remarkable. Given 1 Peter's focus on the constitution and mission of the people of God, it is not surprising that it draws heavily on Exod. 19.5-6, calling the recipients 'a chosen race, a kingdom priesthood, a holy nation, a people for his treasured acquisition'.

Like most commentators, Marcar directs attention to the priesthood language in 1 Peter 2, saying only briefly that the 'first and last of these titles are drawn from Isa. 43.20-21, while the middle two come from Exod. 19.6' (Marcar, p. 176). However, the precise form of 1 Peter's reference to his audience as 'a

---

[2] For a compelling case that the 'prophet like Moses' of Deut. 18 should not be interpreted as a singular Messianic figure, and therefore that Jesus does not fulfill this role, see D. I. Block, 'A Prophet Like Moses: Another Look at Deuteronomy 18:9-22', in *The Triumph of Grace: Literary and Theological Studies in Deuteronomy and Deuteronomic Themes* (Eugene, OR: Cascade, 2017), pp. 349–73.

[3] This example is based on my unpublished MA thesis: C. J. Imes, '"Treasured Possession": Peter's Use of the Old Testament in 1 Peter 2:9–10 (MA thesis, Gordon-Conwell Theological Seminary, 2011).

people for his treasured acquisition' deserves further exploration. A comparison with several other intertexts is instructive.[4]

1 Pet. 2.9	Exod. 19.5-6a	Isa. 43.20-21	Mal. 3.17
ὑμεῖς δὲ γένος ἐκλεκτόν, βασίλειον ἱεράτευμα, ἔθνος ἅγιον, λαὸς εἰς περιποίησιν, ὅπως τὰς ἀρετὰς ἐξαγγείλητε τοῦ ἐκ σκότους ὑμᾶς καλέσαντος εἰς τὸ θαυμαστὸν αὐτοῦ φῶς·	καὶ νῦν ἐὰν ἀκοῇ ἀκούσητε τῆς ἐμῆς φωνῆς καὶ φυλάξητε τὴν διαθήκην μου ἔσεσθέ μοι λαὸς περιούσιος (סגלה) ἀπὸ πάντων τῶν ἐθνῶν ἐμὴ γάρ ἐστιν πᾶσα ἡ γῆ· ὑμεῖς δὲ ἔσεσθέ μοι βασίλειον ἱεράτευμα καὶ ἔθνος ἅγιον.	εὐλογήσει με τὰ θηρία τοῦ ἀγροῦ σειρῆνες καὶ θυγατέρες στρουθῶν ὅτι ἔδωκα ἐν τῇ ἐρήμῳ ὕδωρ καὶ ποταμοὺς ἐν τῇ ἀνύδρῳ ποτίσαι τὸ γένος μου τὸ **ἐκλεκτόν** λαόν μου ὃν **περιεποιησάμην** (יצרתי לי) **τὰς ἀρετάς** μου διηγεῖσθαι.	καὶ ἔσονταί μοι λέγει κύριος παντοκράτωρ εἰς ἡμέραν ἣν ἐγὼ ποιῶ εἰς περιποίησιν (סגלה) καὶ αἱρετιῶ αὐτοὺς ὃν τρόπον αἱρετίζει ἄνθρωπος τὸν υἱὸν αὐτοῦ τὸν δουλεύοντα αὐτῷ.
But you are **a chosen race**, a kingdom priesthood, **a holy nation**, a people for his treasured acquisition, so that you may announce the **praiseworthiness** of the one who called you out of darkness into his marvelous light.	And now, if you will listen to my voice and keep my covenant, you will be my treasured people above all the nations, for the whole earth is mine. But you will be for me a kingdom of priests and a holy nation.	The beasts of the field will praise me and the daughters of ostriches, because I have given water in the desert and rivers in the dry land to quench my **race**, my **chosen** people, which I have **acquired** that they may declare my **praiseworthiness**.	And they will be mine, says the Lord Almighty, on the day when I make [them] as an acquisition and I will choose them as a man chooses his son to serve him.

Exodus 19.5-6 provides the primary conceptual backdrop of 1 Peter's message. Of the four titles used in 1 Pet. 2.9, two are drawn directly from this passage, along with the phrase ὑμεῖς δέ that introduces a contrast.[5] Exodus 19 contrasts

---

[4] The conventions used in the chart are as follows: agreement with between column 1 and 2 is represented by underline style; agreement between column 1 and 3 is represented by **bold style**; agreement between column 1 and 4 is represented by shading. Alterations of these conventions (e.g., italics or broken underline) represent verbal similarity but not verbatim agreement.

[5] On their own these two words are not unusual enough to constitute an allusion, but since the rest of the passage is clearly built around Exod. 19.5-6, the likelihood of intentionality is greater. See also

Israel and the nations, while 1 Peter uses the phrase to separate those who those who trust in Christ from those who reject his message. Already in this echo we may observe a subtle shift. The lines between 'who's in' and 'who's out' have shifted. Ethnicity is no longer the determining factor. Faithful obedience is (see 1 Pet. 1.2; 2.7; 4:17).

First Peter's use of both γένος ('race') and ἔθνος ('nation') to describe his addressees is striking; in fact, they do *not* share common ancestry or political allegiance. The audience represented 'a veritable melting-pot' of cultures, both Gentile and Jewish.[6] In Christ their ethnic differences were set aside and they were brought together as a people, a new race that transcended physical origin, elected by God for a purpose. Their elect status (ἐκλεκτόν) is mentioned first in the list of titles to emphasize their identification with Jesus, who was said to be ἐκλεκτόν ('elect') in 1 Pet. 2.4.[7]

Marcar is correct that γένος ἐκλεκτόν loosely echoes Isa. 43.20, the only other passage in the Greek Scriptures containing these two words in the same verse, though not adjacently.[8] In Isa. 43.21, God specifies the purpose for Israel's election, 'that they may declare my praiseworthiness [τὰς ἀρετάς]'. First Peter echoes this purpose in v. 9 using the same term: 'so that you may announce the praiseworthiness [τὰς ἀρετάς] of the one who called you out of darkness into his marvelous light'.[9] This second echo to Isaiah strengthens the likelihood of the first. The two passages share an additional lexeme in common: 1 Peter uses the nominal form (περιποίησιν) of the verb περιεποιησάμην from Isa. 43.21. Understandably, then, Marcar concludes that Isa. 43.21 is the primary source for the title λαὸς εἰς περιποίησιν in 1 Pet. 2.9.

However, the matter is not so simple. Why does 1 Peter's title differ from both Exod. 19.5 and Isa. 43.21, when 1 Peter demonstrably evokes both texts? In fact, the precise term for 'treasured possession' has shifted along a similar trajectory to ὑμεῖς δέ discussed above. Rather than refer to the people as λαὸς περιούσιος, using the most common translation of the Hebrew סגלה, 1 Peter refers to his audience as λαὸς εἰς περιποίησιν. The sense is similar: a περιούσιος is a special possession,

---

J. H. Elliott, *The Elect and the Holy: An Exegetical Examination of I Peter 2:4-10 and the Phrase βασίλειον ἱεράτευμα* (NovTSup, 12; Leiden: Brill, 1966), p. 39.

[6] Among other things, Schutter points to the urbanization present in the area where the letter was directed as evidence of this. He claims, 'Regarding the intended recipients, their ethnic composition was likely to be as diverse as that of the provinces in view'. W. Schutter, *Hermeneutic and Composition in 1 Peter* (WUNT, 2/30; Tübingen: Mohr Siebeck, 1989), p. 8.

[7] See J. N. D. Kelly, *The Epistles of Peter and of Jude* (BNTC; Peabody, MA: Hendrickson, 1999), p. 97.

[8] Deuteronomy 7.6 and 10.15 are similar, but contain no direct verbal parallels. The indisputable allusion to Isa. 23.21 later in this verse makes the likelihood of this allusion stronger.

[9] Here 1 Peter draws loosely on Isaiac 'light' imagery; YHWH promised in Isaiah that those living in darkness would be brought out into the light (see Isa. 9.1; 42.16). Goppelt is probably correct that the use of the rare word ('marvelous') may have been under the influence of LXX Ps. 117.23, which 1 Pet. 1.7 quoted earlier. L. Goppelt, *A Commentary on 1 Peter* (ed. F. Hahn; trans. J. Alsup; Grand Rapids: Eerdmans, 1993), p. 150. In Ps. 117 the psalmist speaks of the rejected stone that becomes the chief cornerstone (v. 22), and calls that work of God 'marvelous', celebrating the one who came 'in the name of YHWH' and has 'given us light' (v. 23).

while a περιποίησιν is also a possession. However, the latter focuses attention on the act of acquisition, rather than the status of possession, a nuance reinforced by the preposition εἰς.[10]

The word λαός itself is significant, because the Septuagint reserved it for occasions when *God's* people, the Jews, were in view.[11] For 1 Peter to call readers God's λαός is a radical claim for a church of mixed ethnicity. However, 1 Peter's choice of περιποίησιν rather than περιούσιος to convey the elect status of the letter's recipients seems puzzling, given the otherwise precise allusion to LXX Exod. 19.5-6 in 1 Pet. 2.9. In LXX Exod. 19.5, סגלה is translated by λαὸς περιούσιος, a phrase found in only five places in the LXX (Exod. 19.5; 23.22 LXX; Deut. 7.6; 14.2; 26.18). Every time it corresponds to the Hebrew סגלה or עם סגלה.[12] Given the rich cultural and theological significance of the word סגלה, it will be helpful to outline the uses and meaning of סגלה before considering why 1 Peter does not employ this precise phrase—λαὸς περιούσιος—most commonly used to translate it.

סגלה is a relatively rare word, occurring only eight times in the HB. Twice it refers to the king's personal treasury (1 Chron. 29.3; Eccl. 2.8). Six times it is used metaphorically to designate Israel as YHWH's treasure (Exod. 19.5; Deut. 7.6; 14.2; 26.18; Ps. 135.4; Mal. 3.17). To grasp the significance of סגלה as a title, two lines of inquiry are helpful. Since it is not entirely clear how a nation could be equated with a private savings account, Old Testament scholars have sought clarification of its precise meaning though the study of cognate words in other languages.[13] As in Hebrew, the cognate terms for סגלה in Akkadian (*sikiltu*) and Ugaritic (*sglt*) denote accumulated wealth, but were also used metaphorically to describe a vassal in a covenant relationship as one belonging to and treasured by his lord, or at the very least one who carries particular covenant obligations. According to Hans Wildberger, 'סְגֻלָּה almost became a technical term in the OT describing Yahweh's ownership of Israel'.[14]

A second line of inquiry regarding Israel's covenant status relates to the narratological structure of Exodus. With careful attention to the contours of the story, a symmetrical pattern emerges between Moses' life and the nation of Israel. Moses' escape from Pharaoh, flight through the wilderness, encounter with YHWH at

---

[10] Halas' argument for a dynamic εἰς in 1 Pet. 2.9, indicating that the people are *becoming* God's treasured possession, overstretches the evidence. S. Halas, 'Sens dynamique de l'expression "λαὸς εἰς περιποίησιν" en 1 P 2,9', *Bib* 65, no. 2 (1984), pp. 254–58 (254).

[11] Kelly, *The Epistles of Peter and of Jude*, p. 99. Elliott, *The Elect and the Holy*, pp. 40–41. The presence of λαός here may also explain 1 Peter's choice of γένος earlier in the verse, when λαός would have been a more natural translation of the MT (though a departure from the LXX).

[12] Excluding LXX Exod. 23.22 since there is no corresponding Hebrew text.

[13] M. Greenberg, 'Hebrew sᵉgullā: Akkadian sikiltu', *JAOS* 71 (1951), pp. 172–74. H. Huffmon and S. Parker, 'A Further Note on the Treaty Background of Hebrew *Yāda'*", *BASOR* 184 (1966), pp. 36–38 (37 n. 12). J. Hoftijzer, 'Une lettre du roi hittite', in *Von Kanaan bis Kerala* (Kevelaer: Butzon & Bercker, 1982), pp. 379–87 (379–80). A more recent epigraphic analysis is found in D. Pardee, 'A Further Note on PRU V, No. 60: Epigraphic in Nature', in K. Bergerhof, M. Dietrich, and O. Loretz (eds.), *Ugarit-Forschungen* (IJASP, 13; Butzon & Bercker, 1981), pp. 151–56. D. Wiseman, 'Abban and Alalaḫ', *JCS* 12 4 (1958), pp. 124–29.

[14] H. Wildberger, 'סְגֻלָּה', in *TLOT*, p. 2:272. H. Wildberger, *Jahwes Eigentumsvolk: Eine Studie zur Traditionsgeschichte und Theologie des Erwählungsgedankens* (ATANT, 37; Zurich: Zwingli, 1960).

Horeb, and commissioning as God's representative in Exod. 2.1–4.28 mirrors the Israelite experience in Exod. 4.29–20.21.

At the mountain, YHWH revealed himself more fully and commissioned the Israelites as his servants to represent him among the nations. In Exod. 19.4-6, YHWH applied three titles to the Israelites that set them apart from the nations for this representative role: treasured possession (סגלה), kingdom of priests, and holy nation. It is no wonder that 1 Peter gravitates toward Exodus 19 in order to describe the identity and mission of the New Testament people of God. It is the most profound election text in the HB.

However, as already noted, 1 Peter deviates from LXX Exod. 19.5 in the case of סגלה. The key to this mystery lies in careful investigation of his alternate lexeme, περιποίησιν. περιποίησις occurs three times in the LXX as a noun (meaning 'possession' or 'save') and 31 times in its verbal form (meaning 'to acquire' or 'to be kept alive').[15] περιποίησις is far more common than περιούσιος. Since Exodus 19 is clearly in mind, as the previous allusions show, why use the more common περιποίησις rather than the unambiguous λαὸς περιούσιος to refer to the covenant status of the people of God? We may consider the evidence the other way around: of the six occurrences of סגלה referring to Israel in the HB, the LXX renders סגלה as λαὸς περιούσιος four times (Exod. 19.5; Deut. 7.6; 14.2; 26.18), and once as περιουσιασμόν ('treasure', Ps. 135.4). Here is the key point: only once is סגלה rendered as περιποίησιν in the LXX—Mal. 3.17—and not just περιποίησιν, but εἰς περιποίησιν, exactly the phrase used to describe the church in 1 Pet. 2.9.

While the other metaphorical uses of סגלה share the common characteristic of referring to the entire nation of Israel as YHWH's treasured possession,[16] in Malachi the situation has changed. There a faithful remnant of the nation, those who fear YHWH and are recorded in the 'book of remembrance' (3.16), will become the סגלה, distinguishing anew between the righteous and the wicked (3.18). A deliberate act of redemption is required. Is it any wonder that 1 Peter echoes this passage in particular? It is the most suitable expression available to describe God's new redemptive act in Christ for all nations. While the other occurrences of סגלה (and therefore, περιούσιος) speak of Israel as already being Yahweh's סגלה, Mal. 3.17 looks to a future day when God will act to save a new סגלה, made up of only a righteous, God-fearing remnant. In other words, 1 Peter's lexical choice bears theological significance.[17]

To summarize, 1 Peter's phrase λαὸς εἰς περιποίησιν arises from a trio of OT texts: Exod. 19.5 lists the titles given to the Jewish nation as a result of their covenant status as the people of God, providing the covenant context for election. Isaiah 43.20-21 expresses the purpose of Israel's election, also calling them a

---

[15] The Hebrew words standing behind these uses of περιποιέω can be roughly divided into two categories, those that have to do with acquiring property (e.g., Isa. 43.21; Gen. 31.18), and those that relate to preserving someone's life (e.g., Num. 22.33; 2 Chron. 14.12; Isa. 31.5).

[16] Significantly, in Deuteronomy the second generation of those rescued from Egypt are called YHWH's סגלה. A new generation inherited the elect status of their parents, in spite of their parents' apostasy.

[17] Malachi's focus on the fear of YHWH aligns with 1 Peter's emphasis on fearing God (1 Pet 1.17; 2.17).

λαός, but lacking a direct lexical connection with the Hebrew סגלה from Exod. 19.5. LXX Malachi 3.17 has περιποίησις rather than the expected περιούσιος for סגלה, facilitating an association with Isa. 43.21, while at the same time giving OT support to the idea that God would someday select a righteous remnant as his treasured possession.[18] Israel's apostasy had jeopardized her status as Yahweh's covenant people. A fresh beginning was needed.

For 1 Peter, what Malachi announced as a future work of grace had been realized through the work of Jesus, the Messiah. Now believing Gentiles could be included within the remnant and called his people. The word סגלה, which is the linguistic basis for 1 Peter's adaptation of Mal. 3.17, implies far more than simply 'belonging' to God. Comparison with Akkadian and Ugaritic cognates has shown it to be a covenant term to indicate a vassal with special prerogatives to represent the king. Those who are the סגלה are endowed with the task of proclaiming the 'praiseworthiness' of YHWH to the nations and living in such a way that his holiness is evident by their behavior.

From 1 Peter's perspective, membership in this select group is no longer delineated along ethnic lines, but is based on believing loyalty to Jesus, the Messiah. As the apostle Peter explains in Acts 15.7-11, the gift of the Spirit to Gentile believers signals their full membership in the covenant. Believing Gentiles are incorporated together with faithful Jews to make up 'a chosen race, a kingdom priesthood, a holy nation, a people for his treasured acquisition' (1 Pet. 2.9). Along with so many other examples in this volume, this case study reinforces the indispensability of the book of Exodus for New Testament theology, the complexity of intertextual allusions by New Testament writers, and the rewards that come through careful exploration.

---

[18] Other thematic connections between Malachi and 1 Peter strengthen the case for the influence of Malachi on Peter. E.g., 'the day' of judgment (Mal. 4.1-5 and 1 Pet. 1.17; 2.12), the refining fire of God (Mal. 3.2-3 and 1 Pet. 1.6-7; 4.12), God as Father (Mal. 1.6; 2.10 and 1. Pet. 1.17), the election of God's people (Mal. 1.2-3 and 1 Pet. 1.1; 2.9-10), living before the Gentiles (Mal. 1.11 and 1 Pet. 2.12), and a concern for God's name (Mal. 1.11; 3.16; 4.2 and 1 Pet. 4.14-16).

Bibliography

Achtemeier, P. J. *1 Peter: A Commentary on First Peter* (Minneapolis: Fortress, 1996).
Adams, S. A., and S. M. Ehorn, 'Composite Citations: A Conclusion', in S. A. Adams and S. M. Ehorn (eds.), *Composite Citations in Antiquity*. Vol. 2, *New Testament Uses* (LNTS, 593; London: Bloomsbury T&T Clark, 2018), pp. 209–49.
Adams, S. A., and S. M. Ehorn (eds.). *Composite Citations in Antiquity*. Vol. 1, *Jewish, Graeco-Roman, and Early Christian Uses* (LNTS, 525; London: Bloomsbury T&T Clark, 2016).
Aejmelaeus, A. 'Septuagintal Translation Techniques – A Solution to the Problem of the Tabernacle Account', in *On the Trail of Septuagint Translators: Collected Essays* (Leuven: Peeters, rev. edn, 2007 [originally published in 1990]), pp. 107–21.
Aejmelaeus, A. 'What Can We Know about the Hebrew *Vorlage* of the Septuagint?', in *On the Trail of the Septuagint Translators: Collected Essays* (Leuven: Peeters, rev. edn, 2007 [originally published 1987]), pp. 71–106.
Aejmelaeus, A., and Tuukka Kauhanen (eds.). *The Legacy of Barthélemy: 50 Years after Les Devanciers d'Aquila* (Göttingen: Vandenhoeck & Ruprecht, 2017).
Albright, W. F. 'New Light on Early Recensions of the Hebrew Bible', in F. M. Cross and S. Talmon (eds.), *Qumran and the History of the Biblical Text* (Cambridge, MA: Harvard University Press, 1975), pp. 140–46.
Aletti, J.-N., S. J., *Saint Paul Épître aux Éphésiens: Introduction, traduction et commentaire* (ÉBib, 42; Paris: J. Gabalda, 2001).
Alexander, P. S. 'Retelling the Old Testament', in D. A. Carson and H. G. M. Williamson (eds.), *It is Written: Scripture Citing Scripture. Essays in Honour of Barnabas Lindars* (Cambridge: Cambridge University Press, 1988), pp. 99–121.
Alkier, S. 'Intertextuality and the Semiotics of Biblical Texts', in R. B. Hays, S. Alkier and L. A. Huizenga (eds.), *Reading the Bible Intertextually* (Waco, TX: Baylor University Press, 2009), pp. 3–21.
Allen, D. M. *Deuteronomy and Exhortation: A Study in Narrative Re-Presentation* (WUNT, 2/238; Tübingen: Mohr Siebeck, 2008).
Allen, D. M. 'More than Just Numbers: Deuteronomic Influence in Hebrews 3:7–4:11', *TynBul* 58 (2007), pp. 129–49.
Allen, O. W. *Fortress Biblical Preaching Commentaries: Matthew* (Lanham: Fortress, 2013).
Allison, D. C., Jr. 'Eldad and Modad', *JSP* 21 (2011), pp. 99–131.
Allison, D. C., Jr. *James* (ICC; London: Bloomsbury, 2013).
Allison, D. C., Jr. *The New Moses: A Matthean Typology* (Minneapolis: Fortress, 1993).
Allison, D. C., Jr. *Studies in Matthew: Interpretation Past and Present* (Grand Rapids: Baker, 2005).

Anderson, K. L. *'But God Raised Him from the Dead': The Theology of Jesus's Resurrection in Luke-Acts* (PBM; Milton Keynes: Paternoster, 2006).
Andriessen, P. C. B. 'La Teneur Judéo-Chrétienne de He 1 6 et II 14B-III 2', *NovT* 18 (1976), pp. 293–313.
Archer, G., and G. Chirichigno. *Old Testament Quotations in the New Testament* (Chicago: Moody, 1983).
Ashley, T. R. *The Book of Numbers* (NICOT; Grand Rapids: Eerdmans, 1993).
Attridge, H. W. *The Epistle to the Hebrews: A Commentary on the Epistle to the Hebrews* (Hermeneia; Philadelphia: Fortress, 1989).
Aune, D. E. *Revelation 1–5* (WBC, 52A; Dallas: Word Books, 1997).
Aune, D. E. *Revelation 6–16* (WBC, 52B; Nashville: Thomas Nelson, 1998).
Backhaus, K. *Der Hebräerbrief* (RNT; Regensburg: Friedrich Pustet, 2009).
Baden, J. S. *The Composition of the Pentateuch: Renewing the Documentary Hypothesis* (New Haven: Yale University Press, 2012).
Bailey, D. P. 'Jesus as the Mercy Seat: The Semantics and Theology of Paul's Use of *Hilasterion* in Romans 3:25' (Ph.D. diss., University of Cambridge, 1999).
Ball, D. M. *'I Am' in John's Gospel: Literary Function, Background and Theological Implications* (JSNTSup, 124; Sheffield: Sheffield Academic, 1996).
Barclay, J. M. G. '"I will have mercy on whom I have mercy": The Golden Calf and Divine Mercy in Romans 9-11 and Second Temple Judaism', *EC* 1 (2010), pp. 82–106.
Barclay, J. M. G. 'Mirror-Reading a Polemical Letter: Galatians as a Test Case', *JSNT* 31 (1987), pp. 73–93.
Barmash, P. 'Out of the Mists of History: The Exaltation of the Exodus in the Bible', in P. Barmash and W. D. Nelson (eds.), *Exodus in the Jewish Experience: Echoes and Reverberations* (New York: Lexington Books, 2015), pp. 1–22.
Barrett, C. K. *The Gospel According to St. John* (Philadelphia: Westminster, 2nd edn, 1978).
Barthélemy, D. *Les devanciers d'Aquila* (VTSup, 10; Leiden: Brill, 1963).
Bartholomä, P. F. 'Did Jesus Save the People out of Egypt? A Re-examination of a Textual Problem in Jude 5', *NovT* 50 (2008), pp. 143–58.
Bauckham, R. *The Climax of Prophecy: Studies on the Book of Revelation* (Edinburgh: T&T Clark, 1993).
Bauckham, R. *God Crucified: Monotheism and Christology in the New Testament* (Didsbury Lectures 1996; Carlisle: Paternoster, 1998).
Bauckham, R. *Jesus and the God of Israel: God Crucified and Other Studies on the New Testament's Christology of Divine Identity* (Grand Rapids: Eerdmans, 2008).
Bauckham, R. *Jude, 2 Peter* (WBC, 50; Grand Rapids: Zondervan, 1983).
Bauckham, R. 'The Spirit of God in Us Loathes Envy: James 4:5', in G. N. Stanton *et al.* (eds.), *The Holy Spirit and Christian Origins: Essays in Honor of James D. G. Dunn* (Grand Rapids: Eerdmans, 2004), pp. 270–81.
Beale, G. K. *The Book of Revelation: A Commentary on the Greek Text* (NIGTC; Grand Rapids: Eerdmans, 1999).
Beale, G. K. 'The Cognitive Peripheral Vision of Biblical Authors', *WTJ* 76 (2014), pp. 263–93.
Beale, G. K. 'Colossians', in G. K. Beale and D. A. Carson (eds.), *Commentary on the New Testament Use of the Old Testament* (Grand Rapids: Baker, 2007), pp. 841–70.
Beale, G. K. *John's Use of the Old Testament in Revelation* (JSNTSup, 166; Sheffield: Sheffield Academic, 1998).

Beale, G. K. *The Temple and the Church's Mission: A Biblical Theology of the Dwelling Place of God* (NSBT; Downers Grove, IL: InterVarsity, 2004).
Beale, G. K. *The Use of Daniel in Jewish Apocalyptic Literature and in the Revelation of St. John* (Lanham, MD: University Press of America, 1984).
Beasley-Murray, G. R. *John* (WBC, 36; Waco, TX: Word, 2nd edn, 1999).
Beaton, R. *Isaiah's Christ in Matthew's Gospel* (SNTSMS, 123; Cambridge: Cambridge University Press, 2002).
Beckwith, I. T. *The Apocalypse of John: Studies in Introduction, with a Critical and Exegetical Commentary* (New York: Macmillan, 1919).
Beetham, C. A. *Echoes of Scripture in the Letter of Paul to the Colossians* (BIS, 96; Leiden: Brill, 2008).
Belleville, L. L. 'Tradition or Creation? Paul's Use of the Exodus 34 Tradition in 2 Corinthians 3.7-18', in C. A. Evans (ed.), *Paul and the Scriptures of Israel* (Sheffield: Sheffield Academic, 1993), pp. 165-86.
Bernstein, M. J. 'Torah and its Study in the Targum of Psalms', in Y. Elman and J. S. Gurock (eds.), *Ḥazon Naḥum: Studies in Jewish Law, Thought, and History Presented to Dr. Norman Lamm on the Occasion of his Seventieth Birthday* (Noboken, N.J.: Yeshiva University Press, 1997), pp. 39–67.
Berthelot, K., and T. Legrand. *La bibliothèque de Qumrân, vol. 2, Torah: Exode - Lévitique - Nombres: Édition et traduction des manuscrits hébreux, araméens et grecs* (Paris: Cerf, 2010).
Best, E. *A Critical and Exegetical Commentary on Ephesians* (ICC; Edinburgh: T&T Clark, 1998).
Black, M. 'Critical and Exegetical Notes on Three New Testament Texts: Hebrews 6:11, Jude 5, James 1:27', in W. Eltester *et al.* (eds.), *Apophoreta: Festschrift für Ernst Haenchen zu seinem siebzigsten Geburtstag* (Berlin: A. Töpelmann, 1964), pp. 39–45.
Blenkinsopp, J. *Isaiah 40–55* (AB, 19A; New York: Doubleday, 2002).
Block, D. I. 'A Prophet Like Moses: Another Look at Deuteronomy 18:9-22', in *The Triumph of Grace: Literary and Theological Studies in Deuteronomy and Deuteronomic Themes* (Eugene, OR: Cascade, 2017), pp. 349–73.
Blount, B. K. *Can I Get a Witness? Reading Revelation through African American Culture* (Louisville: Westminster John Knox, 2005).
Blount, B. K. *Revelation: A Commentary* (Louisville: Westminster John Knox, 2009).
Bock, D. L. *Luke* (BECNT; 2 vols.; Grand Rapids: Baker, 1994, 1996).
Bock, D. L. *Proclamation from Prophecy and Pattern: Lucan Old Testament Christology* (JSNTSup, 12; Sheffield: JSOT, 1987).
Boesak, A. *Comfort and Protest* (Philadelphia: Westminster, 1987).
Bogaert, P.-M. 'L'importance de la Septante et du "Monacensis" de la Vetus Latina pour l'exégèse du livre de l'Exode (chap. 35–40)', in M. Verveene (ed.), *Studies in the Book of Exodus: Redaction-Reception-Interpretation* (Leuven: Leuven University Press, 1996), pp. 399–428.
Bogaert, P.-M. 'L'orientation du parvis du sanctuaire dans la version grecque de l'Exode (*Ex.*, 27,9-13 LXX)', *AC* 50 (1981), pp. 79–85.
Boismard, M.-E. *Moses or Jesus: An Essay in Johannine Christology* (trans. B. T. Viviano; Minneapolis: Fortress, 1993).
Borchert, G. L. *John* (NAC, 25A; Nashville: Broadman & Holman, 1996).
Borgen, P. *Bread from Heaven: An Exegetical Study of the Concept of Manna in the Gospel of John and the Writings of Philo* (NovTSup, 10; Leiden: Brill, 1965).
Boring, M. E. *Revelation* (Int, 43; Louisville: John Knox, 1989).

Bovon, F. *Luke* (trans. C. M. Thomas; Hermeneia; 3 vols.; Minneapolis: Fortress, 2002, 2012, 2013).
Boxall, I. *Discovering Matthew: Content, Interpretation, Reception* (Grand Rapids: Eerdmans, 2015).
Boxall, I. *The Revelation of St John* (BNTC; London: Continuum, 2006).
Breytenbach, C. 'Zeus und der lebendige Gott: Anmerkungen zu Apostelgeschichte 14:11-17', *NTS* 39 (1993), pp. 396–413.
Brooke, A. E., and N. McLean. *The Old Testament in Greek According to the Septuagint, Vol. 1, Part II* (Cambridge: Cambridge University Press, 1909).
Brown, J. K. 'Genesis in Matthew's Gospel', in M. J. J. Menken and S. Moyise (eds.), *Genesis in the New Testament* (LNTS, 466; London: Bloomsbury T&T Clark, 2012), pp. 42–59.
Brown, J. K. 'Justice, Righteousness', in J. B. Green, J. K. Brown, and N. Perrin (eds.), *Dictionary of Jesus and the Gospels* (Downers Grove, IL: InterVarsity, 2nd edn, 2013), pp. 463–67.
Brown, J. K. *Matthew* (TTCS; Grand Rapids: Baker, 2015).
Brown, J. K. 'Metalepsis: The Intersection of Two Stories', in B. J. Oropeza and S. Moyise (eds.), *Exploring Intertextuality: Diverse Strategies for New Testament Interpretation of Texts* (Eugene, OR: Cascade, 2016), pp. 29–41.
Brown, J. K. *Scripture as Communication: Introducing Biblical Hermeneutics* (Grand Rapids: Baker Academic, 2007).
Brown, J. K., and K. A. Roberts. *The Gospel of Matthew* (THNTC; Grand Rapids: Eerdmans, 2019).
Brown, R. E. *The Gospel According to John I–XII* (AB, 29A; Garden City, NY: Doubleday, 1966).
Brown, R. E. *The Gospel According to John XIII–XXI* (AB, 29B; Garden City, NY: Doubleday, 1970).
Bruce, F. F. *The Epistles to the Colossians, to Philemon, and to the Ephesians* (NICNT; Grand Rapids: Eerdmans, 1984).
Bruning, B. 'The Making of the Mishkan' (Ph.D. diss.; University of Notre Dame, 2014).
Brunson, A. C. *Psalm 118 in the Gospel of John: An Intertextual Study of the New Exodus Pattern in the Theology of John* (WUNT, 2/158; Tübingen: Mohr Siebeck, 2003).
Burge, G. 'Commandment', in J. B. Green, J. K. Brown, and N. Perrin (eds.), *Dictionary of Jesus and the Gospels* (Downers Grove, IL: InterVarsity, 2nd edn, 2013), pp. 149–52.
Burge, G. *The Gospel of John* (NIVAC; Grand Rapids: Zondervan, 2000).
Caird, G. B. 'The Descent of Christ in Ephesians 4, 7–11', in F. L. Cross (ed.), *Studia Evangelica II. Papers Presented to the Second International Congress on New Testament Studies held at Christ Church Oxford, 1961* (Berlin: Akademie-Verlag, 1964), pp. 535–45.
Caird, G. *The Revelation of St John the Divine* (BNTC, London: A. & C. Black, 2nd edn, 1984).
Calvin, J. *The Acts of the Apostles* (2 vols.; Edinburgh: St. Andrew's Press, 1966).
Campbell, A. F. 'Psalm 78: A Contribution to the Theology of Tenth Century Israel', *CBQ* 41 (1979), pp. 51–79.
Campbell, D. A. *Framing Paul: An Epistolary Biography* (Grand Rapids: Eerdmans, 2014).
Cannon, G. E. *The Use of Traditional Materials in Colossians* (Macon, GA: Mercer University Press, 1983).

Capes, D. B. *The Divine Christ: Paul, the Lord Jesus, and the Scriptures of Israel* (Grand Rapids: Baker, 2018).
Carson, D. A. '1 Peter', in G. K. Beale and D. A. Carson (eds.), *Commentary on the New Testament Use of the Old Testament* (Grand Rapids: Baker, 2007), pp. 1015–45.
Carson, D. A. *The Gospel According to John* (PNTC; Grand Rapids: Eerdmans, 1991).
Carson, D. A. 'James', in G. K. Beale and D. A. Carson (eds.), *Commentary on the New Testament Use of the Old Testament* (Baker: Grand Rapids, 2007), pp. 997–1014.
Carter, W. *Matthew and the Margins: A Socio-political and Religious Reading* (Sheffield: Sheffield Academic, 2000).
Carter, W. 'Paying the Tax to Rome as Subversive Praxis: Matthew 17.24-27', *JSNT* 76 (1999), pp. 3–31.
Casey, J. S. 'Exodus Typology in the Book of Revelation' (Ph.D. Diss., Southern Baptist Theological Seminary, 1981).
Ceresko, A. R. 'The Rhetorical Strategy of the Fourth Servant Song (Isaiah 52:13–53:12): Poetry and Exodus-New Exodus', *CBQ* 56 (1994), pp. 42–55.
Charles, R. H. *A Critical and Exegetical Commentary on the Revelation of St. John* (2 vols.; Edinburgh: T&T Clark, 1920).
Childs, B. *The Book of Exodus: A Critical, Theological Commentary* (OTL; Philadelphia: Westminster, 1974).
Chilton, B. 'Greek Testament, Aramaic Targums, and Questions of Comparison', *AS* 11 (2013), pp. 225–51.
Ciampa, R. E. 'Scriptural Language and Ideas', in S. E. Porter and C. D. Stanley (eds.), *As It Is Written: Studying Paul's Use of Scripture* (SBLSymS, 50; Atlanta: Society of Biblical Literature, 2008), pp. 41–58.
Collins, A. Y. *Mark* (Hermeneia; Minneapolis: Fortress, 2007).
Collins, N. *Jesus, the Sabbath and the Jewish Debate: Healing on the Sabbath in the 1st and 2nd Centuries CE* (LNTS, 474; London: Bloomsbury T&T Clark, 2014).
Cook, J. 'Exodus 38 and Proverbs 31: A Case of Different Order of Verses and Chapters in the Septuagint', in M. Vervenne (ed.), *Studies in the Book of Exodus: Redaction-Reception-Interpretation* (Leuven: Leuven University Press, 1996), pp. 537–49.
Cranfield, C. E. B. *A Critical and Exegetical Commentary on the Epistle to the Romans, Volume II: Romans IX–XVI and Essays* (ICC; London: T&T Clark, 1979).
Cranfield, C. E. B. *The Gospel According to Saint Mark* (CGTC, 2; Cambridge: Cambridge University Press, 1963).
Crawford, S. W. *Rewriting Scripture in Second Temple Times* (Grand Rapids: Eerdmans, 2008).
Croasmun, M. *The Emergence of Sin: The Cosmic Tyrant in Romans* (New York: Oxford University Press, 2017).
Cross, F. M. 'The Evolution of a Theory of Local Texts', in *Qumran and the History of the Biblical Text* (Cambridge, MA: Harvard University Press, 1975), pp. 306–20.
Cross, F. M. 'The History of the Biblical Text in the Light of Discoveries in the Judaean Desert', in *Qumran and the History of the Biblical Text* (Cambridge, MA: Harvard University Press, 1975), pp. 177–95.
Daly-Denton, M. *David in the Fourth Gospel: The Johannine Reception of the Psalms* (AGJU, 47; Leiden: Brill, 2004).
Daube, D. *The New Testament and Rabbinic Judaism* (London: Athlone, 1956).
Davids, P. H. *The Letters of 2 Peter and Jude* (PNTC; Grand Rapids: Eerdmans, 2006).

Davies, W. D. 'Paul and the New Exodus', in C. A. Evans and S. Talmon (eds.), *The Quest for Context and Meaning: Studies in Biblical Intertextuality in Honor of James A. Sanders* (New York: Brill, 1997), pp. 443–63.

Davies, W. D., and D. C. Allison Jr. *Matthew* (ICC; 3 vols.; London: T&T Clark, 1988, 1991, 1997),

Davila, J. R. 'Text-Type and Terminology: Genesis and Exodus as Test Cases', *RevQ* 16/61 (1993), pp. 3–37.

Davis, K. 'Caves of Dispute: Patterns of Correspondence and Suspicion in the Post-2002 "Dead Sea Scrolls" Fragments', *DSD* 24 (2017), pp. 229–70.

Davis, K., I. Rabin, I. Feldman, M. Krutzsch, H. Rimon, and Å. Justnes, T. Elgvin, M. Langlois. 'Nine Dubious "Dead Sea Scrolls" Fragments from the Twenty-First Century', *DSD* 24 (2017), pp. 189–228.

Debel, H. 'Envisioning the "Editions" of Exodus: Reconstructing the Growth of a Literary Chain of Tradition', in H. Ausloos and B. Lemmelijn (eds.), *A Pillar of Cloud to Guide: Text-critical, Redactional, and Linguistic Perspectives on the Old Testament in Honour of Marc Vervenne* (BETL, 269; Leuven: Peeters, 2014), pp. 363–78.

Decker, R. J. *Temporal Deixis of the Greek Verb in the Gospel of Mark with Reference to Verbal Aspect* (SBG, 10; New York: Lang, 2001).

Dentan, R. C. 'The Literary Affinities of Exodus XXXIV 6f', *VT* 13 (1963), pp. 34–51.

DeRouchie, J. S. 'Making the Ten Count: Reflections on the Lasting Message of the Decalogue', in J. S. DeRouchie, J. Gile, and K. J. Turner (eds.), *For Our Good Always: Studies on the Message and Influence of Deuteronomy in Honor of Daniel I. Block* (Winona Lake, IN: Eisenbrauns, 2013), pp. 415–40.

deSilva, D. A. 'Five More Papyrus Fragments from a Greek Codex of Exodus', *BIOSCS* 40 (2007), pp. 1–29.

deSilva, D. A., with M. P. Adams. 'Seven Papyrus Fragments of a Greek Manuscript of Exodus', *VT* 56 (2006), pp. 143–70.

Deterding, P. E. 'Exodus Motifs in First Peter', *ConJ* 7, no. 2 (1981), pp. 58–65.

De Troyer, K. 'The Textual Character of the *Exodus Codex* of the Schøyen Collection (*MS* 187; RA 866)', *AnaPap* 23-24 (2011–2012), pp. 57–79.

Dibelius, M., and H. Conzelmann. *The Pastoral Epistles: A Commentary on the Pastoral Epistles* (Hermeneia; Philadelphia: Fortress, 1972).

DiMattei, S. 'Biblical Narratives', in S. E. Porter and C. D. Stanley (eds.), *As It Is Written: Studying Paul's Use of Scripture* (Atlanta: Society of Biblical Literature, 2008), pp. 59–93.

Docherty, S. E. 'Composite Citations and Conflation of Scriptural Narratives in Hebrews', in S. A. Adams and S. M. Ehorn (eds.), *Composite Citations in Antiquity*. Vol. 2, *New Testament Uses* (LNTS, 593; London: Bloomsbury T&T Clark, 2018), pp. 190–208.

Docherty, S. E. *The Use of the Old Testament in Hebrews: A Case Study in Early Jewish Bible Interpretation* (WUNT, 2/260; Tübingen: Mohr Siebeck, 2009).

Dodd, C. H. *The Interpretation of the Fourth Gospel* (Cambridge: Cambridge University Press, 1953).

Doering, L. *Ancient Jewish Letters and the Beginnings of Christian Epistolography* (WUNT, 1/298; Tübingen: Mohr Siebeck, 2012).

Doering, L. 'Gottes Volk: Die Adressaten als "Israel" im Ersten Pestrusbrief', in D. du Toit (ed.), *Bedrängnis und Identität: Studien zu Situation, Kommunikation und Theologie des 1. Petrusbriefes* (BZNW, 200; Berlin: de Gruyter, 2013), pp. 81–113.

Doering, L. '"You are a Chosen Stock...": The Use of Israel Epithets for the Addressees in First Peter', in Y. Furstenberg (ed.), *Jewish and Christian Communal Identities in the Roman World* (Leiden: Brill, 2016), pp. 243–76.
Dohmen, C. 'Decalogue', in T. B. Dozeman, C. A. Evans, and J. N. Lohr (eds.), *The Book of Exodus: Composition, Reception, and Interpretation* (VTSup, 164; Leiden: Brill, 2014), pp. 193–219.
Dohmen, C. *Exodus 19–40* (HThKAT, 5; Freiburg: Herber, 2nd edn, 2012).
Donaldson, T. L. 'The Vindicated Son: A Narrative Approach to Matthean Christology', in R. N. Longenecker (ed.), *Contours of Christology in the New Testament* (Grand Rapids: Eerdmans, 2005), pp. 110–21.
Downing, F. G. 'Common Ground with Paganism in Luke and in Josephus', *NTS* 28 (1982), pp. 546–59.
Dozeman, T. B. *Commentary on Exodus* (Grand Rapids: Eerdmans, 2009).
Dozeman, T. B., T. Römer, and K. Schmid (eds.). *Pentateuch, Hexateuch, or Enneateuch? Identifying Literary Works in Genesis through Kings* (Atlanta: Society of Biblical Literature, 2011).
Dunn, J. D. G. *The Epistles to the Colossians and Philemon* (NIGTC; Grand Rapids: Eerdmans, 1996).
Dunn, J. D. G. 'Rom 7:14-25 in the Theology of Paul', *TZ* 31 (1975), pp. 257–73.
Dunn, J. D. G. *Romans 9–16* (WBC, 38B; Dallas: Word Books, 1988).
Dunn, J. D. G. *Theology of the Apostle Paul* (Grand Rapids: Eerdmans, 1998).
Dunnill, J. *Covenant and Sacrifice in the Letter to the Hebrews* (SNTSMS, 75; Cambridge: Cambridge University Press, 1993).
Durham, J. I. *Exodus* (WBC, 3; Waco, TX: Word, 1987).
Easter, M. C. *The Faith and Faithfulness of Jesus in Hebrews* (SNTSMS, 160; Cambridge: Cambridge University Press, 2014).
Egan, P. T. *Ecclesiology and the Scriptural Narrative of 1 Peter* (Eugene, OR: Pickwick, 2016).
Ehorn, S. M. 'The Citation of Psalm 68(67).19 in Ephesians 4.8 within the Context of Early Christian Uses of the Psalms' (Ph.D. diss., University of Edinburgh, 2015).
Ehorn, S. M. 'The Use of Psalm 68(67).19 in Ephesians 4.8: A History of Research', *CBR* 12 (2013), pp. 96–120.
Ehrman, B. D. *Forgery and Counterforgery: The Use of Literary Deceit in Early Christian Polemics* (New York: Oxford University Press, 2012).
Eisenbaum, P. M. *The Jewish Heroes of Christian History: Hebrews 11 in Literary Context* (SBLDS, 156; Atlanta: Scholars Press, 1997).
Ellingworth, P. *The Epistle to the Hebrews: A Commentary on the Greek Text* (NIGTC; Grand Rapids: Eerdmans, 1993).
Elliott, J. H. *1 Peter: A New Translation with Introduction and Commentary* (AB, 37B; New Haven: Yale University Press, 2000).
Elliott, J. H. *The Elect and the Holy: An Exegetical Examination of 1 Peter 2:4-10 and the Phrase Βασίλειον ἱεράτευμα* (NovTSup, 12; Leiden: Brill, 1966).
Enns, P. *Exodus* (NIVAC; Grand Rapids: Zondervan, 2000).
Enns, P. *Exodus Retold: Ancient Exegesis of the Departure from Egypt in Wis 10:15-21 and 19:1-9* (HSS, 57; Atlanta: Scholars Press, 1997).
Enns, P. 'The "Moveable Well" in 1 Cor 10:4: An Extrabiblical Tradition in an Apostolic Text'. *BBR* 6 (1996), pp. 23–38.
Estelle, B. D. *Echoes of Exodus: Tracing a Biblical Motif* (Downers Grove, IL: InterVarsity, 2018).

Evans, C. A. *Ancient Texts for New Testament Studies: A Guide to the Background Literature* (Peabody, MA: Hendrickson, 2005).
Evans, C. A. 'Praise and Prophecy in the Psalter and in the New Testament', in P. W. Flint and P. D. Miller, Jr. (eds.), *The Book of Psalms: Composition and Reception* (VTSup, 99; Leiden: Brill, 2005), pp. 551–79.
Evans, C. A. *To See and Not Perceive: Isaiah 6:9–10 in Early Jewish and Christian Interpretation* (JSOTSup, 64; Sheffield: JSOT, 1989).
Falk, D. K. *The Parabiblical Texts: Strategies for Extending the Scriptures in the Dead Sea Scrolls* (London: T&T Clark, 2007).
Farrer, A. M. *A Rebirth of Images: The Making of St. John's Apocalypse* (Westminster: Dacre, 1949).
Fee, G. D. 'Old Testament Intertextuality in Colossians: Reflections on Pauline Christology and Gentile Inclusion in God's Story', in S.-W. Son (ed.), *History and Exegesis: New Testament Essays in Honor of E. Earle Ellis for his 80th Birthday* (London: T&T Clark, 2006), pp. 201–22.
Fekkes, J. *Isaiah and Prophetic Traditions in the Book of Revelation* (Sheffield: JSOT, 1994).
Feldmeier, R. *The First Letter of Peter: A Commentary on the Greek Text* (Waco, TX: Baylor University Press, 2008).
Finlan, S. *The Background and Content of Paul's Cultic Atonement Metaphors* (Atlanta: Society of Biblical Literature, 2004).
Finn, A. H. 'The Tabernacle Chapters', *JTS* 16 (1915), pp. 449–82.
Fishbane, M. *Biblical Text and Texture: A Literary Reading of Selected Texts* (Oxford: Oneworld, 1979).
Fishbane, M. 'The "Exodus" Motif/The Paradigm of Historical Renewal', in M. Fishbane (ed.), *Text and Texture: A Literary Reading of Selected Texts* (Oxford: One World, 1998), pp. 121–40.
Fitzmyer, J. *Luke* (AB, 28A-B; 2 vols.; Garden City, NY: Doubleday, 1981, 1985).
Fletcher, M. *Reading Revelation as Pastiche: Imitating the Past* (LNTS, 571; London: Bloomsbury T&T Clark, 2017).
Flusser, D. '"Do not commit adultery", "Do not murder"', *Text* 4 (1964), pp. 220–24.
Flusser, D. '"Today if You will Listen to His Voice": Creative Jewish Exegesis in Hebrews 3–4', in B. Uffenheimer and H. G. Reventlow (eds.), *Creative Biblical Exegesis: Christian and Jewish Hermeneutics Through the Centuries* (JSOTSup, 59; Sheffield: JSOT, 1988), pp. 55–62.
Fossum, J. 'Kyrios Jesus as the Angel of the Lord in Jude 5-7', *NTS* 33 (1987), pp. 226–43.
Foster, P. 'Who Wrote 2 Thessalonians? A Fresh Look at an Old Problem', *JSNT* 35 (2012), pp. 150–75.
Fowl, S. E. *Ephesians: A Commentary* (NTL; Louisville: Westminster John Knox, 2012).
Fox, R. M. (ed.). *The Reverberations of the Exodus in Scripture* (Eugene, OR: Pickwick, 2014).
Fraenkel, D. 'Übersetzungsnorm und literarische Gestaltung—Spuren individueller Übersetzungstechnik in Exodus 25ff. + 35ff.', in L. Greenspoon and O. Munnich (eds.), *VIII Congress of the International Organization for Septuagint and Cognate Studies, Paris, 1992* (SCS, 41; Atlanta: Scholars Press, 1995), pp. 73–87.
France, R. T. *Matthew* (NICNT; Grand Rapids: Eerdmans, 2007).
Freed, E. D. 'Who or What Was before Abraham in John 8:58?', *JSNT* 17 (1983), pp. 52–59.
Gall, A. F. von. *Der Hebräische Pentateuch der Samaritaner* (Giessen: Töpelmann, 1918).

Gallus, L. 'The Exodus Motif in Revelation 15–16: Its Background and Nature', *AUSS* 46 (2008), pp. 21–43.
Garland, D. E. *1 Corinthians* (BECNT; Grand Rapids: Baker, 2003).
Garland, D. E. 'The Temple Tax in Matthew and the Principle of Not Giving Offense', in D. Bauer and M. Alan Powell (eds.), *Treasures New and Old: Recent Contributions to Matthean Studies* (Atlanta: Scholars Press, 1996), pp. 68–98.
Garrett, D. A. *A Commentary on Exodus* (KEL; Grand Rapids: Kregel Academic, 2014).
Garrett, D. A. 'Veiled Hearts: The Translation and Interpretation of 2 Corinthians 3', *JETS* 53 (2010), pp. 729–72.
Garrett, S. R. 'Exodus from Bondage: Luke 9:31 and Acts 12:1-24', *CBQ* 52 (1990), pp. 656–80.
Gathercole, S. J. 'Torah, Life, and Salvation: Leviticus 18:5 in Early Judaism and the New Testament', in C. A. Evans (ed.), *From Prophecy to Testament: The Function of the Old Testament in the New* (Peabody, MA: Hendrickson, 2004), pp. 126–45.
Gelardini, G. *Deciphering the Worlds of Hebrews: Collected Essays* (NovTSup, 184; Leiden: Brill, 2021).
Gempf, C. H. 'Mission and Misunderstanding: Paul and Barnabas in Lystra (Acts 14:8-20)', in A. Billington, M. M. B. Turner, and T. Lane (eds.), *Mission and Meaning (Festschrift Peter Cotterell)* (Carlisle: Paternoster, 1995), pp. 56–69.
Gese, M. *Das Vermächtnis des Apostels: die Rezeption der paulinischen Theologie im Epheserbrief* (WUNT, 2/99; Tübingen: Mohr Siebeck, 1997).
Glasson, T. F. *Moses in the Fourth Gospel* (SBT, 40; London: SCM, 1963).
Gooding, D. W. *The Account of the Tabernacle: Translation and Textual Problems of the Greek Exodus* (TS, 6; Cambridge: Cambridge University Press, 1959).
Goodrich, J. K. 'Until the Fullness of the Gentiles Comes In: A Critical Review of Recent Scholarship on the Salvation of "All Israel" (Romans 11:26)', *JSPL* 6 (2016), pp. 5–32.
Goppelt, L. *A Commentary on 1 Peter* (ed. F. Hahn; trans. J. Alsup; Grand Rapids: Eerdmans, 1993).
Goranson Jacob, H. *Conformed to the Image of His Son: Reconsidering Paul's Theology of Glory in Romans* (Downers Grove, IL: IVP, 2018).
Gough, H. *The New Testament Quotations Collated with the Scriptures of the Old Testament* (London: Walton & Maberly, 1855).
Green, J. B. *The Gospel of Luke* (NICNT; Grand Rapids: Eerdmans, 1997).
Green, J. B. 'The Problem of a Beginning: Israel's Scriptures in Luke 1–2', *BBR* 4 (1994), pp. 61–85.
Greenberg, M. 'Hebrew sᵉgullā: Akkadian sikiltu', *JAOS* 71 (1951), pp. 172–74.
Grindheim, S. 'The Work of God or of Human Beings: John 6:29', *JETS* 59 (2016), pp. 63–66.
Gruen, E. S. *Heritage and Hellenism: The Reinvention of Jewish Tradition* (Berkeley: University of California Press, 1998), pp. 41–72.
Grundmann, W. *Das Evangelium nach Matthäus* (HThKNT, 1; Berlin: Evangelische Verlagsanstalt, 1968).
Guelich, R. A. *Mark 1–8:26* (WBC, 34A; Grand Rapids: Zondervan, 2015).
Gundry, R. H. *Mark: A Commentary on His Apology for the Cross* (Grand Rapids: Eerdmans, 2000).
Gundry, R. H. *Matthew: A Commentary on His Literary and Theological Art* (Grand Rapids: Eerdmans, 1982).
Gunkel, H. *Die Psalmen* (Göttingen: Vandenhoeck & Ruprecht, 5th edn, 1968).

Gupta, N. K. 'A Spiritual House of Royal Priests, Chosen and Honored: The Presence and Function of Cultic Imagery in 1 Peter', *PRSt* 36 (2009), pp. 61–76.

Gurtner, D. M. *Exodus: A Commentary on the Greek Text of Codex Vaticanus* (BSCS; Leiden: Brill, 2013).

Gurtner, D. M. '"Fasting" and "Forty nights": The Matthean Temptation Narrative (4:1-11) and Moses Typology', in C. A. Evans and H. D. Zacharias (eds.), *'What Does the Scripture Say': Studies in the Function of Scripture in Early Judaism and Christianity*, vol. 1: *The Synoptic Gospels* (LNTS, 470; London: Bloomsbury T&T Clark, 2012), pp. 1–11.

Gurtner, D. M. 'LXX Syntax and the Identity of the NT Veil', *NovT* 47 (2005), pp. 344–53.

Gurtner, D. M. *The Torn Veil: Matthew's Exposition of the Death of Jesus* (SNTSMS, 139; Cambridge: Cambridge University Press, 2007).

Guthrie, G. H. *2 Corinthians* (BECNT; Grand Rapids: Baker, 2015).

Haenchen, E. *The Acts of the Apostles* (Oxford: Blackwell, 1971).

Hafemann, S. J. 'God's Salvation "Once and for All" in Jude 5 and the Covenant Argumentation of 2 Peter 1:3-11: Confirming One's Election in the CE', in K.-W. Niebuhr and R. W. Wall (eds.), *The Catholic Epistles and Apostolic Tradition: A New Perspective on James to Jude* (Waco, TX: Baylor, 2009), pp. 331–42.

Hafemann, S. J. *Paul, Moses, and the History of Israel: The Letter/Spirit Contrast and the Argument from Scripture in 2 Corinthians 3* (WUNT, 2/81; Tübingen: Mohr Siebeck, 1995).

Hafemann, S. J. 'Paul and the Exile of Israel in Galatians 3–4', in J. M. Scott (ed.), *Exile: Old Testament, Jewish, and Christian Conceptions* (Leiden: Brill, 1997), pp. 329–71.

Hagner, D. A. *Matthew* (WBC, 33A-B; 2 vols.; Dallas: Word, 1993, 1995).

Hahn, S. W. 'Covenant, Oath, and the Aqedah: Διαθήκη in Galatians 3:15-18', *CBQ* 67 (2005), pp. 79–100.

Hakala, D. L. 'Jesus Said, "Keep the Commandments", and the Rich Man Asked, "Which Ones?": The Decalogue as a Law Summary in the Story of the Rich Man', in C. A. Evans and J. J. Johnston (eds.), *Searching the Scriptures: Studies in Context and Intertextuality* (LNTS, 543; London: Bloomsbury T&T Clark, 2015), pp. 171–90.

Halas, S. 'Sens dynamique de l'expression "λαὸς εἰς περιποίησιν" en 1 P 2,9', *Bib* 65 (1984), pp. 254–58.

Halpern-Amaru, B. *The Perspective from Mt. Sinai: The Book of Jubilees and Exodus* (JAJSup, 21; Göttingen: Vandenhoeck & Ruprecht, 2015).

Hamm, D. 'Acts 3:12-26: Peter's Speech and the Healing of the Man Born Lame', *PRSt* 11 (1984), pp. 199–217.

Hamm, D. 'The Freeing of the Bent Woman and the Restoration of Israel: Luke 13:10-17 as Narrative Theology', *JSNT* 31 (1987), pp. 23–44.

Hardy, T. *Jude the Obscure: A Critical Edition* (ed. Norman Page; London: Norton & Company, 2nd edn, 1999).

Harris, W. H., III. 'The Ascent and Descent of Christ in Ephesians 4:9–10', *BSac* 151 (1994), pp. 198–214.

Harris, W. H., III. *The Descent of Christ: Ephesians 4:7-11 and Traditional Hebrew Imagery* (AGJU, 32; Leiden: Brill, 1996).

Harstine, S. *Moses as a Character in the Fourth Gospel: A Study of Ancient Reading Techniques* (JSNTSup, 229; Sheffield: Sheffield Academic, 2002).

Hays, R. B. *Echoes of Scripture in the Gospels* (Waco, TX: Baylor University Press, 2016).

Hays, R. B. *Echoes of Scripture in the Letters of Paul* (New Haven: Yale University Press, 1989).

Helyer, L. R. 'The *Prōtotokos* Title in Hebrews', *SBT* 6 (1976), pp. 3–28.
Hemer, C. J. *The Letters to the Seven Churches of Asia in Their Local Setting* (JSNTSup, 11; Sheffield: JSOT, 1989).
Hickling, C. J. A. 'Paul's Use of Exodus in the Corinthian Correspondence', in R. Bieringer (ed.), *The Corinthian Correspondence* (Leuven: Peeters, 1996), pp. 367–76.
Hoehner, H. W. *Ephesians: An Exegetical Commentary* (Grand Rapids: Baker, 2002).
Hoftijzer, J. 'Une lettre du roi hittite', in *Von Kanaan bis Kerala* (Kevelaer, Germany: Butzon & Bercker, 1982), pp. 379–87.
Hoffmann, M. R. *The Destroyer and the Lamb: The Relationship Between Angelomorphic and Lamb Christology in the Book of Revelation* (WUNT, 2/203; Tübingen: Mohr Siebeck, 2005)
Hofius, O. *Katapausis: Die Vorstellung vom endzeitlichen Ruheort im Hebräerbrief* (WUNT, 1/11; Tübingen: Mohr Siebeck, 1970).
Hooker, M. D. *The Gospel According to St. Mark* (BNTC; Peabody, MA; Hendrickson, 1992).
Hoppe, R. *Epheserbrief, Kolosserbrief* (SKKNT, 10; Stuttgart: Katholisches Bibelwerk, 1987).
Hoskins, P. M. *That Scripture Might Be Fulfilled: Typology and the Death of Christ* (Longwood, FL: Xulon, 2009).
Howard, G. 'Hebrews and the Old Testament Quotations', *NovT* 10 (1968), pp. 208–16.
Huffmon, H., and S. Parker, 'A Further Note on the Treaty Background of Hebrew *Yada*'', *BASOR* 184 (1966), pp. 36–38.
Hughes, P. E. *A Commentary on the Epistle to the Hebrews* (NICNT; Grand Rapids: Eerdmans, 1977).
Idestrom, R. G. S. 'Echoes of the Book of Exodus in Ezekiel', *JSOT* 33 (2009), pp. 489–510.
Imes, C. J. *'Treasured Possession': Peter's Use of the Old Testament in 1 Peter 2:9–10* (MA thesis: Gordon-Conwell Theological Seminary, 2011).
Jack, A. *Texts Reading Texts, Sacred and Secular* (JSNTSup, 179; Sheffield: Sheffield Academic, 1999).
Jastram, N. 'A Comparison of Two "Proto-Samaritan" Texts from Qumran: 4QpaleoExod^m and 4QNum^b', *DSD* 5 (1998), pp. 264–89.
Jauhiainen, M. *The Use of Zechariah in Revelation* (WUNT, 2/199, Tübingen: Mohr Siebeck, 2005).
Jewett, R. *Romans: A Commentary* (Hermeneia; Minneapolis: Fortress, 2007).
Jobes, K. H. *1 Peter* (Grand Rapids: Baker Academic, 2005).
Johns, L. L. *The Lamb Christology of the Apocalypse of John: An Investigation into Its Origins and Rhetorical Force* (WUNT, 2/167; Tübingen: Mohr Siebeck, 2003).
Johnson, L. T. *The First and Second Letters to Timothy: A New Translation with Introduction and Commentary* (AB, 35A; New York: Doubleday, 2001).
Johnson, L. T. *Hebrews: A Commentary* (NTL; Louisville: Westminster/John Knox, 2006).
Jones, W. H. S. *Pliny, Natural History 28–32* (LCL, 418; Cambridge, MA: Harvard University Press, 1963).
Kahle, P. E. *The Cairo Geniza* (Oxford: Blackwell, 2nd edn, 1959).
Kahle, P. E. 'Untersuchungen zur Geschichte des Pentateuchtextes', *TSK* 88 (1915), pp. 399–439.
Kee, H. C. 'The Function of Scriptural Quotations and Allusions in Mark 11–16', in E. E. Ellis and E. Gräßer (eds.), *Jesus and Paulus* (Festschrift W. G. Kümmel; Göttingen: Vandenhoeck & Ruprecht, 1975), pp. 165–88.

Keener, C. S. *Acts: An Exegetical Commentary* (4 vols.; Grand Rapids: Baker, 2012–2015).
Keener, C. S. *A Commentary on the Gospel of Matthew* (Grand Rapids: Eerdmans, 1999).
Keener, C. S. *The Gospel of John* (Peabody, PA: Hendrickson, 2003).
Keener, C. S. *The IVP Bible Background Commentary: New Testament* (Downers Grove, IL: InterVarsity, 2nd edn, 2014).
Keesmaat, S. C. *Paul and His Story: (Re)Interpreting the Exodus Tradition* (LNTS, 181. Sheffield: Sheffield Academic, 1999).
Kelly, J. N. D. *The Epistles of Peter and of Jude* (BNTC; Peabody, MA: Hendrickson, 1999).
Kibbe, M. H. *Godly Fear or Ungodly Failure? Hebrews 12 and the Sinai Theophanies* (BZNW, 216; Berlin: De Gruyter, 2016).
Kilgallen, J. J. 'The Sadducees and Resurrection from the Dead: Luke 20,27-40', *Bib* 67 (1986), pp. 478–95.
Kim, K. 'Studies in the Relationship between the Samaritan Pentateuch and the Septuagint' (Ph.D. diss., Hebrew University of Jerusalem, 1994).
Kleinig, J. W. *Hebrews* (ConC; St. Louis: Concordia, 2017).
Koester, C. R. *Hebrews: A New Translation with Introduction and Commentary* (AB, 36; New York: Doubleday, 2001).
Koester, C. R. *Revelation: A New Translation with Introduction and Commentary* (AB, 38A; New Haven: Yale University Press, 2014).
Koester, C. R. *Symbolism in the Fourth Gospel* (Minneapolis: Fortress, 2nd edn, 2003).
Kowalski, B. *Die Rezeption Des Propheten Ezechiel in Der Offenbarung Des Johannes* (Stuttgart: Verlag Katholisches Bibelwerk, 2004).
Kooij, A. van der. 'Preservation and Promulgation: The Dead Sea Scrolls and the Textual History of the Hebrew Bible', in N. Dávid, A. Lange, K. de Troyer, and S. Tzoeref (eds.), *The Hebrew Bible in Light of the Dead Sea Scrolls* (FRLANT, 239; Göttingen: Vandenhoeck & Ruprecht, 2012), pp. 29–40.
Köstenberger, A. J. 'Diversity and Unity in the New Testament', in S. J. Hafemann (eds.), *Biblical Theology: Retrospect and Prospect* (Downers Grove, IL: InterVarsity, 2002), pp. 144–58.
Köstenberger, A. J. *Encountering John* (EBS; Grand Rapids: Baker, 2nd edn, 2013).
Köstenberger, A. J. 'Jesus as Rabbi in the Fourth Gospel', *BBR* 8 (1998), pp. 97–128.
Köstenberger, A. J. 'Jesus the Good Shepherd Who Will Also Bring Other Sheep (John 10:16): The Old Testament Background of a Familiar Metaphor', *BBR* 12 (2002), pp. 67–96.
Köstenberger, A. J. *John* (BECNT; Grand Rapids: Baker, 2004).
Köstenberger, A. J. 'John', in G. K. Beale and D. A. Carson (eds.), *Commentary on the New Testament Use of the Old Testament* (Grand Rapids: Baker, 2007), pp. 415–512.
Köstenberger, A. J. 'Lifting Up the Son of Man and God's Love for the World: John 3:16 in Its Historical, Literary, and Theological Contexts', in A. J. Köstenberger and R. W. Yarbrough (eds.), *Understanding the Times: New Testament Studies in the 21st Century* (Wheaton, IL: Crossway, 2011), pp. 141–59.
Köstenberger, A. J. *The Missions of Jesus and the Disciples According to the Fourth Gospel* (Grand Rapids: Eerdmans, 1998).
Köstenberger, A. J. 'The Seventh Johannine Sign: A Study in John's Christology', *BBR* 5 (1995), pp. 87–103.
Köstenberger, A. J. *A Theology of John's Gospel and Letters* (BTNT; Grand Rapids: Zondervan, 2009).

Köstenberger, A. J. 'What Does It Mean to Be Filled with the Spirit? A Biblical Investigation', *JETS* 40 (1997), pp. 229–40.

Kovacs, J. L., and C. Rowland. *Revelation: The Apocalypse of Jesus Christ* (BBC; Malden, MA: Blackwell, 2004).

Kraft, H. *Die Offenbarung Des Johannes* (HNT, 16a; Tübingen: Mohr Siebeck, 1974).

Kratz, R. G. 'The Analysis of the Pentateuch: An Attempt to Overcome Barriers of Thinking', *ZAW* 128 (2016), pp. 529–61.

Kraus, W., and M. Karrer. *Septuaginta Deutsch* (Stuttgart: German Bible Society, 2009).

Kupfer, C. *Mit Israel auf dem Weg durch die Wüste: Eine leserorientierte Exegese der Rebellionstexte in Exodus 15:22–17:7 und Numeri 11:1–20:13* (OTS, 61; Leiden: Brill, 2012).

Kupp, D. D. *Matthew's Emmanuel: Divine Presence and God's People in the First Gospel* (New York: Cambridge University Press, 1996).

Kuyper, L. J. 'Grace and Truth: An Old Testament Description of God and Its Use in the Johannine Gospel', *Int* 18 (1964), pp. 3–13.

Lacomara, A. 'Deuteronomy and the Farewell Discourse (Jn 13:31–16:33)', *CBQ* 36 (1974), pp. 65–84.

LaCoste, N. 'Waters of the Exodus: Jewish Experiences with Water in Ptolemaic and Roman Egypt' (Ph.D. diss., University of Toronto, 2016).

Lane, W. L. *Hebrews 9–13* (WBC, 47B; Dallas: Word, 1991).

Lange, A., and M. Weigold. *Biblical Quotations and Allusions in Second Temple Jewish Literature* (Göttingen: Vandenhoek & Ruprecht, 2011).

Larkin, W. J. *Ephesians* (BHGNT; Waco, TX: Baylor University Press, 2009).

Le Boulluec, A., and P. Sandevoir, *La Bible d'Alexandrie 2: L'Exode* (Paris: Cerf, 1989).

Levison, J. R. 'Spirit, Holy', in John J. Collins and D. C. Harlow (eds.), *Eerdmans Dictionary of Early Judaism* (Grand Rapids: Eerdmans, 2010), pp. 1252–54.

Lierman, J. *The New Testament Moses: Christian Perceptions of Moses and Israel in the Setting of Jewish Religion* (WUNT, 2/173; Tübingen: Mohr Siebeck, 2004).

Lincoln, A. T. *Ephesians* (WBC, 42; Dallas: Word, 1990).

Lincoln, A. T. 'The Use of the OT in Ephesians', *JSNT* 14 (1982), pp. 16–57.

Lindars, B. *New Testament Apologetic* (London: SCM, 1961).

Lohmeyer, E. *Die Brief an die Philipper, and die Kolosser und an Philemon* (KEK, 9; Göttingen: Vandenhoeck & Ruprecht, 1930).

Lohse, E. *Der Brief an die Römer* (Göttingen: Vandenhoeck & Ruprecht, 2003).

Longacre, D. 'A Contextualized Approach to the Hebrew Dead Sea Scrolls Containing Exodus' (Ph.D. diss., University of Birmingham, 2015), pp. 229–36.

Longacre, D. Review of *Dead Sea Scrolls Fragments in the Museum Collection*, edited by E. Tov, K. Davis, and R. Duke. *JTS* 69 (2018), pp. 265–67.

Longenecker, R. N. *Biblical Exegesis in the Apostolic Period* (Grand Rapids: Eerdmans, 2nd edn, 1999).

Louw, J. P., and E. A. Nida. *Greek–English Lexicon of the New Testament Based on Semantic Domains* (New York: United Bible Societies, 2nd edn, 1989).

Luz, U., J. E. Crouch, and H. Koester. *Matthew 1–7: A Commentary* (Minneapolis: Fortress, 2007).

Luz, U., and H. Koester, *Matthew 21–28: A Commentary* (Minneapolis: Fortress, 2005).

Malatesta, E. J. *Interiority and Covenant: A Study of EINAI EN and MENEIN EN in the First Letter of Saint John* (AnBib, 69; Rome: Biblical Institute, 1978).

Mallen, P. 'Genesis in Luke-Acts', in M. J. J. Menken and S. Moyise (eds.), *Genesis in the New Testament* (LNTS, 466; London: Bloomsbury T&T Clark, 2012), pp. 60–82.

Mallen, P. *The Reading and Transformation of Isaiah in Luke-Acts* (LNTS, 367; London: T&T Clark, 2008).
Marcar, K. 'The Quotations of Isaiah in 1 Peter: A Text-Critical Analysis', *TC: A Journal of Biblical Textual Criticism* 21 (2016), pp. 1–22.
Marcos, N. F., and M. V. S. Díaz-Caro (eds.). *La Biblia griega Septuaginta I: Pentateuco* (BEB, 125; Salamanca: Ediciones Sígueme, 2008).
Marcus, J. *Mark 1–8: A New Translation with Introduction and Commentary* (AB, 27A; New Haven, CT: Yale University Press, 2010).
Marshall, I. H. 'Acts', in G. K. Beale and D. A. Carson (eds.), *Commentary on the New Testament Use of the Old Testament* (Grand Rapids: Baker, 2007), pp. 513–606.
Marshall, I. H. *Gospel of Luke: A Commentary on the Greek Text* (NIGTC; Exeter: Paternoster, 1978).
Martin, R. P. *2 Corinthians* (WBC, 40; Grand Rapids: Zondervan, 2014).
Martínez, F. G., and E. J. C. Tigchelaar. *The Dead Sea Scrolls Study Edition* (Leiden: Brill, 1999).
Massonet, J. *L'épître aux Hébreux* (Commentaire Biblique: Nouveau Testament, 15; Paris: Cerf, 2016).
Mathewson, D. *A New Heaven and a New Earth: The Meaning and Function of the Old Testament in Revelation 21:1–22:5* (JSNTSup, 238; London: Sheffield Academic, 2003).
Mbuvi, A. M. *Temple, Exile and Identity in 1 Peter* (LNTS, 345; London: T&T Clark, 2007).
McCaulley, E. *Sharing in the Son's Inheritance: Davidic Messianism and Paul's Worldwide Interpretation of the Abrahamic Land Promise in Galatians* (LNTS, 608; London: Bloomsbury T&T Clark, 2019).
McDonough, S. M. *YHWH at Patmos: Rev. 1:4 in its Hellenistic and Early Jewish Setting* (WUNT, 2/107; Tübingen: Mohr Siebeck, 1999).
McNamara, M. *The New Testament and the Palestinian Targum to the Pentateuch* (Rome: Pontifical Biblical Institute, 1966).
McNamara, M. *Targum and Testament Revisited: Aramaic Paraphrase of the Hebrew Bible* (Grand Rapids: Eerdmans, 2nd edn, 2010).
Meeks, W. A. *The Prophet-King: Moses Traditions and the Johannine Christology* (NovTSup, 14; Leiden: Brill, 1967).
Menken, M. J. J. *Old Testament Quotations in the Fourth Gospel: Studies in Textual Form* (CBET, 15; Kampen: Kok, 1996).
Menken, M. J. J. 'The Provenance and Meaning of the Old Testament Quotation in John 6:31', *NovT* 30 (1988), pp. 39–56.
Menken, M. J. J., and S. Moyise. *The Minor Prophets in the New Testament* (LNTS, 377; London: T&T Clark, 2009)
Menken, M. J. J., and S. Moyise. *Genesis in the New Testament* (LNTS, 466; London: T&T Clark, 2012).
Metzger, B. *A Textual Commentary on the Greek New Testament* (London: United Bible Societies, 1971).
Michaels, J. R. *1 Peter* (WBC, 49; Waco, TX: Word Books, 1988).
Middleton, P. *The Violence of the Lamb: Martyrs as Agents of Divine Judgement in the Book of Revelation* (LNTS, 586; London: Bloomsbury T&T Clark, 2018).
Milne, P. 'Psalm 23: Echoes of the Exodus', *SR* 4 (1974), pp. 237–47.
Minutoli, D., and R. Pintaudi. '*Esodo* (IV 16-VII 21) in un codice di papiro della collezione Martin Schøyen (*MS* 187)', *AnaPap* 23-24 (2011–2012), pp. 17–55.

Moffitt, D. M. *Atonement and the Logic of Resurrection in the Epistle to the Hebrews* (NovTSup, 141; Leiden: Brill, 2011).

Moffitt, D. M. 'Modelled on Moses: Jesus' Death, Passover, and the Defeat of the Devil in the Epistle to the Hebrews', in M. Sommer, E. Eynikel, V. Niederhofer, and E. Hernitscheck (eds.), *Mosebilder: Gedanken zur Rezeption einer literarischen Figur im Frühjudentum, frühen Christentum und der römisch-hellenistischen Literatur* (WUNT, 1/390; Tübingen: Mohr Siebeck, 2017), pp. 279–97.

Moffitt, D. M. 'Perseverance, Purity, and Identity: Exploring Hebrews' Eschatological Worldview, Ethics, and In-Group Bias', in J. Kok, T. Nicklas, D. T. Roth, and C. M. Hays (ed.), *Sensitivity to Outsiders: Exploring the Dynamic Relationship between Mission and Ethics in the New Testament and Early Christianity* (WUNT, 2/364; Tübingen: Mohr Siebeck, 2014), pp. 357–81.

Moffitt, D. M. 'Wilderness Identity and Pentateuchal Narrative: Distinguishing between Jesus' Inauguration and Maintenance of the New Covenant in Hebrews', in K. M. Hockey, M. N. Pierce, and F. Watson (eds.), *Muted Voices of the New Testament: Readings in the Catholic Epistles and Hebrews* (LNTS, 565; London: Bloomsbury T&T Clark, 2017), pp. 153–71.

Moloney, F. J. *The Gospel of John* (Collegeville, MN: Liturgical, 1998).

Moo, D. J. *The Letters to the Colossians and to Philemon* (PNTC; Grand Rapids: Eerdmans, 2008).

Moody, D. 'God's Only Son: The Translation of John 3:16 in the Revised Standard Version', *JBL* 72 (1953), pp. 213–19.

Moritz, T. *A Profound Mystery: The Use of the Old Testament in Ephesians* (NovTSup, 85; Leiden: Brill, 1996).

Moritz, T. 'The Psalms in Ephesians and Colossians', in S. Moyise and M. J. J. Menken (eds.), *The Psalms in the New Testament: The New Testament and the Scriptures of Israel* (London: T&T Clark, 2004), pp. 181–95.

Morris, L. *The Gospel According to John* (Grand Rapids: Eerdmans, 1971).

Motyer, J. A. *The Prophecy of Isaiah* (Downers Grove, IL: InterVarsity, 1993).

Motyer, S. *Your Father the Devil? A New Approach to John and 'the Jews'* (PBM; Carlisle: Paternoster, 1997).

Moule, C. F. D. 'The Christology of Acts', in L. E. Keck and J. L. Martyn (eds.), *Studies in Luke-Acts* (London: SPCK, 1968), pp. 159–85.

Mowvley, H. 'John 1^{14-18} in the Light of Exodus 33^7–34^{35}', *ExpTim* 95 (1984), pp. 135–37.

Moyise, S. 'Composite Citations in the Gospel of Mark', in S. A. Adams and S. M. Ehorn (eds.), *Composite Citations in Antiquity*. Vol. 2, *New Testament Uses* (LNTS, 593; London: Bloomsbury T&T Clark, 2018), pp. 16–33.

Moyise, S. 'Isaiah in 1 Peter', in S. Moyise and M. Menken (eds.), *Isaiah in the New Testament* (London: T&T Clark, 2005; repr. 2007), pp. 175–88.

Moyise, S. *The Old Testament in the Book of Revelation* (JSNTSup, 115; Sheffield: Sheffield Academic, 1995).

Moyise, S. 'Quotations', in S. E. Porter and C. D. Stanley (eds.), *As It Is Written: Studying Paul's Use of Scripture* (SBLSymS, 50; Atlanta: Society of Biblical Literature, 2008), pp. 15–28.

Moyise, S. 'Singing the Song of Moses and the Lamb: John's Dialogical Use of Scripture', *AUSS* 42 (2004), pp. 347–60.

Moyise, S., and M. J. J. Menken, *Deuteronomy in the New Testament* (LNTS, 358; London: T&T Clark, 2007).

Moyise, S., and M. J. J. Menken, *Isaiah in the New Testament* (London: T&T Clark, 2005).

Moyise, S., and M. J. J. Menken, *The Psalms in the New Testament* (London: T&T Clark, 2004).
Mussies, G. *The Morphology of Koine Greek, as Used in The Apocalypse of St. John: A Study in Bilingualism* (Leiden: Brill, 1971).
Najman, H. 'Decalogue', in J. J. Collins and D. C. Harlow (eds.), *The Eerdmans Dictionary of Eary Judaism* (Grand Rapids: Eerdmans, 2010), pp. 526–28.
Nelson, R. D. 'Studies in the Development of the Text of the Tabernacle Account' (Ph.D. diss.; Harvard University, 1986).
Neyrey, J. H. *2 Peter, Jude* (AB, 37C; New Haven, CT: Doubleday, 1993).
Nicholson, G. C. *Death as Departure: The Johannine Descent–Ascent Schema* (SBLDS, 63; Chico, CA: Scholars Press, 1983).
Nilsen, T. D. 'Memories of Moses: A Survey through Genres', *JSOT* 41 (2017), pp. 287–312.
Nolland, J. *The Gospel of Matthew* (NIGTC; Grand Rapids: Eerdmans, 2005).
Nolland, J. *Luke 9:21–18:34* (WBC, 35B; Dallas, TX: Word, 1993).
Novenson, M. V. *Christ among the Messiahs: Christ Language in Paul and Messiah Language in Ancient Judaism* (Oxford: Oxford University Press, 2012).
Orr, W. F. and J. A. Walther. *I Corinthians: A New Translation with Introduction and Commentary* (AB; New Haven: Yale University Press, 1976).
Osburn, C. D. 'The Text of Jude 5', *Bib* 62 (1981), pp. 107–115.
Oswalt, J. N. *The Book of Isaiah 40–66* (NICOT; Grand Rapids: Eerdmans, 1998).
Oudersluys, R. C. 'Exodus in the Letter to the Hebrews', in J. L. Cook (ed.), *Grace Upon Grace: Essays in Honor of Lester J. Kuyper* (Grand Rapids: Eerdmans, 1975), pp. 143–52.
Pao, D. W. *Acts and the Isaianic New Exodus* (BSL; Grand Rapids: Baker, 2002).
Pao, D. W., and E. Schnabel. 'Luke', in G. K. Beale and D. A. Carson (eds.), *Commentary on the New Testament Use of the Old Testament* (Grand Rapids: Baker, 2007), pp. 251–414.
Pardee, D. 'A Further Note on PRU V, No. 60: Epigraphic in Nature', in K. Bergerhof, M. Dietrich, and O. Loretz (eds.), *Ugarit-Forschungen* (IJASP, 13; Butzon & Bercker, 1981), pp. 151–56.
Paulien, J. *Decoding Revelation's Trumpets: Literary Allusions and Interpretation of Revelation 8:7–12* (Berrien Springs: Andrews University Press, 1988).
Pendrick, G. 'Μονογενής', *NTS* 41 (1995), pp. 587–600.
Penner, K., (ed.). *The Lexham English Septuagint* (Bellingham, Lexham, 2019).
Perkins, L. J. 'Exodus', in A. Pietersma and B. G. Wright (eds.), *A New English Translation of the Septuagint* (Oxford: Oxford University Press, 2007), pp. 43–81.
Perkins, L. J. 'Kingdom, Messianic Authority and the Re-constituting of God's People – Tracing the Function of Exodus Material in Mark's Narrative', in T. R. Hatina (ed.), *Biblical Interpretation in Early Christian Gospels.* Vol. 1, *The Gospel of Mark* (LNTS, 304; London: T&T Clark, 2006), pp. 100–15.
Pietersma, A. 'Yohanah and his brother', in L. H. Shiffmann and J. C. VanderKam (eds.), *Encyclopedia of the Dead Sea Scrolls*, vol. 2 (Oxford: Oxford University Press, 2000), pp. 1000–1001.
Platt, D. *Exalting Jesus in Matthew* (Nashville: B&H Academic, 2013).
Popper, J. *Der biblische Bericht über die Stiftshütte: ein Beitrag zur Geschichte der Composition und Diaskeue des Pentateuch* (Leipzig: Heinrich Hunger, 1862).

Porter, S. E. 'Allusions and Echoes', in S. E. Porter and C. D. Stanley (eds.), *As It Is Written: Studying Paul's Use of Scripture* (SBLSymS, 50; Atlanta: Society of Biblical Literature, 2008), pp. 29–40.

Porter, S. E. 'Can Traditional Exegesis Enlighten Literary Analysis of the Fourth Gospel? An Examination of the Old Testament Fulfillment Motif and the Passover Theme', in C. A. Evans and W. R. Stegner (eds.), *The Gospels and the Scriptures of Israel* (JSNTSup, 104; Sheffield: Sheffield Academic, 1994), pp. 396–428. Repr. as Chapter 8 in *John, His Gospel, and Jesus: In Pursuit of the Johannine Voice* (Grand Rapids: Eerdmans, 2015).

Prigent, P. *Commentary on the Apocalypse of St. John* (trans. Wendy Pradels; Tübingen: Mohr Siebeck, 2004).

Propp, W. H. C. *Exodus 1–18* (AB, 2; New York: Doubleday, 1999).

Pryor, J. W. *John: Evangelist of the Covenant People* (Downers Grove, IL: InterVarsity, 1992).

Rahlfs, A., and R. Hanhart. *Septuaginta* (Stuttgart: Deutsche Bibelgesellschaft, rev. edn, 2006).

Ricard, P. *Apocalypse: A People's Commentary on the Book of Revelation* (New York: Orbis, 1998).

Ridderbos, H. N. *The Gospel of John* (trans. J. Vriend; Grand Rapids: Eerdmans, 1997).

Ringe, S. H. 'Luke 9:28-36: The Beginning of an Exodus', *Semeia* 28 (1983), pp. 83–99.

Robar, E. 'Unmarked Modality and Rhetorical Questions in Biblical Hebrew', in N. Vidro, R. Vollandt, E.-M. Wagner, and J. Olszowy-Schlanger (eds.), *Studies in Semitic Linguistics and Manuscripts: A Liber Discipulorum in Honour of Professor Geoffrey Khan* (SSU, 30; Uppsala: Uppsala University Press, 2018), pp. 75–97.

Roberts, A. J., and A. Wilson. *Echoes of Exodus: Tracing Themes of Redemption through Scripture* (Wheaton, IL: Crossway, 2018).

Robinson, J. A. T. 'The Most Primitive Christology of All?', *JTS* n.s. 7 (1956), pp. 177–89.

Römer, T. 'Exode et Anti-Exode: La nostalgie de l'Egypte dans les traditions du désert', in T. Römer (ed.), *Lectio difficilior probabilior? l'exégèse comme expérience de décloisonnement* (BDBAT, 12; Heidelberg: Wiss.-theol. Seminar, 1991), pp. 155–72.

Rowe, C. K. *Early Narrative Christology: The Lord in the Gospel of Luke* (Grand Rapids: Baker, 2009).

Rowe, C. K. *World Upside Down: Reading Acts in the Graeco-Roman Age* (Oxford: Oxford University Press, 2009).

Ruiz, J.-P. *Ezekiel in the Apocalypse: The Transformation of Prophetic Language in Revelation 16,17–19,10* (Frankfurt am Main: Peter Lang, 1989).

Rusam, D. 'Deuteronomy in Luke-Acts', in S. Moyise and M. J. J. Menken (eds.), *Deuteronomy in the New Testament* (LNTS, 358; London: Bloomsbury T&T Clark, 2007), pp. 63–81.

Ryan, J. J. 'Jesus and Synagogue Disputes: Recovering the Institutional Context of Luke 13:10-17', *CBQ* 79 (2017), pp. 41–59.

Safrai, S., and M. Stern. *Compendia Rerum Iudaicarum ad Novum Testamentum: The Jewish People in the First Century II* (Leiden: Brill, 1976).

Salvesen, A. 'Exodus', in J. K. Aitken (ed.), *T&T Clark Companion to the Septuagint* (London: Bloomsbury T&T Clark, 2015), pp. 29–42.

Sanders, E. P. 'Did Paul's Theology Develop?', in J. R. Wagner, C. K. Rowe, and A. K. Grieb (eds.), *The Word Leaps the Gap: Essays on Scripture and Theology in Honor of Richard B. Hays* (Grand Rapids: Eerdmans, 2008), pp. 325–50.

Sanderson, J. E. *An Exodus Scroll from Qumran: 4QpaleoExod*ᵐ *and the Samaritan Tradition* (HSS, 30; Atlanta: Scholars Press, 1986).
Sandmel, S. 'Parallelomania', *JBL* 81 (1962), pp. 1–13.
Scharlemann, M. H. 'Exodus Ethics: Part One: 1 Peter 1:13-16', *ConJ* 2 (1976), pp. 165–70.
Scheiber, A. 'Ihr sollt kein Bein dran zerbrechen', *VT* 13 (1963), pp. 95–97.
Schlatter, A. von. *Das Alte Testament in der johanneischen Apokalypse.* (Gütersloh: Bertelsmann, 1912).
Schlier, H. *Der Brief an die Epheser* (Düsseldorf: Patmos-Verlag, 1957).
Schnabel, E. J. *Acts* (ZECNT, 5; Grand Rapids: Zondervan, 2012).
Schnackenburg, R. *Gospel According to St. John* (3 vols.; London: Burns & Oates, 1968, 1980, 1982).
Schorch, S. 'A Critical *editio maior* of the Samaritan Pentateuch: State of Research, Principles, and Problems', *HBAI* 2 (2013), pp. 100–20.
Schuchard, B. G. *Scripture Within Scripture: The Interrelationship of Form and Function in the Explicit Old Testament Citations in the Gospel of John* (SBLDS, 133; Atlanta: Scholars Press, 1992).
Schürer, E., G. Vermes, F. Millar, and M. Goodman, *The History of the Jewish People in the Age of Jesus Christ (175 BC–AD 135)* (4 vols.; Edinburgh: T&T Clark, rev. edn, 1973–1986).
Schüssler Fiorenza, E. *The Book of Revelation: Justice and Judgement* (Minneapolis: Fortress, 1998).
Schutter, W. *Hermeneutic and Composition in 1 Peter* (WUNT, 2/30; Tübingen: Mohr Siebeck, 1989).
Schwankl, O. *Die Sadduzäerfrage (Mk 12, 18-27 parr): Eine exegetisch-theologische Studie zur Auferstehungserwartung* (BBB, 66; Frankfurt: Athenäum, 1987).
Scott, J. M. *Adoption as Sons of God: An Exegetical Investigation into the Background of* ΥΙΟΘΕΣΙΑ *in the Pauline Corpus* (WUNT, 2/48; Tübingen: Mohr Siebeck, 1992).
Scott, J. M. '"And Then All Israel Will Be Saved" (Rom 11:26)', in J. M. Scott (ed.), *Restoration: Old Testament, Jewish, & Christian Perspectives* (Leiden: Brill, 2001), pp. 489–526.
Screnock, J. *Traductor Scriptor: The Old Greek Translation of Exodus 1–14 as Scribal Activity* (VTSup, 174; Leiden: Brill, 2017).
Seifrid, M. A. 'Romans', in G. K. Beale and D. A. Carson (eds.), *Commentary on the New Testament Use of the Old Testament* (Grand Rapids: Baker, 2007), pp. 607–94.
Selby, G. S. *Martin Luther King and the Rhetoric of Freedom: The Exodus Narrative in America's Struggle for Civil Rights* (Waco, TX: Baylor University Press, 2008).
Sellin, G. *Der Brief an die Epheser* (KEK, 8; Göttingen: Vandenhoeck & Ruprecht, 2008).
Senior, D. *Matthew* (ANTC; Nashville: Abingdon, 1998).
Shin, B. C. *New Exodus in Hebrews* (ANTS; London: Apostolos, 2016).
Sieffert, E. L. 'Die Heilsbedeutung des Leidens und Sterbens Christi nach dem ersten Brief des Petrus', *JDT* 20 (1875), pp. 371–440.
Slater, T. B. *Christ and Community: A Socio-Historical Study of Christology of Revelation* (JSNTSup, 178; Sheffield: Sheffield Academic, 1999).
Smith, D. L. 'The Uses of "New Exodus" in New Testament Scholarship: Preparing a Way through the Wilderness', *CBR* 14 (2016), pp. 207–43.
Snodgrass, K. 'Streams of Tradition Emerging from Isaiah 40:1-5 and Their Adaptation in the New Testament', *JSNT* 8 (1980), pp. 24–45.
Sommer, M. *Der Tag der Plagen* (WUNT, 2/387; Tübingen: Mohr Siebeck, 2015).

Son, H. *Praising God Beside the Sea: An Intertextual Study of Revelation 15 and Exodus 15* (Eugene, OR: Wipf & Stock, 2017).
Spencer, F. S. *Acts* (Readings; Sheffield: Sheffield Academic, 1997).
Sperber, A. (ed.). *The Bible in Aramaic: Based on Old Manuscripts and Printed Texts, Volumes I–III* (Leiden: Brill, 2004).
Stanley, C. D. *Paul and the Language of Scripture: Citation Technique in the Pauline Epistles and Contemporary Literature* (SNTSMS, 74; Cambridge: Cambridge University Press, 1992).
Stanley, C. D. 'Paul's "Use" of Scripture: Why the Audience Matters', in S. E. Porter and C. D. Stanley (eds.), *As It Is Written: Studying Paul's Use of Scripture* (SBLSymS, 50; Atlanta: Society of Biblical Literature, 2008), pp. 125–55.
Stanley, C. D. '"The Redeemer Will Come ἐκ Σιων": Romans 11.26-27 Revisited', in C. A. Evans and J. A. Sanders (eds.), *Paul and the Scriptures of Israel* (Sheffield: Sheffield Academic, 1993), pp. 118–42.
Starling, D. 'Ephesians and the Hermeneutics of the New Exodus', in R. M. Fox (ed.), *Reverberations of the Exodus in Scripture* (Eugene, OR: Pickwick, 2014), pp. 139–59.
Stec, D. M. *The Targum of Psalms: Translated, with a Critical Introduction, Apparatus, and Notes* (ArBib, 16; London: T&T Clark, 2004).
Stegner, W. R. 'Jesus' Walking on the Water: Mark 6.45-52', in C. A. Evans and W. R. Stegner (eds.), *The Gospels and the Scriptures of Israel* (JSNTSup, 104; Sheffield: Sheffield Academic, 1994), pp. 212–34.
Steyn, G. J. 'Deuteronomy in Hebrews', in S. Moyise and M. J. J. Menken (eds.), *Deuteronomy in the New Testament* (LNTS, 358; London: T&T Clark, 2007), pp. 152–68.
Steyn, G. J. *A Quest for the Assumed LXX Vorlage of the Explicit Quotations in Hebrews* (FRLANT, 235; Göttingen: Vandenhoeck & Ruprecht, 2011).
Stinespring, W. F. 'Testament of Isaac: A New Translation and Introduction', in J. H. Charlesworth (ed.), *The Old Testament Pseudepigrapha* (2 vols.; New York: Doubleday, 1983, 1985), pp. 1:903–11.
Stockhausen, C. K. *Moses' Veil and the Glory of the New Covenant: The Exegetical Substructure of II Cor. 3,1–4,6* (AnBib, 116. Rome: Pontificio Instituto Biblico, 1989).
Stökl Ben Ezra, D. *The Impact of Yom Kippur on Early Christianity: The Day of Atonement from Second Temple Judaism to the Fifth Century* (WUNT, 2/163; Tübingen: Mohr Siebeck, 2003).
Strauss, M. L. *The Davidic Messiah in Luke-Acts: The Promise and its Fulfillment in Lukan Christology* (JSNTSup, 110; Sheffield: Sheffield Academic, 1995).
Svebakken, H. *Philo of Alexandria's Exposition of the Tenth Commandment* (SPM, 6; Atlanta: Society of Biblical Literature, 2012).
Swete, H. B. *The Apocalypse of St. John* (London: Macmillan, 1906).
Swete, H. B. *The Old Testament in Greek according to the Septuagint, Vol. 1* (Cambridge: Cambridge University Press, 1901).
Tabb, B. J. *Suffering in Ancient Worldview: Luke, Seneca and 4 Maccabees in Dialogue* (LNTS, 569; London: Bloomsbury T&T Clark, 2017).
Tal, A., and M. Florentin. *The Pentateuch: The Samaritan Version and the Masoretic Version* (Tel Aviv: Haim Rubin, 2010) (Hebrew).
Talbert, C. H. *Reading John* (Reading the New Testament; New York: Crossroad, 1992).
Tate, M. A. *Psalms 51–100* (WBC, 20; Dallas: Word, 1990).
Thackeray, H. St. J. *The Relation of St. Paul to Contemporary Jewish Thought* (London: Macmillan, 1900).
Thielman, F. *Ephesians* (BECNT; Grand Rapids: Baker, 2010).

Thiessen, M. 'Hebrews and the End of Exodus', *NovT* 49 (2007), pp. 353–69.
Thiessen, M. *Paul and the Gentile Problem* (New York: Oxford University Press, 2016).
Thiselton, A. C. *The First Epistle to the Corinthians* (NIGTC; Grand Rapids: Eerdmans, 2000).
Thomas, K. J. 'The Old Testament Citations in Hebrews', *NTS* 11 (1965), pp. 303–25.
Tilling, C. *Paul's Divine Christology* (Grand Rapids: Eerdmans, 2012).
Tov, E. 'The Dead Sea Scrolls and the Textual History of the Masoretic Bible', in N. Dávid, A. Lange, K. de Troyer, and S. Tzoeref (eds.), *The Hebrew Bible in Light of the Dead Sea Scrolls* (FRLANT, 239; Göttingen: Vandenhoeck & Ruprecht, 2012), pp. 41–53.
Tov, E. 'From 4QReworked Pentateuch to 4QPentateuch (?)', in M. Popović (ed.), *Authoritative Scriptures in Ancient Judaism* (JSJSup, 141; Leiden: Brill, 2010), pp. 73–91.
Tov, E. *Textual Criticism of the Hebrew Bible* (Minneapolis; Fortress, 3rd edn, 2012).
Tromp, J. 'Jannes and Jambres (2 Timothy 3,8-9)', in A. Graupner (ed.), *Moses in Biblical and Extra-Biblical Traditions* (BZAW, 372; Berlin: de Gruyter, 2007), pp. 211–26.
Turner, D. L. *Matthew* (BECNT; Grand Rapids: Baker Academic, 2008).
Ulrich, E. *The Dead Sea Scrolls and the Developmental Composition of the Bible* (VTSup, 169; Leiden: Brill, 2015), pp. 187–94.
Ulrich, E. *The Biblical Qumran Scrolls: Transcriptions and Textual Variants* (VTSup, 134; Leiden: Brill, 2010).
Vaux, R. de. *Studies in Old Testament Sacrifice* (trans. J. Bourke and R. Potter; Cardiff: University of Wales Press, 1964).
Vanlaningham, M. G. *Christ, the Savior of Israel: An Evaluation of the Dual Covenant and* Sonderweg *Interpretations of Paul's Letters* (Edition Israelogie, 5; Berlin: Peter Lang, 2012).
Villiers, P. De. 'The Composition of Revelation 14:1–15:8: Pastiche or Perfect Pattern?', *Neot* 38 (2004), pp. 209–49.
Wade, M. L. *Consistency of Translation Techniques in the Tabernacle Accounts of Exodus in the Old Greek* (SCS, 49; Atlanta: SBL, 2003).
Walker, P. W. L. *Jesus and the Holy City: New Testament Perspectives on Jerusalem* (Grand Rapids: Eerdmans, 1996).
Walker, W. O. '2 Corinthians 3:7-18 as a Non-Pauline Interpolation', *JSPL* 3 (2013), pp. 195–217.
Wall, R. W. 'The Acts of the Apostles', in L. E. Keck (ed.), *Acts–First Corinthians* (NIB, 10; Nashville: Abingdon, 2002), pp. 1–368.
Wallace, D. B. *Grammar beyond the Basics: An Exegetical Syntax of the New Testament* (Grand Rapids: Zondervan, 1996).
Walton, S. 'A Tale of Two Perspectives? The Temple in Acts', in T. D. Alexander and S. J. Gathercole (eds.), *Heaven on Earth: The Temple in Biblical Theology* (Carlisle: Paternoster, 2004), pp. 135–49.
Wasserman, E. *The Death of the Soul in Romans 7: Sin, Death, and the Law in Light of Hellenistic Moral Psychology* (WUNT, 2/256; Tübingen: Mohr Siebeck, 2008).
Wasserman, T. *The Epistle of Jude: Its Text and Transmission* (CB, 43; Stockholm, Sweden: Almqvist & Wiksell International, 2006).
Watts, J. D. W. *Isaiah* (WBC, 25; Waco, TX: Word, 1987).
Watts, R. E. *Isaiah's New Exodus in Mark* (WUNT, 2/88; Tübingen: Mohr Siebeck, 1997).
Wellhausen, J. *Die Composition des Hexateuchs und der historischen Bücher des Alten Testaments* (Berlin: G. Reimer, 3rd edn, 1899).

Weinrich, W. C. *Revelation* (ACCSNT, 12; Downers Grove, IL: InterVarsity, 2005).
Westfall., D. M. 'Substitution and Participation in the Writings of Paul: A Study of Four Texts' (Ph.D. diss, University of St Andrews, 2018).
Westfall., D. M. '"Thine Be the Glory"': Christ the Mercy Seat in Romans 3:25'. Paper presented at the St Andrews Symposium for Biblical and Early Christian Studies. St Andrews, Scotland, 2018.
Wevers, J. W. 'The Building of the Tabernacle', *JNSL* 19 (1993), pp. 123–31.
Wevers, J. W. *Notes on the Greek Text of Exodus* (SCS, 30; Atlanta: Scholars Press, 1990).
Wevers, J. W. 'PreOrigen Recensional Activity in the Greek Exodus', in D. Fraenkel, U. Quast, and J. W. Wevers (eds.), *Studien zur Septuaginta—Robert Hanhart zu Ehren. Aus Anlaß seines 65. Geburtstages* (MSU, 20; Göttingen; Vandenhoeck & Ruprecht, 1990), pp. 121–39.
Wevers, J. W. *Text History of the Greek Exodus* (MSU, 21; Göttingen: Vandenhoeck & Ruprecht, 1992).
Wevers, J. W., with the help of U. Quast, *Septuaginta*: *Vetus Testamentum Graecum Auctoritate Academiae Scientiarum Gottingensis editum, vol. II, 1 – Exodus* (Göttingen: Vandenhoeck & Ruprecht, 1991).
White, S. A. 'The All Souls Deuteronomy and the Deacalogue', *JBL* 109 (1990), pp. 193–206.
Wikgren, A. P. 'Some Problems in Jude 5', in B. L. Daniels and M. J. Suggs (eds.), *Studies in History and Text of the New Testament in Honor of Kenneth Willis Clark* (Salt Lake City: University of Utah Press, 1967), pp. 147–52.
Wildberger, H. *Jahwes Eigentumsvolk: Eine Studie zur Traditionsgeschichte und Theologie des Erwählungsgedankens* (ATANT, 37; Zurich: Zwingli, 1960).
Williams, C. H. 'Composite Citations in the Gospel of John', in S. A. Adams and S. M. Ehorn (eds.), *Composite Citations in Antiquity*. Vol. 2, *New Testament Uses* (LNTS, 593; Bloomsbury T&T Clark, 2018), pp. 94–127.
Wink, W. 'Beyond Just War and Pacifism: Jesus' Nonviolent Way', *RevExp* 89 (1992), pp. 197–214.
Winter, B. W. 'On Introducing Gods to Athens: An Alternative Reading of Acts 17:18-20', *TynBul* 47 (1996), pp. 71–90.
Winter, P. 'Μονογενής παρὰ Πατρός', *ZRGG* 5 (1953), pp. 335–65.
Wiseman, D. 'Abban and Alalaḫ', *JCS* 12 4 (1958), pp. 124–29.
Witherington, B., III. *Letters and Homilies for Hellenized Christians*. Vol. 1, *A Socio-Rhetorical Commentary on Titus, 1–2 Timothy, and 1–3 John* (Downers Grove, IL: InterVarsity, 2006).
Witherington, B., III. *The Letters to Philemon, the Colossians, and the Ephesians: A Socio-Rhetorical Commentary on the Captivity Epistles* (Grand Rapids: Eerdmans, 2007).
Wold, B. G. 'Memory in the Dead Sea Scrolls: Exodus, Creation and Cosmos', in S. C. Barton, L. T. Stuckenbruck, and B. G. Wold (eds.), *Memory in the Bible and Antiquity: The Fifth Durham–Tübingen Research Symposium (Durham, September 2004)* (WUNT, 1/212; Tübingen: Mohr Siebeck, 2007), pp. 47–74.
Wolff, C. *Der zweite Brief des Paulus an die Korinther* (THKNT, 8; Berlin: Evangelische Verlagsanstalt, 1989).
Wolter, M. *Der Brief an die Römer (Teilband 1: Röm 1–8)* (EKKNT, 6.1; Neukirchen-Vluyn: Neuchkirchener Verlag, 2014).
Wolter, M. *The Gospel According to Luke* (Baylor-Mohr Siebeck Studies in Early Christianity; 2 vols.; Waco, TX: Baylor University Press, 2016–2017).

Works, C. S. *The Church in the Wilderness: Paul's Use of Exodus Traditions in 1 Corinthians* (WUNT, 2/379; Tübingen: Mohr Siebeck, 2014).
Wright, N. T. 'God Put Jesus Forth: Reflections on Romans 3:24-26', in D. M. Gurtner, G. Macaskill, and J. T. Pennington (eds.), *In the Fullness of Time: Essays on Christology, Creation and Eschatology in Honor of Richard Bauckham* (Grand Rapids: Eerdmans, 2016), pp. 135–61.
Wright, N. T. 'The Letter to the Romans: Introduction, Commentary, and Reflections', in L. E. Keck (ed.), *The New Interpreter's Bible* (Nashville: Abingdon, 2002), pp. 393–770.
Wright, N. T. *The New Testament and the People of God* (COQG, 1; Minneapolis: Fortress, 1992).
Wright, N. T. *Paul and the Faithfulness of God* (COQG, 4; Minneapolis: Fortress, 2013).
Wright, N. T. *Paul: In Fresh Perspective* (Minneapolis: Fortress, 2009).
Wright, N. T. *Pauline Perspectives: Essays on Paul, 1978–2013* (Minneapolis: Fortress, 2013).
Wycherley, R. E. 'St Paul at Athens', *JTS* n.s. 19 (1968), pp. 619–21.
Young, E. J. *The Book of Isaiah* (NICOT; 3 vols.; Grand Rapids: Eerdmans, 1972).
Zahn, M. *Rethinking Rewritten Scripture: Composition and Exegesis in the 4QReworked Pentateuch Manuscripts* (STDJ, 95; Leiden: Brill, 2011).
Zevit, Z. 'Exodus in the Bible and the Egyptian Plagues', *BHD* (2011), n.p., https://www.biblicalarchaeology.org/daily/biblical-topics/exodus/exodus-in-the-bible-and-the-egyptian-plagues.

Contributors

Jeannine K. Brown (Ph.D., Luther Seminary) is Professor of New Testament at Bethel Seminary (USA) and author of *The Gospels as Stories* (Baker) and several commentaries on Matthew (Eerdmans; Baker). She is a member of the Committee on Bible Translation, the standing committee for the New International Version.

Seth M. Ehorn (Ph.D., University of Edinburgh) currently teaches Greek language and linguistics at Wheaton College and is co-editor of *Composite Citations in Antiquity*, 2 vols. (Bloomsbury T&T Clark, 2016, 2018). His most recent publications include *2 Maccabees 1–7* (2020) and *2 Maccabees 8–15* (2022) in the Baylor Handbook on the Septuagint series.

Michelle Fletcher (Ph.D., King's College London) is Associate Lecturer at the University of Kent and a Research Associate at King's College London. Among her publications, she is the author of *Reading Revelation as Pastiche: Imitating the Past* (Bloomsbury, 2017) and is also working on The Visual Commentary of Scripture (King's College).

Daniel M. Gurtner (Ph.D., University of St Andrews) is external affiliate at the Centre for the Study of Judaism and Christianity in Antiquity, St Mary's University (London, UK). He has written extensively on the Gospels and their interface with the Hebrew Bible and Second Temple Judaism. He is currently writing the Word Biblical Commentary on the Gospel of Matthew.

Carmen Joy Imes (Ph.D., Wheaton College) is Associate Professor of Old Testament at Biola University (USA) and author of *Bearing YHWH's Name at Sinai: A Reexamination of the Name Command of the Decalogue* (2018).

Andreas J. Köstenberger (Ph.D., Trinity Evangelical Divinity School) is Research Professor of New Testament and Biblical Theology and Director of the Center of Biblical Studies at Midwestern Baptist Theological Seminary (USA). He is the founder of Biblical Foundations and author of *A Theology of John's Gospel and Letters* (2009).

Drew Longacre (Ph.D., University of Birmingham) is a Postdoctoral Researcher on the European Research Council project 'The Hands that Wrote the Bible: Digital Palaeography and Scribal Culture of the Dead Sea Scrolls' at the Qumran Institute, University of Groningen.

Katie Marcar (Ph.D., Durham University) is a Teaching Fellow in Biblical Languages at the University of Otago (New Zealand) and among her publications are articles in *New Testament Studies* and *TC: A Journal of Biblical Textual Criticism*.

David M. Moffitt (Ph.D., Duke University) is Reader in New Testament Studies at the University of St Andrews (Scotland), author of *Atonement and the Logic of Resurrection in the Epistle to the Hebrews* (2011), and co-editor of *Son, Sacrifice, and Great Shepherd: Studies on the Epistle to the Hebrews* (2020).

Brian J. Tabb (Ph.D., London School of Theology) is Academic Dean and Associate Professor of Biblical Studies at Bethlehem College & Seminary (USA), general editor of *Themelios*, and author of *Suffering in Ancient Worldview: Luke, Seneca, and 4 Maccabees in Dialogue* (2017).

Steve Walton (Ph.D., University of Sheffield) is Professor of New Testament at Trinity College, Bristol (UK), and a former Secretary of the British New Testament Society.

David M. Westfall (Ph.D., University of St Andrews) is Assistant Professor of Theology at Dordt University (USA).

Index of References

Genesis		2.11-15	33	3.14	58, 96,
4.1-12	41	2.11-12	76		101, 185–
8.21	53	2.11	76		7, 200
9.4	100	2.13	77	3.15-16	56, 62, 73
12.1-3	74	2.14	62, 77, 78,	3.15	50, 54, 62,
12.3	53		82		71–3
13.10-11	179	2.15-22	77	3.16	8, 61, 74,
13.14-17	140	2.15	77		158
15.3-8	111	2.18	10	3.17-26	74
15.13-18	111	2.22	75, 77	3.17	8
15.13-14	75	2.23-25	8, 122	3.19-20	8
15.13	111	2.24	8, 158	3.19	74
15.14	81	3	60, 72, 74	3.24	51
17.1-21	111	3.1–4.17	72	3.25	123, 213
17.9-14	100	3.1-10	73	4.1	56
22.18	74	3.1-2	56	4.5	74
26.4	74	3.1	10, 66	4.10-12	117
26.25	74	3.2	55, 66, 77,	4.15	56, 59
31.18	209		78	4.18	119
31.53	74	3.3-4	52, 77	4.19	33
		3.3	52	4.21	123
Exodus		3.5	78	4.22-23	8, 33
1–15	32	3.6	10, 50, 54,	4.22	88, 122,
1–4	105		56, 57, 62,		152
1–3	75		71–4, 78	4.23	112, 158
1.1–12.42	7	3.7-10	8	4.24-26	8
1.5	76	3.7	78	4.29–20.21	209
1.8	76	3.8	8, 78, 152	4.31	8, 61
1.10	76	3.10-12	8	5.2	9
1.11	10, 23	3.10	78	5.18	112
1.13-14	112	3.12	46, 73, 75,	5.23	140
1.16	18, 19		81, 112	6.1	8, 56, 61,
1.22	33, 76	3.13–4.17	82		103
2.1–4.28	209	3.13-15	9, 10	6.3	9, 11
2.1-15	146	3.13-14	101	6.4	8
2.2	76	3.13	72, 73	6.5	8, 112
2.5-10	76	3.14	38	6.6-8	140

Exodus (cont.)		9.6-7	8	12.17	8, 58		
6.6	8, 61, 103, 140, 173	9.10-11	198	12.19	113		
		9.12	8, 123	12.21	113		
6.6-7	8, 158	9.13	112	12.23	154		
6.7-8	158	9.14	8, 9	12.25	8		
6.7	8–10, 91	9.15	8	12.27	8, 64, 113		
6.8	8	9.16	7, 123	12.31	112, 158		
6.9	13	9.18	56, 59	12.33	56		
6.13	8	9.19	13	12.37	10, 39		
6.23	36	9.24	198	12.39	8		
6.26-27	8	9.26	8	12.40	111		
7–12	37	9.29	9	12.41-42	8		
7–11	100, 184, 197, 199, 200	9.30	9	12.43–18.27	7		
		9.35	123	12.44	100		
		10.1-2	102	12.46	105		
7.1	29	10.1	8, 123	12.48-49	100		
7.2	46	10.2	9, 13	12.51	9		
7.3	78, 82, 123, 152	10.3	112, 158	13	64		
		10.7-8	112	13.2	4, 62–4		
7.4-5	8	10.11	112	13.3-4	8		
7.4	8	10.14	56, 59	13.3	2, 8, 113		
7.5	9	10.20	8, 123	13.5	112, 152		
7.7-21	198	10.22	198	13.7	113		
7.8-13	141, 143, 144	10.23	8	13.8-9	8		
		10.24	112	13.9	8		
7.9	153	10.26	112, 158	13.11-16	2		
7.11-12	141	10.27	8, 123	13.11	56, 152		
7.12	142	11.1	56	13.12	4, 62–4		
7.16	112, 158	11.3	13	13.13-15	8		
7.17	9	11.6	56, 59	13.13-14	64		
7.18	13	11.7	8, 9	13.14-15	64		
7.22	123, 142	11.9-10	153	13.14	8		
7.26	112	11.10	8, 123	13.15	123		
7.29	13	12–13	16	13.16	8		
8.1	13, 158	12	62, 93, 146, 190, 192, 193, 174, 191	13.17	10		
8.3-6	198			13.21-22	67, 114		
8.10	8			14–15	33		
8.15	123	12.5		14	78, 82, 114		
8.16	112	12.6	56, 58	14.4	9, 10, 123		
8.18	9	12.10	106	14.5	112		
8.19	13, 62	12.11	62	14.8	8, 123		
8.22	8	12.11	172	14.11	8		
9–16	123	12.12	7	14.12	112		
9.1	112, 158	12.14-20	56, 58	14.13-31	38		
9.3	8	12.14	8	14.13	56, 58		
9.4	8	12.15	113	14.17-18	10		
9.5	13	12.16	62	14.17	123		

14.18	9	16.15	97, 188,	19.13	148
14.19-20	114		200	19.16	88
14.19	51, 66, 67	16.16	120	19.18	45
14.21-31	146	16.18	39, 119,	19.19	88
14.21-22	58		120	20	31
14.21	38	16.23-26	9	20.1-17	8, 79
14.24	57, 67, 114	16.19-20	119	20.1	167
14.25	8	16.31	188	20.2-6	9
14.30	8, 38, 140	16.32-34	189	20.2	8, 71
14.31	194, 195	16.32	8	20.3-11	43
15	16, 184,	16.33	188	20.4-6	135
	193–5,	16.35	10, 35, 55,	20.4	88
	200		56, 152,	20.5	9, 112,
15.1-18	8, 10, 193		188		165, 167,
15.1	195	16.36	10		168
15.3-4	193, 194	17	105, 114	20.8-11	9
15.3	8	17.1-7	115	20.8-10	55, 56, 84
15.4-7	194	17.1	85	20.8-9	62, 68, 69
15.6	8	17.2-3	115	20.10	57, 62, 69
15.8	38	17.2	62, 85, 99	20.11	62, 83
15.9	8	17.3	85, 103	20.12-16	4, 50, 54,
15.11	7, 8, 193,	17.4	10		62, 70
	194	17.6	105	20.12	5, 42, 50,
15.12	8	17.7	85, 115		52, 128,
15.13	8, 121, 173	18.1	8		133–7,
15.14-16	194	18.3-4	77		144
15.16	8, 103	18.11	8, 10	20.13-15	165, 181
15.17	152	18.25	13, 56, 57	20.13-14	166
15.19	58	19–40	8	20.13	40, 100
15.24	115	19	206, 209	20.14	40, 41
16–24	32, 46	19.1–40.38	7	20.17	13, 120,
16	39, 114,	19.1-9	122		121, 137
	119	19.1-6	79	20.19	13
16.1-18	38	19.1	8, 67, 177	20.20	58
16.1	8, 39	19.3	66, 128	20.21-16	43
16.2	115	19.4-6	209	20.21	13, 29
16.3	39	19.5-6	8, 128,	20.22–23.33	9, 65
16.4	98, 119		176, 181,	20.23	9
16.6	8, 9		205, 206,	20.24	13
16.7-8	115		208	21.2	112
16.7	10, 67	19.5	91, 141,	21.6	112
16.10	10, 67, 92,		207–9,	21.10	54
	119		210	21.16	42, 50,
16.12	9	19.6	175–7,		52–4
16.13-14	39		192, 205	21.17	42, 53
16.14-18	38	19.8	9	21.24	40, 41
		19.12-13	146	22.1	62

Exodus (cont.)			157, 171,	29.25	132
22.10	56		172, 181,	29.26-37	45
22.20	8		190	29.32–40.38	21
22.27	53, 62, 85	24.9-11	37	29.35	46
22.28	53, 85	24.9	56	29.38	175
23.4-5	41	24.12	10	29.41	132
23.5	72	24.13	66	29.45-46	88
23.7	29	24.15-16	56	29.46	8–10
23.9	8	24.15	58	30.1-10	13
23.10	13	24.16-18	92	30.6	45
23.12	56	24.16-17	10, 67	30.7	62
23.13	9	24.16	58, 67, 88	30.13-16	44
23.14	58	24.17	67	30.35	56
23.15	8	24.18	24, 55, 56,	31.3	139
23.18	56, 113		66, 67	31.13-17	55
23.20-33	65	24.29	67	31.13	57
23.20-23	66	25–40	13, 32, 43,	31.14-16	9
23.20	50, 51, 55,		44	31.14	56, 57
	62, 65, 66,	25–39	44	31.15	57
	87, 152	25–31	20, 22, 23	31.18	10, 89, 117
23.22	65, 141,	25.8-9	89	32–34	75, 82,
	176, 208	25.8	46, 80		110, 122,
23.23	50, 51, 65	25.11-13	44		125, 179,
23.24-25	112	25.17-18	44		180
23.24	9	25.22	46	32–33	146
23.28	56	25.24-26	44	32.1-35	9
23.29	56	25.28-31	44	32.1	79
23.30	56	25.36-39	44	32.4-6	79
23.31	10, 56	25.40	80, 146,	32.6	115
23.32-33	9		148–50,	32.8	9
23.32	65		157	32.9-14	35
23.33	112	26.31-33	45, 56, 59,	32.10	8
24	36, 151,		62	32.11-12	8
	159, 172	26.31	56	32.11	8, 103
24.1-4	58	26.33	45	32.12-13	158
24.1-2	128	26.35	13	32.13	8
24.1	56	26.36-37	45	32.15-16	117
24.3	9, 171	27.21	80	32.15	119
24.4	10	28.4-7	24	32.16	10
24.5	171	28.7	26	32.24	66
24.6-11	58	28.22	26	32.26-29	8
24.6	37	28.23-28	20, 26	32.28	115
24.7-8	9	29	45, 132	32.30-32	35
24.7	10, 171,	29.1	132	32.31	9, 119
	172	29.18	132	32.32-33	79
24.8	37, 56, 59,	29.20-21	172	32.32	62
	62, 115,	29.20	171, 171	32.33	8
	150–2,	29.21	13	32.34	50, 51

Index of References

33–34	100, 104, 107	34.29-30	67	4.31	132
		34.29	117	5.20-26	54
33.1	8, 158	34.30-33	117	6.1-7	54
33.2	51, 56, 66	34.30	117	6.17	113
33.3	80, 82	34.31	119	8.21	132
33.5	80, 82	34.34	117, 118	8.30	172
33.6	10	34.35	117	12.3	100
33.7	89	35–40	19, 20, 22, 23	12.6	64
33.8-9	119			12.8	64
33.9	89	35.2-3	9	13.2	105
33.11	88	35.31-32	139	14.1-7	172
33.12-17	35	36.8-40	20	14.10	175
33.13	9, 10	36.8-34	20, 26	16–17	203
33.16-18	117	37.1–38.7	21	17.4	132
33.18–34.7	10	37.1-6	20	17.6	132
33.18-19	90	37.2	26	17.10-14	100
33.18	67, 92	37.7-21	20	19.1	175
33.19	123, 125	37.10-15	26	19.18	43, 167
33.20	99, 141	37.17-28	26	20.9	53
33.22	89	37.25-28	21	23.18	175
34.1-4	57	38.1-17	21	24.11	53
34.1	10, 117	38.9-23	20	24.14	53
34.4	66, 118	38.11	26	24.15	53
34.5-8	10, 125	38.17	26	24.23	53
34.5-7	57	38.18-21	20	26.1	82
34.6-7	8, 57, 125	38.22-24	21	26.12	91
34.6	56–8, 90, 165, 169, 181	38.22	23	26.20	82
		38.26	44		
		39.2-31	20	*Numbers*	
34.7	55–7	39.14–40.32	21	6.10	64
34.8	57	39.16	21	6.14	175
34.9-10	125	39.19	45	9.12	105
34.9	82, 125	39.43	10	10.29	10
34.10	9, 125	40.3	45	11	39, 168
34.11-28	9	40.5	21	11.1	103
34.11	56	40.21	45	11.6	188
34.12	9	40.23	55, 57	11.7-9	97
34.14	9	40.24	21	11.7	188
34.15-16	9	40.28-29	67	11.9	188
34.18	8	40.29	67	11.24-29	168
34.20	8	40.34-35	10, 89	11.33-34	98
34.21	55, 57	40.34	9, 56, 58, 88, 92	12.2-8	88
34.24	56			14	179, 180
34.27-28	10	40.35	67	14.10	89
34.28-29	117			14.11	102, 179
34.28	24, 56, 71, 89	*Leviticus*		14.12	179
		2.11	113	14.18	169
34.29-35	10, 67, 117	2.12	132	14.22-23	179

Numbers (cont.)		5.16	52, 134	18.5	74		
14.22	102	5.17-20	54	18.15	66, 81, 97,		
14.27-28	179	5.17-18	165		100		
14.27	103	5.18	13	18.16	99, 167		
14.29	103	5.21	120, 121	18.18-19	74		
14.32-34	24	5.22	89, 117,	18.18	97, 100		
14.33-35	179		167	18.22-23	74		
15.7	132	6–8	24	21.8	173		
16.41-50	115	6.10	74	22.7	134, 136		
17.1-5	23	6.12	2	23.4	53		
17.6	103	6.16	116	23.14	88		
17.20	103	6.21	103	24.1-4	42		
18.15-16	64	6.22	102, 152	24.7	76		
20.2-13	115	7.6	141, 207–9	25.5-6	42		
20.3	99	7.8	103, 173	25.5	71		
20.11	105	7.19	103	26.8	103, 152		
21.4-9	94, 115	7.21	88	26.17-18	91		
21.5-6	116	8.2	35	26.18	141, 208,		
21.8-9	93	8.3	188		209		
21.9	93	8.14	2	27.2-7	13		
22.33	209	8.16	188	28.27	198		
25.1-9	115	9	148	28.35	198		
25.9	115	9.6	82	28.46	152		
26.52-56	140	9.7	2	28.59-60	193, 194		
27.15-18	101	9.9-11	117	29.2-4	102, 103		
27.17	101, 102	9.9	24	29.2	152		
27.18-23	141	9.10	117	29.3	102		
27.18	102	9.19	148	29.13	74		
28.3	175	9.13	82	32	194, 195		
29.1	175	9.25-26	35	32.4	115, 194,		
33.4	7	9.26	103, 173		195		
33.38	67	9.29	103	32.15	115		
		10.1-2	117	32.18	115		
Deuteronomy		10.3	66	32.30	115		
1.3	46	10.15	207	32.31	115		
3.24	103	10.21	69	32.39	59, 101		
4	148	11.2	103	33.2	111		
4.3	152	11.3	152	34	195		
4.12	99	11.29	13	34.1	88		
4.13	117	11.30	13	34.10-12	195		
4.24	99	12.16	100	34.11	102, 152		
4.34	102, 103	13.1-3	100				
5.4	167	14.2	141, 208,	*Joshua*			
5.5	66		209	5.12	10, 188		
5.12-13	69	15.7 LX	54	19.19	140		
5.15	103	15.15	173	24.9	53		
5.16-20	54, 70	18	96, 205				

Index of References

Judges	
1.16	10
4.11	10
5.3	39
9.27	53
16.25	123
20.13	76

1 Samuel	
3.13	53
17.43	53
21.1	57
29.28	136

2 Samuel	
7.6	89
7.12-14	111
7.23	173
16.5	53
16.7	53
16.9	53
16.10	53
16.11	53
16.13	53
19.21	53

1 Kings	
1.48	39
2.8	53
3.1	53
6–7	4
6.1	67
8.10-11	89
11.20	136
15.4	123
17	83
19.11	58

2 Kings	
2.24	53
10.6	136
13	83

1 Chronicles	
29.3	208

2 Chronicles	
9.8	123
14.12	209
23.10	123
30.9	169
30.15-17	114

Nehemiah	
9.15	98, 188
9.17	169
9.20	188
13.2	53
13.25	53

Job	
1.6-12	154
2.1-6	154
3.1	53
9.5	58
9.8	96
9.11	96

Psalms	
2.7-8	111
2.8	111
15.2	89
22.4	140
25.6	169
25.10	90
26.3	90
26.8	89
27.4-6	89
33.21	106
34	105
34.19-22	105
34.20	105, 106
35	194
40.10	90
40.11	169
40.14	39
41.13	39
43.3	89
49.16	131
51.1	169
62.4	53
64.9	152
67.19	128
68.19	128, 130
74.7	89
77.16	96
77.18	116
77.19	96
77.20	102
77.25	188, 189
77.43	152
78	98, 198
78.12-39	97
78.12-16	97
78.17-20	97
78.18	98, 116
78.21-22	98
78.23-31	98
78.23-24	97
78.24	97, 98, 188
78.25	189
78.27	98
78.29-31	98
78.41	98
78.43-53	197
78.52	102
78.56	98
80.1	101
83.12	90
84.1	89
84.11	90
86	194
86.8-10	193, 194
86.9-10	194
86.10	193
86.15	169
90.2	101
91.16	136
95	148, 162
98	194
98.1	193, 194
98.2	193, 194
102.16	89
103.8	169
104.27	152
104.38	67
105.5	193
105.20	120
105.40	97, 98, 188
106.18	115

Psalms (cont.)		10.9	82	43.21	207, 209, 210
106.21	2	10.24	92		
109.28	53	10.26	92	43.25	57, 101
110.2-4	194	11.11-16	171	44.1-2	128
111	194	11.16-18	92	44.6	186
113-118	102	14.1	128	44.22-23	173
113.1	67	19.1	82	45.7	84
117	207	19.19-25	171	45.12	84
117.22	207	20.3	90, 152	45.13	173
117.23	207	23.21	207	45.18	84
118	102	26.19	144	46.4	101
118.22	176	27.9	124	46.6	82
118.25	102	28.16	176	47.8-9	101
118.26	102	31.7	82	48.12	101, 186
134.9	152	31.5	209	48.14	103
135.4	208, 209	32.15	69	48.20-21	171
139	194	32.18	69	49.5-6	57
145	194	32.20	69	52.6	9
145.6	84	35.1	91	49.7	128
145.17	194, 195	35.8-10	91	49.26	92
148.6	123	40–55	50, 92, 101	51.5	103
149.6	123	40–48	90	51.9-11	171
		40	90	51.9	103
Proverbs		40.1-11	39, 91	51.11	173
3.34	168	40.1-9	90	52.3-4	173
16.6	90	40.1-2	92	52.3	173
20.20	53	40.1	87, 91	52.10	103
24.33	53	40.3-5	87	52.13–53.12	92, 95
29.1	82	40.3	91, 92	52.13	95
29.4	123	40.5	92	52.15	103
34.34	53	40.10	103	53	174
		40.12–44.12	91	53.1	103
Ecclesiastes		40.25-26	84	53.6	174
2.8	208	40.28	84	53.7	93, 174, 191
7.22	53	41.4	58, 101, 186		
7.23	53			53.11-14	128
10.20	53	42.5	84	54.13	99
		43.2	58	59.20-21	124
Isaiah		43.10	101, 186	60.1-3	92
1–39	90	43.13	101	60.1-2	144
6.1-13	91	43.16-21	171	61.1-2	69
6.9	91	43.20-21	176, 177, 205, 206, 209	61.6	178
6.10	103			63.5	103
8.6	91			63.10	128
8.14-15	176	43.20	207	63.11	102
8.18	152			63.14	102

64.13	97	*Daniel*		*Haggai*	
65–66	92	5.4	82	1.8	51
66.16	92	5.23	82		
66.23-24	92	6.27	82	*Malachi*	
		8	191	1.2-3	210
Jeremiah		9.4	194	1.6	210
1.6	186	9.11	194	1.11	210
2.6-7	92	10.12	58	2.10	210
7.22	92			2.17	66
7.25	92	*Hosea*		3	51
10	194	2.16-17	92	3.1	50, 51, 65, 66, 87
10.6-7	193	2.19	169		
10.7	194	2.25	176	3.2-3	210
11.4	92	6.6	43	3.2	66
11.7	92	9.12	136	3.5	54
14.13	186	11.1	33, 92, 122	3.9	54
15.10	53	12.10	92	3.16	209, 210
16.14-15	171	12.14	92	3.17	206, 208–10
16.21	9	13.4-5	92		
17.12	89			3.18	209
23.7-8	171	*Joel*		3.22-23	66
31	159	2.13	169	3.22	66
31.32	159			3.23	51
38.31-35	156	*Amos*		4.2	210
38.31-34	158	2.9-10	92	4.5-6	66
38.32	156	3.1-2	92	4.5	51, 66
38.33	117	9.7	92		
39.17	186			Apocrypha/Deutero-Canonical Works	
39.20-21	152	*Jonah*			
		4.2	169	*Tobit*	
Lamentations				12	194
3.22	169	*Micah*			
		2.12-13	102	*Judith*	
Ezekiel		6.4	92	8.18	82
9–11	91	6.8	43		
10.4	89	7.14-15	171	*Wisdom of Solomon*	
11.19	117			3.2	67
20.33-38	171	*Nahum*		8.8	152
20.41	178	1.3	169	10.16	152
34.13	101			14.8	82
36.25-26	94	*Habakkuk*		16.6-7	94
36.26-27	117	3.3	92	16.9	59
37.27-28	89			16.20	98, 188
43.2-4	51	*Zephaniah*			
45.18-25	114	2.15	101		

Index of References

Ecclesiasticus
3.1-16	136
3.1	136
3.11	53
4.1	54
16.11	82
16.7-10	179
17.13	99
29.6	54
29.7	54
34.21	54
34.22	54
45.5	99
48.10	57

Baruch
2.11	152
2.30	82

1 Maccabees
3.44	169
3.55	57
4.51	59
6.17	136
9.23-27	89

2 Maccabees
1.2	74
2.4-7	188, 189
2.8	58
2.17	177
7.27	136

NEW TESTAMENT
Matthew
1–2	32
1.2	36
1.6	36
1.11-12	36
1.11	36
1.16	36
1.17	36
1.23	45, 46
2	31, 33, 35
2.13	33
2.15	31, 33, 36
2.16	33
2.19-21	36
2.20	24, 33, 36
2.21	24, 36
3.2	39
3.8	92
4	35
4.1-11	38
4.1-2	24
4.1	24
4.2	24, 56
4.4	24
4.7	24
4.10	24
5–7	37
5.8	41
5.17	43
5.20	43
5.21-48	41
5.21-46	40
5.21-26	41
5.21-22	166
5.21	40, 165
5.27-28	41, 166
5.27	40, 165
5.37	44
5.38	40
5.39	41
5.43-44	41
5.45-48	41
5.48	41
6.24	43
7.12	43
8–9	37, 38
8.1-17	37
8.4	42
8.16	37
8.17	38
8.18-22	37
8.23–9.8	37
8.23-27	38
8.24	38
8.25	38
8.26	38
9.9-17	37
9.13	43
9.18-34	37
9.18-26	38
9.18-19	37
9.20-22	37
9.23-26	37
11.13	43
12.17	43
13.33	113
14	38
14.13-33	38
14.15-21	39
14.15	39
14.17	39
14.20	39
14.21	39
14.22-33	38
14.24	38
14.27	38
14.30	38
14.32	38
15.1-2	42
15.3-9	42
15.4	42, 43
15.14	42
15.29-31	39
15.31	39
15.32-39	39
15.32	39
15.33	39
15.34	39
15.37	39
15.38	39
16.6	113
16.11-12	113
16.17	100
17	43
17.3-5	42
17.24-27	44
17.24	44
18.6-9	44
18.20	46
19.7	42
19.8	42
19.16-22	43
19.17	43
19.18-19	42, 70
19.18	165, 166
19.21-22	43
20.28	173

22.23	71	8.15	113	2.1-2	81		
22.24	42	8.28	51	2.20	75		
22.32	74	8.31-33	96	2.21-22	64		
22.34-40	43	9.2-7	58	2.22-24	64		
22.40	43	9.2	56, 58	2.22-23	4, 62–4		
23	44	9.7	56, 58, 67	2.23	61, 64, 86, 87		
23.2	42	9.11-13	51				
23.16-22	44	9.30-32	96	2.24	64		
23.16	42, 44	9.49	56, 58	2.25	4, 87		
23.18-19	44	10	54, 55	2.27	64		
23.19	45	10.17-22	137	2.41	62		
23.23	43	10.17	137	2.52	81		
23.24	42	10.19	43, 48, 50, 53, 54, 70, 165, 166	3.3-17	66		
24	197			3.4-6	87		
24.24	96			3.22	82		
26.2	36	10.20	54	4.1-14	82		
26.17	36	10.35-45	96	4.2	56		
26.20-30	39, 40	10.45	59, 173	4.16	68		
26.28	36, 39	11.17	48	4.18	69		
27.50	45	12.18	71	4.31-37	68		
27.51	45	12.19	48	4.31	68		
27.52-53	45	12.26	50, 54, 56, 72	4.38-39	68		
28.20	46			5.25	75		
		12.29	135	6.5	68		
Mark		12.31	167	6.6-11	68		
1.2-3	48	12.32	48	6.6	68		
1.2	50, 55	12.40	56	7.16	75		
1.3	50	13.11	56, 59	7.18-23	65		
1.11	48	13.19	56	7.19-20	65		
1.13	55, 56	13.22	100	7.24-35	65		
2.7	55–7	13.24-26	48	7.27	4, 61, 62, 65, 66, 86, 87		
2.8-12	56	14.12-25	58				
2.24	55, 56	14.12-13	56				
2.26-27	56	14.12	56, 58	7.28	66		
2.26	55	14.22-23	58	9.12-15	65		
2.27	55, 56	14.24	56, 59	9.16	65		
3.6	56, 57	14.62	48	9.18-20	66		
3.14	56	15.38	56, 59	9.21-22	66		
3.27-28	57			9.22	67		
6.15	51	*Luke*		9.23-27	66		
6.44	39	1.9	62	9.27	66		
6.48	56, 96	1.17	66	9.28-33	4, 62, 66		
6.50	56, 58	1.35	64, 67	9.28	66		
7.10	48, 50, 52, 53	1.51	61, 103	9.29	67		
		1.68	61, 65	9.31	4, 67, 87		
7.11	55	1.78	65	9.32	67		
8.9	39	2	81	9.34	67		

Luke (cont.)		20.33	71	3.16	90, 94, 95
9.35	66, 67	20.34-36	72	3.17-18	92
9.44	67	20.37-38	62, 72	3.17	93
9.51	66, 67	20.37	4, 61, 63,	3.18	90
10.20	62		72, 74	3.19-21	94
10.25	70	20.38	4, 72, 87	3.31	98, 99
10.27	167	22.1	62	3.36	94
11.20	62	22.7	62	4.14	94
12.1	113	22.20	37, 62	4.24	88
12.14	62	23.45	63	4.34	95
12.35	62, 172	23.47	75	4.36	94
13.10-17	68	23.56	62	4.42	93
13.10-11	69	24	87	5.8-12	93
13.10	68	24.26	67	5.24	94
13.12-16	4, 87	24.44	61, 67, 87	5.26	94
13.12-13	69			5.37-47	99
13.13	75	*John*		5.37	99
13.14	4, 62, 68,	1.1-18	89	5.39	94, 99
	69	1.1	204	5.45-47	96, 97, 204
13.15	69	1.4	94	5.47	100
13.16	69	1.10	93	6	90, 96,
13.17	69	1.12	88, 94		107, 189
13.21	113	1.14-18	100	6.1-15	4, 97, 98
13.28	74	1.14	89, 90, 107	6.14	96, 97
14.1-6	68	1.16-17	89, 107	6.15	97
17.15	75	1.16	89	6.16-24	96
18.9-14	70	1.17	89, 90, 97	6.20	4, 96
18.15-17	70	1.18	90	6.25-58	97
18.16-17	71	1.19–12.50	4, 90	6.25	97
18.18-23	70	1.23	4, 90, 92,	6.26-27	97
18.18-20	62		107	6.26	97, 98
18.18	70	1.29	4, 93, 106,	6.27	94, 100
18.20	4, 53, 61,		107, 174,	6.28	97
	70, 71,		191	6.29	97
	165, 166	1.36	4, 93, 106,	6.30	97
18.22-33	70		107, 174,	6.31	97, 98,
18.25	71		191		188, 204
18.28-29	70	1.45	96, 204	6.32-33	99
18.30	70, 71	2.11	89	6.32	98–100
18.31-33	82	2.13-22	90	6.33	98, 99
18.37	71	2.16	93	6.40	94
18.43	75	3.5	94	6.41-71	107
19.8	62	3.13	98, 99	6.41	99, 103
20.1-26	71	3.14-15	94, 107	6.44	99
20.27	71	3.14	4, 93, 99	6.45-46	99
20.28	71	3.15-18	94	6.45	97, 99
20.29-33	71	3.15	94	6.46	99

6.49	188	12.28	95	2.22	83	
6.50-51	100	12.32	95, 99	2.43	83	
6.52	100	12.33	96	3.13	4, 62, 72,	
6.53-58	100	12.34	95		74	
6.54	94	12.37-40	99, 102,	4.1	71	
6.55	100		107	4.21	75	
6.59	97	12.37	90, 102,	4.30	83	
6.60-71	99		103	5.9	85	
6.60	96	12.38-41	99	5.12	83	
6.61	99, 103	12.39	103	5.15	67	
6.66	96	12.40	103	5.17	71	
6.68	94	12.41	89	6.8	83	
7.19	4, 100	12.47	92	6.11-14	80, 81	
7.21-23	100	12.50	94	6.13-14	75, 83	
7.22	4, 100	13–17	4, 96, 104	7	4, 62, 72,	
7.31	4, 100, 107	13.1–21.25	4, 104		75, 77–9,	
7.40	96	13.1	95		83, 87, 204	
8.12	4, 101	13.19	204	7.2-53	75	
8.24	101	13.31-32	75, 89	7.2-8	75, 81	
8.28	95, 101	13.34-35	104, 107	7.3	81	
8.42	98	14.2-3	104, 107	7.6-7	81	
8.47	98	14.13	89	7.6	75, 87	
8.54	75	14.15-24	104, 107	7.7	75, 81	
8.56	102	16.14	75	7.9-16	75	
8.58	101, 180,	16.28	95	7.13	74	
	204	17.1	75, 89, 95	7.14	74, 76	
9.3	89	17.2	94	7.15	74	
9.28	100	17.3	94	7.17-44	75	
10.3-4	101, 104	17.4-5	89	7.17-19	61, 81	
10.7-10	102	17.4	95	7.17	81, 87	
10.10	94	17.5	89, 95, 104	7.18-22	81	
10.16	99	17.24	95	7.18-19	81	
10.18	93	17.26	88	7.18	76, 80, 81	
10.24-25	102	18–19	104	7.19	76	
10.28	94	19.14	93	7.20-21	61	
11.4	89	19.24	4, 104, 105	7.20	76, 81	
11.25	94	19.29	105, 107	7.21	76, 80, 81	
11.40	89	19.30	95	7.22-23	74	
11.41-42	102	19.33-36	107	7.22	81	
11.49-51	93	19.33	105	7.23-29	81	
11.51-52	99	19.34	105	7.23	76	
12.13	4, 101, 107	19.36	93, 104–6,	7.24	76, 81	
12.23-33	89		173	7.25	61	
12.23-26	96	20.30-31	90, 97	7.26	77, 80	
12.23	95			7.27-29	81	
12.25	94	*Acts*		7.27-28	77, 80	
12.28-29	88	1.20	85	7.27	78, 82	

248   *Index of References*

Acts (cont.)		17.2	85	7.14	121
7.28	81	17.10-12	86	7.24-25	121
7.29	77, 80	17.16	84	8.1-2	121
7.30-34	72, 82	17.22	84	8.14-17	122
7.30	61, 77, 81	17.24	4, 62, 82–4	8.15	121
7.31	77	17.29	84	8.18	120
7.32	55, 74, 78, 81, 82	17.30	84	8.19	122
		18.18	86	8.21-23	121
7.33-34	78, 80	20.16	86	8.21	120
7.34	81, 82	21.20	75	8.23	122
7.35	77, 78, 80–2	21.21	86	9–11	109, 116, 120, 122, 126
		21.22-24	86		
7.36	62, 78, 82, 152	21.26	86		
		21.28	86	9	123–5
7.37	81, 82	23.1-3	85	9.3	122
7.38-42	82	23.5	4, 62, 85, 87	9.4-5	122
7.38	62, 79, 80, 82, 152			9.6-13	122
		23.6-8	71	9.14-18	122
7.39-42	82			9.15	109, 123, 125
7.39-41	81	*Romans*			
7.39	81	1–8	120	9.16	123
7.40	79–81	1.16-17	123	9.17	109, 123
7.41	79, 80	1.23	120, 121	9.22-24	123
7.42	86	2.7	120	11	122
7.44-50	81	2.10	120	11.7	124
7.44	62, 80, 81	3.7	120	11.25-32	123, 124
7.45-53	75	3.9	121	11.25-27	124
7.45	180	3.10-18	125	11.26-27	124, 125
7.48	82	3.23-25	121	11.30-32	124
7.51-52	82	3.23	120, 121	13.8-10	167
7.51	80–2	3.24-25	121	13.9	109, 120, 165, 166
7.52	82	3.25	121		
7.53	111	4–8	121	15.15	124
8.32-35	174	4.13	122	15.20-21	103
8.32	191	4.20	120	15.24	124
13.16-41	86	5.2	120		
13.33	86	6.1-6	121	*1 Corinthians*	
10.1–11.18	85	6.3	114	1.13-17	114
11.18	75	6.4	120	5	113, 114
14.11	83	6.14-22	121	5.6-8	113
14.15	4, 62, 83, 84	6.18-19	121	5.7	105, 173, 191
		7.6	121		
15.7-11	210	7.7-11	121	5.11	113
15.7-9	85	7.7	109, 120, 121, 137, 138	5.12-13	113
15.10	4, 62, 85			10	114, 116, 117
15.15	86				
17.2-3	86	7.12-14	121	10.1-11	114, 144

10.1-4	115	4.7	111	*1 Timothy*	
10.4	115, 180	4.21-31	112	1.6	143
10.5-11	115	4.24-25	112	1.13	143
10.5	180	5.9	113	4.3	143
10.6	180	5.13	112	4.7	143
10.7	109	5.14	167	6.4	143
10.9	180			6.5	143
10.11	145	*Ephesians*		6.16	141
11.17-34	113	1.3-14	128		
11.23-26	115	1.4	128	*2 Timothy*	
11.25	37	1.5	128	1.6	141
11.31-34	113	1.7	128	2.25	143
13.13	114	1.11	128	3	141
15.50	100	1.24	128	3.1-5	141
		2.19-22	132	3.1	141
2 Corinthians		4.8	128–32,	3.6	141
3	116, 126		144	3.8-9	5, 141–4
3.2	117	4.30	128	3.8	141, 142
3.4-5	117	5.2	132, 133	3.9	142
3.7-18	117	5.14	144	3.16	144
3.7-13	144	6.1-2	137	11.22	67
3.7	118	6.1	133, 134		
3.13	118	6.2-3	5, 128,	*Titus*	
3.16	118		133, 134,	1.10	143
3.18	118		138, 144	2.14	141
4.4	118	6.2	135, 137,	3.3	143
4.6	118		138		
8	119	6.3	134, 137	*Hebrews*	
8.15	109, 119	6.4	136	1–4	152, 156
9	119	6.12	100	1–2	153
		6.14	172	1	155, 156
Galatians		6.22	135	1.2	159
1.16	100			1.6	152
3	112	*Colossians*		1.8	151
3.13	111	1	140	1.14	193
3.15	111	1.9-14	139	2–4	156, 160
3.16	111	1.9-10	139	2	155
3.17	110	1.12-14	128, 139	2.2	111, 148,
3.18	111	1.12	139, 140		152, 155
3.19	111, 152	1.13	139, 140	2.4	153, 155
3.22-25	112	1.14	139	2.5	152, 153,
3.27	114, 115	1.15	139		161
4	111	3.20	133	2.6	151
4.1-9	112			2.12	151
4.3	111	*2 Thessalonians*		2.14-18	153, 155
4.4-5	111	2.9	96	2.14-16	153, 154
4.6-7	111			2.14	100

Hebrews (cont.)		11.13-16	161	1.17	173, 210
2.15	154	11.19	148	1.18-19	173
3–4	148, 153,	11.23-29	147, 160	1.18	174, 175
	159, 193	11.23-28	146	1.19	105, 174,
3.1-6	155	11.26	160, 180		175, 191
3.7–4.13	155	11.27	148	2	205
3.7–4.11	144, 155	11.28	153, 154	2.4-10	173, 175
4.7	151	11.29	146	2.4-5	176
4.8-10	102	11.39-40	160, 161	2.5	172, 175,
4.8	104, 180	12	160		181
4.14-16	150	12.2	104	2.6-8	175, 176
4.14	104, 157	12.5-6	152	2.7	207
4.16-19	161	12.18-24	147, 160	2.9-10	175, 176,
4.16	161	12.18-19	146		205, 210
5–7	156	12.22-24	161	2.9	172, 175,
6.1	193	12.26	151		176, 178,
6.5	161	12.28	161		181, 205–
6.20	104	13.11-12	159		10
7.21	151	13.14	161	2.12	178, 210
7.25	150, 157	13.22	147	2.17	210
8–9	158, 159			2.22-25	174
8	156	*James*		2.23	174
8.1-4	150, 157	2.1-7	167	2.25	174
8.1-2	150	2.8	167	3.1-2	178
8.5	146, 148,	2.10	167	3.15-16	178
	150, 157	2.11	165, 167,	4.12	210
8.8-12	157		181	4.14-16	210
8.8-11	151	2.23	167	4.17	207
8.9	156	4	168	5.13	170
9	157	4.5	165, 167,		
9.1-11	150		168, 181	*2 Peter*	
9.1-5	157	4.6	167, 168	2.1-10	178
9.4	188	4.10	168	2.9	178
9.12-14	159	5.11	165, 168,		
9.15-20	158		169, 181	*1 John*	
9.19-20	157			2.2	93
9.20	146, 150,	*1 Peter*		4.10	93
	157	1.1	170, 210	4.14	93
9.24-26	150, 159	1.2	171, 172,	5.6-8	105
9.28	161, 162		181, 207		
10.16	151	1.6-7	210	*Jude*	
10.19-22	161	1.7	207	3	179
10.25	161	1.10-12	169	4	179
10.30	152	1.13	173, 181	5–7	178
10.37	161	1.15-16	175, 178	5	178–81
11	160	1.16-17	177		
11.10	161	1.17-19	173, 181		

Revelation		22.3	190	2.21	57
1–3	197	22.20	187	2.23-27	57
1.4	5, 185–7, 200			2.25	57
		PSEUDEPIGRAPHA		6.11	59
1.5	198	*1 Enoch*		10.17	154
1.6	177	70.4	55	16.18	177
1.8	186	90.9-13	191	17.16-17	154
1.17	200			23.29	154
2.17	5, 185, 188, 189	*2 Baruch*		27.22	74
		6.5-10	188	33.20	177
3.20-21	189	6.7-10	189	48	198
4.8	186	6.7	59	48.4–49.4	154
5	185, 190–2	29.8	98, 188	48.4	152
5.6	93, 192	59.3	58	48.12	152
5.9	93, 192	77.7	169	49.13	106
5.10	177, 192			50.7	57
5.12	93	*3 Baruch*			
6.1–8.1	195	4.14	35	*Liber antiquitatum biblicarum*	
7.17	93				
8.2–9.21	195	*3 Maccabees*		9.7	152
11.9	189	2.4-7	179	10.7	115
11.15-18	195	6.4	58	11.8	57
11.17	186			11.15	115
12	185	*4 Maccabees*		19.8	169
12.11	93	7.19	55, 72	20.8	1158
13.8	93	8.23	54	47.1	142
15	5, 185, 193, 194, 199, 200	16.25	55, 72		
				Life of Adam and Eve	
		4 Ezra		6.1	35
15.1-4	195	1.19	188		
15.1	195, 199	7.132-33	169	*Odes of Solomon*	
15.3-4	193, 194			12.1	74
15.3	193–5	*Apocalypse of Abraham*			
15.4-7	194	12.1-2	35	*Prayer of Manasseh*	
15.4	194, 195	17.10	169	1	74
16	5, 185, 195, 197–200			1.1	55
		Aristobulus		*Sibylline Oracles*	
16.5	186	1.17	67	3.49	98
17	200	*Joseph and Aseneth*		7.149	177
17.14	93	2.8	59		
18	198	11.10	169	*Testament of Benjamin*	
19.7	93			12.4	67
19.9	93	*Jubilees*			
20.6	177	1.4	56	*Testament of Isaac*	
21.22-23	93	1.27-29	111	4.4	35
22.1-3	93	2.17-19	57		

Testament of Joseph		*4QExod^b*		68.19	129, 131,
19.8-9	191	frgs. 3 ii,			132, 134
		5-6 i ll. 4-5	55	81.11	132
Testament of Judah				121.8	132
19.3	169	*11Q9*		127.2	132
		13.12	133	139.2-3	132
Testament of Levi		57.4	57	144.12	132
11.4-6	177				
		CD		Mishnah	
Testament of Moses		2.17–3.12	179	*'Abot*	
3.9	74			1.1	41
		CD-A		2.1	43
Testament of Naphtali		4.12-13	143	3.2	46
3.4-5	179	5.17-19	142	3.5	85
		5.18-19	143	3.6	46
Testament of Simeon				5.4-5	37
9.1	67	Mediaeval Manuscripts			
		MS 72	25	*Menaḥot*	
Dead Sea Scrolls		MS 85	25	85a	142
1Q28a		MS 91	25		
1.28–2.1	57	MS 94–96	25	*'Ohalot*	
2.21-22	57	MS 128	25	3.5	105
		MS 130	25		
1QH		MS 318	25	*Pesaḥim*	
19.29	169	MS 321	25	5.5-8	105
		MS 344	25	5.7	102
1QHa		MS 376	25	9.3	102
20.11-12	89	MS 628	25	10.7	102
		MS 630	25		
1QM		MS 805	24-6	*Sanhedrin*	
11.9-10	28			10.3	179
		Targums			
1QS		*Targum Onqelos*		*Šeqalim*	
5.15	29	Num. 21.16-20	115	2.1	44
8.9	132				
		Targum Pseudo-Jonathan		*Sukkah*	
4Q377		Deut. 32.39	186	3.9	102
frg. 2		Exod. 1.15	142		
col. 2.10-11	58	Exod. 7.11	142	Talmuds	
		Num. 22.22	142	*b. Sanhedrin*	
4Q504				99a	100
1-2 ii 8-12	28	*Targum Psalms*			
		1.2	132	*b. Sukkah*	
4Q511		19.8	132	37b	102
frag. 52	169	49.16	132		
frag. 54-55	169	51.17	132	*t. Soṭah*	
frag. 57-59	169	53.3	158	13.2-4	89

Midrash

Exodus Rabbah
9.7	142
29.9	99

Leviticus Rabbah
15.2	105

Mekilta Exodus
19.2	88

Numbers Rabbah
11.2	188

Qoheleth Rabbah
1.9	188

Tanḥuma Ki Tisa, 19
on Exod. 32	142, 143

Philo

De Abrahamo
56	177

De decalogo
51	166
94	44
121-137	166
142-143	137
168-171	166
173	137

Quod deterius potiori insidari soleat
118	98

De fuga et inventione
1.83	53

Hypothetica
7.2	53

Legum allegoriae
1.40	29
2.21	115
3.102	149
3.169-76	98

De migratione Abrahami
1.174	51

De mutatione nominum
259-60	98

Quaestiones et solutiones in Exodum
1.15	113
2.14	113
2.36	151

Quis rerum divinarum heres sit
173	166
191	98, 119
79	98

De sobrietate
66	177

De somniis
1.140-44	111

De specialibus legibus
1.293	113
2.243	53
2.261	137
2.262	137
3.8	166
3.182	41
4.78	137

De vita Mosis
1.92	142
1.105	67
2.248	67

Josephus

Antiquities
2.309	67
2.312	67
2.320	67
2.325	67
3.6.4 ss 122-29	59
3.91-92	166
3.245	102
3.296	188
4.21	188
5.72	67
11.5.2 ss133	57
15.134-37	111

War
5.5.4-5 ss212-219	59
6.5.3 ss 288-300	59

Christian Works

1 Clement
23.3	168

2 Clement
11.2	168

Acts of Pilate
5.1	142

Barnabas
4.6-14	115
12.8	180
20.1	166

Martyrdom of Polycarp
9.2	81

Shepherd of Hermes
Vis 2.3.4	168

Classical Sources

Andrew of Caesarea
Commentary on the Apocalypse
1.4	186
16.21	197

Appian
Bella civilia
1.9.83	198
4.1.4	198

Apuleius
Apologia
90.6   142

Cassius Dio
Historia Romana
37.25.2   198

Clement of Alexandria
Paedagogus
1.60.3   181

Eusebius
Praeparatio evangelica
9.8   142

Irenaeus
Adversus haereses
4.30.4   197

Justin
Dialogus cum Tryphone
24.2   181
75.12   181

Origen
Contra Celsum
4.51   142

Commentary on Matthew
23.37   142
29.9   142

Pausanias
Graeciae descriptio
10.12.10   186

Pliny the Elder
Naturalis historia
30.2.11   142, 143

Plutarch
Alexander
31.4   198

Victorinus of Petovium
5.2   190

Index of Authors

Achtemeier, P. J. 169, 171–6
Adams, M. P. 27
Adams, S. A. 48, 138
Aejmelaeus, A. 17, 18, 20, 23
Albright, W. F. 13
Aletti, J.-N. 130
Alexander, P. S. 80
Alkier, S. 113
Allen, D. M. 147, 153, 160, 161
Allen, O. W. 41
Allison, D. C. 32, 33, 35–9, 41, 166–9
Anderson, K. L. 74
Andriessen, P. C. B. 144, 152
Archer, G. 72
Ashley, T. R. 105
Attridge, H. W. 151, 153, 160
Aune, D. E. 185, 186, 188, 189, 194, 198

Backhaus, K. 150
Baden, J. S. 11
Bailey, D. P. 121
Ball, D. M. 101
Barclay, J. M. G. 116, 122, 125
Barmash, P. 1
Barrett, C. K. 93, 94, 99, 101, 104, 105
Barthelémy, D. 17
Bartholomä, P. F. 179, 180
Bauckham, R. 84, 116, 167, 178–81, 191–5
Beale, G. K. 34, 89, 139, 183, 186–9, 193–5
Beasley-Murray, G. R. 96, 99, 101
Beaton, R. 32
Beckwith, I. T. 189
Beetham, C. A. 139, 140
Belleville, L. L. 116, 118
Bernstein, M. J. 132
Berthelot, K. 29
Bertram, G. 95

Best, E. 130
Black, M. 179
Blenkinsopp, J. 90, 92
Block, D. I. 205
Blount, B. K. 185, 187
Bock, D. L. 64, 66, 68, 75
Boesak, A. 185
Bogaert, P.-M. 20, 22, 23
Boismard, M.-E. 97
Borchert, G. L. 93, 100
Borgen, P. 99
Boring, M. E. 189
Bovon, F. 64, 67
Boxall, I. 40, 195–7
Breytenbach, C. 84
Brooke, A. E. 27
Brown, J. K. 32, 34, 36, 39–41, 43, 45
Brown, R. E. 102, 103, 105
Bruce, F. F. 140
Bruning, B. 23
Brunson, A. C. 102
Büchsel, F. 173
Burge, G. 43, 93, 101, 105

Caird, G. 130, 197
Calvin, J. 86
Campbell, A. F. 97
Campbell, D. A. 127
Cannon, G. E. 139
Capes, D. B. 116
Carson, D. A. 89, 92, 94–7, 101–3, 166, 171
Carter, W. 35, 37, 39, 40, 44
Casey, J. S. 192
Ceresko, A. R. 1
Charles, R. H. 183
Childs, B. 66, 178
Chilton, B. 130
Chirichigno, G. 72

Ciampa, R. E. 133
Collins, A. Y. 52–4, 56–8
Collins, N. 69
Conzelmann, H. 144
Cook, J. 22
Cranfield, C. 51
Crawford, S. W. 14
Croasmun, M. 121
Cross, F. M. 13
Crouch, J. E. 34

Daly-Denton, M. 98
Daube, D. 105, 106
Davids, P. H. 178, 180
Davids, W. D. 178
Davies, W. D. 36–9, 109
Davila, J. R. 13
Davis, K. 14
De Troyer, K. 27
de Vaux, R. 105
De Villiers, P. 196
DeRouchie, J. S. 71
Debel, H. 11
Decker, R. J. 51
Dentan, R. C. 169
deSilva, D. A. 27
Deterding, P. E. 169, 173, 174
Díaz-Caro, M. V. S. 28
DiMattei, S. 110, 111
Dibelius, M. 144
Docherty, S. E. 148
Dodd, C. H. 95
Doering, L. 169–72
Dohmen, C. 134, 136
Donaldson, T. L. 35
Downing, F. G. 84
Dozeman, T. B. 12, 177, 178
Duke, R. 14
Dunn, J. D. G. 121, 122, 124, 136, 139
Dunnill, J. 153
Durham, J. I. 51, 66, 105

Easter, M. C. 153
Egan, P. T. 169, 170, 174
Ehorn, S. M. 48, 105, 130–2, 138
Ehrman, B. D. 127
Eisenbaum, P. M. 153
Ellingworth, P. 150, 151
Elliott, J. H. 171, 173–7, 207, 208
Enns, P. 29, 31, 43, 54, 115

Estelle, B. D. 62, 109
Evans, C. A. 63, 72, 103, 130

Falk, D. K. 14
Farrer, A. M. 182, 198
Fee, G. D. 139
Fekkes, J. 183
Feldmeier, R. 171
Finlan, S. 132
Finn, A. H. 20, 22
Fishbane, M. 2, 171
Fitzmyer, J. 64, 72
Fletcher, M. 183–5, 194, 198, 199
Florentin, M. 16
Flusser, D. 148, 165
Fossum, J. 179
Foster, P. 127
Fowl, S. E. 130
Fox, R. M. 29
Fraenkel, D. 20
France, R. T. 37, 44
Freed, E. D. 101

Gall, A. F. von 16
Gallus, L. 197
Garland, D. E. 44, 46, 115
Garrett, D. A. 66, 67
Garrett, S. R. 68
Gathercole, S. J. 70
Gelardini, G. 144
Gempf, C. H. 84
Gese, M. 133
Glasson, T. F. 97
Gooding, J. K. 20, 22
Goodman, M. 80
Goodrich, J. K. 124
Goppelt, L. 207
Goranson Jacob, H. 120
Gough, H. 72
Green, J. B. 64, 69
Greenberg, M. 208
Grindheim, S. 97
Gruen, E. S. 2
Grundmann, W. 37
Guelich, R. A. 51
Gundry, R. H. 37, 51
Gunkel, H. 97
Gupta, N. K. 169, 172, 174, 178
Gurtner, D. M. 28, 34, 35, 45, 51, 56, 65
Guthrie, G. H. 118

Haenchen, E. 86
Hafemann, S. J. 112, 118, 179, 180
Hagner, D. A. 34, 39, 41
Hahn, S. W. 110
Hakala, D. L. 70
Halas, S. 208
Halpern-Amaru, B. 29
Hamm, D. 69, 75
Hanhart, R. 27
Hardy, T. 1
Harris, W. H. III 130
Harstine, S. 97
Hays, R. B. 33, 35, 37, 48, 52, 58, 60, 62, 64, 66, 87–9, 105, 108, 110, 119, 133, 139
Helyer, L. R. 160
Hemer, C. J. 189
Hickling, C. J. A. 109
Hoehner, H. W. 133, 135
Hoffmann, M. R. 192
Hofius, O. 162
Hoftijzer, J. 208
Hooker, M. D. 51
Hoppe, R. 139
Hoskins, P. M. 105
Howard, G. 152
Huffmon, H. 208
Hughes, P. E. 153

Idestrom, R. G. S. 1
Imes, C. J. 205

Jack, A. 183
Jastram, N. 13
Jauhiainen, M. 183
Jewett, R. 122, 123, 125
Jobes, K. H. 171, 172, 174
Johns, L. L. 191
Johnson, L. T. 142, 151
Jones, W. H. 143

Kahle, P. E. 17
Karrer, M. 28
Kauhanen, T. 17
Kee, H. C. 56
Keener, C. S. 37, 38, 81, 83, 84, 92, 96
Keesmaat, S. C. 109, 120
Kelly, J. N. D. 207, 208
Kibbe, M. H. 147, 153, 156

Kilgallen, J. J. 72
Kim, K. 13
Kleinig, J. W. 150
Koester, C. R. 34, 45, 100, 153, 160, 196–8
Koester, H. 34
Kooij, A. van der 14
Köstenberger, A. J. 88–91, 95–7, 99–101, 104, 107, 110
Kovacs, J. L. 190, 197
Kowalski, B. 183
Kraft, H. 187
Kratz, R. G. 11
Kraus, W. 28
Kupfer, C. 1
Kupp, D. D. 46
Kuyper, L. J. 90

LaCoste, N. 29
Lacomara, A. 104
Lane, W. L. 160
Lange, A. 29
Larkin, W. J. 135
Le Boulluec, A. 28
Legrand, T. 29
Levison, J. R. 89
Lierman, J. 97
Lincoln, A. T. 128, 135, 136, 144
Lindars, B. 102
Lohmeyer, E. 139
Lohse, E. 122, 141
Longacre, D. 12
Longenecker, R. N. 131
Louw, J. P. 41
Luz, U. 34, 45

Malatesta, E. J. 104
Mallen, P. 32, 74
Marcar, K. 170
Marcos, N. F. 28
Marcus, J. 50
Marshall, I. H. 64, 73, 80
Martínez, F. G. 28, 143
Martin, R. P. 118, 119
Massonet, J. 150
Mathewson, D. 183
Mbuvi, A. M. 169
McCaulley, E. 111
McDonough, S. M. 185–7
McLean, N. 27

McNamara, M. 142, 186
Meeks, W. A. 97, 100
Menken, M. J. J. 3, 97, 98, 106
Metzger, B. 180, 181
Michaels, J. R. 170, 171, 174–7
Middleton, P. 191
Millar, F. 80
Milne, P. 1
Minutoli, D. 27
Moffitt, D. M. 147, 152, 154, 157
Moloney, F. J. 101, 105
Moo, D. J. 140
Moody, D. 90
Moritz, T. 129, 130, 133, 136, 144
Morris, L. 99, 101, 191
Motyer, J. A. 91
Motyer, S. 101
Moule, C. F. D. 74
Mowvley, H. 90
Moyise, S. 3, 48, 128, 164, 174, 183, 194, 195
Mussies, G. 183

Najman, H. 165
Nelson, R. D. 22
Neyrey, J. H. 178
Nicholson, G. C. 95
Nida, E. A. 41
Nilsen, T. D. 42
Nolland, J. 34, 42, 67
Novenson, M. V. 110

Orr, W. F. 114
Osburn, C. D. 179, 180
Oswalt, J. N. 90–2, 103
Oudersluys, R. C. 144

Pao, D. W. 62, 65, 67, 69, 70, 72, 87
Pardee, D. 208
Parker, S. 208
Paulien, J. 183
Pendrick, G. 90
Penner, K. 28
Perkins, L. J. 28, 49, 52, 56, 59, 60
Pietersma, A. 143
Pintaudi, R. 27
Platt, D. 33
Popper, J. 19, 22
Porter, S. E. 104, 110, 127, 128, 164, 165
Prigent, P. 189

Propp, W. H. C. 105
Pryor, J. W. 88, 104

Quast, U. 27, 51, 111

Rahlfs, A. 27
Reasoner, M. 125
Ricard, P. 185, 196, 198
Ridderbos, H. N. 95, 99, 101–3
Ringe, S. H. 67
Römer, T. 1, 12
Robar, E. 9
Roberts, A. J. 40, 61, 109
Roberts, K. A. 39–41, 43
Robinson, J. A. T. 74
Rowe, C. K. 62, 84
Rowland, C. 190, 197
Ruiz, J.-P. 183
Rusam, D. 74
Ryan, J. J. 69

Safrai, S. 136
Salvesen, A. 17
Sanders, E. P. 136
Sanderson, J. E. 13
Sandevoir, P. 28
Sandmel, S. 131
Scharlemann, M. H. 169
Scheiber, A. 105
Schlatter, A. von 182
Schlier, H. 138
Schmid, K. 12
Schnabel, E. 65, 67, 69, 70, 72, 80
Schnackenburg, R. 100, 101
Schorch, S. 16
Schürer, E. 80
Schüssler Fiorenza, E. 193
Schuchard, B. G. 103, 106
Schutter, W. 207
Schwankl, O. 72
Scott, J. M. 111, 124
Screnock, J. 23
Seifrid, M. A. 125
Selby, G. S. 1
Sellin, G. 133
Senior, D. 38
Shin, B. C. 144
Sieffert, E. L. 172
Slater, T. B. 190, 192
Smith, D. L. 2, 109

Snodgrass, K. 91
Sommer, M. 183, 196, 197
Son, H. 184, 185, 192, 194
Spencer, F. S. 81
Sperber, A. 151
Stanley, C. D. 125, 138, 164
Starling, D. 128, 138
Stec, D. M. 129
Stegner, W. R. 49
Stern, M. 136
Steyn, G. J. 147, 149, 150, 157
Stinespring, W. F. 35
Stökl Ben Ezra, D. 121
Stockhausen, C. K. 117
Strauss, M. L. 67, 68
Svebakken, H. 137
Swete, H. B. 27, 189

Tabb, B. J. 72, 87
Tal, A. 16
Talbert, C. H. 100
Tate, M. A. 97, 98
Thackeray, H. St. J. 131
Thielman, F. 130, 133
Thiessen, M. 112, 161
Thiselton, A. C. 113, 114
Thomas, K. J. 150, 151
Tigchelaar, E. J. C. 28, 143
Tilling, C. 116
Tov, E. 14, 23
Tromp, J. 143
Turner, D. L. 39, 46

Ulrich, E. 14, 16, 23

Vanlaningham, M. G. 124
Vermes, G. 80

Wade, M. L. 20, 23
Walker, P. W. L. 82
Walker, W. O. 116
Wall, R. W. 75
Wallace, D. B. 42
Walther, J. A. 114
Walton, S. 75
Wasserman, E. 121, 179
Wasserman, T. 178–81
Watts, J. D. W. 90–2
Watts, R. E. 1, 48, 52
Weigold, M. 29
Weinrich, W. C. 186, 189, 190, 197
Wellhausen, J. 11
Westfall, D. M. 121
Wevers, J. W. 19, 24, 27, 50, 52, 55, 63, 111, 149
White, S. A. 165
Wikgren, A. P. 179
Wildberger, H. 208
Williams, C. H. 106
Wilson, A. 61, 109
Wink, W. 41
Winter, B. 84
Wiseman, D. 208
Witherington, B., III 135, 142
Wold, B. G. 2
Wolff, C. 118, 119
Wolter, M. 67, 121
Works, C. S. 109
Wright, N. T. 2, 102, 120–2, 138
Wycherley, R. E. 84

Young, E. J. 91

Zahn, M. 14
Zevit, Z. 7

www.ingramcontent.com/pod-product-compliance
Lightning Source LLC
Chambersburg PA
CBHW062126300426
44115CB00012BA/1830